Rationality and Pluralism

Leading psychologist, lecturer and author Windy Dryden has compiled his most valuable writings on Rational Emotive Behaviour Therapy from the last 35 years. This collection reveals the thinking, concepts and practical experience that have made Dryden one of the most respected and cited REBT authorities of our time.

Dryden has authored or edited nearly 200 books and established Europe's first Masters in REBT. While his primary allegiance remains with REBT, he has published extensively on CBT and the wider issues of psychotherapy.

Dryden's pluralistic perspective on REBT comes through in such seminal pieces as:

- 'The therapeutic alliance in rational-emotive individual therapy'
- 'Compromises in rational-emotive therapy'
- 'Adapting CBT to a broad clientele'
- 'Unconditional self-acceptance and self-compassion'.

Windy Dryden is Professor of Psychotherapeutic Studies at Goldsmiths, University of London.

World Library of Mental Health series

The *World Library of Mental Health* celebrates the important contributions to mental health made by leading experts in their individual fields. Each author has compiled a career-long collection of what they consider to be their finest pieces: extracts from books, journals, articles, major theoretical and practical contributions, and salient research findings.

For the first time ever the work of each contributor is presented in a single volume so readers can follow the themes and progress of their work and identify the contributions made to, and the development of, the fields themselves.

Each book in the series features a specially written introduction by the contributor giving an overview of his career, contextualizing his selection within the development of the field, and showing how his own thinking developed over time.

Rationality and Pluralism

The selected works of Windy Dryden

Windy Dryden

Routledge
Taylor & Francis Group
LONDON AND NEW YORK

First published 2013
by Routledge
27 Church Road, Hove, East Sussex BN3 2FA

Simultaneously published in the USA and Canada
by Routledge
711 Third Avenue, New York, NY 10017

Routledge is an imprint of the Taylor & Francis Group, an informa business

British Library Cataloguing in Publication Data
A catalogue record for this book is available from the British Library

Library of Congress Cataloging in Publication Data
Dryden, Windy.
[Works. Selections]
Rationality and pluralism : the selected works of Windy Dryden / Windy Dryden.
pages cm
Includes bibliographical references and index.
1. Rational emotive behavior therapy. I. Title.
RC489.R3D827 2013
616.89'142–dc23

2012031397

ISBN: 978–0–415–63478–6 (hbk)
ISBN: 978–0–203–07001–7 (ebk)

Typeset in Sabon
by RefineCatch Ltd, Bungay, Suffolk

I dedicate this book to Dr Janet Stockdale, who taught me as an undergraduate at the London School of Economics (1969–1972) and who went beyond the call of duty in my hour of need. Without her kindness, I would not have finished my first degree and my life would have taken a very different path. Thank you, Jan.

CONTENTS

PREFACE

In this preface, I will say a little about myself and my development as a therapist. This will help put into context the selected writings that appear in this collection.

I was born in Hackney in East London in 1950, an only child to two loving parents. I grew up in a household where one aunt lived in the same house as my parents and me, and the other aunt lived nearby. I had, in effect, three loving mothers! I went to a Jewish school before transferring late to a primary school because there was too much religious education at the former. I was, at that time, not good at mixing, but being an only child, I had learned to enjoy my own company. I developed a stammer early on in life and this further hampered my social development and led to teasing and light bullying at grammar school. I remember wondering why someone who was nice to me one-to-one could join with other boys a few minutes later and tease me about my speech. This was the roots of my later interest in social psychology. Also, as I found a lot of the teasing hurtful, I became familiar with the world of feelings and this was the roots of my later interest in counselling and psychotherapy.

At school I was particularly interested and adept at languages and did Russian, Latin and French at A Level. However, with my stammer I realised that I could not be an interpreter and I was not interested in a career in translation so looked further afield and decided to study Psychology at university. Before leaving school, I was able to overcome my anxiety about speaking in public because of my stammer and did so by applying techniques that were very similar in nature to those I were to discover later when I encountered REBT (see Chapter 14). In 1968, I began a degree in Psychology at Nottingham University, but dropped out after a month because I was homesick. I then did a few menial jobs before going on *ulpan* in Israel which involved an intensive study of Modern Hebrew and work on a kibbutz. This experience helped to me to grow up and prepared me to study for a Social Psychology degree at the London School of Economics. I emerged from this with an upper second, but no idea of what I wanted to do next.

At the leaving 'do' after our results were posted, our Head of Department, Professor Hilde Himmelweit, announced that there were a number of bursaries for people who wanted to do a PhD in Psychology at other London colleges and in an impulsive moment I applied for and was awarded a Social Science Research Council (SSRC) to study for a degree at Bedford College, University of London[1] in Regents Park. I began this in 1972. Around that time I had developed an interest in the human potential movement that was prevalent at the time and went to a number of encounter groups. Partly due to this and partly due to the writings of Sidney

Jourard (1968, 1971) who had written on the topic of self-disclosure, I became interested in this subject and decided to study it for my PhD. I was later to return to this topic as it related to therapy (see Chapter 9).

During this period, I developed an interest in counselling and began to do a counselling course at the South West London College and worked as a voluntary counsellor at Nightline, a telephone counselling service for students, and as a Samaritan. In 1974, I applied for and was awarded a Department of Education and Science (DES) State bursary to study for a one year full-time Diploma in Counselling in Educational Settings course at the University of Aston in Birmingham. This course was basically person-centred in orientation, but also had a module on behaviour therapy. While I resonated with person-centred theory, I preferred the more active-directive therapeutic style of behaviour therapy. I was also impressed with the ideas of Albert Ellis, the founder of REBT, but did not act on this interest at that point. I was awarded the Diploma in June 1975 and was fortunate to be in the right place at the right time and was appointed to a Lectureship in Counselling at Aston to teach on the course on which I had just been a student.

I mentioned earlier that I was dissatisfied with person-centred practice, so in 1977, I began a two-year Training Programme in Psychodynamic Psychiatry and Psychotherapy. Centre for Postgraduate Psychiatry, Uffculme Clinic, Birmingham. This was largely a theoretical course and I only completed the first year because I resonated neither with psychodynamic theory nor with its practice. Instead, I went to New York to do several training courses in REBT at what is now the Albert Ellis Institute and served as Ellis's co-therapist in several of his groups during August 1978[2] and began a two-year part-time MSc in Psychotherapy at the University of Warwick. This course was eclectic in nature and widened my horizons about the theory and practice of psychotherapy and set the stage for my later interests in eclecticism, integration and pluralism in psychotherapy. In 1981, a day after I got married, I began a six month sabbatical at the Center for Cognitive Therapy at the University of Pennsylvania in Philadelphia under the auspices of Aaron T. Beck, the founder of Cognitive Therapy (CT). I was trained and saw patients in CT, but maintained my links with the Albert Ellis Institute by travelling there every Wednesday and seeing patients there (see Chapter 4).

On my return to England, I encountered a fundamental shift in the funding of higher education which resulted in me taking voluntary redundancy from my lectureship at Aston in 1983, although I stayed there in a part-time capacity for a while helping to bring the Diploma course to a sad end. It took me two years to find another full-time job and after 54 job rejections in 1985, I was appointed to a lectureship in psychology at what is now Goldsmiths, University of London where I have remained ever since. I used REBT to help myself deal with these rejections (see Chapter 14) and doing so helped me to become more psychologically resilient (see Chapter 17).

I was originally appointed at Goldsmiths to establish a Masters in Counselling which I did, but after running first a three-year part-time course and then a two-year, part-time version, in 1995 I re-focused my training efforts and established Europe's first Masters in REBT, a two-year part-time programme which is still running as I write.[3]

While my primary allegiance has been to REBT as the pieces in this collection testify, I have also maintained a broad view on psychotherapy. Indeed, my publications are split between REBT/CBT and more broader issues in psychotherapy and I have often brought the latter to bear on the former (see Chapters 3, 8, 18 and 20). My publishing career began in 1977 and I am still active today. So far I have authored or edited nearly 200 books, either by myself or with colleagues, and my 200th book should be published soon after this collection has appeared.

While my publications are both focused (on REBT/CBT) and more broad (on general issues in psychotherapy), I decided to select only from the former body of work for this collection since I am perhaps best known as an REBT scholar. Having said that, as you will see, I take a broad view on REBT and on re-reading the pieces I consider that my pluralistic perspective on this topic area comes through in this collection. Incidentally, my recent interest has been on pluralism in counselling and psychotherapy (see Dryden, 2012) and I look forward to teaming up with Mick Cooper and John McLeod (2011) in developing this emerging field through various publishing projects. At 62, there is still life left in this old rational dog!

Windy Dryden
London and Eastbourne
June 2012

Notes

1 Later this college merged with Royal Holloway College in Egham to become the Royal Holloway and Bedford New College. Very soon after the College dropped the Bedford connection to much sadness and consternation.
2 I completed my training in REBT in 1981.
3 In May 2012.

References

Cooper, M., and McLeod, J. (2011). *Pluralistic counselling and psychotherapy*. London: Sage.
Dryden, W. (2012). Pluralism in counselling and psychotherapy: Personal reflections on an important development. *European Journal of Psychotherapy and Counselling*, *14*, 103–111.
Jourard, S.M. (1968). *Disclosing man to himself*. Princeton, NJ: Van Nostrand.
Jourard, S.M. (1971). *Self-disclosure. An experimental analysis of the transparent self*. New York: Wiley.

ACKNOWLEDGEMENTS

The author wishes to thank the following:

Chapter 1 – Sage for permission to reprint Dryden, W. (2012) Rational emotive behaviour therapy. In C. Feltham and I. Horton (Eds), *The Sage handbook of counselling and psychotherapy*. London: Sage (pp. 298–301).

Chapter 2 – Springer for permission to reprint Dryden, W. (1979) Past messages and disputations: The client and significant others. *Rational Living*, 14(2): 26–28.

Chapter 5 – Springer for permission to reprint Dryden, W. (1986) Language and meaning in RET. *Journal of Rational-Emotive Therapy*, 4(2): 131–142.

Chapter 6 – Springer Publishing Company for permission to reprint Dryden, W. (1986) Vivid methods in rational-emotive therapy. In A. Ellis and R. Grieger (Eds), *Handbook of rational-emotive therapy. Volume* 2. New York: Springer (pp. 221–245).

Chapter 7 – Taylor & Francis for permission to reprint Dryden, W. (1987) The therapeutic alliance in rational-emotive individual therapy. In W. Dryden, *Current issues in rational-emotive therapy*. London: Croom Helm (pp. 59–71).

Chapter 8 – Taylor & Francis for permission to reprint Dryden, W. (1987) Compromises in rational-emotive therapy. In W. Dryden, *Current issues in rational-emotive therapy*. London: Croom Helm (pp. 72–87).

Chapter 9 – Springer for permission to reprint Dryden, W. (1990) Self-disclosure in rational-emotive therapy. In G. Stricker and M. N. Fisher (Eds). *Self-disclosure in the therapeutic relationship*. New York: Plenum (pp. 61–74).

Chapter 10 – Springer for permission to reprint Dryden, W. (1994) Reason and emotion in psychotherapy: Thirty years on. *Journal of Rational-Emotive & Cognitive-Behavior Therapy*, 12(2): 83–99.

Chapter 11 – PCCS Books for permission to reprint Dryden, W. (1998) Rationality, outrageous ideas and sensitivity. In W. Dryden (Ed.), *Are you sitting uncomfortably: Windy Dryden live and uncut*. Ross-on-Wye: PCCS Books.

Chapter 12 – John Wiley & Sons for permission to reprint Dryden, W. (1998) Understanding persons in the context of their problems: A rational emotive behaviour therapy perspective. In M. Bruch and F.W. Bond (Eds), *Beyond diagnosis: Case formulation approaches in CBT*, Chichester: John Wiley & Sons (pp. 43–64).

Chapter 13 – *Romanian Journal of Cognitive and Behavioral Psychotherapies* for permission to reprint Dryden, W. (2001) My idiosyncratic practice of REBT. *Romanian Journal of Cognitive and Behavioral Psychotherapies*, 1(1): 17–30.

Chapter 14 – Sage for permission to reprint Dryden, W. (2001) How rational am I? Self-help using rational emotive behaviour therapy. In E. Spinelli and S. Marshall (Eds), *Embodied theories*. London: Continuum (pp. 28–42).

Chapter 15 – The Association for Rational Emotive Behaviour for permission to reprint Dryden, W. (2002) REBT's situational ABC model. *The Rational Emotive Behaviour Therapist*, 10(1): 4–14.

Chapter 16 – Oxford University Press for permission to reprint Dryden, W. (2005) The personal therapy experiences of a rational emotive behaviour therapist. In J. D. Geller, J. C. Norcross and D. E. Orlinsky (Eds), *The psychotherapist's own psychotherapy*. New York: Oxford University Press (pp. 98–113).

Chapter 17 – Springer for permission to reprint Dryden, W. (2007) Resilience and rationality. *Journal of Rational-Emotive & Cognitive-Behavior Therapy*, 25(3): 213–226.

Chapter 18 – Taylor & Francis for permission to reprint Dryden, W. (2009) The importance of choice in therapy: From the perspective of a, hopefully flexible, CBT practitioner. *European Journal of Psychotherapy and Counselling*, 11: 311–322.

Chapter 19 – Springer for permission to reprint Dryden, W. (2011) Albert Ellis and rational emotive behavior therapy: A personal reflection. *Journal of Rational-Emotive & Cognitive-Behavior Therapy*, 29(4): 211–219.

Chapter 20 – Sage for permission to reprint Dryden, W. (2012) Adapting CBT to a broad clientele. In W. Dryden and R. Branch (Eds), *The CBT handbook*. London: Sage (pp. 214–230).

Chapter 21 – Springer for permission to reprint Dryden, W. (2012, in press) Dealing with procrastination: The REBT approach and a demonstration session. *Journal of Rational-Emotive & Cognitive-Behavior Therapy*, 30(4): 1–18.

Chapter 22 – Springer for permission to reprint Dryden, W. (in press) Unconditional self-acceptance and self-compassion. In M. E. Bernard (Ed.), *Self-acceptance*. New York: Springer.

Every effort has been made to contact copyright-holders for:

Chapter 3 – Dryden, W. (1982) Rational-emotive therapy and eclecticism. *The Counsellor*, 3(5), 15–22.

Chapter 4 – Dryden, W. (1984) Rational-emotive therapy and cognitive therapy: A critical comparison. In M. A. Reda and M. J. Mahoney (Eds), *Cognitive psychotherapies: Recent developments in theory, research and practice*. Cambridge, MA: Ballinger (pp. 81–99).

Please advise the publisher of any errors or omissions, and these will be corrected in subsequent editions.

CHAPTER 1

RATIONAL EMOTIVE BEHAVIOUR THERAPY

(Albert Ellis, 1913–2007)

C. Feltham and I. Horton (Eds) (2012) *The Sage handbook of counselling and psychotherapy*. London: Sage (pp. 298–301)

As this volume of selected works is structured around my publications in the area of Rational Emotive Behaviour Therapy (REBT), a therapeutic approach which is best placed within the cognitive-behavioural tradition of counselling and psychotherapy, I decided to begin the collection with this piece. The article serves as a basic introduction to and overview of REBT which sets the rest of the book in context.

Brief history

Rational emotive behaviour therapy (REBT) was founded in 1955 by Albert Ellis, an American clinical psychologist who had become increasingly disaffected with psychoanalysis in which he trained in the late 1940s. Originally the approach was called rational therapy (RT) because Ellis wanted to emphasize its rational and cognitive features. In doing so, Ellis demonstrated the philosophical influences (largely Stoic) on his thinking. In 1961 he changed its name to rational-emotive therapy to show critics that it did not neglect emotions, and over 30 years later (in 1993) Ellis renamed the approach yet again, calling it rational emotive behaviour therapy to show critics that it did not neglect behaviour.

In 1962 Ellis published *Reason and Emotion in Psychotherapy*, a collection largely of previously published papers or previously delivered lectures, but which became a seminal work in the history of psychotherapy. Most of REBT's major present-day features are described in this book: the pivotal role of cognition in psychological disturbance; the principle of psychological interactionism where cognition, emotion and behaviour are seen as interacting, not separate, systems; the advantages of self-acceptance over self-esteem in helping clients with their disturbed views of their selves; and the importance of an active-directive therapeutic style, to name but a few.

Albert Ellis died in 2007 after an unfortunate period during which he was in dispute on a number of issues with the institute that continues to bear his name. Despite this, the legacy that Ellis left REBT and the wider field of psychotherapy is untarnished and unquestioned.

REBT is practised all over the world and has many different therapeutic, occupational and educational applications. However, it tends to live in the shadow of Beck's cognitive therapy, an approach to cognitive-behaviour therapy which has attracted a greater number of practitioners and is more academically respectable.

Basic assumptions

Rationality is a concept that is normally applied to a person's beliefs. Rational beliefs, which are deemed to be at the core of psychological health, are flexible or non-extreme, consistent with reality, logical, and both self and relationship enhancing. Irrational beliefs, which are deemed to be at the core of psychological disturbance, are rigid or extreme, inconsistent with reality, illogical, and both self and relationship defeating.

There are four types of rational belief: non-dogmatic preferences ('I want to be approved of, but I don't have to be'); non-awfulizing beliefs ('It's bad to be disapproved of, but it isn't the end of the world'); discomfort tolerance beliefs ('It is difficult to face being disapproved of, but I can tolerate it'); and acceptance beliefs (e.g. self-acceptance, 'I can accept myself if I am disapproved of'; other acceptance, 'You are not horrible if you disapprove of me'; and life acceptance, 'Even though this tragedy happened, life is not all bad and comprises good, bad and neutral events').

Similarly, there are four types of irrational belief: rigid demands ('I must be approved of'); awfulizing beliefs ('If I'm disapproved of, it's the end of the world'); discomfort intolerance beliefs ('I can't tolerate being disapproved of'); and depreciation beliefs (e.g. self-depreciation, 'I am worthless if I am disapproved of'; other depreciation, 'You are horrible if you disapprove of me'; and life depreciation, 'Life is all bad because this tragedy happened').

REBT advocates a situational 'ABC' model of psychological disturbance and health. 'A' stands for adversity, which occurs within a situation and can be actual or inferred. 'A' represents the aspect of the situation that the person focuses on and evaluates. 'B' stands for belief (rational or irrational). 'C' stands for the consequences of holding a belief about A and can be emotional, behavioural and cognitive. Thus, 'As' do not cause 'Cs' but contribute to them. 'Bs' are seen as the prime but not the only determiners of 'Cs'.

Holding a rational belief about an 'A' leads to healthy emotions, functional behaviour, and realistic and balanced subsequent thinking. Holding an irrational belief about the same 'A' leads to unhealthy emotions, dysfunctional behaviour, and unrealistic subsequent thinking that is highly skewed to the negative.

REBT's view of human nature is realistic. Humans are seen as having the potential for both rational and irrational thinking. The ease with which we transform our strong desires into rigid demands suggests that the tendency towards irrational thinking is biologically based, but can be buffered or encouraged by environmental contexts.

Clients often have the unfortunate experience of inheriting tendencies towards disturbance and being exposed to their parents' disturbed behaviour. REBT is optimistic and realistic here. It argues that if such clients work persistently and forcefully to counter their irrational beliefs and act in ways that are consistent with their rational beliefs, then they can help themselves significantly. However, REBT also acknowledges that most clients will not put in this degree of effort over a long period of time and will therefore fall far short of achieving their potential for psychological health.

Origin and maintenance of problems

People are disturbed not by events but by the rigid and extreme views that they take of them. This means that while negative events contribute to the development of disturbance, particularly when these events are highly aversive, disturbance occurs when people bring their tendencies to think irrationally to these events.

REBT does not have an elaborate view of the origin of disturbance. Having said this, it does acknowledge that it is very easy for humans when they are young to disturb themselves about highly aversive events. However, it argues that even under these conditions people react differently to the same event and thus we need to understand what a person brings to and takes from a negative activating event. People learn their standards and goals from their culture, but disturbance occurs when they bring their irrational beliefs to circumstances where their standards are not met and their pursuit of their goals is blocked.

REBT has a more elaborate view of how disturbance is maintained. It argues that people perpetuate their disturbance for a number of reasons including the following:

- They lack the insight that their disturbance is underpinned by their irrational beliefs and think instead that it is caused by events.
- They wrongly think that once they understand that their problems are underpinned by irrational beliefs, this understanding alone will lead to change.
- They do not work persistently to change their irrational beliefs and to integrate the rational alternatives to these beliefs into their belief system.
- They continue to act in ways that are consistent with their irrational beliefs.
- They lack or are deficient in important social skills, communication skills, problem-solving skills and other life skills.
- They think that their disturbance has payoffs that outweigh the advantages of the healthy alternatives to their disturbed feelings and/or behaviour.
- They live in environments which support the irrational beliefs that underpin their problems and they think that as this is the case they cannot do anything to help themselves.

Change

REBT therapists consider that the core facilitative conditions of empathy, unconditional acceptance and genuineness are often desirable, but neither necessary nor sufficient for constructive therapeutic change. For such change to take place, REBT therapists need to help their clients to do the following:

- realize that they largely create their own psychological problems and that while situations contribute to these problems, they are in general of lesser importance in the change process
- fully recognize that they are able to address and overcome these problems
- understand that their problems stem largely from irrational beliefs
- detect their irrational beliefs and discriminate between them and their rational beliefs
- question their irrational beliefs and their rational beliefs until they see clearly that their irrational beliefs are false, illogical and unconstructive while their rational beliefs are true, sensible and constructive
- work towards the internalization of their new rational beliefs by using a variety of cognitive (including imaginal), emotive and behavioural change methods
- refrain from acting in ways that are consistent with their old irrational beliefs

- extend this process of challenging beliefs and using multimodal methods of change into other areas of their lives and to commit to doing so for as long as necessary.

All this is best done when effective REBT therapists develop, maintain and suitably end a good working alliance with clients (Dryden, 2009). This involves:

- therapists and clients having a good working bond
- therapists and clients sharing a common view of the determinants of the latter's problems and how these can best be addressed
- therapists and clients working towards agreed goals
- therapists and clients executing agreed tasks designed to facilitate goal achievement.

Skills and strategies

REBT therapists see themselves as good psychological educators and therefore seek to teach their clients the ABC model of understanding and dealing with their psychological problems. They stress that there are alternative ways of addressing these problems and strive to elicit from their clients informed consent at the outset and throughout the counselling process. If they think that a client is better suited to a different approach to therapy, they do not hesitate to effect a suitable referral.

REBT therapists frequently employ an active-directive counselling style and use both Socratic and didactic teaching methods. However, they vary their style from client to client. They begin by working with specific examples of identified client problems and help their clients to set healthy goals. They employ a sequence of steps in working on these examples which involves using the situationally based ABC framework, challenging beliefs and negotiating suitable homework assignments with their clients.

Helping clients to generalize their learning from situation to situation is explicitly built into the counselling process. So too is helping clients to identify, challenge and change core irrational beliefs which are seen as accounting for disturbance across a broad range of relevant situations.

A major therapeutic strategy involves helping clients to become their own therapists. In doing this, REBT therapists teach their clients how to use a particular skill such as challenging irrational beliefs, model the use of this skill, and sometimes give the clients written instructions on how to use the skill on their own. Constructive feedback is given to encourage the refinement of the skill. As clients learn how to use the skills of REBT for themselves, their therapists adopt a less active-directive, more prompting therapeutic style in order to encourage them to take increasing responsibility for their own therapeutic change.

REBT may be seen as an example of theoretically consistent eclecticism in that its practitioners draw upon procedures that originate from other counselling approaches, but do so for purposes that are consistent with REBT theory. REBT therapists are judiciously selective in their eclecticism and avoid the use of methods that are inefficient, or mystical, or of dubious validity.

REBT therapists have their preferred therapeutic goals for their clients, namely to help them to change their core irrational beliefs and to develop and internalize a set of core rational beliefs. However, they are ready to make compromises with their clients on these objectives when it becomes clear that their clients are unable or unwilling to change their core irrational beliefs. In such cases, REBT therapists help their clients by encouraging them to change their distorted inferences, to effect behavioural changes without necessarily changing their irrational beliefs, or to remove themselves from negative activating events.

Research evidence

There is quite a lot of research indicating that psychological disturbance is correlated with irrational beliefs (see Dryden et al., 2009), but studies indicating that these beliefs are at the core of disturbance have yet to be carried out. Most scales which measure irrational and rational beliefs are deficient in one respect or another and there is a need to develop a scale with excellent psychometric properties.

Numerous studies on the effectiveness of REBT have been carried out and various meta-analyses of REBT outcome studies have been conducted which have come to different conclusions about the effectiveness of REBT. Well-controlled trials of REBT need to be done with clinical populations, employing well-trained REBT therapists who can be shown to adhere to a properly designed REBT competency scale. Such a scale has recently been published (Dryden et al., 2010).

References

Dryden, W. (2009) *Skills in Rational Emotive Behaviour Counselling and Psychotherapy*. London: Sage.

Dryden, W., David, D. and Ellis, A. (2009) Rational emotive behavior therapy. In K.S. Dobson (ed.), *Handbook of Cognitive-Behavioral Therapies* (3rd edn, pp. 226–76). New York: Guilford.

Dryden, W., Beal, D., Jones, J. and Trower, P. (2010) *Journal of Rational-Emotive & Cognitive-Behavior Therapy*, 28 (4), whole issue.

Ellis, A. ([1962] 1994) *Reason and Emotion in Psychotherapy* (rev. edn). New York: Birch Lane.

Recommended reading

Dryden, W. (ed.) (1995) *A Rational Emotive Behaviour Therapy Reader*. London: Sage.

Dryden, W. (2001) *Reason to Change: A Rational Emotive Behaviour Therapy (REBT) Workbook*. Hove: Brunner-Routledge.

Dryden, W., DiGiuseppe, R. and Neenan, M. (2010) *A Primer on Rational Emotive Behaviour Therapy* (3rd edn). Champaign, IL: Research Press.

Ellis, A. (2001) *Overcoming Destructive Beliefs, Feelings, and Behaviors*. Amherst, NY: Prometheus.

CHAPTER 2

PAST MESSAGES AND DISPUTATIONS

The client and significant others

Rational Living, 14(2): 26–28 (1979)

This piece is one of the first articles that I wrote on REBT and the first to be published in *Rational Living*, the house organ of what is now known as the Albert Ellis Institute. I pointed out in this book's introduction that I have always striven to take a pluralistic perspective on REBT and this article nicely demonstrates this. Its basic thesis is that, while REBT therapists do not routinely take their clients back to their past, they can certainly do this, particularly when clients think that this will be therapeutic for them. However, as they do this, they need to guard against teaching clients that the past can cause present disturbance. Rather past events,or more accurately the inferences that one has formed of past events, can and often do contribute to such disturbance. How this is dealt with is the subject of the article.

Rational-emotive therapy (RET) is a comprehensive treatment approach which aims to deal with the three basic modalities of human dysfunctioning—cognitive, emotive, and behavioral. Indeed, its multimodal focus is what initially attracted me to RET. However, with regard to another important dimension in psychotherapy—time perspective—rational-emotive theory is less comprehensive in its recommendations. In listening to many tapes of RET practitioners and in participating in discussions with faculty, fellows, and practicum students during a two-month stay at the Institute for Rational-Emotive Therapy in New York in the summer of 1978, I have noted that the large majority claim (at least within earshot of others!) to follow Ellis's (1977) teachings with regard to time perspective (p. 27):

> The rational therapist for the most part ignores connections between the client's early history and his present disturbances. He does not believe that the client was made neurotic by his past experiences, but by his own unrealistic and overdemanding *interpretations* of these experiences.

Thus, when clients want to discuss their past experiences, they are generally instructed by the therapist that the reason they are anxious, depressed, angry, or guilty now is because they are *right now* reindoctrinating themselves with the beliefs they had acquired in the past. Broadly speaking, this is a sound approach and leads the focus of RET practice to be present-centered and future-oriented. However, I am a little concerned with the apparent absolutistic manner in which people have interpreted Ellis in this regard. I believe that with *some* clients, therapeutic movement is delayed by the practitioner's strong reluctance to consider past material. This reluctance is also evident in the RET literature; as far as I am aware, only Dombrow (1973) has made a similar plea for working with past material in RET.

My first thesis is that, while I concur with Ellis's view that "for the most part," exploring connections between the client's earlier history and his present disturbance may not be particularly helpful, with *some* clients exploring past material can actually enhance therapeutic movement. My second thesis is that the therapist can effectively do this by helping clients to dispute the irrationality implicit in the messages they received in the past from significant others. This has the additional effect of enabling clients to recognize and accept the fallibility of those who were assumed to be infallible or omnipotent. To put it in a theoretical perspective, clients are helped to dispute the irrational belief suggested by Hauck (1967): "the idea that beliefs held by respected authorities or society must be correct and therefore should not be questioned" (p. 2).

I believe that, interestingly enough, rational-emotive therapists are not loathe to help clients dispute the irrationality implicit in messages they are receiving from people in their lives at present and the messages they may receive from people in the future. Of course, this is not the major focus of therapeutic intervention, since the practitioner will then proceed to help clients to dispute the irrationality implicit in the messages they give themselves in response to the irrational messages received from others. Thus, the principle of disputing the irrationality in others' messages is not altogether foreign to RET practice, although it would be viewed as an inelegant solution. While not foreign to RET practice, this procedure has received little attention in the RET literature. Moreover, while at present we have very little research evidence showing the superior effectiveness of elegant over inelegant RET solutions, the possibility may exist that such inelegant solutions may enhance therapeutic movement in some clients and may thus deserve consideration.

To illustrate the thesis that helping some clients dispute the irrationality implicit in messages received from people in the past may facilitate therapeutic movement, I will briefly discuss the case of Mary, a very intelligent, 32-year-old Irish woman whom I saw in a University Health Service setting. Mary had suffered from severe feelings of worthlessness for many years. She had previously received therapeutic help from a kindly Irish psychiatrist who "boosted her ego" temporarily. Needless to say, such "progress" was short-lived. In the traditional RET manner, I attempted to show Mary that her depression stemmed from the strict demands she placed on herself and the resulting self-downing which accompanied her failures to live up to these demands. However, Mary seemed more interested in talking at length about the inhumane treatment she had received from her parents when she was younger—she had been cruelly beaten, often for little reason, and particularly when she made mistakes. My repeated and forceful attempts to guide her to the view that her present disturbance was caused by present self-indoctrination did not lead to therapeutic progress. However, movement did occur after I had worked with Mary for a short period of time, helping her to analyze and dispute the irrationality implicit in the messages she had received from her parents in the past. In my opinion, this enabled her to become more receptive to the view that it was not the parents' messages at A which caused her disturbance at C, but her own interpretations of the messages at B, with which she was now reindoctrinating herself. Mary's response to my change of therapeutic attack was illuminating. She claimed that the occasions when we analyzed and disputed her parents' irrationality were helpful in that "I felt freed then to look at what I am doing to myself now."

In conclusion, while I have pointed out the advantages of helping some clients to dispute the irrationality implicit in messages received from significant others—1. it may help initially resistant clients to later respond more favorably to present-centered/future-oriented RET; 2. it has educational value in teaching that significant others are not infallible and have their own irrational beliefs; and 3. it helps make RET even more multimodal in approach—I also want to emphasize some potential dangers. First, if not sensitively handled, the client may conclude that A really does cause C. Thus, it is important to stress to the client that whatever irrational messages were communicated to him by significant others, he is still responsible for causing his own emotional disturbance by communicating equally irrational messages to himself. Second (and related to the first issue) clients may begin to severely *blame* significant others for causing their problems. This is not a problem if the issue of blame is then handled in the traditional RET manner. Finally, delving into the past may lead the practitioner and his client into blind alleys and encourage the former to collude with the latter's attempts to avoid self-responsibility.

Nonetheless, if the above problems are competently handled, it is my contention that the strategy of helping the client to analyze and dispute the irrationality in past (present and future) messages from significant others does have its place in RET practice with certain clients.

References

Dombrow, R. On the use of early childhood material in rational-emotive therapy. *Rational Living*, 1973, 8(1), 17–18.

Ellis, A. A rational approach to interpretation. In Ellis, A. and Grieger, R. (eds.): *Handbook of rational-emotive therapy*. New York: Springer, 1977.

Hauck, P. Challenge authority: for thy health's sake. *Rational Living*, 1967, 2(1), 1–3.

CHAPTER 3

RATIONAL-EMOTIVE THERAPY AND ECLECTICISM

The Counsellor, 3(5): 15–22 (1982)

In 1978, I began my training in REBT at what is now known as the Albert Ellis Institute. At the same time I began a two-year, part-time Masters course in Psychotherapy at the University of Warwick. This course, which was run by John and Marcia Davis, was an eclectic-based course and taught me to look at counselling and psychotherapy from a broad perspective. This paper, which was published in 1982, two years after I completed the MSc programme, outlines how eclecticism informed my practice of REBT. Five years later, I published a piece on how I saw REBT as being a theoretically-consistent approach to eclecticism (Dryden, 1987).

Reference

Dryden, W. (1987). A case of theoretically consistent eclecticism: Humanizing a computer 'addict'. In J. C. Norcross (Ed.), *Casebook of eclectic psychotherapy*. New York: Brunner/Mazel (pp. 221–237).

Eclecticism has been defined as "consisting of that which has been selected from diverse sources, systems or styles" (American Heritage Dictionary of the English Language, 1971) and much has been recently written on eclectic approaches in psychotherapy (e.g. Dryden, 1980a; Garfield, 1980; Lazarus, 1976 and Shostrom, 1976). However, there have been few attempts to clarify the decisions that clinicians make in broadening their therapeutic repertoire by selecting from diverse therapeutic orientation. The aim of this paper is to show what guides rational-emotive therapists in such endeavours.

Rational-emotive theory states that much emotional disturbance stems from the faulty inferences and irrational evaluations that patients make in endeavouring to make sense of themselves, other people and the world (Wessler and Wessler, 1980). Examples of faulty inferences have been detailed by Beck et al. (1979) and include arbitrary inferences, overgeneralizations and selective abstractions. Irrational evaluations are based on a philosophy of demandingness which hinders patients from achieving their long-term goals and restricts their opportunities to live effectively and creatively in the world. Such demands are couched in terms of musts, shoulds, oughts and have to's, i.e. absolutistic demands on self, others and the world. The major task of rational-emotive therapists is to help patients correct their faulty inferences and to replace their demanding philosophy with a desiring philosophy, i.e. one which is characterized by wants, preferences and wishes. To achieve their basic task, rational-emotive therapists focus on cognitive, affective and behavioural factors and consequently R.E.T. has been described as a comprehensive system of psychotherapy (Ellis and Abrahms, 1978).

Rational-emotive therapists then are guided by a particular theory of emotional disturbance and personality change (Ellis, 1978) and thus can be contrasted with eclectic therapists who de-emphasize theory (e.g. Lazarus, 1976). Theory is considered important by rational-emotive therapists for a number of reasons. First, theory provides testable propositions for empirical study. Second, as Frank (1970) has shown, theory helps therapists gain emotional support from others with similar views and thus helps sustain the therapist's morale. The third and most important reason is that theory helps guide therapists in their work, helps them correctly select particular therapeutic procedures and gives them a framework for determining the consequences of such procedures. Eysenck (1970) also stresses the need for theory in psychotherapy and warns that without a theoretical framework the practice of eclectic therapists would be characterized by "a mish-mash of theories, a hugger-mugger of procedures, a charivaria of therapies and a gallimaufry of activities having no proper rationale and incapable of being tested or evaluated" (p. 145).

Therapeutic practice

In the execution of their major task—affecting cognitive change, rational-emotive therapists attempt to engage patients in a concrete and situationally-based exploration of their problems. To encourage concreteness, therapists tend to use an implicit ABCDE framework in exploring their patients' problems. Point "A" in the framework represents an event or the patients' perceptions and inferences concerning that event, "B" represents the patient's beliefs or evaluations about the phenomenal event, while "C" stands for the emotional and behavioural consequences of the patient's belief. At point "D" the therapist's task is to help the patient challenge his faulty inferences and irrational evaluations and replace them with more realistic and rational cognitions which leads to emotional and behavioural change at point "E".

In practice rational-emotive therapists tend to start at point "C". The major goal here is to help patients acknowledge their feelings (without dwelling on them) and to identify their actions. In doing so the therapist may very well use procedures derived from other therapeutic systems. For example, if a patient experiences difficulty in acknowledging feelings, the rational-emotive therapist might employ a gestalt awareness exercise of psychodramatic technique with the specific purpose at this stage of encouraging the patient to acknowledge feelings.

After helping the patient to correctly identify emotional and behavioural responses, the therapist shifts her attention to the context in which such responses arise (point A). Exploration at this point involves the therapist paying attention to the patient's description of the relevant context. The patient is helped to describe his perception of the relevant situation fairly briefly. The therapist tends not to dwell upon those events and discourages the patient from presenting too many or problem-irrelevant contexts. The goal of the therapist is to aid the patient in adequately framing the problem so that she can assist in the identification and correction of presently held faulty inferences and beliefs. In practice the context tends to be either one that is anticipated or one of recent occurrence and thus R.E.T. tends to be a present and future-oriented therapy. Rational-emotive therapists tend not to focus on events that have occurred in the distant past since it is argued that such exploration does not aid the correction of presently-held faulty cognitions (Ellis, 1962). However, Dryden (1979) has found that in certain circumstances such exploration does assist the therapist in her dissuasion strategies with some patients. Thus understanding the likely origins of presently-held beliefs may motivate such patients to change such beliefs. The point at issue here is that the purpose of exploring such past events is to facilitate the disputing of *presently* held inferences and beliefs.

At point B in the ABCDE framework, the therapist's task is to help the patient identify the irrational evaluations that the latter employs in appraising the relevant context. Here the therapist is not limited to verbal interventions such as: "what are you saying to yourself?", which are often seen in therapy transcripts. In fact, in the author's experience a common answer to such questions is—"nothing". In addition to psychodrama (Nardi, 1979) and gestalt methods, various role-playing and imagery methods may be used as an aid to facilitate the discovery of irrational beliefs. Indeed, client-centre procedures for some patients may be employed. Such patients find the less active-directive style implicit in such procedures helpful in exploring and discovering meanings and beliefs (DiLoreto, 1971). Rather than abandon R.E.T. for client-centred therapy, an eclectic rational-emotive therapist would vary her therapeutic style but not the theoretical underpinnings of her system.

Point D in the framework is also called the dissuasion process (Wessler and Wessler, 1980). On attempting to dissuade the patient, the therapist may use a wide variety of cognitive, imaginal, affective, and behavioural methods, and may suggest similar procedures for the patient to use between sessions as the latter strives to put into practice in his everyday life what he has learned in therapy (point E).

Theory-inspired guidelines for choosing appropriate therapeutic procedures

Thus far it has been argued that rational-emotive therapists may choose from a range of cognitive, experiential and behavioural methods to facilitate his task of working within the ABCDE framework. However rational-emotive therapists are mindful of possible negative effects of employing certain procedures and by no means would employ all available procedures. There are a number of issues that rational-emotive therapists have in mind when deciding whether or not to employ a particular therapeutic procedure.

(a) **Helping patients get better rather than feel better.** One basic aim of rational-emotive therapists is to promote long-term philosophically-based change as opposed to helping patients feel better in the short-term. Thus rational-emotive therapists may deliberately avoid being unduly warm towards their patients and would be wary of employing cathartic methods. The hazard of undue therapist warmth is that it may lead to increased long-term dependence in a patient who may then believe that they are worthwhile because the therapist is acting very warmly towards them. However if the therapist or other significant people act coldly towards the patient, he may then conclude that he is worthless. Thus, undue therapist warmth, although patients feel better when so exposed, tends to distract clients from dealing with the more difficult task of accepting themselves unconditionally (Ellis, 1977). For this reason an intense relationship between therapist and patient is generally avoided. The therapist strives to establish and maintain a working relationship with her patient and strives to accept the patient as a fallible human being without being unduly warm towards him.

Cathartic methods have the short-term value of encouraging relief of pent-up feelings, but in the long-term if not employed sparingly and briefly often encourage patients to practise their already well-ingrained irrational philosophies. For example, cathartic procedures which place emphasis on the ventilation of intense angry feelings (e.g. pounding a cushion) run the risk of encouraging processes of blaming which are according to rational-emotive theory a feature of the irrational philosophy underlying anger. Rational-emotive therapists might employ such procedures when they wish to help patients to acknowledge their feelings, but the patient would then be quickly encouraged to consider the philosophy underlying such feelings.

(b) **Self-esteem vs. self-acceptance.** In R.E.T., self-esteem is defined as a form of global self-rating and is to be avoided since according to rational-emotive theory it has problematic long-term implications for patients. Procedures based on self-esteem notions encourage patients to define themselves as worthwhile or competent so long as they gain approval or succeed at valued tasks. They are thus prone to defining themselves as worthless and incompetent if they receive disapproval or fail at the same task. Furthermore, rational-emotive theory states that it is nonsensical to give humans global ratings since they are on-going, complex ever-changing organisms who defy such ratings. As an alternative, rational-emotive therapists not only endeavour to get patients accepting themselves as on-going, complex, ever-changing fallible human beings but also encourage them to rate their traits, aspects, and behaviour but not their selves. Many procedures do not in fact discourage patients from making such global self-ratings. For example, many therapists give patients homework assignments which are designed to encourage the patient to succeed. Thus a patient who succeeds at approaching a woman at a discotheque may conclude that because he has been able to do this, perhaps he is not worthless after all. The implication would be that if he failed in his assignment then this would be a confirmation of his worthlessness. Rational-emotive therapists by contrast may at times encourage patients to deliberately go out and fail since such a failure experience presents them with opportunities to work on accepting themselves as fallible humans rather than sub-humans when they fail. In reality, rational-emotive therapists suggest both success and failure-oriented homework assignments to their patients.

(c) **Anger vs. annoyance.** Rational-emotive theory clearly distinguishes between anger and annoyance. Annoyance results when something occurs which we view as a trespass on our personal conceptual domain, which we strongly dislike but which we refrain from demanding should not have happened. There is an absence of blaming of self, other or the world for the deed, i.e. the deed is rated but the perpetration of the deed is accepted. In contrast anger stems from the jehovian demand that the trespass should not have occurred and the trespasser is damnable. Therapists from other persuasions often do not make such a clear distinction and thus the therapeutic procedures which they employ may encourage the full expression and ventilation of anger rather than annoyance. If this occurs then rational-emotive therapists would avoid using these procedures. As mentioned earlier, while the full expression and ventilation of anger helps the person feel better it often encourages adherence to a long-term and damaging anger-creating philosophy. In R.E.T., procedures are used to help patients to fully acknowledge their anger but then they are encouraged to dispute the underlying philosophy.

(d) **Desensitization vs. implosion.** Rational-emotive therapists face a choice of two different approaches when the issue of suggesting homework assignments to patients arises. They can either suggest that patients gradually face their fears and overcome their problems in a slow stepwise fashion while minimizing discomfort (desensitization). Or they can suggest that patients take a risk and forcefully confront their fears and their problems while tolerating discomfort (implosion).

Rational-emotive therapists very definitely favour implosion-based assignments since they help patients overcome their "low frustration tolerance" (L.F.T.) or "discomfort anxiety", constructs which according to rational-emotive theory play a central role in preventing change (Wessler 1978; Ellis, 1980). Consequently such therapists would avoid helping patients to gradually and painlessly overcome their problems because such procedures are viewed as encouraging patients to cling to their philosophy of L.F.T. which actually decreases their chances of maintaining therapeutic improvement and increases the possibility of relapse (Ellis, 1980).

Due to the somewhat unusual stance taken on the above issues rational-emotive therapy has proved rather difficult to combine with other methods derived from different theoretical origins. Garfield and Kurtz (1977) make a similar observation, noting in their study of 154 clinicians' eclectic views that R.E.T. was occasionally combined with learning theory-based approaches but was not combined with psychoanalytic, neo-analytic, Rogerian, humanistic or Sullivanian orientations.

Therapeutic style

Ellis (1976) speaking for rational-emotive theory argues that humans have great difficulty maintaining the changes that they make more easily in the short term because of the strong biological basis to irrational thinking. Because of this difficulty. Ellis urges rational-emotive therapists to adopt an active-directive, forceful and persistent therapeutic style and also encourage their patients to be equally active, forceful and persistent with themselves. However, is such a style beneficial with a wide range of patients? Or should rational-emotive therapists vary their therapeutic style with different patients? If the latter is to be advised, what criteria should be employed to assist rational-emotive therapists in these important decisions?

The first question remains unanswered since we lack research which has systematically studied the effects of active-directive R.E.T. across a wide range of patients. There is however some research evidence concerning different therapeutic styles with different patients which has relevance for R.E.T. practitioners. DiLoreto (1971) in a study using socially anxious patients found that active-directive R.E.T. was more effective with introverts than extroverts in the sample while client-centred therapy was more effective with extroverts. This suggests that R.E.T. practitioners might effectively adopt a less directive more reflective style of R.E.T., when working with socially anxious extroverts. Morley and Watkins (1974) carried out a treatment study with speech anxious patients. They found that active-directive R.E.T. benefited external locus of control patients most, while internal locus of control patients profited most from a modified R.E.T. approach where rational and irrational beliefs relevant to speech anxiety were merely presented and not challenged in the usual fashion. To what extent these findings can be generalized to other patient populations remains unclear. We must also wait for studies to consider Ellis' point often made in practice that the stronger patients adhere to irrational philosophies the more forceful the therapist had better be.

Carson (1969) advocates an interpersonally-based system to help the therapist vary her interpersonal style according to the patient's own style. Unproductive interlocking interactional patterns arise when the therapist adopts a manner of relating which confirms the patient in his own self-defeating style. The therapist's task is to adopt an interpersonal style which (a) does not reinforce the patient's dysfunctional style and (b) provides a disconfirming experience for the patient. For example, with a passive patient it would be important for the rational-emotive therapist to refrain from adopting a very active style which might reinforce the patient's self-defeating passivity.

Thus, rational-emotive therapists had better be mindful of Eschenroeder's (1979) question: "Which therapeutic style is most effective with what kind of client?" (p. 5).

Therapeutic modalities

Rational-emotive theory holds that the important modalities of human experience—cognitive (verbal and imaginal), affective and behavioural are overlapping rather than separate systems (Ellis, 1962). However it may be important for R.E.T. practitioners to vary the emphasis they place in working within the various modalities with different patients. What criteria might be important as guides to decision-making in this area, bearing in mind that the ultimate goal is a common one (i.e. to effect philosophical changes)? One set of criteria might be the ability of patients to handle verbal concepts. The author's own experience of working as a counselling psychologist in a working-class region is that with those patients who find it difficult using words it is important for therapists to focus on the behavioural modality both within and between sessions. When teaching rational concepts, important with such patients, then it is essential to use the visual mode of communication as an adjunct to the verbal mode. Thus, I use pen and paper a lot, sketching diagrams to facilitate such patients' understanding of difficult rational concepts. In addition, I have devised a number of visual models to illustrate rational concepts (Dryden, 1980b). When patients employ words to protect them from emotional experience, i.e. when they employ intellectualization as a major defensive style, then rational-emotive therapists might more effectively focus on the experiential modality helping such patients to acquaint themselves with that mode of experience from which they have shielded themselves. If therapists spend too much time engaging such patients in traditional rational-emotive socratic dialogue then they may well reinforce their patients' defensive style. Such speculations of course need to be tested.

Beutler (1979) has suggested a system which combines therapeutic modalities and styles in determining whether certain therapies are more effective than others with patients on three major patient dimensions. The first dimension is symptom complexity. If symptoms are circumscribed Beutler (1979) hypothesizes that a greater behavioural focus would be more effective, whereas if they are more complex a greater cognitive focus is needed. The second dimension is defensive style, the therapist needs to emphasize the behavioural modality in therapy whereas cognitive interventions are required with patients utilizing an internal defensive style. The third dimension taps the degree to which external events are construed as representing a threat to the person's autonomy-reactance. If the patient is high on the reactance dimension i.e. if he is pre-disposed to view external events as autonomy-endangering, then the therapist would be more productive if she adopted a less directive, more experiential therapeutic style. If the patient is low on this dimension then greater therapist direction with a more behavioural focus is needed. Beutler (1979) reviewed empirical studies relevant to his hypotheses but found only meagre to moderate support for these hypotheses. However, these hypotheses were not tested directly and Beutler's system remains a promising one in that it provides the rational-emotive therapist with some guidelines as to possible variations in style and modality focus with different patients.

In conclusion, it has been shown how R.E.T. practitioners employ rational-emotive theory as a guide in their choice of a wide array of therapeutic interventions. In addition, the argument was advanced that R.E.T. practitioners had better take into account patient characteristics in making decisions concerning therapeutic style and modality-focus. However, the central purpose of the eclectic R.E.T. practitioner remains the modification of faulty inferences and irrational beliefs.

References

The American Heritage Dictionary of the English Language (1971). New York: American Heritage.

Beck, A. T., Rush, A. J., Shaw, B. F. and Emery, G. (1979). *Cognitive Therapy of Depression*. New York: Wiley.

Beutler, L. E. (1979). Toward specific psychological therapies for specific conditions. *Journal of Consulting and Clinical Psychology*, 47, 882–897.

Carson, R. C. (1969). *Interaction Concepts of Personality* London: George Allen & Unwin.

DiLoreto, A. E. (1971). *Comparative Psychotherapy: An Experimental Analysis*. Chicago: Aldine-Atherton.

Dryden, W. (1979). Past messages and disputations: the client and significant others. *Rational Living*, 14 (1), 26–28.

Dryden, W. (1980a). "Eclectic" approaches in individual counselling: some pertinent issues. *The Counsellor*, 3, 24–30.

Dryden, W. (1980b). Nightmares and fun. Paper given at the Third National Conference on Rational-Emotive Therapy, June, New York.

Ellis, A. (1962). *Reason and Emotion in Psychotherapy*. New York: Lyle Stuart.

Ellis, A. (1976). The biological basis of human irrationality. *Journal of Individual Psychology*, 32, 145–168.

Ellis, A. (1977). Intimacy in psychotherapy. *Rational Living*, 12 (2), 13–19.

Ellis, A. (1978). Toward a theory of personality. In R. J. Corsini (ed.), *Readings in Current Personality Theories*. Illinois: F. E. Peacock.

Ellis, A. (1980). The philosophic implications and dangers of some popular behavior therapy techniques. Invited address to the World Congression Behavior Therapy, July, Jerusalem.

Ellis, A. and Abrahms, E. (1978). *Brief Psychotherapy in Medical and Health Practice*. New York: Springer.

Eschenroeder, G. (1979). Different therapeutic styles in rational-emotive therapy. *Rational Living*, 14 (2), 3–7.

Eysenck, H. J. (1970). A mish-mash of theories. *International Journal of Psychiatry*, 9, 140–146.

Frank, J. D. (1970). Psychotherapists need theories. *International Journal of Psychiatry*, 9, 146–149.

Garfield, S. L. (1980). *Psychotherapy: An Eclectic Approach*. New York: Wiley.

Garfield, S. L. and Kurtz, R. (1977). A study of eclectic views. *Journal of Consulting and Clinical Psychology*, 45, 78–83.

Lazarus, A. A. (1976). *Mutimodal Behavior Therapy*. New York: Springer.

Morley, E. L. and Watkins, J. T. (1974). Locus of control and effectiveness of two rational-emotive therapy styles. *Rational Living*, 9 (2), 22–24.

Nardi, T. J. (1979). The use of psychodrama in R.E.T. *Rational Living*, 14 (1), 35–38.

Shostrom, E. L. (1976). *Actualizing Therapy: Foundations for a Scientific Ethic*. San Diego: Edits.

Wessler, R. A. and Wessler, R. L. (1980). *The Principles and Practice of Rational-Emotive Therapy*. San Francisco: Jossey-Bass.

CHAPTER 4

RATIONAL-EMOTIVE THERAPY AND COGNITIVE THERAPY

A critical comparison*

M. A. Reda and M. J. Mahoney (Eds) (1984) *Cognitive psychotherapies: Recent developments in theory, research and practice*. Cambridge, MA: Ballinger (pp. 81–99).

In 1981, I spent a six months' sabbatical at the Center for Cognitive Therapy, University of Pennsylvania in Philadelphia under the auspices of Aaron T. Beck, the originator of Cognitive Therapy (CT). I was the first person in Britain to do an extended training in CT. In addition to being trained in CT and seeing patients in that method at the Center's Mood Clinic, during the sabbatical, I also sat in on and participated in CT sessions conducted by Dr David Burns, the author of the best-selling self-help book, *Feeling Good* (Burns, 1980) and went one day a week to what is now known as the Albert Ellis Institute to see patients at their clinic using REBT. Thus, at the time, I was practising both CT and REBT in different contexts. It thus seemed to me a good idea to write a piece critically comparing CT and REBT building on my experiences and based on the extant published literature. The article that appears here is the result.

Reference

Burns, D. D. (1980). *Feeling good: the new mood therapy*. New York: William M. Morrow.

A critical comparison between two approaches to psychotherapy is offered in this chapter. In comparing rational-emotive therapy with cognitive therapy I have utilized the writings of both Aaron Beck and Albert Ellis, other statements by Beck and Ellis that have not been published, the views of experienced and highly trained rational-emotive therapists and cognitive therapists, and my own views concerning the differences and similarities between rational-emotive therapy and cognitive therapy based on my experiences of being trained at both the Institute for Rational-Emotive Therapy in New York and the Center for Cognitive Therapy in Philadelphia. My aim in this comparative review is to consider the developmental history, theoretical and philosophical underpinnings, and practical components of the two approaches.

At the outset it is important to note that Ellis (1979, 1980a) states that there are two forms of RET: general RET, which he claims is synonymous with cognitive behavior therapy (CBT) (Ellis, 1980a), and specialized RET, which he claims differs from CBT in several important respects.[1]

* I am grateful to the following people with whom I discussed some of the issues that appear in this chapter or who gave feedback on early drafts: Aaron T. Beck, Ray DiGiuseppe, Albert Ellis, Art Freeman, Ray Harrison, Ira Herman, George Lockwood, Sue Walen, Richard Wessler, Ruth Wessler, and Jeff Young. However, only I am responsible for the chapter's content.

Development

Both rational-emotive therapy and cognitive therapy were developed as a result of their founders' dissatisfaction with psychoanalytic theory and practice. However, while Ellis has developed RET mainly outside the formal academic arena, Beck has remained firmly within it. This factor may partially account for the different emphases apparent in the work of Beck and Ellis. Ellis used to be in private practice and is now executive director of two nonprofit institutes. The Institute for Rational-Emotive Therapy has a clinic where lengthy diagnostic interviews are not carried out. Over the years Ellis and his colleagues have seen patients representing the broad spectrum of emotional disorders. RET, then, has developed without Ellis and his colleagues focusing on any one specific emotional disorder for special and intensive empirical study and without them carrying out rigorously designed outcome studies. Beck and his colleagues on the other hand have spent much of their time and attention studying the psychological processes of the depressive disorders and have carried out rigorously designed outcome studies on the cognitive therapy of depression. Beck and his team are now adopting a similar approach to the study of anxiety disorders. In their clinic lengthy diagnostic interviews are carried out.

These differences are reflected in the different emphases of Beck's and Ellis's writings. Ellis has written extensively on a wide variety of psychotherapeutic issues and the spectrum of the emotional disorders. He has written widely on the philosophical and theoretical underpinnings of RET (Ellis, 1976, 1978, 1979b), has steadily over the years published books and articles on the *general* strategy and specific techniques used in RET (Ellis, 1958, 1962, 1968, 1971, 1975, 1979d) but somewhat surprisingly has not written much on the practice of RET over the course of treatment. He has recently published a treatment manual, 23 years after the inception of RET (Ellis & Abrahms, 1978).

In contrast, Beck's writings lack the breadth and variety of Ellis's, but reflect the in-depth study replete with his own group's experimental work that is lacking in the work of Ellis (Beck, 1963, 1964, 1967, 1973; Beck et al., 1979). Beck (1976) has written a more general text on the emotional disorders but on closer inspection focuses mainly on the depressive and anxiety disorders. In this publication anger is covered only briefly, while shame and guilt are not given coverage at all. Beck has not written extensively on the philosophical underpinnings of cognitive therapy but unlike Ellis has written on the practice of cognitive therapy over the course of treatment and has published three treatment manuals where therapeutic style, strategy, and technique are specifically described.

Any comparison between rational-emotive therapy and cognitive therapy must be placed in a historical context that illustrates the different interest and emphases in the work of the founding fathers. These differences do account for some of the differences in the current status of the two approaches.

Theoretical and philosophical underpinnings

Images of the person and the acquisition of emotional disturbance

All approaches to psychotherapy are based on either explicit or implicit images of human beings. Such images do have a direct influence on the practice of therapy although such a relationship is of course confounded by other variables. Ellis (1976, 1978, 1979b) has spelled out in detail the image of the person that underlies his practice of specialized RET. In contrast, Beck does not address himself to this issue in his writings, preferring to focus on the theoretical and experimental factors associated with depression and anxiety.

Ellis (1976, 1978) has consistently emphasized the biological basis of irrationality which he claims underlies most emotional disturbance. Indeed he writes: "RET-oriented personality theory hypothesises that probably 80 per cent of the variance of human behaviour rests on biological bases and about 20 per cent on environmental training" (Ellis, 1978, p. 304). It is difficult to determine to what extent this view is shared by rational-emotive therapists and to what extent adhering to this viewpoint influences therapeutic practice.[2]

Beck's (1967, 1976) earlier work appeared to emphasize important early learning experiences in the development of cognitive schemas that leave a person vulnerable to emotional disorders. In his more recent work, however, more emphasis is given to the influence of premorbid personality (Beck, in press) and biological factors (Beck, Note 1) in the development of emotional disorders.

Both Ellis and Beck have made similar statements concerning the acquisition of emotional disturbance. Ellis (1978, 1979b) considers there to be a multiplicity of origins of personality and presumably of emotional disturbance. In the same vein Beck (in press) argues that it is counterproductive to speak of *the* cause of the affective disorders. He argues that there are a host of possible predisposing and precipitating factors in the development of depression. While making similar statements concerning the acquisition of emotional disturbance, it is clear that Beck and Ellis differ in their views concerning the *ultimate* determinants of emotional disturbance with Ellis stressing biological factors and Beck stressing significant learning experiences albeit against the background of a specific biological disposition (Herman, Note 2). Such differences show up in how Beck and Ellis talk about the development of emotional disturbance. While Beck talks and writes in terms of human beings *learning* dysfunctional underlying assumptions, Ellis talks in terms of human beings *teaching* themselves irrational beliefs (and being biologically prone to do so). A common Ellis message to his patients is "It's got zero to do with your mother and father; you taught yourself that nonsense." While Ellis exaggerates in this way in order to make a point, such a remark does capture his distaste for theories that make significant learning experiences primary in explaining the development of emotional disturbance.

Although Ellis stresses humans' biological tendency toward irrationality, he has an optimistic view of human potential for change:

> People . . . have an unusual capacity to change their cognitive and behavioral processes so that they can (a) choose to react differently from the way they usually do, (b) refuse to upset themselves about almost anything that may occur, and (c) train themselves so that they can semiautomatically remain minimally disturbed for the rest of their lives.
>
> (Ellis, 1979a, p. 2)

Thus if human beings apply themselves they can achieve considerable results. Beck, a priori, must have faith in the ability of humans to overcome their emotional problems, but he has not written about this potential for change. It is difficult to imagine him writing in the same vein as Ellis, however. Beck's view on this issue seems to me to be a traditional one, that human beings can achieve a fair measure of emotional health while overcoming significant barriers. Ellis's view is less traditional, saying that human beings can achieve a considerable measure of emotional health while overcoming gigantic barriers.

The nature of emotional disturbance

Both Beck and Ellis have acquired their reputations for giving cognitive factors primacy in accounting for emotional disturbance, and both stress that cognitions, feelings, and behaviors interrelate. In addition both point to underlying cognitive structures as being at the root of emotional disturbance. They do not agree as to the nature of these underlying cognitive structures, however. For Ellis the root of emotional disturbance is a set of "musturbatory ideologies" toward self, others, and life conditions in general (Ellis, 1977a). Such ideologies take the form of evaluations (as opposed to inferences) (Wessler & Wessler, 1980; Wessler, 1982) and are absolutist and grandioise in nature. Ellis calls these structures ideologies because he wishes to stress their philosophical nature. Such ideologies, he claims, are responsible for the inferential cognitive distortions that Beck et al. (1979) so carefully document, although this claim has yet to be studied. Beck (Beck et al., 1979; Kovacs & Beck, 1978) agrees that maladaptive underlying cognitive structures are responsible for patients' cognitive distortions about self, experiences, and future but does not agree with Ellis that these underlying assumptions or cognitive schema are invariably musturbatory and evaluative in nature. Beck (1976) does say that these assumptions tend to be absolute in nature as well as being characterized by such distortions as exaggeration and overgeneralization. Beck (1976, pp. 255–256) gives nine examples of underlying assumptions that predispose people to depression. While seven of these assumptions are evaluative in nature, two are inferential statements about reality ("If somebody disagrees with me, it means he does not like me" and "If I don't take advantage of every opportunity to advance myself, I will regret it later"). This list is also quoted in Beck et al. (1979) and Coleman and Beck (1981), so it is possible to argue that this is still Beck's viewpoint. Thus we see that whereas rational-emotive therapists tend to distinguish clearly between inferential (or what Ellis calls observations) and evaluative processes (Wessler and Wessler, 1980; Wessler, 1982), cognitive therapists do not make such a clear distinction.

Ellis's viewpoint on emotional disturbance is centered on two basic themes. These I call "ego disturbance" and "discomfort disturbance." Emotional disturbance is due to human beings' failure to acknowledge or accept their human fallibility and their failure to adopt a tolerant attitude toward discomfort. Thus Ellis tends to view disturbance in terms of two fundamental processes. Although Beck and other cognitive therapists (Beck et al., 1979; Burns, 1980) outline a number of faulty information-processing styles or cognitive distortions that are reflected in underlying assumptions, they tend to emphasize the idiosyncratic nature of these assumptions and do not specify such distinct fundamental processes. Thus whereas rational-emotive therapists tend to think in terms of finite clusters of irrational beliefs, cognitive therapists tend to think in terms of an infinite number of underlying assumptions (Herman, Note 2).[3]

Another difference between rational-emotive therapy and cognitive therapy that is derived from the writings of Beck and Ellis and my observations is that Ellis clearly distinguishes between what he calls appropriate and inappropriate emotions, wheras cognitive therapists in general do not. For example, Ellis (1977b) in reviewing Beck's (1976) *Cognitive Therapy and the Emotional Disorders* notes that Beck uses *sadness* "as a term for all kinds of states ranging from mild regret to severe self-damning" (p. 295).[4] Ellis's clear distinction between appropriate and inappropriate feelings stems from his clear distinction between "healthy" rational beliefs and "unhealthy" irrational beliefs. While no comparatively simple criteria have been described in the cognitive-therapy literature for distinguishing between dysfunctional and functional underlying assumptions, Young (Note 3), a cognitive therapist, does employ criteria for distinguishing between functional and dysfunctional thoughts, feelings, and behaviors.

Ellis in his writings (e.g., Ellis, 1979b; Ellis & Abrahms, 1978) emphasizes that humans often disturb themselves about their disturbance and that this is a significant feature of both his theory and his practice. Whereas cognitive therapists acknowledge the prevalence of this process in anxiety disorders (anxiety about anxiety), the corresponding process in depression (depression about depression) is not prominently featured.

Beck and cognitive therapists on the other hand highlight inferential cognitive distortions prominently in their ideas about disturbance and as targets for change in their practical interventions. For example, negative predictions about the future are regarded as a primary factor in depression and highly influential in the production of suicidal ideations. Ellis does acknowledge the influence of such distortions, but these do not occupy a central role in his theorizing and practice.

Perpetuation of emotional disturbance

Beck et al. (1979) argue that depressed persons perpetuate their pain-inducing and self-defeating attitudes despite objective evidence of positive features in their lives. They argue that humans utilize cognitive schema and faulty information-processing styles to edit out various potentially disconforming experiences and distort such experiences to fit in with the activated cognitive schema. As a result alternatives are not explored and new behaviors not attempted. Thus the person is likely to have familiar experiences that further perpetuate the disturbance (Herman, Note 2). Although Ellis would not disagree with this view, his arguments concerning the perpetuation of emotional disturbance highlight the view that "most people have a natural tendency to resist basic personality change" (Ellis, 1979c, p. 51). He and Wessler (1978) argue that *low frustration tolerance* (LFT) is at the root of such perpetuation. We have already seen that cognitive therapists do not highlight this process in their writings. Ellis argues that most human beings have a natural affinity for comfort and thus opt for the relative comfort of short-term, self-defeating goals and in so doing miss out on the potential change-producing but uncomfortable experiences that striving for their long-term self-enhancing goals would afford.

The nature of emotional health and goals of therapy

Ellis's image of the emotionally healthy individual is firmly rooted in a "clinical-humanistic-atheistic" philosophy (Ellis, 1980b). His position is that if human beings are to experience emotional health they had better identify their self-enhancing life goals and work consistently toward them. Furthermore he specifies the subgoals that will enable humans to be successful in their primary goal. These are (1) self-interest, (2) social interest, (3) self-direction, (4) tolerance, (5) flexibility, (6) acceptance of uncertainty, (7) commitment, (8) scientific thinking, (9) self-acceptance, (10) risk-taking, and (11) non-utopianism (Ellis, 1979c, pp. 55–57). Ellis considers that the goals of specialized rational-emotive therapy had better be directed to help patients achieve these eleven subgoals and thus help them achieve what he calls a "profound philosophic change," while recognizing that in a large number of cases the therapist will have to settle for more conservative goals as in general RET. Furthermore Ellis states that a major goal of RET is to help patients use what he calls "the scientific method" in the future to test out hypotheses about self, others, and the world.

Beck has not addressed himself in detail to describing the characteristics of emotionally healthy individuals. He does say, however, that cognitive-therapy techniques are designed to help people "identify, reality-test and correct maladaptive distorted conceptualizations and the dysfunctional beliefs (schemas) underlying those cognitions" (Beck et al., 1979, p. 4). Emotionally healthy individuals are presumably, then, viewed as highly adept at such skills. From this, the goal of cognitive therapy can be seen as helping patients acquire and develop such skills—which is more ambitious than Beck's subsequent statement: "the goal of cognitive therapy is to relieve emotional distress and the other symptoms of depression" (Beck et al., 1979, p. 35).

It is doubtful that cognitive therapists generally adhere to a well-organized common philosophical position and consequently do not specify an equivalent list of subgoals. It is doubtful that they would have such aspirations. Indeed as Young (Note 3) says, cognitive therapists place much more emphasis on modifying expectations than changing philosophies. At times cognitive therapists share Ellis's views on self-acceptance, that a person had better accept himself not rate himself, but as Ellis has pointed out, they do not consistently take this position (Ellis, 1977b). However, implicit in their writings is the high regard given to the value of realistic thinking and of functionality of thoughts, behaviors, and emotions that may prove to be the cornerstones of any future theorizing concerning the philosophical underpinnings of cognitive therapy. Young (Note 3) adopts two major criteria in helping patients determine the functionality of their thoughts, feelings, and behaviors: (1) Is it causing the patient unwanted symptoms? and (2) is it hurting others unnecessarily? The overlap between this concept of functionality and Ellis's concept of rationality, which he defines as that which aids and abets one's long-term goals of survival and happiness, is apparent.

Views on change processes

Both Beck and Ellis agree that for thoroughgoing cognitive change, repeated rethinking and responding to dysfunctional cognitions is necessary. However, while Ellis argues that therapists had better help patients do this forcefully and energetically, Beck does not address himself directly to the issue of force in any of his writings. By implication, however, force is not advocated within the therapeutic style of collaborative empiricism that is characteristic of cognitive therapy. Burns (1980), a cognitive therapist, however, does describe and use freely a technique that he calls "externalization of voices."[5] It requires patients to respond to their own dysfunctional cognitions in an energetic manner.

Although both Beck and Ellis stress the importance of behavior change in effecting cognitive change, Beck and other cognitive therapists have traditionally advocated helping patients to try out new behaviors in a graded fashion, being careful not to expose them to undue discomfort. Cognitive change is deemed to occur when the patient processes and integrates the outcome of these behavioral assignments that are likely to be designed to test out his hypotheses. Ellis is likely to favor behavioral assignments that repeatedly expose patients "at a jump" to uncomfortable and feared situations, arguing that for patients who will do it, these experiences bring about the greatest amount of cognitive change and help patients raise their level of frustration tolerance. Since cognitive therapists value highly the stance of "collaborative empiricism," they are likely to negotiate behavioral assignments that the patient feels he is able to handle. These are unlikely to be too demanding. It is my experience that a number of rational-emotive therapists adopt this approach rather than that of Ellis.

However, Beck, in recent writings on shame, advocates that the person needs to have "shameful" experiences in order to begin to see that such experiences are tolerable. Furthermore Beck (Note 4) has said that although graded task assignments are recommended for use with depressed patients, exposure assignments are more effective with anxious patients. Thus there seems to be a rapprochement in viewpoints on this issue.

Practical issues

Therapeutic style

A variety of RET therapists have made the point that it is not necessary to adopt Ellis's forceful style with most patients in order to practice effective RET (Walen et al., 1980; Wessler & Wessler, 1980), and Ellis himself acknowledges that RET can be practiced in many different styles, including one normally associated with client-centered therapists. However, Ellis (1979f) considers that the preferred therapeutic style of rational-emotive therapists is one emphasizing both active-directiveness and therapeutic forcefulness. One main reason why Ellis advocates forcefulness as a preferred therapeutic style is that he believes human irrationality has a strong biological basis that had better be forcefully combatted. In contrast, while Beck stresses that in the short-term treatment of depressed patients, active-directiveness is a preferred style, collaboration, rather than confrontation, is to be regarded as one of the most important hallmarks of cognitive therapy. Indeed as Young and Beck (1982) say, "cognitive therapy . . . consists of a particular therapeutic *style*, as well as a set of techniques." In this therapeutic style, called *collaborative empiricism*, the therapist explains to the patient the rationale for everything done during the session. Patient and therapist set an agenda at every session. The therapist helps the patient identify and question maladaptive cognitions through guided discovery. He or she frequently pauses and asks for feedback from the patient to determine the impact of the therapeutic interventions and basically clues the patient into whatever is happening in the therapeutic endeavor. This style has influenced the practice of some rational-emotive therapists (e.g., Wessler & Wessler, 1980). Whenever I have heard Ellis's therapy sessions, while he does endeavor to develop a collaborative relationship with his clients, he does not by this definition adhere to the stance of collaborative empiricism. Ellis (Note 5) has said that with patients who are relatively undisturbed and nondefensive, it is possible to take such a stance in RET, but he would like to know exactly how Beck and his colleagues deal with what he calls "difficult customers," namely the resistant, disturbed, and defensive clients, who he says constitute most of his clinical caseload. He hypothesizes that adopting the collaborative empirical stance with such patients would have less effect than adopting a forceful stance. Young (Note 3) has said, however, that with patients who are particularly rigid in their thinking a confrontative style can be employed in cognitive therapy when collaborative empiricism has been exhausted. Such a confrontative style is used only as a last resort.

Therapeutic strategy

Rational-emotive therapists and cognitive therapists differ in the speed with which therapists and patients move toward the identification and modification of underlying maladaptive assumptions. In cognitive therapy the initial task of the therapist in dealing with a patient's cognitions is to help him identify and correct his automatic thoughts. These thoughts are ones the patient can identify first and are only the tip of the cognitive iceberg. Self-monitoring is repeated until tentative hypotheses can be developed concerning both secondary and primary assumptions underlying these automatic thoughts. These hypotheses are either confirmed or rejected as the result of the collection of more data. Such an approach is lengthy and is usually reserved for the middle to later stages of therapy. This entire procedure is based on the principle of *induction* since the cognitive therapist does not claim to know at the outset the nature of the patient's cognitions, which is centrally related to his emotional disturbance. He thus chips away from the outer layer of the automatic thoughts to the inner core of the basic assumption. On the other hand Ellis claims that he can quickly discern the patient's cognitions that are centrally related to his problem: namely the absolutist evaluations that are either couched in the form of a "must" or in the form of a grossly exaggerated negative conclusion. Thus it can be seen that Ellis is operating according to the principle of *deduction*. Ellis tends to refer to the patient's automatic thoughts (as defined by Beck) only briefly and as a means to identify these irrational beliefs. Whereas Ellis is likely to go straight for the patient's evaluative thinking and then deal with any remaining inferential distortions after doing so, Beck and cognitive therapists in general are more likely to deal with inferential cognitive distortions initially and only later, if at all, deal with the patient's evaluative thinking. I say "if at all" because, as we have seen, patients' primary underlying assumptions do not in cognitive therapy necessarily take the form of evaluations. This difference may be a distinguishing feature between rational-emotive therapists and cognitive therapists in general.

While I have outlined differences between rational-emotive therapists' and cognitive therapists' typical stategic approaches, it is worth noting that rational-emotive therapists claim more leeway in deviating from the typical. In response to Beck et al.'s criticism of rational-emotive therapists that they often do not establish a solid data base against which the patient's conclusions can be tested, Ellis says that:

> although RET therapists are not required to do this as you seem to do it, they can easily choose to do so. In many instances I would proceed almost exactly as your therapists did in the dialogue given in this section of the manual; in other instances, I might possibly proceed to discussing the patient's worth or her catastrophizing—and in the course of doing so derive the "solid data base" information. In a few other cases, I might help her to fully accept herself or to stop catastrophizing without the data base information brought out in your instance—but with various other kinds of information brought out. RET does *not* have one special way of questioning and disputing.
>
> (Ellis quoted in Beck et al., 1979, p. 154)

It is my view that in specialized RET, therapists would more likely proceed straight to patients' evaluative beliefs while in general RET, they could and often do proceed as cognitive therapists would. One of the major reasons why cognitive therapists do not deviate from a standardized sequence of treatment procedures is that their outcome studies require standardized treatment. Both rational-emotive and cognitive therapists need to be more mindful of the question: "Is an early focus on inferential or evaluative cognitions likely to be more effective with this particular client?"

Therapeutic techniques

There are a number of differences between rational-emotive therapists and cognitive therapists in technique. While Ellis claims that virtually every behavioral and cognitive technique that has ever been invented is used in general RET and thus presumably all the techniques that cognitive therapists have devised would fall under the rubric of general RET, I shall confine my statements to a comparison between specialized RET and cognitive therapy.

While both rational-emotive therapists and cognitive therapists make use of inductive questioning or the Socratic dialogue method, I have observed that cognitive therapists are likely to persist longer with this method than rational-emotive therapists. The latter do tend to use explanations more frequently than do cognitive therapists, and faced with patients who do not seem to benefit from Socratic dialogue are likely to dispense with this method sooner.

Both rational-emotive therapists and cognitive therapists are well known for asking their patients to look for evidence for their irrational evaluations and faulty inferences respectively. A feature of Ellis's practice in particular, rational-emotive therapists are likely to ask for evidence of statements where no corroborating evidence is likely to exist. Thus when a rational-emotive therapist asks a patient: "Where is the evidence that you *must* succeed?" he knows a priori that there is in all probability no evidence that could corroborate such a statement. There are no behavioral experiments, for example, that a patient and therapist could construct, the results of which could in fact corroborate such a statement. Thus rational-emotive therapists quite often ask patients for evidence concerning their irrational evaluations—matters that more appropriately belong to the realm of ideology.[6] These are questions a patient can in fact answer while sitting in the therapist's armchair using reason alone. Ellis (Note 5) has said that one main reason why he asks patients for evidence supporting their irrational beliefs is that patients often regard such beliefs as facts. Cognitive therapists are more likely to ask patients for evidence concerning their inferences (hypotheses) where data can be gathered from the outside world to corroborate or falsify the hypotheses.

Thus, if a patient predicts that he will be laughed at when he walks into a room full of people, the cognitive therapist and patient can construct an experiment to test the validity of such a hypothesis. Cognitive therapists are not noted for asking patients for evidence concerning matters belonging to the realm of ideology. They prefer to limit their discussion of such matters to questioning patients concerning the functionality of adhering to such beliefs. Taking this example further, when a rational-emotive therapist asks the patient: "Where is the evidence that it would be terrible if you are laughed at?" he knows there is in all probability only one answer to this question. He can further show the patient in the session that there is in all probability only one answer. The patient can even acknowledge the "correct" ideological position. Paradoxically, the patient will probably only believe in the "correct" ideological position if he practices adhering to the new position in the outside world.

One of the most important technical procedures that cognitive therapists appear to have in their armamentarium is the Daily Record of Dysfunctional Thoughts (DRDT) form. This has been verified by Herman (Note 2). By contrast, although there are a number of written homework forms that have been devised by rational-emotive therapists, these are neither employed consistently nor seen as a major therapeutic change agent. This may be because rational-emotive therapists do not pay as much attention to the role of automatic thoughts in emotional disturbance as do cognitive therapists.

While both Beck and Ellis recommend the use of imagery techniques, Beck and other cognitive therapists employ a wider range of imagery methods than does Ellis who employs mainly rational-emotive imagery (Ellis & Abrahms, 1978) and sexual imagery in the treatment of sexual problems. However, other rational-emotive therapists such as Wessler (Wessler & Wessler, 1980; Wessler, Note 6) are more similar to cognitive therapists in employing a wide variety of imagery procedures.

As we have seen, rational-emotive therapists and cognitive therapists are likely to favor different types of behavioral assignment. Cognitive therapists are more likely to employ behavioral assignments in the service of helping patients to test faulty inferences or hypotheses (for example, they can be used quite early on in the treatment of a severely withdrawn, depressed patient who believes that he could not read even a sentence of a book). Rational-emotive therapists, and Ellis in particular, are likely to employ behavioral assignments, primarily in the service of changing evaluations. As a result, such behavioral assignments often aim to recreate patients' worst fears so as to enable them to see that they can cope with the worst. As we have seen, Ellis often advocates behavioral assignments based on the principle of flooding in order to help patients raise their level of frustration tolerance. He would criticize the use of graded behavioral assignments, which are used in cognitive therapy particularly with depressed patients, as often doing little to change a patient's low frustration tolerance. In fact he argues that such graded task assignments communicate the implicit message "Yes, you do need to go slowly, you cannot stand to expose yourself to more discomfort than this" (Ellis, 1980c). Cognitive therapists would counter that to urge most patients (particularly those who are depressed) to full exposure would threaten the therapeutic alliance and be against the spirit of collaborative empiricism. However cognitive therapists and patients could very well negotiate flooding assignments if so desired within such collaborative guidelines. It is my impression, however, that they do not do so frequently although they aim to do this in their future work with anxious patients.

Since cognitive therapists adhere to the collaborative empiricism stance, this prohibits the use of certain techniques that rational-emotive therapists would employ. For example, paradoxical procedures are not advocated in cognitive therapy since the explanation of the rationale underlying a paradoxical procedure would in fact negate the impact of the procedure. Furthermore cognitive therapists are not encouraged to use the somewhat flamboyant and dramatic interventions rational-emotive therapists sometimes employ, which, while possibly having a great amount of therapeutic impact for the patient, may backfire (Dryden, Note 7). In this regard rational-emotive therapists are greater risk-takers than cognitive therapists. In addition, rational-emotive therapists make more of a concerted effort to use humor in their interventions to help patients take life less seriously. As DiGiuseppe (Note 8) has said, rational-emotive therapists are freer than cognitive therapists to use a wide range of educational and social psychological methods to help change maladaptive cognitions and beliefs.

Finally in the correction of maladaptive basic assumptions, cognitive therapists are likely to emphasize pragmatic arguments to help patients change the nature of these assumptions and are less likely than rational-emotive therapists to help patients see the philosophical errors inherent in their assumptions. Rational-emotive therapists use both pragmatic and philosophical arguments in helping patients to give up their irrational beliefs.

Conclusion

Rational-emotive therapy's strengths lie in the fact that it is based on a well-developed and well-articulated set of philosophical formulations provided primarily by Albert Ellis. Until very recently, rational-emotive therapists have not had recourse to a treatment manual and even now such guidelines as have been provided in these manuals (Ellis & Abrahms, 1978; Walen et al., 1980) lack the specificity of those provided for cognitive therapists (e.g., in Beck et al., 1979), especially over the whole course of therapy.

Cognitive therapy's strengths lie in the careful work that has gone into the development of clear and precise treatment manuals that can be used in outcome studies. Its weaknesses lie in the fact that such practical advances have far outstripped the development of its philosophical underpinnings. This could be a focus for future work.

There are signs that rational-emotive therapists are being influenced by the activities of Beck and his colleagues and also vice versa. One of the strengths of cognitive therapy has been the careful attention that Beck and his colleagues have paid to maximizing the use of valuable therapeutic time. Thus agenda-setting and careful attention to the development and maintenance of the collaborative working alliance are features that some rational-emotive supervisors are now encouraging their supervisees to employ (Walen et al., 1980; Wessler & Wessler, 1980). Conversely as cognitive therapists adopt the same careful study of anxiety disorders as they have of depressive disorders, they will learn the value of encouraging patients to take greater behavioral risks in overcoming one of the major bases of anxiety disorders: discomfort anxiety (there is some evidence that this is already happening). Indeed cognitive therapists have a lot to learn from Albert Ellis about discomfort anxiety, and there are signs that they are beginning to do so. This process of mutual influence will continue given greater contact between rational-emotive therapists and cognitive therapists.

Notes

1 These ways are "Cognitively, it has a pronounced philosophic emphasis, includes a humanistic-existentialist outlook, strives for pervasive and long-standing rather than symptomatic change, tries to eliminate all self-ratings, stresses anti*must*urbatory rather than anti-empirical disputing methods, recognizes the palliative aspects of cognitive distraction, discourages problem solving that is not accompanied by changes in clients' basic belief system, and emphasizes secondary as well as primary symptoms of emotional disturbance. Emotively it stresses the discrimination of appropriate from inappropriate emotions, emphasizes methods of working directly with and on emotions, encourages forceful emotive interventions, and uses relationship procedures that heavily stress unconditional rather than conditional positive regard. Behaviorally, it favors penalization as well as reinforcement, is partial to in vivo desensitization and flooding and makes sure that skill training is done within a philosophic framework of trying to help clients make basic changes in their irrational beliefs." (Ellis, 1980a)

2 Throughout this chapter it should be noted that the extent to which rational-emotive therapists and cognitive therapists agree with the views expressed by Ellis and Beck, respectively, is not known. This remains a fruitful area for research.

3 Herman's view has recently been challenged by Freeman (Personal Communication, 1982) who claims that cognitive therapists think in terms of finite clusters of underlying assumptions, while acknowledging their idiosyncratic nature.

4 Beck (Note 4) says that Ellis has misinterpreted him on this point. Burns (1980), however, does distinguish between sadness and depression.

5 Alternatively called the "point-counterpoint" technique (Young, Note 3).

6 Here it is again to be noted that Ellis (1977a) refers to such irrational evaluations as "ideologies."

Reference notes

1 Beck, A. T. Speculations regarding the biology of mental disorders. Unpublished paper. Center for Cognitive Therapy, 1982.
2 Herman, I. Personal communication, 1981.
3 Young, J. Personal communication, 1982.
4 Beck, A. T. Personal communication, 1982.
5 Ellis, A. Personal communication, 1981.
6 Wessler, R. L. Alternative conception of rational-emotive therapy: Toward a philosophically neutral psychotherapy. Paper presented at 12th European Congress of Behaviour Therapy. Rome, Italy, September 5, 1982.
7 Dryden, W. The evocative function of rational-emotive therapists: Vivid RET. Manuscript in preparation.
8 DiGiuseppe, R. Personal communication, 1982.

References

Beck, A. T. Thinking and depression, 1: Idiosyncratic content and cognitive distortions. *Archives of General Psychiatry*, 1963, *9*, 324–333.

Beck, A. T. Thinking and depression, 2: Theory and therapy. *Archives of of General Psychiatry*, 1964, *10*, 561–571.

Beck, A. T. *Depression: Clinical, experimental, and theoretical aspects*. New York: Hoeber, 1967.

Beck, A. T. *The diagnosis and management of depression*. Philadelphia: University of Pennsylvania Press, 1973.

Beck, A. T. *Cognitive therapy and the emotional disorders*. New York: International Universities Press, 1976.

Beck, A. T. Cognitive therapy of depression: New perspectives. In P. Clayton (Ed.), *Depression*. New York: Raven Press, in press.

Beck, A. T., Rush, A. J., Shaw, B. F., & Emery, G. *Cognitive therapy of depression*. New York: Guilford Press, 1979.

Burns, D. D. *Feeling good: The new mood therapy*. New York: William Morrow, 1980.

Coleman, R. E., & Beck, A. T. Cognitive therapy for depression. In J. F. Clarkin and H. I. Glazin (Eds.), *Depression: Behavioral and directive intervention strategies*. New York: Garland, 1981.

Ellis, A. Rational psychotherapy. *Journal of General Psychology*, 1958, *59*, 35–49.

Ellis, A. *Reason and emotion in psychotherapy*. New York: Lyle Stuart, 1962.

Ellis, A. *Growth through reason*. Palo Alto, Calif.: Science and Behavior Books, 1971.

Ellis, A. The rational-emotive approach to sex therapy. *The Counseling Psychologist*, 1975, *5*, 14–21.

Ellis, A. The biological basis of human irrationality. *Journal of Individual Psychology*, 1976, *32*, 145–168.

Ellis, A. The basic clinical theory of rational-emotive therapy. In A. Ellis and R. Grieger (Eds.), *Handbook of rational-emotive therapy*. New York: Springer, 1977. (a)

Ellis, A. Review of A. T. Beck's Cognitive therapy and the emotional disorders, New York: International Universities Press, 1976. *Behavior Therapy*, 1977, *8*, 295–296. (b)

Ellis, A. Toward a theory of personality. In R. J. Corsini (Ed.), *Readings in current personality theories*. Itasca, Ill.: F. E. Peacock, 1978.

Ellis, A. Rational-emotive therapy. In A. Ellis and J. M. Whiteley (Eds.), *Theoretical and empirical foundations of rational-emotive therapy*. Monterey, Calif.: Brooks/Cole, 1979. (a)

Ellis, A. Toward a new theory of personality. In A. Ellis and J. M. Whiteley (Eds.), *Theoretical and empirical foundations of rational-emotive therapy*. Monterey, Calif.: Brooks/Cole, 1979. (b)

Ellis, A. The theory of rational-emotive therapy. In A. Ellis and J. M. Whiteley (Eds.), *Theoretical and empirical foundations of rational-emotive therapy*. Monterey, Calif.: Brooks/Cole, 1979. (c)

Ellis, A. The practice of rational-emotive therapy. In A. Ellis and J. M. Whiteley (Eds.), *Theoretical and empirical foundations of rational-emotive therapy*. Monterey, Calif.: Brooks/Cole, 1979. (d)

Ellis, A. Rejoinder: Elegant and inelegant RET. In A. Ellis and J. M. Whiteley (Eds.), *Theoretical and empirical foundations of rational-emotive therapy*. Monterey, Calif.: Brooks/Cole, 1979. (e)

Ellis, A. The issue of force and energy in behavioral change. *Journal of Contemporary Psychotherapy*, 1979, *10*, 83–97. (f)

Ellis, A. Rational-emotive therapy and cognitive behavior therapy: Similarities and differences. *Cognitive Therapy & Research*, 1980, *4*, 325–340. (a)

Ellis, A. Psychotherapy and atheistic values: A response to A. E. Bergin's "Psychotherapy and religious values." *Journal of Consulting & Clinical Psychology*, 1980, *48*, 635–639. (b)

Ellis, A. The philosophic implications and dangers of some popular behaviour therapy techniques. Invited address to the World Congress of Behavior Therapy, Jerusalem, July 15, 1980. (c)

Ellis, A., & Abrahms, E. *Brief psychotherapy in medical and health practice*. New York: Springer, 1978.

Kovacs, M., & Beck, A. T. Maladaptive cognitive structures in depression. *American Journal of Psychiatry*, 1978, *135*, 525–533.

Walen, S. R., DiGiuseppe, R., & Wessler, R. L. *A practitioner's guide to rational-emotive therapy*. New York: Oxford University Press, 1980.

Wessler, R. A. The neurotic paradox: A rational-emotive view. *Rational Living*, 1978, *13*, 9–12.

Wessler, R. A., & Wessler, R. L. The principles and practice of rational-emotive therapy. San Francisco: Jossey-Bass, 1980.

Wessler, R. L. Varieties of cognitions in the cognitively-oriented psychotherapies. *Rational Living*, 1982, *17*, 3–10.

Young, J. E., & Beck, A. T. Cognitive therapy: Clinical applications. In A. J. Rush (Ed.), *Short-term psychotherapies for depression*. Chichester, England: Wiley, 1982.

CHAPTER 5

LANGUAGE AND MEANING IN RET

Journal of Rational-Emotive Therapy, 4(2): 131–142 (1986)

REBT theory comprises a number of concepts, all of which have a specific meaning in that theory. This meaning is often at variance with how these concepts are generally understood and, as such, if the therapist does not take care to ensure that the client understands and agrees with the REBT meaning of a particular concept, then therapeutic misunderstanding and miscommunication will often ensue. In the piece that follows, I focus on and discuss the issue of language and meaning in REBT theory. Using the working alliance framework which became a feature of my later publications, language and meaning in REBT theory is a topic that can be best placed in the 'views' domain of the alliance and when the therapist clarifies the client's understanding of REBT-based concepts he or she is carrying out important work within the 'tasks' domain of that alliance.

Abstract

The same verbal labels can have different semantic meaning. RET often assigns idiosyncratic meaning to commonplace words and misunderstandings between therapists and clients may result. In this article the issue of language and meaning in RET is discussed with special reference to feeling words, rational and irrational concepts, and the language of change. Some therapeutic strategies are suggested to help therapists develop shared meaning frameworks with their clients.

In this article the issue of language and meaning in rational-emotive therapy will be discussed—a topic which has received scant attention in the RET literature. For example, two of the major texts in rational-emotive therapy (Walen, DiGiuseppe & Wessler, 1980; Wessler & Wessler, 1980) devote a little over a page to this issue. Wessler and Wessler (1980) make the important point which encapsulates the argument that will be made in this article. "Since all words are abstractions and subject to varying denotations and connotations, it is important that we use a shared vocabulary with a client—specifically, that we define our terms and check out the meanings of the client's terms—and try to keep the dialogue as concrete as possible" (p. 179). In addition to understanding the client's language, it is equally important that the therapist ensures that the client understands the therapist's use of language. Since therapist language can be best construed as "A" in the ABC framework, it is likely then to be interpreted idiosyncratically by the client who will then proceed to make evaluations about such interpretations. Thus, the possibilities for misunderstanding are legion. RET is often misconstrued by fellow professionals given the different meanings that can be attributed to the term "rational." Young (1975) has argued that people often construe rational to mean cold, logical and unemotional whereas in RET rational is defined as "that which aids and abets our clients' basic goals and purposes." However, this use of the word "rational" is not commonly held and if unexplained will often lead to wrong impressions being created in the minds of both non-RET therapists and clients.

The language of feeling

RET theory states that when people do not get what they want and are *not* insisting that they get what they want, then they are liable to experience negative emotions. To the extent that these emotions stem from rational beliefs and are deemed to motivate people to recover and to set new goals for themselves or to pursue old ones that are blocked, these emotions are deemed to be constructive. In RET terminology specific words exist for these constructive emotions and these are contrasted with emotions that are deemed to be destructive, not only because they stem from absolutistic musturbatory evaluations (musts, shoulds, oughts, have to's, etc.) but also because most of the time they inhibit clients from achieving their basic goals and purposes. Thus in RET "anxiety" is considered to be destructive and "concern" is deemed to be constructive. However, when listening to clients' accounts of their own problems, it is important that RET therapists remember that the ways in which clients spontaneously (i.e. before RET) use language, particularly with regard to feeling words, may suggest different meanings to that denoted by RET language.

Thus opportunities for confusion and misunderstanding that arise when we consider the ways in which feeling words are used by clients and RET therapists are many. Consider the term "anxiety." Anxiety in RET terminology is deemed to result when there exists a threat to the client's personal domain, a threat which is absolutistically evaluated as "terrible" or "awful" and which absolutely *must* not occur. Concern is deemed to result when the client does not evaluate this perceived threat in an absolutistic manner, but instead believes: "I really don't want this threat to occur but if it does, it does." Such a belief will result in the person concluding that if the threat does occur it would be unfortunate and bad rather than (absolutistically) awful and terrible. However, clients do not make this distinction spontaneously. They may, for example, report feeling concern when a cognitive analysis reveals that they are, in RET terms, anxious. Conversely, other clients will report feeling "anxious" when they are, according to RET theory, experiencing strong concern since they do not make absolutistic irrational evaluations. For example, one of my clients consistently used the term anxiety to refer to keenness. Had I assumed that his use of the term anxiety was in fact synonymous with the RET use of the term anxiety I would have wasted a lot of therapeutic time by seeking to find irrational evaluations which did not exist. I might have also assumed that the client was a D.C. (difficult customer) because he would not admit to such irrational evaluations.

An additional issue needs to be considered when the term "anxiety" is subjected to an analysis of its meaning. Although a client may agree that his or her feelings of anxiety stem from the irrational belief: "This perceived threat must not occur," the client may not agree with the therapist's position that such feelings are destructive. Indeed, many clients consider that anxiety (in the RET sense) will in fact motivate them to carry out a given task. Whether anxiety will motivate them to *better* performances is, of course, the issue which needs to be addressed. However, for RET therapists to assume that once anxiety has been elicited the client will necessarily wish to change feelings of anxiety to those of concern overlooks an important fact—namely that clients make inferences and evaluations about their feelings. As DiGiuseppe (1984) has shown, some people consider that good things might happen or bad things might not happen as a result of experiencing (in RET terms) destructive negative feelings. This is one good reason why it is often helpful to discuss with clients their goals for change (Wessler & Wessler, 1980). To assume that the client wishes to change a destructive negative emotion without checking that this is the case may be a recipe for therapeutic failure.

Depression, according to RET theory, is a destructive negative emotion which occurs when clients evaluate some loss to their personal domain as absolutistically awful or terrible, conclusions which stem from the belief "This loss must not occur or must not be as bad as it is." It is contrasted with the constructive negative emotion, sadness which occurs when such losses are evaluated as bad but without the concomitant "must." Again, clients regularly refer to their own feelings of sadness when they are really, in RET terms, depressed and vice versa! Continuing the analysis outlined above concerning the implications of destructive negative feelings, some depressed clients construe this painful emotion as a sign of acute sensitivity (in a productive sense) and may view a therapist's attempts to help them to give up their depression as an attempt to make them less sensitive—efforts they would stubbornly resist. Thus, again, it is important for rational-emotive therapists to be aware that some clients create private meanings about their feelings of depression which may refer to positive implications of this emotion rather than the negative implications held by their therapists.

Guilt, according to RET theory occurs when clients break their moral or ethical codes and absolutistically insist that this must not have occurred. Such individuals damn themselves as bad individuals for committing such "bad" acts. The rational alternative to guilt is often expressed in the RET literature as remorse, regret, or sorrow. These emotions are deemed to occur when the bad act is viewed as bad but when the person concerned does not demand "I must not have done this bad thing" or conclude "I am bad for doing it." Rather the person accepts him or herself as a fallible human being while, and this is important, not excusing him or herself from acting badly. Clients often misconstrue their therapists' interventions when the emotion of guilt is targeted for change, particularly when therapists do not check out with their clients that this is a troublesome emotion for them. Thus, some clients may accuse the RET therapist of encouraging them to do bad things or, less problematically, not discouraging them from doing bad things because they use guilt in a different way than their therapists. In addition, clients often believe that guilt, in the RET use of the word, will actually protect them from doing bad things in the future rather than, as is argued in RET theory, encouraging them to do bad things. In this latter analysis once one has damned oneself and regards oneself as bad, this will lead to the person committing more rather than less bad acts. As Ellis puts it "How can a shit be deshitified?"

Anger is a particularly troublesome emotion since it often has several meanings. Anger, according to RET theory is regarded as being a destructive negative emotion which stems from an absolutistic evaluation that the other person must not break my rule or must not act as badly as they do, in fact, act. It is contrasted with the appropriate alternative feeling annoyance which is regarded as being constructive and stems from the belief "I don't like your bad behavior but there is no reason why you must not act this way and you are not a worm (or any other sub-human term that the client uses) for acting badly." It is important to realize as DiGiuseppe

(1984) has done that people often consider that if they are not angry by definition they will then allow other people to dominate them. In a sense they believe "I have to be angry in order to protect myself from other people's bad influence." If RET therapists do not first clearly distinguish between the RET meanings of anger and annoyance for their clients then the latter may view their attempts to change anger to annoyance as (1) advice to act less powerfully in the social arena or (2) suggestions that they would be wise to experience *less* strong emotions and thus to deny the strength of their rational desires. RET theory holds that annoyance is not necessarily less intense than anger, but clients often conclude that it is. This is, of course, not the true intention of RET therapists, but without discussing these distinctions *before* implementing disputing strategies, client "resistance" is likely to occur, although, of course, it is not resistance but the results of a poorly designed therapeutic intervention.

Ellis (personal communication) has recently advocated that in order to get over these semantic problems with respect to the term that "anger," damning anger (an inappropriate emotion) be distinguished from non-damning anger (an appropriate emotion). Again, if this distinction is not made then the client who positively values "anger" will be unlikely to give up his "positive" emotion. However, if the therapist can help the person to realize that there are different types of anger and that non-damning anger is in fact productive and damning anger, unproductive, then the client is at least liable to listen to the therapist, whereas in the previous scenario the client may well switch off from the therapist who is viewed as a person who is trying to encourage the client to relinquish a "positive" emotion.

Similar arguments can be used when jealousy is the focus for discussion and the distinction between destructive and constructive jealousy can usefully be introduced to clients who, while experiencing the negative behavioral, emotional and interpersonal consequences of destructive jealousy, nevertheless regard their feelings of jealousy as evidence that they really love their partner. If a therapist encourages such a person to work on giving up feelings of jealousy without making distinctions between its destructive and constructive forms, then the person is likely to "resist" the therapist who in their mind is advocating they relinquish their feelings of love for their partner.

Premise language

Wessler and Wessler (1980) have argued that a person's beliefs can be put in the form of a syllogism which contains both a premise and a conclusion. Thus, "I must do well" is a premise and "If I don't do well I would be worthless" would be the conclusion that stems from the premise. It is apparent that semantic confusion can often result when RET therapists refer to such terms as "musts, shoulds, oughts, have to's, etc." A major problematic area here concerns the conditionality of these terms. Thus, the term "I must do well in order to pass my exams" is a conditional phrase and not therefore irrational because the person is outlining the conditions which have to be met in order for an outcome to be achieved. Indeed, novice RET therapists who are only too delighted to have identified a "must" in the client's thinking, wrongly assume that all "musts" are irrational and, therefore, to be targeted for change. This is certainly not the case. It is to be underscored at this point that Rational-Emotive Therapists are only interested in targeting for change irrational "musts", i.e. those that are absolutistic in nature, especially when they are implicated in feelings that the client wishes to change. This latter point is important. I have often heard RET therapists doing sound RET but not therapeutic RET. Here therapists have in fact identified absolutistic musts and are using correct disputational strategies to help the client to give them up, but the problem is that the client does not want to change his or her destructive negative emotions or dysfunctional behaviour.

The term "should" is particularly problematic. As Vertes (1971) has shown, the word "should" has several different semantic meanings. It can mean, of course, I absolutely should. It can also mean, I preferably should. It also has an empirical meaning (e.g. given the conditions that exist in the world at this present time, the sun should come up in the morning). It can also refer to matters of recommendation (e.g. "You really should go and see Chariots of Fire"). I have on more than one occasion heard novice RET therapists challenge such non-absolutistic "shoulds": "Why *must* you go and see Chariots of Fire?" "Because I like it" the client replies. 'But why must you have what you like?" retorts the therapist. This elementary therapeutic error would not occur if therapists learn not to confuse the word with its meaning.

A particular problem is encountered when the word "Right" is used in therapy in sentences such as: "He has no right to act that way." I have sometimes heard RET therapists involve themselves in unproductive discussions with their clients concerning the non-absolutistic meaning of the word "Right". "You have the right to do anything, you have the right to rape and murder if that's your inclination" is an example. While this is theoretically correct (this statement really means that there is no law in the universe to suggest that the person must not rape or pillage), the word "Right" is extremely problematic and in my experience will often be construed by clients as meaning that the therapist is either actively advocating these activities or refusing to condemn their "badness." Such is the confusion about the term "Right," that RET therapists might be well advised to drop this from their vocabulary, at least in therapy.

Similar problems can occur when relative or rational beliefs are considered. Thus RET therapists often teach their clients that the rational form of "must" is "I want to" or "I would prefer to." While this is correct, it is not the only way of expressing a relative belief. Thus, the term "It would be better" is also a rational belief but one which does not indicate that the person may actually *want* to carry out the activity in question. Take, for example, the student who believes that they absolutely must pass an exam. A therapist in trying to help such a client discriminate between their preferences and demands correctly helps the person see that they *want* to pass the exam but they do not have to. But what if the client goes on to express an irrational belief about working to pass the exam? The therapist who tries to help the client to see that while they don't have to work, they would want to work is likely to be using an unproductive strategy which ignores the notion that a person may not want to do what *would be better*. Rational beliefs can then take the form of a desire and, therefore, a client can be encouraged to undertake an activity because of their desire. But a client can also be encouraged to undertake an undesired activity that would be in their best interests because they want the results of doing this activity. Their desire concerns the outcome of the activity and not the process.

Conclusion language

Semantic problems can occur when the language of conclusions is analyzed, particularly when the terms horror, awful, and terrible are considered. These terms in

RET theory are distinguished from terms such as, catastrophe, and tragedy (as in the phrase, tragedies are not awful). In RET terminology, a tragedy is something that occurs which is rated as very bad. Terrible and related terms in RET theory add to the notion of tragedy. Terrible relates to the belief that this tragedy must not occur or must not be as bad as it is. This distinction needs to be carefully made with clients otherwise they may assume that their therapists are being insensitive to their tragedies by trying to show them that such bad events are not *that* bad. Such clients may say "Are you trying to argue that it wasn't that bad for me to lose all my possessions and my family in that fire?" Indeed, my experience in working with people who have recently experienced tragedies such as losing a loved one, or being raped, has shown me that endeavors to teach the client the difference between tragedy and horror may themselves be viewed as insensitive interventions by clients who regard their destructive negative emotions as highly appropriate to the situation.

Semantic confusion can often arise when the term "fallible human being" is being discussed in therapy. First it is important to ascertain that the client actually understands what the term "fallible" means. One of my clients in Birmingham (U.K.) thought that it meant obese and was insulted as I tried to encourage her to accept herself as a fallible human being in such a circumstance. In addition, clients may construe therapists' attempts to encourage them to accept themselves as fallible as encouragement for them to condone their bad actions, or as reasons to excuse future bad actions. When clients view the term fallible as having bad connotations it is hardly surprising when they "resist" their therapists' attempts to encourage them to accept themselves as fallible human beings. Another problem relating to the attitude "fallible human being" is that it may not accurately reflect the source of the client's irrationality. More than one client has said to me: "Yes, I can accept myself as a fallible human being" but shortly after implied: ". . . who *must not* act badly." It is therefore important when planning disputing strategies to look at *both* premise and conclusion forms of the syllogism to ensure that irrationalities are being challenged at both levels.

The associated term "self-acceptance" also has its semantic problems. "Acceptance" is a particularly difficult word because it can often be viewed in clients' minds as meaning "resignation." Thus, by encouraging clients to accept themselves, their resistance may indicate that they perceive that they are being asked to resign themselves to being forever the slob that they think that they are. Acceptance, when viewed as meaning resignation, also conjures up images of inaction whereas in RET self-acceptance is viewed as encouraging clients towards action.

Semantic problems can also arise when issues of self-rating are being discussed with clients. Clients often have their own private ways of rating themselves. It may come as a surprise to most RET therapists that not all clients regard themselves as "shits." In supervising a therapy tape, I heard a RET therapist and his client get into an enormous argument because of the therapist's insistence that the client was calling himself a shit. The client replied, "Listen, I have never, ever in my whole life considered myself a shit and I really don't like your attempts to persuade me thus." Here, the client was being more rational than the therapist! Thus the terms, shit, bad, worthless, less worthy, undeserving, are not synonymous and in fact I have found it very useful to discover the particular form of negative self-rating that clients use. The resulting shared meaning that I have been able to establish with my client has been facilitative in both therapeutic communication and the therapeutic change programme.

The language of change

The language which therapists use when they attempt to help clients change can also lead to semantic confusion and constitute obstacles to therapeutic progress. For example clients may construe the therapist's attempt to have them give up their musts as meaning "Give up your desire." Clients may often assume that the opposite of crucial is indifference. In planning such disputing strategies and while disputing irrational musts, therapists are recommended to keep in mind the importance of using the language of desire during this entire process. The term "homework" can also be extremely problematic because in some clients' minds, certainly in Britain, homework is associated with school and with negative experiences. I often find it helpful to ask the client to give me a word that would capture the notion of the importance of putting into practice between therapy sessions what has been learned in the sessions. Thus, one client came up with the term "training assignment," while another client came up with the term "transfer assignment" to capture the meaning of the phrase usually referred to as homework.

While urging clients to persist at executing assignments, Ellis often exhorts clients to "work and practice, work and practice." This is good advice but can be construed as very negative by clients who already have a high degree of low frustration tolerance. Thus, for some clients, words like persistence or repetition may capture similar meanings but be less negative in connotation. In addition, one of the hidden dangers of urging clients to "work and practice" and to "push themselves hard in therapy" is that some clients may actually consider that their therapists believe that they *have to* do the work or that they *have to* change. In these instances therapists serve as a poor role model in the minds of their clients.

It is important to realise that virtually any word that therapists can use when encouraging people to change may have negative connotations for some clients. It is therefore perhaps a good idea for RET therapists to ask clients at the end of therapy whether in this context they are using any words that the clients are viewing as negative (Beck, Rush, Shaw & Emery, 1979). If I was a client in RET or cognitive therapy I would view the term "agenda" negatively. This is because my mother used to ask me at the beginning of every day "What's on your agenda today, son?" a term which has come to have negative connotations for me.

Using words clients do not understand

RET is best viewed as an educational therapy. Since good education depends on effective communication, it is important that the therapist uses words that clients can understand. My seven years' experience working in a working class community in East Birmingham has taught me to be aware of using a number of words that are in common usage among RET therapists. I have found the following words to be most problematic amongst this population: dysfunctional, fallible, evidence, belief, cognition (to be avoided *almost* at all costs), rational, etc. Such clients will in fact rarely say to you "I'm sorry, I don't understand what that means" but will give various non-verbal cues to non-understanding. Thus, I have detected over the years the following patterns of non-understanding: (a) The Glazed Look. Here the client displays a glazed expression often accompanied by a fixed smile, (b) The Automatic Head Nod. Here clients nod knowingly as if they understand their therapists' RET terminology. If such nodding goes on for longer than 10 seconds without interruption this is a sign that clients may not understand what is being said. If this is accompanied by the knowing smile then it is almost guaranteed that the client doesn't understand a word the therapist is saying.

Towards shared meaning in RET

In this concluding section ways in which RET therapists can strive towards adopting shared meaning frameworks with their clients will be outlined. One important method of checking whether a client has understood the meaning of a concept which the therapist is using is to ask the client for clarification of the client's understanding. Questions like, "I am not sure whether I am making myself clear on this point. Can you put into your own words what you think I am saying?" can be used to good effect in that they encourage clients to be active in the therapeutic process and to use their own language rather than just parroting the language of the therapist. It is especially important for the therapist to pay attention to the non-verbal aspects of the client's responses to such questions. When the client uses exactly the same language as the therapist the way in which the client responds can often serve as a guide to whether or not he or she has understood the therapist's communications. When the client uses the same words as the therapist in answer to such enquiries the therapist can usefully ask "What do you understand by the word, e.g. awful. What other words in your mind are equivalent to this word?" I have found asking for synonyms particularly revealing of clients' misunderstandings of the rational concepts I have been endeavouring to teach them. For example, a common "synonym" that clients use for the term "awful" is "very bad." The latter, of course, is not a synonym for the former in RET theory.

A constructive therapeutic strategy for making clear distinctions between constructive and destructive negative emotions while ensuring that client and therapist have a shared meaning framework while using the same verbal label is to define terms before implementing disputing strategies. In particular, emotions should be linked with their evaluative beliefs in any exposition of terms. For example, while trying to clarify whether a client is angry (damningly angry) or annoyed (non-damningly angry) I might say something like this "O.K. So you say that you are angry. Now, when you are experiencing that emotion, what was more likely to be going through your mind? Did you believe, for example, that that person who did that bad thing was no good and absolutely should not have acted that way, or did you believe that although their behavior was bad, there was no reason why the person must not have acted that way? Also, did you regard *them* as bad or just *their behavior* as bad?" I have found that my clients can often more reliably distinguish between the two emotional states when I include their cognitive definitions than when such definitions are excluded. Clients rarely know spontaneously the RET theoretical distinction between these two emotional states. Thus, when discussing feeling terms with clients (particularly when one is distinguishing between constructive and destructive emotions) strive to include their cognitive counterparts.

RET therapists have much to learn from the work of George Kelly (1955) and his followers in Personal Construct Therapy with respect to discovering the clients' idiosyncratic meaning systems. One such strategy derived from PCT concerns asking clients for polar opposites for their feelings. This is particularly useful while planning and carrying-out disputing strategies since it may help the therapist to discover why clients may not in reality wish to change an emotion that they claim they wish to change and which, according to RET theory, is a destructive negative emotion. Thus, for example, I once worked with a depressed client who claimed not to want to be depressed but was resisting my attempts to help her feel sad, I asked her what she associated in her mind as being the opposite of sad, to which she replied "sensitive." This highly idiosyncratic use of the word "sad" as being in some way equivalent to being insensitive helped me to understand why my client resisted my attempts to encourage her to experience what RET theory stated as constructive negative emotion.

In conclusion I wish to emphasize that therapists should preferably be alert to the idiosyncratic ways in which clients use language and the equally idiosyncratic ways in which they may interpret the rational concepts that RET therapists strive to teach them. It is important for RET therapists to internalize the language system of RET but in doing so they should not assume that their clients will magically share the meaning structure implicit in rational-emotive terminology.

References

Beck, A.T., Rush, A.J., Shaw, B.F. & Emery, G. (1979) *Cognitive therapy of depression*. New York: Guilford.

DiGiuseppe, R. (1984). Thinking what to feel. *British Journal of Cognitive Psychotherapy*, 2 (1), 27–33.

Kelly, G.A. (1955). *The psychology of personal constructs*. Volumes 1 and 2. New York: Norton.

Vertes, R. (1971) The should: A critical analysis. *Rational Living*, 6(2) 22–25.

Walen, S.R., DiGiuseppe, R., & Wessler, R.L. (1980). *A practitioner's guide to rational-emotive therapy*. New York: Oxford University Press.

Wessler, R.A., & Wessler, R.L. (1980). *The principles and practice of rational-emotive therapy*. San Francisco: Jossey-Bass.

Young, H.S. (1975). Rational thinkers and robots. *Rational Living*, 9 (1), 3–7.

CHAPTER 6

VIVID METHODS IN RATIONAL-EMOTIVE THERAPY*

A. Ellis and R. Grieger (Eds) (1986) *Handbook of rational-emotive therapy. Volume 2*. New York: Springer (pp. 221–245)

REBT can be practised in a manner that is flat, boring and mechanical and, when it is, it is rarely effective since clients are not being encouraged to participate in an emotionally engaging process. By contrast, when REBT is practised in a way where its concepts come to life then clients do seem to benefit a lot more. They remember the concepts better and are thus able to retrieve and apply them when they need to. In the early 1980s, I published three linked articles on what I called 'Vivid RE[B]T' and outlined a number of ways in which therapists could make the practice of REBT more therapeutically stimulating for their clients. These three articles were combined into one chapter and it is this collated piece that appears here.

The fundamental goal of rational-emotive therapy is to enable clients to live effective lives by helping them change their faulty inferences and irrational evaluations about themselves, other people, and the world. While there are many ways of achieving this goal, the purpose of this chapter is to highlight ways in which rational-emotive therapists can make the therapeutic process a more vivid experience for their clients so that they may be stimulated to identify and change their faulty inferences and irrational evaluations more effectively. A number of rational-emotive and cognitive therapists have already written on the use of vivid methods in therapy (Arnkoff, 1981; Ellis, 1979; Freeman, 1981; Knaus & Wessler, 1976; Walen, DiGiuseppe, & Wessler, 1980; and Wessler & Wessler, 1980). However, a comprehensive account of the uses, advantages, and limitations of such methods has yet to appear in the literature on rational-emotive therapy. In this chapter, attention will be given to the use of vivid methods in *problem assessment*, vivid *disputing* methods, and vivid ways in which clients may *work through* their emotional and behavioral problems.

Rationale for vivid methods in RET

Rational-emotive therapists aim to help clients achieve their goals through the systematic application of cognitive, emotive, and behavioral methods. However,

* This chapter combines three articles by Dr. Dryden: (1) "Vivid RET: Problem assessment," *Rational Living*, 1983, *18*, 7–12; (2) "Vivid RET: Disputing methods," *Journal of Rational-Emotive Therapy*, 1983, *1*, 9–14, and (3) "Vivid RET: The working through process," *Journal of Rational-Emotive Therapy*, 1984, *1*, 27–31. Reproduced by permission of *Rational Living* and the *Journal of Rational-Emotive Therapy*.

therapist and client rely heavily on verbal dialogue in their in-session encounters. The tone of such dialogue in rational-emotive therapy sessions can be rich, stimulating, and arousing, but it is far too often dry and mundane (as supervisors of novice rational-emotive therapists will testify). While the role of emotional arousal in the facilitation of attitude change is complex (Hoehn-Saric, 1978), it is my contention that the majority of clients can be helped best to reexamine faulty inferences and irrational beliefs if we as therapists gain their full attention and make therapy a memorable experience for them. While there are no studies that are addressed to this point in the rational-emotive therapy literature, there is some suggestion from process-and-outcome studies carried out on client-centered therapy that vivid therapist interventions are associated with successful client outcome and with certain client in-therapy behaviors that have in turn been linked to positive outcome (Rice, 1965; Rice, 1973; Rice & Gaylin, 1973; Rice & Wagstaff, 1967; Wexler, 1975; Wexler & Butler, 1976). At present we do not know whether any client in-therapy behaviors are associated with successful outcome in RET. Yet, it is possible to hypothesize that such client in-session behaviors as attending to and being fully involved in the therapeutic process and making links between in-session dialogue and out-of-session activities will be associated with therapeutic gain in RET. If this proves correct, then it is my further contention that vivid methods in RET may more effectively bring about such client behavior.

Given the dearth of much-needed studies on these points, anecdotal evidence will have to suffice. This involves feedback from my clients, who frequently related incidents of (1) how my own vivid therapeutic interventions helped them to reexamine a variety of their dysfunctional cognitions and (2) how they, with my encouragement, improved by making the working-through process a more stimulating experience for themselves.

It should be stressed at the outset that, while there is a place for vivid methods in RET, these are best introduced into therapy at appropriate times and within the context of a good therapeutic alliance between therapist and client.

Problem assessment

Effective rational-emotive therapy depends initially on the therapist gaining a clear understanding of (1) the client's problems in cognitive, emotional, and behavioral terms and (2) the contexts in which the client's problems occur. To a great extent, the therapist is dependent on the client's verbal reports in gaining such an understanding. It is in this area that many obstacles to progress may appear. Some clients have great difficulty identifying and/or accurately labeling their emotional experiences. Other clients are in touch with and able to report their emotions but find it hard to relate these to activating events (either external or internal). Yet a further group of clients is easily able to report problematic activating events and emotional experiences but has difficulty seeing how these may relate to mediating cognitions. Vivid methods can be used in a variety of ways to overcome such obstacles to a valid and reliable assessment of client problems.

Vividness in portraying activating events

With some clients, traditional assessment procedures through verbal dialogue do not always yield the desired information. When this occurs, rational-emotive therapists often use imagery methods. They ask clients to conjure up evocative images of activating events. Such evocative imagery often stimulates the client's memory concerning her or his emotional reactions or indeed in some instances leads to the reexperiencing of these reactions in the session. While focusing on such images, the client also can begin to gain access to cognitive processes below the level of awareness that cannot be easily reached through verbal dialogue.

One particularly effective use of imagery in the assessment of client problems is that of bringing future events into the present. This is illustrated by the following exchange between myself and a client who was terrified that her mother might die, which led her to be extremely unassertive with the mother.

Therapist: So you feel you just can't speak up to her. Because if you did, what might happen?
Client: Well, she might have a fit.
Therapist: And what might happen if she did?
Client: She might have a heart attack and die.
Therapist: Well, we know that she is a fit woman, but let's go along with your fear for the moment. Okay?
Client: Okay.
Therapist: What if she did die?
Client: I just can't think . . . I . . . I'm sorry.
Therapist: That's okay. I know this is difficult, but I really think it would be helpful if we could get to the bottom of things. Okay? (Client nods.) Look, Marjorie, I want you to imagine that your mother has just died this morning. Can you imagine that? (Client nods and begins to shake.) What are you experiencing?
Client: When you said my mother was dead I began to feel all alone . . . like there was no one to care for me . . . no one I could turn to.
Therapist: And if there is no one who cares for you, no one you can turn to . . .?
Client: Oh, God! I know I couldn't cope on my own.

Instructing clients to imagine vividly something that has been warded off often leads to anxiety itself. It is important to process this anxiety, as it is sometimes related to the client's central problem. Issues like fear of loss of control, phrenophobia, and extreme discomfort anxiety are often revealed when this anxiety is fully assessed. However, some clients do find it difficult to imagine events spontaneously and require therapist assistance.

While imagery methods are now routinely used in cognitive behavior therapy (e.g., Lazarus, 1978), there has been little written on how therapists can stimulate clients' imagery processes. I have used a number of the following vivid methods to try and help clients utilize their potential for imagining events.

Vivid, connotative therapist language

One effective way of helping clients to use their imagery potential is for the therapist to use rich, colorful, and evocative language while aiding clients to set the scene. Unless the therapist has gained prior diagnostic information, he or she is sometimes uncertain about which stimuli in the activating event are particularly related to the client's problem. Thus, it is best to give clients many alternatives. For example, with a socially anxious client I proceeded thus, after attempting without success to get him to use his own potential for imagery.

Therapist: So at the moment we are unclear about what you are anxious about. What I'd like to suggest is that we use your imagination to help us. I will help you set the scene based on what we have already discussed. However, since we have yet to discover detailed factors, some of the things I say might not be relevant. Will you bear with me and let me know when what I say touches a nerve in you?

Client: Okay.

Therapist: Fine. Just close your eyes and imagine you are about to walk into the dance. You walk in and some of the guys there glance at you. You can see the *smirks* on their *mocking* faces and one of them *blows* you a kiss. (Here I am testing out a hypothesis based on previously gained information.) You start to *seethe* inside and . . .

Client: Okay, when you said I was starting to seethe, that struck a chord. I thought I can't let them get away with that but if I let go I'll just go berserk. I started feeling anxious.

Therapist: And if you went berserk?

Client: I couldn't show my face in there again.

Therapist: What would happen then?

Client: I don't know. I . . . It's funny—the way I see it, I would never go out again.

Here I was using words like "smirks," "mocking," "blows," and "seethe" deliberately in my attempt to stimulate the client's imagination. It is also important for the therapist to vary his or her tone so that this matches the language employed.

Photographs

I have at times asked clients to bring to interviews photographs of significant others or significant places. These are kept on hand to be used at relevant moments in the assessment process. I have found the use of photographs particularly helpful when the client is discussing an event in the past that is still bothering her or him. Thus, for example, one client who spoke without feeling about being rejected by his father who died seven years earlier, broke down in tears when I asked him to look at a picture of him and his father standing apart from one another. Feelings of hurt and anger (with their associated cognitions) were expressed, which enabled us to move to the disputing stage.

Other mementoes

In a similar vein, I have sometimes asked clients to bring in mementoes. These may include pictures they have drawn, paintings that have meaning for them, and poems either written by themselves or other people. The important point is that these mementoes are to be related to issues that the client is working on in therapy. A roadblock to assessment was successfully overcome with one client when I asked her to bring in a memento that reminded her of her mother. She brought in a bottle of perfume that her mother was accustomed to wearing. When I asked her to smell the perfume at a point in therapy when the assessment process through verbal dialogue was again breaking down, the client was helped to identify feelings of jealousy toward her mother, which she experienced whenever her mother left her to go out socializing. Moreover, my client was ashamed of such feelings. This issue was centrally related to her presenting problem of depression.

Another of my clients was depressed about losing her boyfriend. I had great difficulty helping her to identify any related mediating cognitions through traditional assessment procedures. Several tentative guesses on my part also failed to pinpoint relevant cognitive processes. I then asked her to bring to our next session anything that reminded her of her ex-boyfriend. She brought in a record of a popular song that had become known to them as "our song." When I played the song at an appropriate point in the interview, my client began to sob and expressed feelings of abandonment, hurt, and fear for the future. Again a vivid method had unearthed important assessment material where traditional methods had failed.

It should be noted from these examples that quite often such dramatic methods lead to the expression of strong affective reactions in the session. This is often an important part of the process, because such affective reactions are gateways to the identification of maladaptive cognitive processes that are difficult to identify through more traditional methods of assessment.

The "interpersonal nightmare" technique

Rational-emotive and cognitive therapists sometimes employ methods originally derived from gestalt therapy and psychodrama to assist them in the assessment phase of therapy. These have been adequately described (Arnkoff, 1981; Nardi, 1979) and will not be discussed here. I would like to describe a related technique I have developed (Dryden, 1980), which I call the "interpersonal nightmare" technique. This technique may be best used with clients who are able to specify only sketchily an anticipated "dreaded" event involving other people but are neither able to specify in any detail the nature of the event nor how they would react if the event were to occur. First the client is given a homework assignment to imagine the "dreaded" event. He or she is told to write a brief segment of a play about it, specifying the exact words that the protagonists would use. The client is encouraged to give full rein to imagination while focusing on what he or she fears might happen. An example will suffice. The following scenario was developed by a 55-year-old woman with alcohol problems who was terrified of making errors at the office where she worked as a typist.

Scene:	Boss's office where he sits behind a very large desk. He has found out that one of the typists has inadvertently filed a letter wrongly and sends for her. She comes in and is made to stand in front of the boss.
Boss:	Have you anything to say in this matter?
Typist (me):	Only that I apologize and will be more careful in the future.
Boss:	What do you mean by saying you will be more careful in the future—what makes you think you have a future? (At this point he starts banging on the desk.) I have never yet met anyone less competent or less suited to the job than you are. You mark my words, I will make life so uncomfortable for you that you will leave. When I took over this job I intended to have the people I wanted working for me, and you are not on that list. I have already gotten rid of two typists, and I shall see that you are the third. Now get out of my office you stupid, blundering fool, and remember I shall always be watching you and you will never know when I shall be behind you.

I then read over the scene with the client, making inquiries about the tone in which she thought her boss would make these statements and asking her to identify which words the boss would emphasize. I then arranged for a local actor who was the same age as the boss to enact the scene realistically on cassette. In the next session I instructed my client to visualize the room in which the encounter might take place. She briefly described the room, paying particular attention to where her boss would be sitting and where she would be standing. I then played her the cassette, which evoked strong feelings of fear of being physically harmed and humiliated. Again, important data had been collected that traditional assessment procedures had failed to uncover.

These examples have shown how rational-emotive methods can employ various visual, olfactory, language, and auditory methods to help clients vividly imagine appropriate activating events. This in turn helps them more easily identify maladaptive emotional experiences and related cognitive processes that are not readily identified through the verbal interchange of the psychotherapeutic interview. It is important to note that the use of such methods is not being advocated for its own sake. They are employed with specific purposes in mind.

Rational-emotive problem solving

Knaus and Wessler (1976) have described a method that they call rational-emotive problem solving (REPS). This method involves the therapist creating conditions in the therapy session that approximate those the client encounters in her or his everyday life and which give rise to emotional problems. Knaus and Wessler contend that this method may be used either in a planned or impromptu fashion and is particularly valuable when clients experience difficulty in identifying emotional experiences and related cognitive processes through verbal dialogue with their therapists. I employed this method with a male client who reported difficulty in acting assertively in his life and claimed not to be able to identify the emotions and thoughts that inhibited the expression of assertive responses. During our discussion I began to search around for my pouch of pipe tobacco. Finding it empty, I interrupted my client and asked him if he would drive to town, purchase my favorite tobacco, adding that if he hurried he could return for the last five minutes of our interview. He immediately got up, took my money and walked out of my office toward his car. I rushed after him, brought him back into my office and together we processed his reactions to this simulated experience.

It is clear that this technique must be used with therapeutic judgment and that its use may threaten or even destroy the therapeutic alliance between client and therapist. However, since rational-emotive therapists value risk taking, they are often prepared to use such techniques when more traditional and less risky methods have failed to bring about therapeutic improvement. It is further important, as Beck et al. (1979) have stressed, for the therapist to ask the client for the latter's honest reactions to this procedure, to ascertain whether it may have future therapeutic value for the client. When a client indicates that she or he has found the rational-emotive problem-solving method unhelpful, the therapist had better then explain the rationale for attempting such a procedure and disclose that he or she intended no harm but was attempting to be helpful. Normally clients respect such disclosures, and in fact the therapist in doing so provides a useful model for the client, namely, that it is possible to nondefensively acknowledge errors without damning oneself. However, with this method, it is apparent that therapists cannot realistically disclose their rationale in advance of initiating the method, since this would detract from its potential therapeutic value.

Dreams

Although Albert Ellis has recently written a regular column for *Penthouse* magazine providing rational-emotive interpretations of readers' dreams, rational-emotive therapists are not generally noted for using dream material. However, there is no good reason why dream material cannot be used in RET as long as (1) it does not predominate in the therapeutic process and (2) the therapist has a definite purpose in mind in using it.

Freeman (1981, pp. 228–229) has outlined a number of further guidelines for the use of dreams for assessment purposes:

1 The dream needs to be understood in thematic rather than symbolic terms.
2 The thematic content of the dream is idiosyncratic to the dreamer and must be viewed within the context of the dreamer's life.
3 The specific language and imagery are important to the meaning.
4 The affective responses to the dreams can be seen as similar to the dreamer's affective responses in waking situations,
5 The particular length of the dream is of lesser import than the content.
6 The dream is a product of and the responsibility of the dreamer.
7 Dreams can be used when the patient appears stuck in therapy.

I inadvertently stumbled on the usefulness of dream material for assessment purposes when working with a 28-year-old depressed student who would frequently reiterate, "I'm depressed and I don't know why." I had virtually exhausted all the assessment methods I knew (including those described in this chapter) to help her identify depressogenic thoughts in situations when she experienced depression, but without success. In a desperate last attempt, I asked her if she could remember any of her dreams, not expecting in the least that this line of inquiry would prove fruitful. To my surprise she said yes, she did have a recurring dream. In this dream she saw herself walking alone along a river bank, and when she peered into the river, she saw a reflection of herself as a very old woman. This image filled her with extreme sadness and depression. On further discussion she said that she believed that this dream meant that she had no prospect of finding any happiness in her life, either in love relationships or in her career and that she was doomed to spend her years alone, ending up as a sad, pathetic, old woman. This account of the dream and subsequent discussion of its meaning enabled me to help her identify a number of inferential distortions and irrational beliefs, which provided the focus for subsequent cognitive restructuring.

Daydreams may also provide important material for assessment purposes. For some people, particular daydreams occur in response to and as compensation for a negative activating event. Thus, one client reported having the daydream of establishing a multinational corporation after failing to sell insurance to prospective customers. The use of such daydreams by clients may not necessarily be dysfunctional but may impede them (as in the preceding example) from getting to the core of their problems. Often daydreams are an expression of our hopes and aspirations, and I have found it valuable to ask clients not only about the content of such material but also what would stop them from actualizing their goals. Much important assessment material is gathered in this manner, in particular concerning ideas of low frustration tolerance.

In vivo *therapy sessions*

Sacco (1981) has outlined the value of conducting therapy sessions in real-life settings in which clients experience emotional difficulties. I have found moving outside the interview room to such settings particularly useful in gaining assessment material when traditional methods have failed to provide such data. For example, I once saw a male student who complained of avoiding social situations. He did so in case others would see his hands tremble. Traditional assessment methods yielded no further data. To overcome this treatment impasse, I suggested to him that we needed to collect more data and we eventually conducted a therapy session in a coffee shop where I asked him to go and get us both a cup of coffee. He refused because he feared that his hands might tremble, but I firmly persisted with my request. He was able to identify a stream of negative cognitions on the way from our table to the service counter. He returned without our coffees but with valuable information, which we processed later in my office. It is important for therapists to explain their rationale for conducting *in-vivo* sessions in advance, in order to gain client cooperation. In addition, obtaining clients' reactions to these sessions is often helpful, particularly if *in-vivo* sessions are planned for use later in the therapeutic process.

Disputing

In this section, various vivid disputing methods will be outlined. The purpose of these methods is (1) to help clients see the untenable basis and dysfunctional nature of their irrational beliefs and to replace them with more rational ones and (2) to help them make more accurate inferences about reality. These methods often demonstrate the rational message powerfully but indirectly, and they do not necessarily call upon the client to answer such questions as "Where is the evidence . . .?"

It is important for the therapist to make certain preparations before initiating vivid disputing methods, since the success of such methods depends upon (1) the client clearly understanding the link between thoughts, feelings, and behaviors and (2) the therapist ascertaining particular biographical information about the client.

Preparing for vivid disputing

The thought-feeling-behavior link

After the therapist has undertaken a thorough assessment of the client's target problem, the next task is to help the client see the connections among thoughts, feelings, and behaviors. Here again vivid methods can be employed. Thus the therapist, while speaking with the client, might pick up a book, drop it to the floor, and continue talking to the client. After a while, if the client has made no comment, the therapist can ask for both affective and cognitive reactions to this incident: Thus, the client is given a vivid here-and-now example of the thought-feeling link.

Biographical information

Before initiating the vivid disputing process, I often find it helpful to gather certain information about the client. I like to find out about my client's *interests, hobbies*, and *work situation*. I have found this information often helps me adapt my interventions, using phrases that will be meaningful to my client, given her or his idiosyncratic life situation. Thus, if my client is passionately interested in boxing, a message utilizing a boxing analogy may well have greater impact than a golfing analogy.

I also find it helpful to discover *who my client admires*. I do this because later I may wish to ask my client how he or she thinks these admired individuals might solve similar problems. This prompts the client to identify with a model to imitate. Lazarus (1978) has employed a similar method with children. For example, I asked a male client to imagine that his admired grandfather experienced public speaking anxiety, and I inquired how he would have overcome it. This helped him identify a coping strategy that he used to overcome his own public speaking anxiety problem. This approach is best used if the client also can acknowledge that the admired individual is fallible and thus prone to human irrationality. In addition, it is important that the client sees the feasibility of imitating the model.

I find it invaluable to ask my clients about their *previous experiences of attitude change*. I try and discern the salient features of such change for possible replication in my in-session disputing strategies. For example, one anxious female client told me she had changed her mind about foxhunting after reading a number of personal accounts offering arguments against foxhunting. As part of my disputing plan, I directed this client to autobiographies of people who had overcome anxiety. Another client claimed she had in the past received help from speaking to people who had experienced problems similar to her own. I arranged for this client to speak to some of my ex-clients who had experienced but overcome comparable problems.

I now propose to outline a number of ways in which rational-emotive therapists can vividly employ disputing techniques. The importance of tailoring interventions to meet the specific, idiosyncratic requirements of clients should be borne in mind throughout.

Vivid disputing methods

Disputing in the presence of vivid stimuli

In a previous article (Dryden, 1983), I outlined a number of ways of vividly portraying activating events to help clients identify their emotional reactions and the cognitive determinants of these reactions. I outlined various visual, language, auditory, and olfactory methods. These same methods can be used as context material in the disputing process. For example, one client brought along a drawing of herself and her mother. She portrayed her mother as a very large, menacing figure and herself as a small figure crouching in fear in front of her mother. I asked the client to draw another picture where she and her mother were of the same height, standing face-to-face, looking each other in the eye. When she brought in this drawing, I inquired how her attitude toward her mother differed in the two pictures. This not only provided her with a demonstration that it was possible for her to evaluate her mother differently but also led to a fruitful discussion in which I disputed some of her irrational beliefs inherent in the first drawing while having her focus on the second.

A similar tactic was employed using the "interpersonal nightmare" technique with the 55-year-old woman mentioned earlier. After disputing some of the irrational beliefs uncovered when the technique was employed for assessment purposes, I repeatedly played the woman the tape while having her dispute some of the irrational beliefs it revealed. A similar method can be used when *in-vivo* sessions are conducted. In my 1983 article I reported the case of a student who was anxious about his hands shaking in public. Both assessment and later disputing of his irrational beliefs were carried out in a coffee bar. Indeed he practiced disputing his irrational beliefs while carrying two shaking cups of coffee back from the service counter to our table. Disputing in the presence of vivid stimuli enables the client to build bridges from in-session to out-of-session situations.

Imagery methods

One very effective imagery method that can be used in the disputing of irrational beliefs is that of time projection (Lazarus, 1978). When a client makes grossly exaggerated negative evaluations of an event, he often stops thinking about it and therefore cannot see beyond its "dreaded" implications. The purpose of time projection is to enable clients to see vividly that time and the world continue after the "dreaded event" has occurred. Thus, for example, a Malaysian student whose tuition fees were paid for by his village concluded that it would be terrible if he failed his exams because he couldn't bear to face his fellow villagers. I helped him to imagine his return to his village while experiencing shame. I then gradually advanced time forward in imagery. He began to see that it was likely that his fellow villagers would eventually come to adopt a compassionate viewpoint toward him, and even if they did not, he could always live happily in another part of the country or in another part of the world.

Imagery methods that focus on helping clients think more carefully and critically about "dreaded" events are also extremely valuable. For example, another client who had a fear of other people seeing his hands shake was asked to imagine going into a bar, ordering a drink, and drinking while his hands shook. He said that he would be extremely anxious about this because other people in the bar would stare at him. He was asked to imagine how many people would stare at him. Would they stare in unison, or would they stare one at a time? He was asked to imagine how often they would stare at him, how long they would stare at him, and how often in the evening they would resume staring at him. He concluded that everybody would not stare at him and those who did stare would possibly only stare for about 30 seconds and he could stand that. This and other methods illustrate that it is possible to simultaneously help clients dispute both their faulty inferences and irrational evaluations. Another technique I employed with this same client was "imagery to exaggeration." He was asked to imagine his hands shaking while consuming drink and with everybody in the bar staring at him continually for three hours. At this point he burst out laughing and realized the exaggerated nature of his inference.

Rational-emotive imagery is a frequently employed technique and has been fully described by Maultsby and Ellis (1974) and Ellis (1979). It often has dramatic impact and thus qualifies as a vivid method. It is worthwhile noting at this point that some clients have difficulty conjuring up images and may have to be trained in a stepwise fashion to utilize this ability. Furthermore, while helpful, it is probably not necessary for clients to imagine with extreme clarity.

The rational-emotive therapist as raconteur

Wessler and Wessler (1980) have outlined the therapeutic value of relating various stories, parables, witty sayings, poems, aphorisms, and jokes to clients. The important factor here is that the therapist modifies the content of these to fit the client's idiosyncratic situation. Telling identical stories to two different clients may well have two different effects. One client may be deeply affected by the story, while for another the story may prove meaningless. It is important that rational-emotive therapists become acquainted with a wide variety of these stories and be prepared to modify them from client to client, without introducing unwarranted distortions.

Active visual methods

Active visual methods combine therapist or client activity with a vivid visual presentation. Young (1980) has outlined one such method, which he uses to help clients see the impossibility of assigning a global rating to themselves. He asks a client to describe some of his behaviors, attributes, talents, and interests. Every answer the client gives Young writes on a white sticky label and sticks the label on the client. This continues until the client is covered with white sticky labels and can begin to see the impossibility of assigning one global rating to such a complex being. Wessler and Wessler (1980) outline similar active visual methods to communicate a similar point. For example, they ask their clients to assign a comprehensive rating to a basket of fruit or a desk. Clients are encouraged to explore actively the components of the fruit basket or desk while attempting to assign a global rating to it.

Visual models

I have previously described the use of visual models I have devised, each of which demonstrates a rational message (Dryden, 1980). For example, I employ a model called the "LFT Splash." In the model a young man is seated at the top of a roller coaster with a young woman standing at the bottom. I tell clients that the young man does not move because he is telling himself that he can't stand the splash. Clients are asked to think what the young man would have to tell himself in order to reach the woman. This model is particularly useful in introducing to clients the idea of tolerating acute time-limited discomfort which, if tolerated, would help them achieve their goals.

Flamboyant therapist actions

A common disputing strategy that rational-emotive therapists use in verbal dialogue when clients conclude they are stupid for acting stupidly is to ask some variant of the question "How are you a stupid person for acting stupidly?" Alternatively, instead of asking such questions, the therapist could suddenly leap to the floor and start barking like a dog for about 30 seconds, resume her or his seat, and then ask the client to evaluate this action. Clients usually say that the action is stupid. The therapist can then ask whether that stupid action makes him or her a stupid person. Such flamboyant actions often enable clients to discriminate more easily between global self-ratings and ratings of behaviors or attributes.

Rational role reversal

Rational role reversal has been described by Kassinove and DiGiuseppe (1975). In this technique, the therapist plays a naive client with an emotional problem that is usually similar to the client's. The client is encouraged to adopt the role of the rational-emotive therapist and help the "client" dispute his or her irrational belief.

As Kassinove and DiGiuseppe point out, this technique is best used after the client has developed some skill at disputing some of his or her own irrational ideas. A related technique has been devised by Burns (1980), which he calls "externalization of voices." In this technique, which is again used after the client has displayed some skill at disputing irrational beliefs, the therapist adopts the irrational part of the client's personality and supplies the client with irrational messages. The client's task is to respond rationally to the irrational messages. When clients show a high level of skill at this, the therapist, in role, can try hard to overwhelm the client with a barrage of quick-fire irrational messages, thus helping the client to develop an automatic ability to respond to his or her own irrational messages. This method also can be used to help clients identify those negative thoughts to which they experience difficulty in responding.

Therapist self-disclosure

Some clients find therapist self-disclosure an extremely persuasive method, while for others it is contraindicated. One way of attempting to ascertain a client's possible reactions to therapist self-disclosure is to include an appropriate item in a pretherapy questionnaire. It may well be wise to avoid using therapist self-disclosure with clients who respond negatively to the item. In any case, the therapist had better ascertain the client's reaction to any self-disclosing statements she or he might make. The research literature on this topic indicates that therapists had better not disclose personal information about themselves too early in the therapeutic process (Dies, 1973). When therapists do disclose information about themselves it is my experience that the most effective forms of self-disclosure are those in which they portray themselves as coping rather than mastery models. Thus, for example, it is better for the therapist to say to the client, "I used to have a similar problem, but this is how I overcame it," rather than to say, "I have never had this problem, because I believe . . ."

Paradoxical therapist actions

This method is often best used when clients, through their actions, communicate messages about themselves to the therapist that are based on irrational beliefs. For example, I once saw a female client who experienced a lot of rheumatic pain but had an attitude of low frustration tolerance toward it. Her behavior toward me in sessions indicated the attitude, "I am a poor soul, feel sorry for me." This prompted me to adopt an overly sympathetic and diligent stance toward her. Thus at the beginning of every session I treated her as if she could hardly walk and escorted her by arm to her chair and made frequent inquiries about her comfort. This eventually prompted her to make statements like, "Don't treat me like a child," "I can cope," or "It's not as bad as all that." I then helped her to identify and dispute some of the original implicit irrational messages. Whenever she began to lapse back into her self-pitying attitude, I began to behave in an overly solicitous manner again, which provided a timely reminder for her to attend to the behavioral components of her philosophy of low frustration tolerance and then to the philosophy itself.

Paradoxical therapist communications

Ellis (1977) has written on the use of humor in RET, where the therapist humorously exaggerates clients' irrational beliefs. He points out the importance of using humor against the irrational belief, rather than as an *ad hominem* attack. Taking clients' beliefs and inferences to an absurd conclusion is another paradoxical technique that can be used. Thus, for example, with clients who are scared that other people may discover one of their "shameful" acts or traits, therapists can take this to its illogical conclusion by saying, "Well there is no doubt about it, they will find out, then they will tell their friends, some of whom will call up the local television station, and before you know it you will be on the six o'clock news." Again, it is important that clients perceive that such communications are being directed against their beliefs rather than against them. Thus, feedback from clients on this matter had better be sought.

Rational songs

Ellis (1977) has written about the use of his now-famous rational songs in therapy. For example, the therapist can hand a client a song sheet and sing, preferably in an outrageous voice, a rational song that has been carefully selected to communicate the rational alternatives to the client's target irrational belief. Since Ellis tends to favor tunes that were written many years ago, it may be more productive for the therapist to rewrite the words to more up-to-date and popular songs, for clients not familiar with some of the "old favorites."

In-session inference tests

Clients are likely to make faulty inferences about their therapist similar to those they make about other people in their lives. For example, one of my clients saw me talking to a fellow therapist at the end of one of our sessions. At our next session she told me that she was anxious about this because she was convinced I had been talking about her and laughing about what she had told me in the session (she was not in fact paranoid). I proceeded to pull out two pieces of paper, kept one for myself and gave the other one to her. I told her that I wanted to find out whether she indeed had extraordinary mind-reading powers. I thus wrote down the word "chicken" on my piece of paper and asked her to concentrate very carefully for the next three minutes and to write down what she thought I was thinking about. I said that I would keep thinking about the word I had written down to make it a fair experiment. After the three minutes, she wrote down the word "baseball." This became known as the "baseball-chicken" interview, which she recalled frequently when she made arbitrary inferences concerning the meaning of other people's behavior.

Using the therapist–client relationship

Wessler (1982) has written that it is important for the rational-emotive therapist to inquire about the nature of his client's reactions to him or her, that is, to examine some of the client's here-and-now attitudes. Little has been written about this approach in the rational-emotive literature, and thus relatively little is known about its potential as a framework for disputing inaccurate inferences and irrational beliefs. Wessler (1982) also advocates that therapists give clients frank feedback about this impact on them and explore whether clients have a similar impact on other people. Such generalizations must of course be made with caution, but such discussion is often a stimulus for clients to become more sensitive to their impact on other people and often leads them to ask other people about their interpersonal impact (Anchin & Kiesler, 1982).

The advantage of using the therapist–client relationship in this way is that it provides both parties with an opportunity to process the client's inferences and beliefs in an immediate and often vivid fashion. The outcome of such strategies is often more memorable for clients than the outcome of more traditional disputing methods, where client inferences and beliefs about recent past events are processed.

Therapist paralinguistic and nonverbal behavior

When rational-emotive therapists want to emphasize a point, one important way of doing so is for them to vary their paralinguistic and nonverbal behavior. For example, Walen et al. (1980, p. 178) note that when Ellis in his public demonstrations talks about something being "awful" he drops his voice several notes, stretches out the word and increases his volume, producing a dreary and dramatic sound, for example, "and it's AWWWWWFULL that he doesn't like me." Later, when he changes the word "awful" to "unfortunate" or a "need" to a "want," Ellis again pronounces the words now reflecting rational concepts in a distinct way. He says the key word slowly, enunciates very clearly, and raises the pitch of his voice as well as the volume. In addition, the therapist might associate some dramatic nonverbal behavior with the paralinguistic clue. For example, when the word "awful" is pronounced, the therapist might sink to the floor, holding his neck as if strangling himself.

Therapeutic markers

Another way of emphasizing a point is to draw the client's attention to the fact that an important point is about to be made. For example, I might say to a client when I want to emphasize a point, "Now I want you to listen extremely carefully to this point because if you miss it it would be awwwfull" (therapist sinks to the floor again). I call such interventions "therapeutic markers." Another way of emphasizing statements is to change one's body position. For example, by moving their torsos forward toward clients, therapists can indicate the importance of their following statements. Whenever I want clients to become aware of important statements they have made, particularly when they make more rational statements at the beginning of the disputing process, I may, for example, pause and say, "Excuse me, could you just repeat what you said—I really want to make a note of this." If I am recording a session, I might say, "Hold on a minute, I really want you to hear what you have just said, I can't believe it myself, I just want to check it out."

Pragmatic disputes

One major way of encouraging clients to surrender their irrational beliefs in favor of more rational ones is to point out to them, and in this context in dramatic terms, the implications of continued adherence to their irrational beliefs. Ellis counsels that for particularly resistant and difficult clients this tactic is often the most effective (Ellis, 1982). Quite often I have heard Ellis tell clients something like, "If you continue to cling to that belief you'll suffer for the rest of your life." Here, as before, he changes his paralinguistic and nonverbal behavior when he states the conclusion, "You'll suffer for the rest of your life." In a similar vein, when clients state that they can't (or rather, won't) change their beliefs, he points out to them the logical implications of not doing so when he says forcefully: "So suffer!" In this regard it would be interesting to determine under what conditions pragmatic disputes are more effective than philosophical ones.

Working through

This final section focuses on how therapists can help clients to vividly work through some of their emotional problems. Ellis (1980) has criticized some popular behavioral techniques on the grounds that they do not necessarily encourage clients to make profound philosophical changes in their lives. In particular he criticizes those methods that encourage the client to confront a dreaded event very gradually. He posits that this gradualism may indeed reinforce some clients low-frustration-tolerance ideas. Whenever possible, then, rational-emotive therapists encourage their clients to act in dramatic and vivid ways because they believe significant attitude change is more likely to follow the successful completion of such tasks. I will outline the vivid methods that clients can put into practice behaviorally and cognitively in their everyday lives. First, however, rational-emotive therapists face a further problem, which has received insufficient attention in the RET literature: how to encourage clients to carry out their homework assignments.

Vivid cues for encouraging clients to do their homework

While some clients conscientiously do the homework assignments they and their therapists have negotiated, other clients do not. It is true that some clients do not follow through on these assignments because of low-frustration-tolerance ideas; still other clients do not follow through, particularly early on in the working-through process, because they require some vivid reminders to initiate this process. With such clients, I have found it particularly helpful to ask them what they generally find memorable in everyday life experiences. For example, some people find the printed word memorable, while others have visual images on which they cue. Yet others focus primarily on auditory stimuli. I find that it is profitable to capitalize on whatever channel the client finds memorable.

Vivid visual cues

There are a number of ways clients can remind themselves to initiate the disputing process. A number of rational-emotive therapists encourage clients to carry around small 3″ × 5″ cards with rational self-statements written on them, to which clients can refer at various times. Other therapists have encouraged clients to write reminders to themselves either to initiate a homework assignment or to refer to a rational message. These clients are encouraged to pin up such messages at various places around the home or in their work situation.

I find it helpful to encourage those clients who find visual images powerful to associate a particular dysfunctional feeling with a visual image that would enable them to initiate the disputing process. Thus one client found it helpful to conjure up a sign in her mind that said "Dispute" when she began to feel anxious. Another client, who was depressed, began to associate the onset of depression with a road sign on which was written "Act now."

Another strategy I have used is to ascertain from clients what, if any, in-session experiences they have found particularly memorable. I try to help them encapsulate some of these experiences as a cue either to initiate the disputing process or to remind themselves of the relevant rational principle to which this experience referred. One client who was prone to thinking himself an idiot for acting idiotically found it memorable when I made strange faces at him to help him get the point that concluding he was an idiot for acting idiotically was an overgeneralization. Whenever he began to make such an overgeneralization in everyday life, he would get the image of my making faces and quickly remember to what this referred. This helped him accept himself regardless of any idiotic act he actually made or thought he might make in the future.

Another client who did virtually no cognitive disputing or behavioral assignments outside the sessions was helped in the following manner. First, this issue was made the focus of therapy. Instead of asking her traditional disputing questions, I asked her to imagine what I would say to her were I to respond to her irrational beliefs. She in fact had understood rational principles because her answers were very good. Her problem was that she would not employ these principles. I then asked her if there was any way she could conjure up a picture of me giving her rational messages at various emotionally vulnerable times in her everyday life. She hit on the idea of imagining that I was perched on her shoulder whispering rational messages into her ear. Additionally she began to carry around a small card that said "Imagine that Dr. Dryden is on your shoulder." This proved a particularly effective technique where all else had failed.

Vivid language

Wexler and Butler (1976) have argued in favor of therapists using expressive language in therapy. I have found that one of the major benefits of using vivid nonprofane language is that clients remember these vivid expressions or catchphrases and use them as shorthand ways of disputing irrational beliefs in their everyday lives. For example, in the case where I helped a client dispute a particular distorted inference by having her attempt to read my mind (the "baseball–chicken" interview), whenever the client concluded that other people were making negative inferences about her without supporting data, she would remember the phrase "baseball and chicken." This served (1) as a timely reminder that she might be making incorrect conclusions from the data at hand, and (2) as a cue for her to start examining the evidence.

In a related technique, the therapist asks the client to give his or her own distinctive name to a faulty psychological process. Wessler and Wessler (1980) give such an example where a client came to refer to himself as "Robert the Rule Maker," to describe his tendency to make demands on himself and other people. A knowledge of clients' subcultural values is particularly helpful here. I work in a working-class area in Birmingham, England, and one word my clients frequently use, which was unfamiliar to me, was the word "mather."[1] I helped one client who was angry with her mother to see her mother as a fallible human being with a worrying problem, and that she could be accepted for this rather than be damned for it. My client suddenly laughed and said, "Yes! I guess my mother is a matherer." I encouraged her to remember this catchy phrase whenever she began to feel angry toward her mother.

Auditory cues

Rational-emotive therapists often make tape recordings of their sessions for clients to replay several times between sessions. This often serves to remind clients of rational principles they have understood in the session but may have since forgotten.

Using personal recording systems, clients also can be encouraged to develop auditory reminders to initiate either cognitive or behavioral homework assignments. In addition, they can be encouraged to put forceful and emphatic rational statements on cassettes and play these while undertaking behavioral assignments. For example, I once saw a client who was anxious about other people looking at her for fear they might think her strange. I suggested that she do something in her everyday life that would encourage people to look at her so she could dispute some of her underlying irrational beliefs. She decided to wear a personal stereo system in the street, which she thought would encourage people to look at her. I suggested that while walking she play a tape on which she had recorded the rational message "Just because I look strange doesn't mean that I am strange."

The use of rational songs in therapy has already been described. Several of my clients have found that singing a particular rational song at an emotionally vulnerable time has been helpful for them. It has reminded them of a rational message they might not ordinarily have been able to focus on while being emotionally distressed. Another client told me that her sessions with me reminded her of a particular song and whenever she hummed this song to herself it helped bring to mind the fact that she could accept herself even though she did not have a man in her life. The song, ironically, was "You're No One Till Somebody Loves You." In fact she rewrote some of the words and changed the title to "You're Someone Even Though Nobody Loves You."

Olfactory cues

It is possible for clients to use various aromas as cues to remind themselves to do a homework assignment or to initiate the disputing process. One client said that she found my pipe tobacco particularly aromatic and distinctive. Since we were both seeking a memorable cue, I suggested an experiment whereby she purchased a packet of my favorite tobacco and carried this around with her to smell at various distressing times. This aroma was associated in her mind with a particular rational message. This proved helpful, and indeed my client claimed that by saying to herself the phrase "Pipe up" she now no longer has to take the tobacco out of her handbag to smell. Just the phrase is enough to remind her of the rational message.

The working-through process

From its inception, RET has strongly recommended that clients undertake "some kind of activity which itself will act as a forceful counterpropagandist agency against the nonsense he believes" (Ellis, 1958). Ellis has consistently stressed that for clients who will agree to do them, dramatic, forceful, and implosive activities remain the best forms of working-through assignments. Such assignments emphasize either cognitively based or behavioral activities.

Cognitive assignments

In cognitive assignments, clients are encouraged to find ways in which they can convince themselves (outside therapy sessions) that rational philosophies which they can acknowledge as correct in therapy sessions are indeed correct and functional for them. Ellis has always urged clients to dispute their ideas vigorously, using such aids as written homework forms (Ellis, 1979). Other vivid cognitive techniques that clients can use include the following.

Rational proselytizing

(Bard, 1973). Here clients are encouraged to teach RET to their friends. In teaching others, clients become more convinced themselves of rational philosophies. This technique, however, had better be used with caution, and clients should be warned against playing the role of unwanted therapist to friends and relatives.

Tape-recorded disputing

In this technique, clients are encouraged to put a disputing sequence on tape. They are asked to play both the rational and irrational parts of themselves. Clients are further encouraged to try and make the rational part more persuasive and more forceful in responding to the irrational part.

Passionate statements

For those clients who are intellectually unable to do cognitive disputing in its classical sense, *passionate rational self-statements* can be used. Here client and therapist work together to develop appropriate rational self-statements that the client can actually use in everyday life. Clients are encouraged to repeat these statements in a very forceful manner instead of in their normal voice tone. Another variation of this technique is to have clients say rational self-statements to their reflection in a mirror, using a passionate tone and dramatic gestures to again reinforce the message.

Behavioral techniques

Behavioral techniques that rational-emotive therapists particularly favor have clients do cognitive disputing in actual settings that vividly evoke their fears. The purpose is to enable clients to have the success experience of doing cognitive disputing while exposing themselves to feared stimuli. In addition, dramatic behavioral assignments are recommended to help clients overcome their low-frustration-tolerance ideas. Here the focus is oriented toward clients changing their dysfunctional attitudes toward their internal experiences of anxiety or frustration. Behavioral assignments include the following.

Shame-attacking exercises

Here the client is encouraged to do some act that she or he has previously regarded as "shameful." The client is encouraged to act in a way that will encourage other people in the environment to pay attention to her or him without bringing harm to self or other people and without unduly alarming others. She or he is encouraged to engage simultaneously in vigorous disputing, such as, "I may look weird, but I'm not weird." In my opinion, one of the drawbacks of encouraging a client to do shame-attacking exercises in a group is that the group serves to reinforce the client positively for doing the exercise. Doing shame-attacking exercises together can become a game that is not taken seriously. However, shame-attacking exercises are extremely valuable in promoting change, and, while humor is an important component, my experience is that greater and longer-lasting change is effected when clients do shame-attacking exercises on their own as part of their individual therapy, without the social support of a group.

Risk-taking assignments

In risk-taking assignments clients are encouraged to do something they regard as being "risky." For example, a client may be encouraged to ask a waiter to replace a set of cutlery because it is too dirty. In preparing clients for risk-taking exercises, identification and disputing of faulty inferences and consequent irrational evaluations needs to be done. The problem, however, is to get the client to prompt the aversive responses from others that he or she predicts will occur. In order for evaluative change to take place the client had better be prepared to do such risk-taking experiences repeatedly over a long period of time so that he or she eventually encounters the "dire" response. This is because such aversive responses from others occur far less frequently than the client predicts. Again the client is encouraged to undertake cognitive disputing along with the behavioral act.

Step-out-of-character exercises

Wessler (1982) has modified this exercise from Kelly (1955). Clients are encouraged to identify desired behavioral goals that are not currently enacted with frequency. For example, one group member chose the goal of eating more slowly, which for him was a desirable, nonshameful, nonrisky exercise, but one that involved monitoring of eating habits and cognitive disputing of low-frustration-tolerance ideas.

In vivo *desensitization*

These methods require clients to confront their fears repeatedly in an implosive manner. For example, clients with elevator phobia are asked to ride in elevators 20 to 30 times a day at the start of treatment, instead of gradually working their way up to this situation either in imagery or in actuality. Again, simultaneous cognitive disputing is urged. Neuman (1982) has written on and presented tapes of short-term group-oriented treatment of phobias. In his groups clients are encouraged to rate their levels of anxiety. The most important goal is for clients to experience a "level 10," which is extreme panic. Neuman continually points out to people that it is important to experience "level 10" because only then can they learn that they can survive and live through such an experience. Similarly, if inroads to severe phobic conditions are to be made, it is important for rational-emotive therapists to work toward helping clients tolerate extreme forms of anxiety before helping clients to reduce this anxiety.

Stay-in-there activities

Grieger and Boyd (1980) have described a similar technique, which they call "stay-in-there" activities, the purpose of which is to have clients vividly experience that they can tolerate and put up with uncomfortable experiences. One of my clients wanted to overcome her car-driving phobia. One of the things she feared was that her car would stall at a set of traffic lights and she would be exposed to the wrath of motorists who were stuck behind her. After eliciting and disputing her irrational ideas in traditional verbal dialogue, I encouraged her actually to turn off her engine at a set of lights and to stay there fur about 20 minutes, thus creating the impression her ear had broken down. Fortunately, the other car drivers did react in an angry fashion and she was able to practice disputing her dire needs for approval and comfort in a situation in which she remained for fully half an hour.

Some clients tend to do these dramatic exercises once or twice and then drop them from their repertoire. Therapists are often so glad and so surprised their clients will actually do these assignments that they do not consistently show them the importance of *continuing* to do them. One of the reasons for continued practice has already been mentioned, namely, that clients are more likely to make inferential changes than evaluative changes by doing these assignments infrequently. This is largely because the "dreaded" event has a far lower probability of occurring than clients think. However, sooner or later, if clients consistently and persistently put into practice these assignments, they may well encounter such events that will provide a context for disputing of irrational beliefs. Thus, if therapists really want to encourage clients to make changes at "B" as well as at "A," they had better be prepared to encourage clients consistently to do these dramatic assignments over a long period of time.

Operant conditioning methods

Ellis (1979) has consistently employed operant conditioning methods to encourage clients to take responsibility for being their own primary agent of change. Here clients are encouraged to identify and employ positive reinforcements for undertaking working-through assignments, and apply penalties when they do not do so. While not all clients require such encouragement, difficult and resistant clients, whose resistance is due to low-frustration-tolerance ideas, can be encouraged to take full responsibility for not putting into practice assignments that would stimulate change. Thus, dramatic experiences like burning a $10 bill, throwing away an eagerly awaited meal, and cleaning a dirty room at the end of a hard day's work are experiences that are designed to be so aversive that clients would choose to do the assignment previously avoided rather than undergo the penalty. Of course clients can, and often do, refuse to do the assignment and refuse to employ operant conditioning methods. However, many clients who have been resistant in the working-through process have, in my experience, begun to move when the therapist adopts this no-nonsense approach.

Limitations of vivid methods in RET

While the basic thesis in this chapter has been to show the possible efficacy of vivid RET, there are, of course, limitations on such an approach.

First, it is important for therapists to determine the impact on clients of introducing vivid methods into the therapeutic process. Thus, using the guidelines of Beck, Rush, Shaw, and Emery (1979), it is perhaps wise for the therapist to ask the client at various points in the therapy to give frank feedback concerning the methods and activities used. While the therapist may not always agree not to use such techniques just because a client has a negative reaction to them, we had better obtain and understand our clients' negative reactions to our procedures.

Second, it is important in the use of vivid dramatic techniques not to overload the client. One vivid and dramatic method carefully introduced into a therapy session at an appropriate time is much more likely to be effective than several dramatic methods employed indiscriminately in a session.

Third, it is important that rational-emotive therapists be clear about the rationale for using vivid methods and not see the use of such methods as a goal in itself. The important thing to remember is that vivid methods are to be used as vehicles for promoting client attitude change and not to make the therapeutic process more stimulating for the therapist. It is also extremely important to ascertain what the client has learned from the vivid methods the therapist has employed. The client will not magically come to the conclusion the therapist wants. It is also important that therapists not promote "false" change in their clients. Change is "false" when the client feels better as a result of some of these vivid methods but does not get better. Ellis (1972) has written an important article on such a distinction. Thus therapists should invariably ask questions like, "What have you learned from doing this vivid method?" and "How can you strengthen this learning experience for yourself outside of therapy?"

Fourth, dramatic and vivid methods are not appropriate for all clients. They are particularly helpful for those clients who use intellectualization as a defense and/or who use verbal dialogue to tie rational-emotive therapists in knots. While there are no data at the moment to support the following hypothesis, I would speculate that dramatic and vivid methods had better not be used with clients who have overly dramatic and hysterical personalities. It is perhaps more appropriate to assist such clients to reflect in a calm and undramatic manner on their experiences than to overstimulate an already highly stimulated personality.

Note

1 This is pronounced "my-the" and means to be worried or bothered.

References

Anchin, J. C., & Kiesler, D. J. (Eds.), *Handbook of interpersonal psychotherapy*. Oxford: Pergamon Press, 1982.

Arnkoff, D. B. Flexibility in practicing cognitive therapy. In G. Emery, S. D. Hollon, and R. C. Bedrosian (Eds.), *New directions in cognitive therapy*. New York: Guilford, 1981.

Bard, J. A. (1973). Rational proselytizing. *Rational Living*, *8*(2), 24–26.

Beck, A. T., Rush, A. J., Shaw, B. F., & Emery, G. (1979). *Cognitive therapy of depression*. New York: Guilford.

Burns, D. D. *Feeling good: The new mood therapy*. New York: Morrow, 1980.

Dies, R. R. Group therapist self-disclosure: An evaluation by clients. *Journal of Counseling Psychology*, 1973, *20*, 344–348.

Dryden, W. Nightmares and fun. Paper presented at the Third National Conference on Rational-Emotive Therapy. New York, June 7, 1980.

Ellis, A. (1959). Rational psychotherapy. *Journal of General Psychology*, *59*, 35–49.

Ellis, A, (1972), Helping people get better, rather than merely feel better. *Rational Living*, *7*(2), 2–9.

Ellis, A. (1977). Fun as psychotherapy, *Rational Living*, *I2*(1), 2–6.

Ellis, A. (1979). The practice of ralional–emotive therapy. In A. Ellis & J. M. Whiteley (Eds.), *Theoretical and empirical foundations of rational-emotive therapy*. Monterey, CA: Brooks/Cole.

Ellis, A. (1980, July 15). *The philosophic implications and dangers of some popular behavior therapy techniques*. Invited address to the World Congress on Behavior Therapy, Jerusalem.

Ellis, A. (1982). Personal communication.

Freeman, A. Dreams and imagery in cognitive therapy. In G. Emery, S. D. Hollon, and R. C. Bedrosian (Eds.), *New directions in cognitive therapy*. New York: Guilford, 1981.

Grieger, R. & Boyd, J. (1980). *Rational-emotive therapy: A skills-based approach*. New York: Van Nostrand Reinhold.

Hoehn-Saric, R. Emotional arousal, attitude change and psychotherapy. In J. D. Frank, R. Hoehn-Saric, S. D. Imber, B. L. Liberman, and A. R. Stone (Eds.), *Effective ingredients of successful psychotherapy*. New York: Brunner/Mazel, 1978.

Kassinove, H., & DiGiuseppe, R. Rational role reversal, *Rational Living*, 1975, *10*(1), 44–45.
Kelly, G. A. (1955). *The psychology of personal constructs*. New York: Norton.
Knaus, W., & Wessler, R. L. Rational-emotive problem simulation. *Rational Living*, 1976, *11*(2), 8–11.
Lazarus, A. A. *In the mind's eye*. New York: Rawson, 1978.
Maultsby, M. C., Jr., & Ellis, A. *Technique for using rational-emotive imagery*. New York: Institute for Rational Living, 1974.
Nardi, T. J. The use of psychodrama in RET. *Rational Living*, 1979, *14*(1), 35–38.
Neuman, F. (Leader), (1982). *An eight-week treatment group for phobics* (Series of eight cassette recordings). White Plains, NY: F. Neuman.
Rice, L. N. Therapist's style of participation and case outcome. *Journal of Consulting Psychology*, 1965, *29*, 155–160.
Rice, L. N. Client behavior as a function of therapist style and client resources. *Journal of Counseling Psychology*, 1973, *20*, 306–311.
Rice, L. N., & Gaylin, N. L. Personality processes reflected in client and vocal style and Rorschach processes. *Journal of Consulting and Clinical Psychology*, 1973, *40*, 133–138.
Rice, L. N., & Wagstaff, A. K. Client voice quality and expressive style as indexes of productive psychotherapy. *Journal of Consulting Psychology*, 1967, *31*, 557–563.
Sacco, W. P. Cognitive therapy in-vivo. In G. Emery, S. D. Hollon, & R. C. Bedrosian (Eds.), *New directions in cognitive therapy*. New York: Guilford. 1981.
Walen, S. R., DiGiuseppe, R., & Wessler, R. L. *A practitioner's guide to rational-emotive therapy*. New York: Oxford University Press, 1980.
Wessler, R. A. (1982, September 5). *Alternative conceptions of rational-emotive therapy: Toward a philosophically neutral psychotherapy*. Paper presented at the twelfth European Congress of Behavior Therapy, Rome.
Wessler, R. A., & Wessler, R. L. (1980). *The principles and practice of rational-emotive therapy*. San Francisco: Jossey-Bass.
Wexler, D. A. A scale for the measurement of client and therapist expressiveness. *Journal of Clinical Psychology*, 1975, *31*, 486–489.
Wexler, D. A., &. Butler, J. M. (1976). Therapist modification of client expressiveness in client-centered therapy. *Journal of Consulting and Clinical Psychology*, 44, 261–265.
Young, H. S. *Teaching rational self value concepts to tough customers*. Paper presented at the Third National Conference on Rational-Emotive Therapy, New York, June 8, 1980.

CHAPTER 7

THE THERAPEUTIC ALLIANCE IN RATIONAL–EMOTIVE INDIVIDUAL THERAPY

W. Dryden (1987) *Current issues in rational-emotive therapy*. London: Croom Helm (pp. 59–71)

When I was studying for the MSc in Psychotherapy at Warwick University (1978–1980), the theoretical framework with which I was most struck and which has had the most influence on my subsequent thinking about the practice of REBT specifically and about the practice of psychotherapy in general is what is generally referred to as working alliance theory (Bordin, 1979). Bordin argued that the working alliance (referred to as the therapeutic alliance in the piece that follows) comprises three components: bonds, goals and tasks – I later added a fourth component that I called 'views' (Dryden, 2006, 2011). This piece was my first systematic attempt to bring working (therapeutic) alliance theory to the practice of REBT. For a more contemporary and extended statement of my views on this subject, see Dryden (2009).

References

Bordin, E. S. (1979). The generalizability of the psychoanalytic concept of the working alliance. *Psychotherapy: Theory, Research and Practice*, 16(3): 252–260.
Dryden, W. (2006). *Counselling in a nutshell*. London: Sage.
Dryden, W. (2009). *Skills in rational emotive behaviour counselling and psychotherapy*. London: Sage.
Dryden, W. (2011). *Counselling in a nutshell. 2nd edition*. London: Sage.

Bordin's (1979) concept of the therapeutic alliance

As a rational-emotive therapist I have found the work of Ed Bordin (1979) on the concept of the therapeutic alliance particularly helpful in developing a basic framework for the conduct of RET. Bordin argues that the therapeutic alliance refers to the complex of attachments and shared understandings formed and activities undertaken by therapists and clients as the former attempt to help the latter with their psychological problems.

Bordin has stressed that there are three major components of the therapeutic alliance: (a) *bonds* – which refer to the interpersonal connectedness between therapist and client; (b) *goals* – which refer to the aims of both therapist and client; and (c) *tasks* – which are activities carried out by both therapist and client in the service of the latter's goals.

I will consider each of these components separately and show that rational-emotive therapists have important clinical decisions to make in each of the three alliance domains so as to individualize therapy for each client and thus maximize therapeutic benefit.

At the outset it should be noted that Bordin (1979) has speculated that effective therapy occurs when therapist and client (a) have an appropriately bonded working relationship; (b) mutually agree on the goals of the therapeutic enterprise; and (c) both understand their own and the other person's therapeutic tasks and agree to carry out these to implement the client's goals.

Bonds

The major concern of rational-emotive therapists in the bond domain should be to establish and maintain an appropriately bonded relationship that will encourage *each* individual client to implement his or her goal-directed therapeutic tasks. It should be underscored that there is no *single* effective bond that can be formed with clients in RET; different clients require different bonds. This observation became clear to me when on a six months' sabbatical at the Center for Cognitive Therapy in Philadelphia in 1981. As reported elsewhere (Dryden, 1984a), I saw two clients on the same afternoon who benefited from a different bonded relationship with me. At 4 p.m. I saw Mrs. G., a fifty-year-old married business woman, who was impressed with my British professional qualifications and whose responses to initial questions indicated that she anticipated and preferred a very formal relationship with her therapist. I provided such a relationship by using formal language, citing the research literature whenever appropriate, wearing a suit, shirt and tie and by referring to myself as Dr. Dryden and to my client as Mrs. G. On one occasion I inadvertently used her first name and was put firmly in my place concerning the protocol of professional relationships. On another occasion I disclosed a piece of personal information in order to make a therapeutic point and was told in no uncertain terms: 'Young man, I am not paying you good money to hear about your problems.' Here, a therapist is faced with the choice of respecting and meeting a client's bond anticipations and preferences or examining the reasons why, for example, this client was so adamantly against her therapist's informality. In my experience the latter strategy is rarely productive and rational-emotive therapists are recommended to fulfil their clients' preferences for therapeutic style as long as doing so does not reinforce the client's psychological problems.

At 5 p.m. on the same afternoon I regularly saw Mr. B., a forty-two-year-old male nurse who indicated that he did not respond well to his previous therapist's neutrality and formality. Our therapy sessions were thus characterized by an informal bond. Before seeing him I would remove my jacket and tie that I wore for Mrs. G.; in sessions we would use our first names and would both have our feet up on my desk. We also developed the habit of taking turns to bring in cans of soda and my client referred to our meetings as 'rap sessions' while I conceptualized my work as therapy within an informal context.

I maintain that Mrs. G. would not have responded well to an informal therapeutic relationship nor would Mr. B. have done as well with a highly formal mode of therapy. Thus, I argue that it is important that rational-emotive therapists pay attention to the question: 'Which bond is likely to be most effective with a particular patient at a given time in the therapeutic process?' Drawing upon social psychological principles, certain writers have argued that some clients show more progress when the therapeutic bond is based on liking and trustworthiness, while other flourish more when the bond emphasizes therapist credibility and expertness (Beutler, 1983; Dorn, 1984; Strong & Claiborn, 1982). Future research in RET, could fruitfully address the issue of which bond is effective with which clients. However, until we have such data, therapists could make decisions about what type of bond to foster on the basis of an early assessment of the client's anticipations and preferences in the bond domain and to try to meet such expectations, at least initially. This is one reason why I would caution novice therapists against emulating the therapeutic style of leading RET practitioners whose bond with clients may be based mainly on prestige and expertness. Rational-emotive therapists should thus be prepared to emphasize different aspects of themselves with different clients in the bond domain, without adopting an inauthentic facade, and to monitor transactions in this domain throughout therapy.

How can this best be done? One way would be to administer a portion of Lazarus's (1981) Life History Questionnaire which focuses on client's expectations regarding therapy. The items: 'How do you think a therapist should interact with his or her clients?' and 'What personal qualities do you think the ideal therapist should possess?' are particularly relevant and could usefully provide impetus for further exploration of this issue at the outset of therapy. If the client has had therapy previously, the current therapist could usefully explore what aspects of the previous therapist (s)' interactive style and behaviour were deemed by the client to be both helpful and unhelpful. Particular emphasis should be placed on the exploration of the instrumental nature of previous therapeutic bonds since statements such as: 'He was warm and caring' are of little use unless the client evaluated these qualities positively and attributed therapeutic progress to these factors.

Furthermore, and for similar reasons, I have found it helpful to explore clients' accounts of people in their lives who have had both positive and negative therapeutic influence on their personal development. Such exploration may provide the therapist with important clues concerning which types of therapeutic bonds to promote actively with certain clients and which bonds to avoid developing with others.

Therapeutic style is another aspect of the bond domain which requires attention. Interpersonally-orientated psychotherapists (e.g. Anchin & Kiesler, 1982) have argued that clinicians need to be aware that therapeutic styles have a 'for better or worse' impact on different clients. Rational-emotive therapists tend to be active and directive in their style of conducting therapy. This therapeutic style may not be entirely productive with both passive clients and, as Beutler (1983) has argued, clients who are highly reactive to interpersonal influence. Clients who tend to be passive in their interpersonal style of relating may 'pull' an increasingly active style from their therapists who may in turn reinforce these clients' passivity with their increased activity. Clients whose psychological problems are intrinsically bound up with a passive style of relating are particularly vulnerable in this regard. It is important that rational-emotive therapists be aware of the danger of becoming enmeshed in such unproductive vicious circles which have unfortunate self-fulfilling prophecy implications for their passive clients. These therapists need to engage their clients productively at a level which constructively encourages increased activity on their part but without threatening them through the use of an *overly* passive style of practising RET.

Beutler (1983) has argued that all approaches to psychotherapy can be viewed as a process of persuasion and this is particularly true of RET practitioners who aim to 'persuade' clients to re-evaluate and change their irrational Beliefs. As such, rational-emotive therapists need to be especially careful in working with clients for whom such persuasive attempts may be perceived as especially threatening (i.e. highly reactant clients). Here it is important that therapists execute their strategies with due regard to helping such clients to preserve their sense of autonomy, emphasizing throughout that these clients are in control of their own thought processes and decisions concerning whether or not to change them. At present, the above suggestions are speculative and await full empirical enquiry, but my clinical work has led me to question the desirability of establishing the same therapeutic bond with all clients and of practising rational-emotive therapy in an unchanging therapeutic style.

Goals

The major concern of rational-emotive therapists in the goal domain of the alliance is to ensure that there is agreement between therapist and client on the client's outcome goals for change. A prerequisite of such agreement concerns clients and therapists arriving at a shared understanding of the clients' most relevant problems as defined by the client (Meichenbaum & Gilmore, 1982). Difficulties may occur here when the therapist uncritically accepts the client's initial accounts of his or her problem since such accounts may well be biased by the client's internalized values, e.g. the views of significant others in the client's life. In addition, although most rational-emotive therapists consider that early goal-setting with the client is important, clients' initial statements about their goals for change may well be coloured by their psychological disturbance as well as by their internalized values concerning what these goals *should* be. Rational-emotive therapists need to walk a fine line between uncritically accepting clients' initial goals for change and disregarding them altogether. A helpful solution here involves establishment and maintenance of a channel of communication between client and therapist which deals with meta-therapy issues (i.e. issues concerning matters relating to therapy itself). Dryden & Hunt (1985), have referred to the activities that occur within this channel as involving negotiations and renegotiations about therapeutic issues. Rational-emotive therapists need to take the main responsibility for keeping this communication channel open in order to monitor clients' goals over time and to determine the reasons for shifts in these goals.

Pinsof & Catherall (1986) have made the important point that clients' goals occur (implicitly or explicitly) in reference to their most important relationships and their therapists need to be mindful of the impact that these systems are likely to have on both the selection of such goals and the client's degree of progress towards goal attainment. Adopting this focus may well possibly mean involving parts of the client's interpersonal system in therapy itself. It also suggests that future theorizing in RET could profitably assign a more central role to interpersonal issues (cf. Kwee & Lazarus, 1986; Safran, 1984).

Tasks

As outlined in Chapter 1, rational-emotive practitioners tend to subscribe to the following therapeutic process. Initially, having agreed to offer help to the client, the therapist attempts to structure the therapeutic process for the client and begins both to assess his or her problems in rational-emotive terms and also to help the client to view his or her problems within this framework. Goals are elicited based on a rational-emotive assessment and therapeutic strategies and techniques are implemented to effect the desired changes. Finally, obstacles to client change are analyzed and, it is hoped, overcome, and therapeutic gains are stabilized and maintained.

Therapists have tasks to execute at each stage in the rational-emotive therapeutic process and these will now be outlined.

Structuring

Effective RET depends in part on each participant clearly understanding their respective responsibilities in the therapeutic endeavour and upon each agreeing to discharge these responsibilities in the form of carrying out therapeutic tasks. It is the therapist's major responsibility to help the client to make sense of this process by providing an overall structure of mutual responsibilities and tasks. It is important to stress that structuring occurs throughout therapy and not just at the outset of the process. Sensitive clinicians who pay attention to alliance issues will structure the process using language which the client can understand and analogies which make sense to each individual person. Thus, it is often helpful to discover clients' hobbies and interests so that apt and personally meaningful structuring statements can be made. Thus, if a client is interested in golf, ascertaining how that person learned the game may be valuable in drawing parallels between the processes of learning coping skills and learning golfing skills. Both involve practice and failures can be realistically anticipated in each activity.

Assessment and conceptualization of clients' problems

During the assessment process, rational-emotive therapists traditionally attempt to gain a full understanding of the cognitive and behavioural variables that are maintaining their clients' problems. During this stage two issues become salient from an alliance theory perspective. First, it is important for therapist and client to arrive at a shared *definition* of the client's problems (i.e. what these problems are). Second, as Meichenbaum & Gilmore (1982) have noted, it is important for them to negotiate a shared *conceptualization* of the client's problem (i.e. an explanation of what accounts for the existence of this problem) so that they can work productively together in the intervention stage of therapy.

When working towards shared problem conceptualization, I argue that it is important for RET therapists to use, wherever possible, the client's own language and concepts, particularly when providing alternative explanations of their problems. This helps therapists to work within the range of what clients will accept as plausible conceptualizations of their problems. If clients' own ideas about the origins of their problems and more particularly what maintain them are ignored, then they may well resist accepting their therapists' conceptualizations. As Golden (1985) has noted, sometimes therapists often have to accept initially, for pragmatic purposes, a client's different (i.e. to the therapist's) conceptualization of his or her problems in order to arrive later at a shared one. In addition, rational-emotive therapists may well privately (i.e. to themselves) conceptualize a client's problems in rational-emotive terms (irrational Beliefs) while publicly (to the client) using the client's conceptualization (e.g. negative self-hypnosis). To what extent the effectiveness of RET is based on negotiation or on the unilateral persuasion attempts of the therapist is a matter for future empirical enquiry

Change tactics

Once the therapist and client have come to a mutually agreed understanding of the client's problems, the therapist then discusses with the client a variety of techniques that the client can use to reach his or her goals. Here it is important to realize that both client and therapist have tasks to execute.

Effective RET in the task domain tends to occur when:

(a) Clients understand what their tasks are.
(b) Clients understand how executing their tasks will help them achieve their goals.
(c) Clients are, in fact, capable of executing their tasks and believe that they have this capability.
(d) Clients understand that change comes about through repeated execution of their tasks.
(e) Clients understand the tasks of their therapists and can see the link between their therapists' tasks, their own tasks and their goals.
(f) Therapists adequately prepare their clients to understand and execute the latter's tasks.
(g) Therapists effectively execute their tasks (i.e. they are skilled in the techniques of RET) and use a wide range of techniques appropriately.
(h) Therapists employ techniques which are congruent with their clients' learning styles. Whilst some clients learn best through action, others learn best through reading bibliotherapy texts, etc.
(i) Therapists employ techniques that clients have selected (from a range of possible procedures) rather than unilaterally selecting techniques without client participation.
(j) Therapists pace their interventions appropriately.
(k) Therapists employ techniques which are potent enough to help clients achieve their goals, (e.g. using exposure methods with clients with agoraphobic problems – Emmelkamp, Kuipers & Eggeraat, 1978).

Failures in RET

I have been practising RET now for over ten years in a variety of settings, I have worked in (a) a university counselling service; (b) a general practice; (c) a National Health Service psychiatric clinic; (d) a local marriage guidance council and (e) private practice. I have seen, in these settings, a wide range of moderately to severely disturbed individuals who were deemed to be able to benefit from weekly counselling or psychotherapy. While I do not have any hard data to substantiate the point, I have found rational-emotive therapy to be a highly effective method of individual psychotherapy with a wide range of client problems.

However, I have of course had my therapeutic failures, and I would like, in this final section, to outline some of the factors that in my opinion have accounted for these failures. I will again use Bordin's (1979) useful concept of the therapeutic working alliance as a framework in this respect.

Goals

I have generally been unsuccessful with clients who have devoutly clung to goals where changes in other people were desired. (In this regard, I have also failed to involve these others in therapy.) I have not been able to show or to persuade these clients that they make themselves emotionally disturbed and that they ought to work to change themselves before attempting to negotiate changes in their relationships with others. It is the devoutness of their Beliefs which seems to me to be the problem here.

Bonds

Unlike the majority of therapists of my acquaintance, I do not regard the relationship between therapist and client to be the sine qua non of effective therapy. I strive to accept my clients as fallible human beings and am prepared to work concertedly to help them overcome their problems, but do not endeavour to form very close, warm relationships with them. In the main, my clients do not appear to want such a relationship with me (preferring to become close and intimate with their significant others). However, occasionally I get clients who do wish to become (non-sexually) intimate with me. Some of these clients (who devoutly believe they need my love) leave therapy disappointed after I have failed either to get them to give up their dire need for love or to give them what they think they need.

Tasks

In this analysis I will assume throughout that therapists are practising RET effectively and thus the emphasis will be on client variables.

My basic thesis here is that when therapist and client agree concerning: (a) the view of psychological disturbance as stated in rational-emotive theory, (b) the rational-emotive view on the acquisition and perpetuation of psychological disturbance, and (c) the rational-emotive view of therapeutic change, such agreements are likely to enhance good therapeutic outcome. Furthermore, the greater the disagreement between the two participants on such matters, the greater the threat that exists to the therapeutic alliance with all the negative implications that this has for good therapeutic outcome. I should say at the outset that this hypothesis has yet to be tested and should thus be viewed sceptically.

I will illustrate my points by using clinical examples from my experience as a therapist.

Conceptualization of psychological disturbance

Rational-emotive theory states that much psychological disturbance can be attributed to clients' devout, absolutistic evaluations (irrational Beliefs) about themselves, other people and life events. RET therapists assume that most clients do not enter therapy sharing this viewpoint and, thus, one of the therapist's major tasks is to persuade the client to adopt this viewpoint if effective RET is to ensue. Of course, not all clients will be so persuaded because they have their own (different) ideas about the nature of their psychological problems and what causes them and are not prepared to relinquish these. In my experience, the following clients are not good candidates for RET unless they change their ideas about the determinants of their problems; those who believe that their problems are caused by (a) external events (including events that happened in childhood), (b) physical, dietary or biochemical factors, (c) repressed basic human impulses, (d) fate or astrological factors and (e) blockages in the body.

I once had a referral from a social worker who confused RET with Reichian therapy. The client specifically wanted to work on his character armour, blockages in which he considered were at the source of his problems. I explained that an error had been made and that I was a rational-emotive therapist and gave him a brief outline of the rational-emotive view of his problems. He responded with incredulity, saying that he hadn't heard such intellectualised clap-trap in a long while and asked me whether I knew of anyone who could really help him. I referred him to a local bioenergetics therapist who, apparently, helped him considerably.

Acquisition and perpetuation of psychological disturbance

Rational-emotive theory de-emphasizes the value of understanding acquisition variables in helping clients change. Rather, it stresses the importance of understanding how people perpetuate their psychological problems. This is because the theory hypothesizes that while past events may well have contributed to clients' psychological disturbance, these did not make them disturbed, since people bring their tendency to make themselves disturbed to these events and experiences. Thus, clients who come to therapy in order to trace their psychological problems back to their roots tend not to benefit greatly from the present-centred and future-orientated focus of RET. Clients who are prepared to look for and challenge their currently held irrational Beliefs do much better in RET than clients who are preoccupied with discovering how they came to hold such Beliefs in the first place.

A 60-year old woman with agoraphobic problems was firmly convinced that the origins of her panic lay in buried childhood feelings towards her parents, who while kindly disposed to my client, had placed undue burdens on her as a child. Not only did we have different views concerning the 'causes' of her present problems, but we differed as to the most appropriate time focus for the therapy. I did discuss her childhood with her, but as a stimulus to help her re-focus on her present disturbance-perpetuating Beliefs, but to no avail. She quit therapy with me and started consulting a Jungian therapist who has seen her now for two years with little impact on her panic disorder.

Views on therapeutic change

RET can be viewed as a therapeutic system which has a 'Protestant Ethic' view of therapeutic change. Clients are urged to 'work and practise' their way to emotional health by using a variety of cognitive, emotive and behavioural methods designed to help them to change their irrational Beliefs. Clients who are not prepared to put in the necessary hard work usually have less successful therapeutic outcomes than clients who challenge repeatedly their irrational Beliefs in thought, feeling and deed.

It follows from the above that RET places most emphasis on the activities that clients initiate and sustain outside therapy as the major agent of change. Clients who consider that change will occur primarily from therapy sessions usually do not gain as much from RET as clients who are in accord with the rational-emotive viewpoint on this matter.

During my six months stay at the Center for Cognitive Therapy in Philadelphia, I saw briefly a client who had heard of cognitive therapy for depression and wished to try it. I was learning this approach at the time and was keen to do it 'by the book'. The client had recently moved to Philadelphia from Los Angeles where she had consulted an experiential therapist with whom she had had a very close relationship which, in my opinion, had encouraged her to be more dependent on love and approval than she was before she consulted him. The client had come to believe that therapeutic change depended on a very warm, close therapeutic relationship in which completing homework assignments and 'Daily Record of Dysfunctional Thoughts' sheets had no place. Despite my attempts to change her views on such matters, she left cognitive therapy to seek another experiential therapist.

Ellis's study on failures in RET

Ellis (1983e) has published some interesting data which tend to corroborate my own experiences of therapeutic failure in RET. He chose fifty of his clients who were seen in individual and/or group RET and were rated by him, and where appropriate by his associate group therapist, as 'failures'. In some ways, this group consisted of fairly ideal RET clients in that they were individuals (1) of above average or of superior intelligence (in Ellis's judgement and that of their other group therapist); (2) who seemed really to understand RET and who were often effective (especially in group therapy) in helping others to learn and use it; (3) who in some ways made therapeutic progress and felt that they benefited by having RET but who still retained one or more serious presenting symptoms, such as severe depression, acute anxiety, overwhelming hostility, or extreme lack of self-discipline; and (4) who had at least one year of individual and/or group RET sessions, and sometimes considerably more.

This group was compared to clients who were selected on the same four criteria but who seemed to benefit greatly from RET. While a complete account of this study – which, of course, has its methodological flaws – can be found in Ellis (1983e), the following results are most pertinent:

1 In its cognitive aspects, RET . . . emphasizes the persistent use of reason, logic, and the scientific method to uproot clients' irrational Beliefs. Consequently, it ideally requires intelligence, concentration, and high-level, consistent cognitive self-Disputation and self-persuasion. These therapeutic behaviours would tend to be disrupted or blocked by extreme disturbance, by lack of organization, by grandiosity, by organic disruption, and by refusal to do RET-type Disputing of irrational ideas. All these characteristics proved to be present in significantly more failures than in those clients who responded favourably to RET.

2 RET also, to be quite successful, involves clients' forcefully and emotively changing their Beliefs and actions, and their being stubbornly determined to accept responsibility for their own inappropriate feelings and to vigorously work at changing these feelings (Ellis & Abrahms, 1978; Ellis & Whiteley, 1979). But the failure clients in this study were significantly more angry than those who responded well to RET; more of them were severely depressed and inactive, they were more often grandiose, and they were more frequently stubbornly resistant and rebellious. All these characteristics would presumably tend to interfere with the kind of emotive processes and changes that RET espouses.

3 RET strongly advocates that clients, in order to improve, do in vivo activity homework assignments, deliberately force them selves to engage in many painful activities until they become familiar and unpainful, and notably work and practise its multimodal techniques. But the group of clients who signally failed in this study showed abysmally low frustration tolerance, had serious behavioural addictions, led disorganized lives, refrained from doing their activity homework assignments, were more frequently psychotic and generally refused to work at therapy. All these characteristics, which were found significantly more frequently than were found in the clients who responded quite well to RET, would tend to interfere with the behavioural methods of RET,

Thus it appears from the above analysis that the old adage of psychotherapy applies to RET: namely that clients who could most use therapy are precisely those individuals whose disturbance interferes with their benefiting from it.

References

Anchin, J.C., & Kiesler, D.J. (Eds.). (1982). *Handbook of interpersonal psychotherapy*. New York: Pergamon.

Bordin, E.S. (1979). The generalizability of the psychoanalytic concept of the working alliance. *Psychotherapy: Theory, Research and Practice*, *16*, 252–260.

Beutler, L.E. (1983). *Eclectic psychotherapy: a systematic approach*. New York: Pergamon.

Dorn, F.J. (1984). *Counseling as applied social psychology: an introduction to the social influence model*. Springfield: IL: Thomas.

Dryden, W. (1984a). Rational-emotive therapy. In W. Dryden (Ed.), *Individual therapy in Britain*. London: Harper & Row.

Dryden, W., & Hunt, P. (1985). Therapeutic alliances in marital therapy. II. Process issues. In W. Dryden (Ed.), *Marital therapy in Britain. Volume 1: context and therapeutic approaches*. London: Harper & Row.

Ellis, A. (1983e). Failures in rational-emotive therapy. In E.B. Foa & P.M.G. Emmelkamp (Eds), *Failures in behaviour therapy*. New York: Wiley.

Ellis, A., & Abrahms, E. (1978). *Brief psychotherapy in medical and health practice*. New York: Springer.

Ellis, A., & Whiteley, J.M. (Eds.). (1978). *Theoretical and empirical foundations of rational-emotive therapy*. Monterey, CA: Brooks/Cole.

Emmelkamp, P.M.G., Kuipers, A.C.M., & Eggeraat, J.B. (1978). Cognitive modification versus prolonged exposure in vivo: A comparison with agoraphobics as subjects. *Behaviour Research and Therapy*, *16*, 33–41.

Golden, W.L. (1985). An integration of Ericksonian and cognitive-behavioral hypnotherapy in the treatment of anxiety disorders. In E.T. Dowd & J.M. Healy (Eds.), *Case studies in hypnotherapy*. New York: Guilford.

Kwee, M.G.T., & Lazarus, A.A. (1986). Multimodal therapy: The cognitive behavioural tradition and beyond. In W. Dryden & W.L. Golden (Eds.), *Cognitive-behavioural approaches to psychotherapy*. London: Harper & Row.

Lazarus, A.A. (1981). *The practice of multimodal therapy*. New York: McGraw-Hill.

Meichenbaum, D., & Gilmore, J.B. (1982). Resistance from a cognitive behavioral perspective. In P.L. Wachtel (Ed.), *Resistance*. New York: Plenum.

Pinsof, W.M., & Catherall, D.R. (1986). The integrative psychotherapy alliance: Family, couple and individual scales. *Journal of Marital and Family Therapy*, *12*, 137–151.

Safran, J.D. (1984). Assessing the cognitive-interpersonal cycle. *Cognitive Therapy and Research*, *8*, 333–347.

Strong, S.R., & Claiborn, C.D. (1982). *Change through interaction*. New York: Wiley-Interscience.

CHAPTER 8

COMPROMISES IN RATIONAL-EMOTIVE THERAPY

W. Dryden (1987) *Current issues in rational-emotive therapy.*
London: Croom Helm (pp. 72–87)

REBT theory holds that if clients identify, challenge and change their irrational beliefs and develop and strengthen their conviction in the rational alternatives to these beliefs, then doing so will help them deal with their psychological disturbance and live more resourcefully. However, for a variety of reasons, clients will not, or believe that they cannot, do this. Consequently, REBT therapists are called upon to make compromises with their preferred way of working, which is to help clients to effect belief change. The following piece deals with this issue and is my view of an early example of my pluralistic perspective on REBT.

Introduction

In this chapter I discuss the notion that while RET therapists prefer to encourage their clients to achieve a profound philosophic change by replacing their irrational Beliefs with rational Beliefs, this is not always possible. In such cases, RET therapists are advised to make various compromises in helping clients deal with their problems in ways which do not involve philosophic change. These alternative strategies are termed 'compromises' in that, while not ideal, they often bear more fruit than the preferred strategies of RET.

I should say at the outset that by RET in this chapter I mean those therapeutic activities which are designed to effect philosophic change – or what Ellis calls 'elegant', 'preferential' or 'specialized' RET. I personally consider that therapeutic activities which are designed to effect other kinds of change (e.g. inferentially-based change, behaviourally-based change or change in Activating events) are best referred to as derived from other approaches to cognitive-behaviour therapy, although Ellis considers such activities to be part of 'inelegant', 'non-preferential' or 'general' RET. Since terms like 'elegant' vs 'inelegant', 'preferential' vs 'non-preferential' etc. are value-laden and may offend other cognitively-orientated practitioners, I prefer to avoid their use and thus distinguish between rational-emotive therapy and other forms of cognitive-behaviour therapy. This distinction is more likely, in my opinion, to promote constructive dialogue among cognitively-orientated therapists than the one employed by Ellis (1980b).

Before discussing the various compromises that RET therapists sometimes are called upon to make, it is first important to distinguish between rational-emotive therapy and other approaches to cognitive-behaviour therapy.

Differences between rational-emotive therapy and other approaches to cognitive-behaviour therapy

As opposed to other approaches to cognitive-behaviour therapy, rational-emotive therapy:

1 Has a distinct philosophic emphasis which is one of its central features and which other forms of cognitive-behaviour therapy appear to omit. Thus, it stresses that humans appraise themselves, others and the world in terms of (a) rational, preferential, flexible and tolerant philosophies and in terms of (b) irrational, musturbatory, rigid, intolerant and absolutistic philosophies.

2 Has an existential-humanistic outlook which is intrinsic to it and which is omitted by most other approaches to cognitive behaviour therapy. Thus, it sees people 'as holistic, goal-directed individuals who have importance in the world just because they are human and alive; it unconditionally accepts them with their limitations, and it particularly focuses upon their experiences and values, including their self-actualizing potentialities' (Ellis, 1980b, p. 327). It also shares the views of ethical humanism by encouraging people to emphasize human interest (self and social) over the interests of deities, material objects and lower animals.

3 Favours striving for pervasive and long-lasting (philosophically-based) rather than symptomatic change.

4 Attempts to help humans eliminate all self-ratings and views self-esteem as a self-defeating concept which encourage them to make conditional evaluations of self. Instead, it teaches people *un*conditional self-acceptance (Ellis, 1972).

5 Considers psychological disturbance to reflect an attitude to taking life 'too' seriously and thus advocates the appropriate use of various humorous therapeutic methods (Ellis, 1977b, 1977c, 1981c) .

6 Stresses the use of antimusturbatory rather than antiempirical Disputing methods. Since it considers that inferential distortions often stem from dogmatic musts, shoulds, etc., rational-emotive therapy favours going to the philosophic core of emotional disturbance and Disputing the irrational Beliefs at this core rather than merely Disputing antiempirical inferences which are more peripheral. Also rational-emotive therapy favours the use of forceful logicoempirical Disputing of irrational Beliefs whenever possible rather than the employment of rationally-orientated, coping self-statements. When feasible, rational-emotive therapy teaches clients how to become their own scientists instead of parroting therapist inculcated rational Beliefs.

7 Gives a more central explanatory role to the concept of discomfort anxiety in psychological disturbance than do other cognitive-behavioural approaches to psychotherapy. Discomfort anxiety is defined as: 'emotional hypertension that arises when people feel (1) that their life or comfort is threatened, (2) that they *must* not feel uncomfortable and *have to* feel at ease and (3) that it is awful or terrible (rather than merely inconvenient or disadvantageous) when they don't get what they supposedly must' (Ellis, 1980b, p. 331). While other cognitive-behavioural approaches to psychotherapy recognise specific instances of discomfort anxieties (e.g. 'fear of fear' – Mackay, 1984), they tend not to regard discomfort disturbance to be as centrally implicated in psychological problems as does rational-emotive therapy.

8 Emphasizes, more than other approaches to cognitive behaviour therapy, that humans frequently make themselves disturbed about their original disturbances. Thus, rational-emotive therapists actively look for secondary symptoms of disturbances and encourage clients to work on overcoming these before addressing themselves to the primary disturbance.

9 Has clearcut theories of disturbance and its treatment, but is eclectic or multimodal in its techniques. However, it favours some techniques (e.g. active Disputing) over others (e.g. cognitive distraction) and strives for profound philosophic change where feasible.

10 Discriminates between 'rational' and 'irrational' negative emotions. Rational-emotive theory considers such negative emotions as sadness, annoyance, concern, regret, and disappointment as 'rational' affective responses to thwarted desires based on a non-devout philosophy of desire and it views them as healthy when they do not needlessly interfere with people's goals and purposes. However, it sees depression, anger, anxiety, guilt, shame/embarrassment, self-pity, and feelings of inadequacy usually as 'irrational' emotions based on absolutistic demands about thwarted desires. Rational-emotive therapy considers these latter feelings as symptoms of disturbance because they very frequently (but not always) sabotage people from pursuing constructively their goals and purposes. Other approaches to cognitive-behaviour therapy do not make such fine discriminations between 'rational' and 'irrational' negative emotions.

11 Advocates therapists giving unconditional acceptance rather than giving warmth or approval to clients. Other cognitive-behaviour therapies tend not to make this distinction. Rational-emotive therapy holds that counsellor warmth and approval have their distinct dangers in that they may unwittingly encourage clients to strengthen their dire needs for love and approval. When RET therapists unconditionally accept their clients they also serve as good role models, in that they also help clients to unconditionally accept themselves.

12 Stresses the importance of the use of vigour and force in counteracting irrational philosophies and behaviours (Dryden, 1984c, Ellis, 1979c). Rational-emotive therapy is alone among cognitive-behavioural approaches to psychotherapy in stressing that humans are, for the most part, biologically predisposed to originate and perpetuate their disturbances and often thus experience great difficulty in changing the ideological roots of these problems. Since it holds this view it urges both therapists and clients to use considerable force and vigour in interrupting clients' irrationalities.

13 Is more selective than most other cognitive-behaviour therapies in choosing behavioural change methods. Thus, it favours the use of penalization in encouraging resistant clients to change. Often these clients won't change to obtain positive reinforcements, but may be encouraged to change to avoid stiff penalties. Furthermore, rational-emotive practitioners have reservations concerning the use of social reinforcement in psychotherapy. They consider that humans are too reinforceable and that they often do the right thing for the wrong reason. Thus, they may change to please their socially reinforcing therapists, but in doing so they have not been encouraged to think and act for their own sake. RET therapists aim to help clients become maximally non-conformist, non-dependent and individualistic and would thus use social reinforcement techniques sparingly. Finally, rational-emotive therapy favours the use of in-vivo desensitization and flooding methods rather than the use of

gradual desensitization techniques since it argues that the former procedures best help clients to raise their level of frustration tolerance (Ellis, 1983c).

Thus, as noted in Chapter 1, the major goal of rational-emotive therapy is an ambitious one: to encourage clients to make a profound philosophic change in the two main areas of ego disturbance and discomfort disturbance. This involves helping clients, as far as is humanly possible, to give up their irrational Beliefs and to replace these with rational Beliefs.

In summary, as was outlined in Chapter 1, in rational-emotive therapy, the major goals are (a) to help clients pursue their long-range basic goals and purposes and to help them do so as effectively as possible by fully accepting themselves and tolerating unchangeable uncomfortable life conditions. Rational-emotive practitioners further strive to help clients obtain the skills which they can use to prevent the development of future disturbance. In encouraging clients to achieve and maintain this profound philosophic change, rational-emotive therapists implement the following strategies. They help their clients see that:

1 Emotional and behavioural disturbances have cognitive antecedents and that these cognitions normally take the form of absolutistic irrational Beliefs. RET therapists train their clients to observe their own psychological disturbances and to trace these back to their ideological roots.
2 People have a distinct measure of self-determination and can thus decide to work at undisturbing themselves. Thus, clients are shown that they are not slaves to their biologically-based irrational thinking processes.
3 People can implement their choices and maximize their freedom by actively working at changing their irrational Beliefs. This is best achieved by employing cognitive, emotive and behavioural methods – often in quite a forceful and vigorous manner (Ellis, 1979d).

With the majority of clients, from the first session onward, RET therapists are likely to use strategies designed to effect profound philosophic change. The therapist begins the process with the hypothesis that this particular client may be able to achieve such change and thus begins to implement rational-emotive methods which he or she will abandon after collecting sufficient data to reject this initial hypothesis. Rational-emotive practitioners regularly implement this viewpoint which is based on the notion that the client's' response to therapy is the best indicator of his or her prognosis.

Compromises

When it is clear that the client is not able to achieve philosophic change, whether on a particular issue or in general, the therapist often uses other cognitive-behavioural therapeutic methods to effect less 'profound' changes. Since, in such cases, these methods yield better results for the client than can be achieved by standard rational-emotive methods, they are regarded as compromises yielding an outcome between no change, on the one hand, and profound philosophical change, on the other.

Inferentially-based change

Inferentially-based change occurs when clients do not change irrational Beliefs but do succeed in correcting distorted inferences such as negative predictions, overly negative interpretation of events and the behaviour of others, etc.

A good example of such change was reported by a therapist of my acquaintance. He was working with a middle aged woman who reported feeling furious every time her ageing father would telephone her and enquire 'Noo, what's doing?' She inferred that this was a gross invasion of her privacy and absolutistically insisted that he had no right to act in this way. The therapist initially intervened with the usual rational-emotive strategy by attempting to Dispute this client's dogmatic Belief and tried to help her see that there was no law in the universe which stated that he must not invade her privacy. Meeting initial resistance, the therapist persisted with different variations of this theme – all to no avail. Changing tack, he began to implement a different strategy designed to help the client question her inference that her father was actually invading her privacy. Given her father's age, the therapist inquired, was it not more likely that his question represented his usual manner of beginning telephone conversations rather than an intense desire to pry into her affairs? This inquiry proved successful in that the client's rage subsided because she began to re-interpret her father's motives.

Another example of inferentially-based change occurred with one of my clients, Robert, who was anxious lest people would stare at him for spilling his drink. His hands would shake whenever he attempted to drink in public. I first employed the customary philosophically-based RET strategy, encouraging him to assume the worst and imagine that people would actually stare at him when he spilled his drink. This yielded his irrational Belief: 'If they stare at me, it would prove that I would be a worthless freak.' However, I could not encourage him to Dispute this Belief successfully and he still adhered strongly to it after my varied Disputing efforts. Changing tack, I took him to several pubs and asked him to observe other people's reactions as I deliberately spilled drinks in public. From this, he came to realise that other people in general did not stare at me when I spilled my drinks and this helped him to change his own inference to: 'It is unlikely that most people will stare at me when I spill my drink.' This inferentially-based change enabled him to order and consume drink in public and reduce his social anxiety although he never did change his aforementioned irrational Belief.

Interestingly, in both examples, although my fellow therapist and I returned to Disputing our clients' irrational Beliefs *after* helping them to modify their distorted inferences, we never succeeded in helping them to change these Beliefs. However, some clients are more willing to re-evaluate their irrational Beliefs after they have been helped to correct distorted inferences. Rational-emotive theory holds that irrational Beliefs are the breeding ground for the development of negative inferences and thus when clients succeed in changing their irrational Beliefs, spontaneous reduction in the negativity of inferences will follow. However, these two examples show that inferentially-based change can occur in the absence of philosophically-based change.

Behaviourally-based change

Behaviourally-based change occurs when clients do not change irrational Beliefs, but improve by effecting constructive changes in behaviour. Such behaviour change, in my experience occurs when clients (a) replace dysfunctional behaviour with constructive behaviour and (b) acquire constructive patterns of behaviour which previously have been absent from their skill repertoire. An example of each follows.

Replacing dysfunctional behaviour with constructive behaviour

Sylvia, a first year university student, sought therapy for extreme examination anxiety. She predicted that she would fail her first year exams, demanded that she must pass them and concluded that should she fail, this would be the 'end of the world'. No amount of Disputing her irrational Beliefs yielded any therapeutic gain, so I shifted attention to her test-taking behaviour. I discovered that Sylvia approached an examination in the following way. She would choose to answer the first question that she knew anything about; she would write everything she knew about that question without first making an answer plan and would often only answer two out of four questions in the entire examination. It thus transpired that her inferences concerning failure were accurate rather than negatively distorted. My subsequent therapeutic approach focused on teaching Sylvia the following examination techniques: allocating sufficient time to answer all questions; analyzing the wording of examination questions; making answer plans; answering all parts of a given question; and dealing with 'mind-blank' experiences through cognitive distraction. With the help of her department, I arranged for Sylvia to take several 'mock' examinations so that she could practise her newly acquired skills with the result that she performed very well in these examinations. These experiences helped Sylvia to predict success in her 'end-of-year' examinations rather than failure. This led to a significant decrease in her examination anxiety. However, although Sylvia did in fact do very well in her exams, she still held the same irrational Beliefs about failure as she did at the outset and did not want to focus on these later as she thought failure to be 'so unlikely that it's not worth considering'.

This example clearly shows that behaviour change often leads to inferentially-based change but not necessarily to philosophically-based change. *Acquiring new skills.* Mrs. Anderson was referred to me with problems of anger and depression. Her husband and two teenage children expected her to go out to work, do all the housework without help and cater to their every whim. She had done this for several years, but had become increasingly angry and depressed. Her anger was based on the irrational Belief that they must not treat her this way and her depression stemmed from the Belief that she was no good for failing to please her family. Traditional rational-emotive Disputing methods failed to yield any therapeutic gains so I shifted the focus of therapy to a discussion of assertion and the value of politely declining to do the bidding of her family. Through role-play methods it transpired that Mrs. Anderson did not have assertive skills in her repertoire since she could only communicate in an aggressive and demanding manner. I thus trained her intensively in polite, negative assertive skills which she was able to put into practice with her family. Surprisingly her family responded quite well to her behaviour, began to share household tasks and made less demands upon her. The result was that Mrs. Anderson's depressed mood lifted appreciably and she became far less angry. As in the other examples in this chapter, I returned to Disputing her irrational Beliefs as outlined above but again without success.

This example shows that a client's behavioural changes can sometimes elicit constructive behaviour from others leading to healthy changes in the interpersonal system of which the client is a part.

Changing activating events

I concluded the above example with the observation that a client's change in behaviour can promote healthy system-based change. However, this does not always occur. In a similar case to that described above, I had to involve the client's husband and children in therapy and encourage them to change their behaviour towards the depressed client, Mrs. Curran, since her own assertive efforts did not on this occasion elicit constructive responses from her family members. Once they changed their behaviour towards Mrs. Curran for the better, her mood lifted accordingly. Again Disputing efforts aimed at helping Mrs. Curran to re-evaluate her irrational Beliefs, pre- and post-improvement, did not lead to philosophically-based change.

In another example of helping clients by promoting changes in Activating events, I helped Mr. Brown to overcome his depression by encouraging him to change his vocation from accountancy to law. He was depressed because he believed: 'I have to enjoy my job in order to be happy.' No amount of Disputing this Belief yielded any therapeutic gain so I switched the focus of the sessions to exploring his vocational interests and aptitudes. This led Mr. Brown to conclude that he would be happier working as a solicitor than as an accountant. Accordingly, he decided to go to law school. Years later, after he qualified as a solicitor, I met Mr. Brown who had effected a successful career change. He still believed that he had to be vocationally satisfied in order to be happy but since he was happy working in the law he considered that there was no need to re-evaluate this irrational Belief.

Challenging but not overwhelming: a compromise in negotiating homework assignments

Ellis (1983c) has recently criticized the use of gradual approaches to helping clients overcome their emotional and behavioural problems. His argument is that the use of gradual methods in psychotherapy and behaviour therapy reinforces 'a philosophy that states or implies that (1) emotional change has to be brought about slowly and cannot possibly occur quickly or suddenly; (2) that it must be practically painless as it is occurring; and (3) that it cannot occur with the use of jarring, painful, flooding methods of therapy' (p.142). Thus, psychotherapeutic gradualism is seen by Ellis as counter-therapeutic in that it basically reinforces clients' discomfort anxiety or philosophy of Low Frustration Tolerance (LFT) which serve to perpetuate rather than ameliorate their problems. He thus prefers wherever possible the use of flooding or 'full-exposure' methods and homework assignments in RET, primarily because they help clients to overcome their discomfort anxiety and to raise their tolerance level for frustration.

However, 'wherever possible' is the important phrase to note here since not all clients will agree to. execute flooding or 'full-exposure' homework assignments. That this should be rational-emotive therapists' initial approach to negotiating homework assignments is not questioned here. In taking this stance, therapists should explain the rationale for this type of homework assignment, emphasize the benefits of such an approach and encourage clients to implement these assignments after thoroughly Disputing clients' LFT ideas. What therapists are in fact saying is: 'Such methods are the most efficient means of helping you achieve your therapeutic goals.' It is not surprising that Ellis should recommend such assignments, given his belief in the value of efficiency in psychotherapy (Ellis, 1980c).

However, no matter how therapists try to encourage (or persuade) some clients to execute 'full-exposure' homework assignments, such clients steadfastly refuse to do so. In the face of such opposition, if therapists persist in their persuasive tactics, they will commit two therapeutic errors. First, they will threaten the therapeutic alliance between themselves and their 'resistant' clients. Bordin (1979) has noted that there are three major components of this alliance – goals, bonds and tasks. In such instances, the therapeutic alliance is likely to break down in the *task* domain. Although therapist and client may have a good collaborative relationship (effective bonds) and agree on the client's goals (shared goals), they disagree about the tasks that the client is prepared to do in order to achieve therapeutic goals. Second, such overly persistent therapists serve as poor role models since they tend to believe that clients *must* be 'efficient' in their approach to therapy and do 'full-exposure' assignments. Paradoxically, these therapists, by insisting that clients execute certain types of homework assignments are in fact being inefficient themselves. A breakdown in the therapeutic alliance often leads to therapeutic impasses which in turn often lead to clients dropping out of treatment.

In such cases, what should therapists preferably do? There is no need to return to therapeutic gradualism, for there is another alternative which allows therapists and clients to effect a working compromise. Whenever I encounter clients who steadfastly refuse to execute 'full-exposure' homework tasks and prefer gradual assignments, I explain this therapeutic compromise. I invite them to choose assignments which are sufficiently *challenging* to discourage reinforcement of their philosophy of Low Frustration Tolerance, but which are not *overwhelming* for them. I explain their choices thus:

> 'There are three ways that you can overcome your fears. The first is like jumping in at the deep end. You expose yourself straightaway to the situation you are most afraid of. The advantage here is that if you can learn that nothing terrible will happen then you will overcome your problems quite quickly. However, the disadvantage is that some people just can't bring themselves to do this and get quite discouraged as a result. The second way is to go very gradually. On the one hand, you only do something that you feel comfortable doing, while on the other, you don't really get an opportunity to face putting up with discomfort which in my opinion, is a major feature of your problem. Also treatment will take much longer this way. The third way is what I call "challenging but not overwhelming". Here you choose an assignment which is sufficiently challenging for you to make progress but not one which you feel would be overwhelming for you at any given stage. Here you are likely to make progress more quickly than with the gradual approach but more slowly than with the "deep end" approach.'

I find that when clients are given an opportunity to choose their own rate of progress, the therapeutic alliance is strengthened. Most clients who refuse to execute 'full exposure' assignments choose the 'challenging but not overwhelming' approach and only very rarely do they opt for gradual desensitization therapy. When they do so I do try to dissuade them and frequently succeed. In the final analysis, however, I have not found it productive to insist that clients choose a particular way of tackling problems that is against their preferences.

Case example

Mary, a 23 year old, single woman came to therapy for help in overcoming her anxiety about eating in public. Typically she had both ego and discomfort anxiety-related Beliefs (Ellis, 1979b, 1980a), and in the early sessions I helped her to identify and Dispute such self-defeating attitudes as: 'I must not be anxious while eating'; 'If other people see me leave my food they will think I'm odd and I need their approval'; 'I am a shameful individual for having this problem'; 'There is something wrong with me because I have a small appetite' and 'I must not make a fuss and draw attention to myself.'

She claimed that her anxiety would be at its peak if she were faced with the prospect of not finishing her food in a crowded, fashionable restaurant. However, although she was successful at verbally Disputing both ego and discomfort-anxiety related Beliefs about this incident in therapy sessions, she could not initially conceive of putting this into practice in this particular setting even though I presented the rationale for 'full-exposure' homework assignments and emphasized the benefits that she would experience as a result. She literally could not imagine herself doing it (a good sign that such an experience would, in her terms, be too traumatic). She enquired whether there was not a painless method for overcoming her problems. I explained the dangers of such 'painless' methods and introduced her to the idea of 'challenging, but not overwhelming' tasks. She agreed, albeit with some reluctance, to select such an assignment. My hunch was that she would have terminated therapy if I had persisted in persuading her to expose herself fully to her anxieties. Over the following weeks she set herself and successfully executed the following 'challenging but not overwhelming' tasks while Disputing her salient irrational Beliefs. These tasks were in temporal order:

1 Eating two squares of chocolate in a public place.
2 Eating a meal of fish and chips on her own in a crowded restaurant, full of strangers.
3 Eating out in a snack bar with her boy-friend.
4 Eating out with her parents in a semi-fashionable restaurant.
5 Eating out with her boy-friend in a fashionable restaurant.
6 Deliberately asking for smaller portions in a fashionable restaurant.
7 Eating out with a large group of friends in a very exclusive restaurant, sending back any portions that were too big.

As I have said, each task was seen by the client as 'sufficiently' challenging but not overwhelming and tasks 5, 6 and 7 were initiated by her in a planned break from therapy. This principle allows clients to take responsibility for their therapy quite early on, once they have fully understood it and experienced initial success. On follow-up, she was able to eat out in a variety of settings with a variety of people without anxiety.

Variations on a theme

While I have not used the 'challenging but not overwhelming' principle in planning a hierarchy of assignments before treatment commences, it can be used in this way. I have not found this necessary because what clients find 'challenging but not overwhelming' changes over time so that the initial hierarchy becomes redundant. Theoretically, therapists could also use SUDS ratings of hierarchy and/or non-hierarchy items, although, again I have not found this necessary.

While I have used this principle mainly in helping clients set appropriately challenging tasks to overcome their anxiety problems, I have also used it successfully in helping depressed clients set appropriately challenging behavioural tasks. In so doing I stress to clients the importance of defining what is challenging in personal terms in relation to their depressed state rather than in relation to their non-depressed state. The successful execution of small tasks deemed personally challenging by depressed clients when they are depressed, is highly encouraging for such clients and makes them more amenable to the subsequent use of more traditional cognitive change procedures (Beck et al., 1979).

In conclusion, the negotiation of 'challenging but not overwhelming' homework assignments is seen as a healthy compromise between therapists and clients when the latter are overly threatened by the prospect of fully exposing themselves to their anxieties. Such tasks enable clients to execute homework assignments without unduly reinforcing their low frustration tolerance ideas and help to preserve the therapeutic alliance between the protagonists. I maintain that in such circumstances it is a highly pragmatic and efficient approach to negotiating homework assignments in that it provides clients with the best available (acceptable) means to achieve therapeutic ends.

Conclusion

In this chapter I have considered the various compromises that RET therapists may be called upon to make when they cannot help their clients achieve philosophically-based change. Rather than persist with traditional rational-emotive methods that do not prove to be effective, RET therapists can still help their clients by encouraging them to change inferences, behaviour or Activating events.

There are, of course, problems associated with such compromises: (1) Clients who succeed in changing negative inferences may later encounter events that realise their inferences. As they have not changed their irrational Beliefs they may make themselves disturbed about such events. Thus the client of my colleague may later discover that her father in fact had been prying into her affairs and my own client with social anxiety (Robert) may later encounter a group of people who will notice his anxiety and stare at him. (2) Clients who do change their behaviour for the better may still encounter events which serve to activate their latent unchanged irrational Beliefs. Thus, Sylvia, my client with examination anxiety, may in the future fail an important examination and Mrs. Anderson's family may again make unreasonable demands upon her. (3) Clients who change or remove themselves from problematic Activating events may later re-encounter such situations which again may activate their latent unmodified irrational Beliefs. Thus, Mrs. Curran's family may later mistreat her and Mr. Brown's enthusiasm for the law may wane. Finally, (4) Clients who overcome their problems by using 'challenging but not overwhelming' methods are still vulnerable to 'overwhelming' situations.

While I have described cases where productive changes in inferences, behaviour and situations have not led to Belief change, other clients do later change their irrational Beliefs after effecting such changes. And yet although RET theory has emphasized the interdependence of ABC factors I have wanted to show here that change, particularly at the level of Beliefs ('B') does not necessarily follow changes achieved at 'A' or 'C'.

The implications of this chapter for empirical study is clear. It would be helpful to research questions such as: (1) 'With what clients, at which stages of the therapeutic process, are Belief change (inference change, behaviour change and situation change) methods appropriate?'; and (2) 'Under which conditions do changes in inferences, behaviour and situations lead to Belief change and when do they not promote such change?'

Finally, given the way I have chosen to distinguish rational-emotive therapy from other approaches to cognitive-behaviour therapy and given my arguments about 'compromises' in RET I conclude with the intriguing notion that RET therapists do not *only* practise RET! Indeed it would be fascinating to research the question: 'When do RET therapists practise RET and when do they not do so?'

References

Beck, A.T., Rush, A.J., Shaw, B.F., & Emery, G. (1979). *Cognitive therapy of depression. New York: Guilford.*

Bordin, E.S. (1979). The generalizability of the psychoanalytic concept of the working alliance. *Psychotherapy: Theory, Research and Practice*, *16*, 252–260.

Dryden, W. (1984c). *Rational-emotive therapy: Fundamentals and innovations*. London: Croom-Helm

Ellis, A. (1972). Helping people get better rather than merely feel better. *Rational Living*, *7*(2), 2–9.

Ellis, A. (1977b). Fun as psychotherapy, *Rational Living*, *12*(1), 2–6.

Ellis, A. (speaker). (1977c). *Conquering dire need for love* (cassette recording). New York: Institute for Rational-Emotive Therapy.

Ellis, A. (1979b). Discomfort anxiety: A new cognitive-behavioral construct. Part 1 *Rational Living*, *14*(2), 3–8.

Ellis, A. (1979c). The practice of rational -emotive therapy. In A. Ellis & J.M. Whitley (Eds), *Theoretical and empirical foundations of rational-emotive therapy*. Monterey, CA: Brooks/Cole.

Ellis, A. (1979d). The issue of force and energy in behavioral change. *Journal of Contemporary Psychotherapy*, *10*(2), 83–97.

Ellis, A. (1980a). Discomfort anxiety: A new cognitive-behavioral construct. Part 2. *Rational Living*, *15*(1), 25–30.

Ellis, A. (1980b). Rational-emotive therapy and cognitive behavior therapy: Similarities and differences. *Cognitive Therapy and Research*, *4*, 325–340.

Ellis, A. (1980c). The value of efficiency in psychotherapy. *Psychotherapy: Theory, Research and Practice*, *17*, 414–419.

Ellis, A. (1981c). The use of rational humorous songs in psychotherapy. *Voices*, *16*(4), 19–26.

Ellis, A. (1983c). The philosophic implications and dangers of some popular behavior therapy techniques. In M. Rosenbaum, C.M. Franks & W. Jaffe (Eds.), *Perspectives on behavior therapy in the eighties*. New York: Springer.

Mackay, D. (1984). Behavioural psychotherapy. In W. Dryden (Ed.), *Individual therapy in Britain*. London: Harper & Row.

CHAPTER 9

SELF-DISCLOSURE IN RATIONAL-EMOTIVE THERAPY

G. Stricker and M. N. Fisher (Eds) (1990) *Self-disclosure in the therapeutic relationship*. New York: Plenum (pp. 61–74)

In 1974, I was awarded a PhD in Social Psychology from the University of London. My thesis title was 'Self-disclosure: some central and peripheral issues'. The subject of my thesis was one of the factors that led me to become interested in counselling and in the same year I began a one year full-time Diploma in Counselling in Educational Settings at the University of Aston in Birmingham. Although I did not publish any papers from my PhD, I never lost my interest in the therapeutic value of self-disclosure – both for client and therapist. Indeed, in the subsequent years I had used self-disclosure as an REBT therapist in showing clients how I dealt with a range of my own problems and life challenges. So, when I was invited to contribute to an edited volume on how I used self-disclosure in REBT, I readily accepted the invitation. The following piece is my contribution to that volume.

In this chapter I will first outline briefly the basic principles of rational-emotive therapy; then consider how rational-emotive therapists view client and therapist self-disclosure; and, finally, deal with common obstacles to such self-disclosure and how these may be overcome.

The basic principles of rational-emotive therapy

Rational-emotive therapy holds that people are disturbed not by events but by their view of events. More specifically the theory postulates that when people are psychologically healthy, they adhere to nondogmatic preferences even though events may go against their preferences (e.g., "I want to be approved by Susan but I don't have to be. It is unfortunate that Susan doesn't like me"). However, when people become psychologically disturbed they tend to make absolute demands out of their preferences (e.g., "Susan must like me. It's terrible that she doesn't"). When people think in such rigid ways they tend to draw irrational conclusions from their dogmatic premises (i.e., their *musts*). Thus they tend to conclude that whenever they do not get what they think they *must* that (1) it is *awful* (meaning more than 100% bad); (2) they *cannot stand* it (meaning that they can never be happy again as long as the "awful" events in their life are present); and (3) they, other people, and/or life conditions are *damnable*. A basic goal of rational-emotive therapists is to help their clients to identify (1) their disturbed emotions and self-defeating behaviors; (2) the events that trigger the irrational beliefs that lead to these disturbed emotions and behaviors; and (3) the irrational beliefs, to which they devoutly cling. After helping clients to identify such irrational beliefs, rational-emotive therapists then encourage them to dispute their irrational beliefs vigorously by using various cognitive, emotive, and behavioral means (Ellis & Dryden, 1987).

The role of rational-emotive therapists in the therapeutic process is usually a direct and educative one. RET therapists strive to teach their clients the ABC theory of emotional disturbance and educate them in their active role in disputing their own irrational beliefs cognitively, emotively, and behaviorally.

The RET approach to client self-disclosure

RET is a structured approach to psychotherapy and, as such, RET therapists generally encourage their clients to disclose themselves, using the ABC framework of psychological disturbance (where *A* = the Activating event, *B* = Belief, and *C* = Emotional and Behavioral Consequences of those beliefs). However, it is recognized that some clients do benefit from disclosing their problems and their feelings about them in a fairly unstructured way in the early stage of therapy.

A typical sequence of structuring client self-disclosure in RET is as follows. First the therapist asks the client to focus on one psychological problem at a time. This may be a problem that the client finds most distressing in his life or one that he wishes to address first in psychotherapy. When both therapist and client agree on the nature of the client's problem in broad terms, the therapist then attempts to assess the client's problem according to the ABC framework. Typically, the therapist starts with *C*, the client's major disturbed emotional response. Here the RET therapist will encourage her client to be as specific as he can about this emotional response. In general, when clients disclose their emotional problems in vague terms such as "I feel upset," "I feel bad," and "I felt miserable," RET therapists attempt to help them to clarify these problems and, in particular, whether the negative emotion was appropriate or inappropriate to the activating event at *A*.

According to RET theory, appropriate negative emotions stem from clients' rational, undogmatic beliefs which are normally expressed in the form of wishes, wants, and preferences. Major negative emotions that stem from these rational beliefs are sadness, concern, annoyance, and regret – emotions that are constructive responses to negative life events and that help people adjust to those events and then to move on with their lives. Such emotions are distinguished from inappropriate negative emotions which, according to RET theory, stem from dogmatic irrational beliefs. Such emotions are anxiety, depression, anger, and guilt – emotions that are seen as being unconstructive responses to negative life events and that inhibit people from adjusting to those events and from getting on with their lives.

While helping the client to distinguish his inappropriate from his appropriate negative emotions at *C*, the therapist will often help the client to distinguish between irrational or rational beliefs at *B*. Assuming that the client has a disturbed inappropriate negative emotion at *C*, the RET therapist will proceed to encourage the client to disclose what was the triggering activating event at *A* in the ABC framework. Here the RET therapist will encourage her client to disclose a *specific* example of the activating event; this is because the client, in real life, reacted to a *specific* activating event and his irrational belief was in fact triggered by such a specific event. The therapist will discourage her client from describing activating events in vague or overly discursive terms, since such disclosures will not aid the identification of specific irrational beliefs at *B*, later in the assessment process.

At this phase of assessment a particularly powerful intervention tool is the use of "inference chaining" (Moore, 1983). In RET theory, *A* stands not only for the event but also for the client's interpretations or inferences about the event, and it often occurs that clients make themselves disturbed not so much about the actual event but about the inferences that they make about the event. In inference chaining the therapist seeks to help the client to identify and disclose the most relevant inference in the chain (i.e., the one that served as a trigger for the irrational belief).

A brief example of inference chaining follows:

Therapist: So at point C you felt anxious. Now what were you anxious about? (Here the therapist encourages the client to disclose what it was about *A* that he was disturbed about.)
Client: I was anxious because I thought that the woman might reject me.
Therapist: And what would be anxiety-provoking in your mind if she did reject you?
Client: All my friends would see this and they would laugh at me.
Therapist: And what would be anxiety-provoking about that in your mind?
Client: Well, if my friends would laugh at me, I would gain the reputation of being a wimp.
Therapist: And if people generally thought of you as a wimp . . .?
Client: Oh my God, I couldn't stand it, that would really be horrible.

In this clinical exchange it can be seen that while the initial reported *A* was rejection, the client was really anxious about the psychological implications of this rejection. Thus, using inference chaining, the therapist structured the client's self-disclosure in a way that helped the client to identify the core aspect of *A* that served as a trigger for his irrational belief: "I must not be thought of as a wimp."

After assessing both *C* and *A*, RET therapists then encourage their clients to identify and disclose the irrational beliefs that account for their psychological disturbance at *C*. There are two major strategies that can be used to identify such irrational beliefs. First is through the use of such open-ended questions as "What were you telling yourself about that experience to make yourself feel anxious?" The problem about this strategy is that clients then disclose aspects of their thought processes that are not irrational beliefs. Thus, they may often disclose automatic thoughts (not in the form of irrational beliefs) and inferences or interpretations that again do not lie at the core of their emotional problem. If this occurs, the rational-emotive therapist will explain to the client why that particular thought would not be sufficient to account for his emotional problem. Through the subsequent use of guided questions and short didactic explanations, the therapist is generally successful in helping the client to identify the major *must* in his thinking which did account for *C*.

A second strategy at this point is to ask questions that are guided by RET theory. Instead of asking: "What were you telling yourself about that experience at *A* to cause your anxiety to point *C*?" the therapist asks such questions as: "What *must* were you telling yourself about *A* that caused *C*?" The danger of using such a strategy is that the therapist may put words into the client's mouth. However, the advantage of this type of theory-guided question is that it encourages the client to identify efficiently the *musts* in his thinking.

At this point the RET therapist has two major tasks. First, while encouraging disclosure of the client's irrational beliefs the therapist will educate the latter concerning the important distinctions between rational and irrational beliefs. Second, it is helpful if the therapist encourages her client to disclose his irrational beliefs both in the form of a premise, i.e., the musts and demands, and the conclusions derived from such premises (i.e., awfulizing, I can't stand it-itis, and damnation).

When the client can see the relationship between his irrational beliefs and his emotional problems at point *C*, the therapist is then in a position to help him to dispute his irrational beliefs and to encourage him to practice doing this outside therapy sessions. To facilitate this the therapist often encourages the client to undertake certain homework assignments, the goal of which is to encourage the client to begin to internalize his new rational philosophy. As therapy proceeds the client's self-disclosure tends to center on (1) reporting back on his experiences of doing homework assignments, and (2) bringing up new problems that are approached in a similar way to that outlined.

It can be seen, then, that rational-emotive therapists do not give their clients free rein to disclose themselves in whatever way they choose. If given such free rein, clients will often bring up irrelevancies, sidetrack themselves, and generally discourage themselves from adopting a problem-solving approach towards their psychological problems. Having said this, the use of clinical flexibility is advised in varying the structure of RET according to the therapeutic requirements of given clients at given points in the therapeutic process. Thus, some clients will require and benefit from a less structured approach on the part of their therapists if they are to disclose their concerns in a meaningful way. This is particularly the case if they are ashamed about disclosing certain experiences.

In addition, the more a client is successful at using RET methods during the middle and end phases of therapy, the less the therapist's role is a direct one and the more she will encourage the client to structure his disclosures for himself during this period. Here the therapist may do little more than to make interventions such as, "OK, that was your *A*, now what was your irrational belief? . . . Fine, how did you challenge that? . . . Good, what was the result of doing that? . . . Fine, what homework assignment did you give yourself? . . . that sounded good." The purpose of this gradual shift in therapeutic style from "active-directive" to "prompting-encouraging" is twofold. First, it helps the client to gain increasing control over the therapeutic process. Second, it encourages the client to be his own therapist so that he can disclose his problems to himself and use the RET method of problem assessment and solution to help himself.

Therapist self-disclosure in RET

One of the basic aspects of the therapist's role in RET is to educate the client in the ABCs of his emotions (Dryden, 1987). As such, however, the therapist will freely disclose her own experiences in the service of making that educational experience a memorable one for her client.

In order to understand fully the RET position on therapist self-disclosure, it is first necessary to outline the RET view of human fallibility (Ellis, 1972) since this is central to such understanding. The RET theory of human fallibility states that all humans are equal in humanity, that there are neither good humans nor bad humans and that no human being is more valuable or more worthy than any other. All people are equal in humanity although they may be unequal in terms of their different traits, behaviors, thoughts, feelings, etc. Thus the RET therapist does not see herself as being more valuable than her client, although she will tend to consider that she is more knowledgeable about understanding emotional problems.

Given that the effective RET therapist would accept herself for her errors and flaws and for past and present emotional disturbances, she will, as often as is therapeutically advisable, show her client how she upset herself about experiences similar to those with which her client is concerned and how she used RET to overcome such emotional disturbances. Note that in choosing this mode of self-disclosure, the RET therapist is providing her client with a coping model of overcoming emotional disturbance and not with a mastery model. The therapist who employs a mastery model approach to self-disclosure will stress that she has never experienced a problem similar to the client's because she thinks rationally about similar events with which the client is struggling. This approach is unproductive because it unduly emphasizes the inequality between therapist and client and deemphasizes their shared humanity.

A coping model of self-disclosure, on the other hand, where the therapist outlines that she too has experienced or is currently experiencing similar emotional disturbances but is able to get over these by using RET methods and techniques, indicates to the client that both therapist and client share the same experiences, although one is more adept at present in overcoming them than the other. Such a coping model emphasizes the shared humanity of the therapist and client while not bela-boring the inequality that exists between therapist and client in the therapeutic enterprise. The therapist who utilizes the coping model of self-disclosure can furthermore outline the *process* of solving emotional problems for the client, and as such self-disclosure can often be a powerful therapeutic tool.

Let me use a personal example to illustrate this. I used to have a very bad stammer and was not only ashamed about this but also anxious about speaking in public because I was scared that if I revealed my stammering in public, other people would laugh at me and I would severely condemn myself if this occurred. I often disclose this fact to clients who not only experience similar problems concerning stammering but who also have problems that are exacerbated by their anxiety that these problems may be revealed publicly. My self-disclosure is often along these lines:

"You know, as we find out more about your problem I am myself reminded of a problem that I used to have which in certain ways is quite similar to yours. I don't know if you've noticed but I have a stammer – here the client usually says, 'Well yes, I have noticed it but it's really not that noticeable' (indeed, I rarely stammer these days although I still have a slight speech hesitancy). I used to have a very bad stammer and hid myself away because I used to tell myself, 'I must not stammer in public. It would be terrible if I did and I couldn't stand it if other people were to see me stammer and to think badly of me.' Well, I struggled with this problem for many years and received much inadequate help from various speech therapists. However, it wasn't until I heard a radio program on which a noted entertainer outlined his own approach to overcoming his stammering problem that I started to overcome mine. This man told how he decided to force himself to speak up in public while reminding himself that if he stammered, he stammered, too bad. This was the first good piece of advice I'd heard on overcoming anxiety about stammering and I resolved to apply this myself. Indeed, although I did not realize it, I used the principles of RET which I'm now going to teach you. What I did was to force myself to enter situations and speak up, but before I did so I prepared myself by telling myself that there is no reason why I must not stammer, and if I did, too bad. On occasion I would speak more vehemently to myself and say things like: 'If I stammer, I stammer, fuck it!' The more I internalized these beliefs, the more I was able to go into situations and speak up. It certainly wasn't easy and I did have setbacks, but I persisted and now I can speak without anxiety in a variety of public situations, including radio and television. I still make myself anxious at times, but when I do, I look for and dispute my irrational beliefs in a very powerful and vigorous way and push myself forward on the basis of my rational beliefs. Even on the odd occasions when I cop out, I refuse to condemn myself and fully accept myself as a person who has opted out at a given moment. So you see, I too have experienced similar problems but have managed to help myself enormously. So I have a lot of faith that if you apply similar techniques you could also gain a lot of benefit from these methods."

While I have presented this personal self-disclosure in uninterrupted form, in practice, parts of it are interspersed with dialogue with the client concerning what he or she can learn from my experience.

It should be noted that this self-disclosure illustrates for the client the rational-emotive approach to therapeutic change. In this personal example I show the client (1) how to identify a personal problem; (2) how to identify the rational belief that underpins the problem; (3) the importance of repetitive and forceful disputing of this belief in situations in which the problem occurs; (4) that setbacks will occur and that under certain circumstances, people will choose to avoid rather than confront their problems; and (5) the importance of accepting themselves when this happens. When the therapist discloses personal information for educative purposes it is important that she ask her client what he can learn from her experience. It should not be forgotten that the purpose of therapist self-disclosure is to aid the learning process of the client. It is not an opportunity for the therapist to boast about her achievements in overcoming personal problems. Rather, the philosophy that should preferably underpin therapist self-disclosure is: "You and I are equal in humanity. At the moment I have more experience and skills in overcoming emotional problems but you can learn this too. It is difficult, but if you persist with it you can experience as much benefit as I did."

Cautions

While therapist self-disclosure does have great therapeutic merits, therapists should not disclose themselves indiscriminately to their clients; and I will now outline circumstances in which it may be preferable for therapists not to disclose themselves to their clients.

First, therapist self-disclosure, like any form of therapist communication, needs to be considered within the wider framework of the therapeutic alliance (Bordin, 1979). For example, in my experience, it is probably not wise for therapists to disclose their own problems and how they overcame them at a very early stage in the therapeutic process. This is so mainly because clients may not view such early self-disclosure as appropriate therapist behavior, and this may threaten the therapeutic alliance (Dies, 1973). This being so, some clients will, however, experience benefit from early therapist self-disclosure and therapists need to use their therapeutic judgment and their knowledge of their client as guides concerning the wisdom of making such disclosures.

Second, RET therapists are cautioned against disclosing themselves to clients who seek a formal relationship with their therapist. I made this mistake once when I disclosed a piece of personal information to a client who responded in this way: "Well, young man, that's all very interesting but I'm not paying you good money to hear about your problems, will you please address yourself to mine." This client wanted her therapist to act in a formal manner and did not value the use of therapist self-disclosure which, parenthetically, does seem to be associated with therapist informality. This is perhaps one reason why RET therapists in general favor therapist self-disclosure in that they favor adopting, whenever possible, an informal therapeutic role with their clients.

Third, RET therapists should be wary about disclosing themselves to clients who might use such information to harm themselves, or their therapists. For example, there are clients who idealize their therapists and for whom disclosure of therapist fallibility may come as a very painful blow, with the result that such clients may make themselves (albeit needlessly) depressed and anxious about this. Other clients may distort the content and the purpose of therapist self-disclosure to discredit the therapist in his or her community. It is difficult for RET therapists to predict which clients will have such negative responses to therapist self-disclosure; but it is possible to gain such information, and certain signs in the clients' psychopathology may provide clues for therapists in this respect.

For example, if a client has a history of extreme anger and vengefulness when their view of a person is threatened, this is perhaps a clue that the therapist may not wish to disclose personal information to the client that may threaten the client's view of the therapist. However, it should be noted that unless there are signs to the contrary, RET therapists do tend to use self-disclosure whenever therapeutically advisable and will often take risks (although not foolhardy risks) in this regard. Of course RET therapists can never guarantee that their self-disclosures will have positive effects. Therapists who demand certainty that their clients will react favorably to their disclosures will probably never self-disclose. Given the fact that RET therapists are not afraid to take calculated risks in therapy, they will take the chance of gaining therapeutic leverage by disclosing their problems and how they overcame them after disputing any demands they may have about this being acceptable to the client.

Now that I have outlined the value and risks of therapist self-disclosure in RET, I would like to emphasize how important it is for therapists to elicit feedback from their clients concerning the impact of their self-disclosures (Beck, Rush, Shaw, & Emery, 1979). Thus at the end of a session during which I have disclosed to a client some of my problems and how I have overcome them, I generally ask the client what impact this had on him, how he felt about my disclosure, what he learned from my disclosure, and whether or not he preferred me to disclose this information. If the therapist establishes her own system of feedback with the client, then it is possible to gauge the likely future benefit of therapist self-disclosure with that client. When a client indicates that therapist self-disclosure is not helpful, then that is perhaps a good guide for the therapist not to disclose her problems and the way she overcame them in future to that client.

Disclosing personal reactions to the client

While I have so far focused on one major feature of therapist self-disclosure, namely disclosure of problems and how these have been overcome, there is another aspect of self-disclosure that I would like to address in this chapter – the issue of providing clients with feedback concerning one's personal reactions to them. When clients talk about such issues as not getting on with people, I look for possible ways in which they may antagonize people by monitoring my own reactions to them in the therapy session. It sometimes occurs that I get a clear indication that a client's mode of interaction with me may if reproduced with other people, lead these other people to shun the client.

For example, one of my clients developed the habit of putting his feet up on my furniture. His presenting problem was that he felt quite lonely and didn't get on with people. I not only shared with him my reaction of displeasure whenever he did this, but was also keen to show him that while I disapproved of his behavior, I did accept him as a person. I told him that while I did not demand that he must not under any circumstances continue to put his feet on my furniture, I would, if he continued to do so, exercise my right to terminate the therapeutic relationship. Later on in the therapeutic process he told me that he really valued my feedback on his interpersonal behavior (although he did not appreciate it at the time!) because he could see in a very clear way the negative impact that he was having on other people.

In this example I have stressed an important aspect of the RET approach to disclosing personal reactions to clients – namely, that it is important to make a distinction between the person's behavior from the person as a whole and to teach this principle to the client. While the client is encouraged to take responsibility for his behavior, he is shown that he does not equal his behavior. Thus when the therapist brings to the client's attention some problematic aspect of his behavior she demonstrates unconditional acceptance of the client as a person but takes a no-nonsense approach to drawing attention to the negative aspects of the client's behavior.

RET therapists are again advised to use clinical judgment before disclosing their personal reactions to their clients. For example, clients who very easily upset themselves about even minor criticisms need to be quite adept at using RET methods to overcome such strong reactions before therapists disclose their negative reactions to problematic aspects of their clients' interpersonal behavior. This is true whether or not such clients ask for such feedback.

In general, whenever clients ask me for my opinion of them, I use this as an opportunity to teach them RET, particularly if I do have a negative reaction to them, and I sometimes disclose this reaction without being asked, as in the example just provided. Such disclosure needs to be made tactfully, and it is important for the therapist to pay attention to the language she uses to disclose her negative reactions to aspects of her clients' behavior. In addition to showing the client that he does not equal his behavior, it is also important that the client be shown that, although he is acting in a way that the therapist finds negative, he does not have to continue to act that way, and that the therapist has faith and confidence that he can improve his behavior. I have personally found the combination of *both* disclosing negative reactions about certain aspects of my clients' behavior in the context of teaching the RET position on (1) the difference between the person and his acts, and (2) the possibility of change *and* providing encouragement, to be especially therapeutic.

Overcoming obstacles to disclosure in clients and therapists

There are many reasons that both clients and therapists do not disclose their experiences, feelings, and problems during the therapeutic process and, in this concluding section, I outline some of the main explanations for disclosure avoidance and what RET therapists can do about this phenomenon.

Clients

In my experience there are three main reasons clients do not disclose their experiences and problems to their therapists in RET: (1) shame, (2) need for the therapist's approval, and (3) reluctance to participate in the therapeutic process.

When clients are ashamed about disclosing their experiences to their therapists they tend to believe that they *must* not have these problems in the first place and that they are in some way unworthy individuals for having them. Thus, rather than disclose both the nature of their original problem to themselves and their therapist, they unwittingly give themselves a second problem (i.e., shame about the original problem) that accounts for their disclosure avoidance. If this is the case, it is important for the RET therapist to deal with the client's shame about the problem before encouraging him to disclose the nature of this problem. If the client does admit to feeling shame, one way of doing this is to label the client's problem "X" and help the client to see that "X" is really the activating event (*A* in the ABC framework) and the feeling at C is shame. The client can then be helped to identify the irrational beliefs at *B* that underpin his experience of shame. If this assessment proves to be correct and the client acknowledges that this is the case, then the RET therapist can deal with the irrational beliefs about the undisclosed problem without having to know what the problem is. Then, having been helped to overcome his shame about the problem, the client may find it easier to disclose the problem to his therapist.

The second reason a client avoids disclosure of his problems is that he fears that if he discloses the problem to the therapist she would somehow disapprove of him and he would condemn himself because he thinks he needs the therapist's approval. First, it is important to ascertain that this is the reason the client does not disclose the true nature of his problems and, if so, this is again dealt with using the ABC framework, with *A* = the prospect of losing the therapist's approval, *B* = "I need the therapist's approval and I am less worthy if I don't have it," and *C* = anxiety. Then the therapist can help the client to dispute and change the irrational beliefs that underpin the anxiety that stops him from disclosing the true nature of his problems. Once again, if this proves successful, the client is likely to disclose his problems after he has overcome his need for the therapist's approval.

The final reason for the client's unwillingness to disclose his problems to his therapist is a general reluctance to being a client in the first place. This often occurs when the client is told that if he does not participate in the therapeutic process, he will incur a penalty, for example, from the courts, or from his partner who may leave the relationship. My approach to this situation is to show the client that there is no reason he has to disclose his problems to me or to participate fully in the therapeutic process and that he has every right not to do so. However, I also point out to the client that since he is choosing to attend, even under duress, he might as well work on a problem as defined by him rather than work on a problem that has been defined for him by a third party. Once the client sees that I am on his side and not on the side of the referring agent, he is more likely to see me as an ally and begin to use the therapeutic process for his own benefit rather than for the benefit of others.

Therapists

RET therapists are usually quite willing to disclose not only their problems and how they have overcome them but also their personal reactions to their clients; although, as I have suggested, such disclosure needs to be made in the context of sound clinical decision making. However, some RET therapists are reluctant to employ self-disclosure in this way and, in my experience in supervising such therapists, there are three main reasons that this occurs: (1) a need to be seen as thoroughly competent by the client; (2) a need for the client's approval; and (3) the belief that therapists should not have psychological problems.

When RET therapists believe that they have to be competent under all conditions, they tend to avoid the appropriate use of therapist self-disclosure because they predict that if they disclose that they have had emotional problems, even though they have overcome them, their clients will judge them as being incompetent; and if this was the case, they would condemn themselves for this. While supervising therapists who have this belief, I have used a double-barreled approach to this problem. First, I encourage the therapist concerned to assume that her worst fear is realized, i.e., that if she discloses herself to her clients they will indeed see her as being incompetent as a therapist. Having encouraged her to imagine that her worst fear has come true, I then help her to see that it is her beliefs (*B*) about this situation (*A*) that leads to her reluctance to self-disclosure at *C*. I then help her to identify and to challenge the irrational belief that underpins this experience, namely: "I must be seen as a competent therapist, otherwise I'm unworthy." When this has been done, the therapist is in a better position to reassess logically the likelihood that her clients will actually see her as incompetent. Here I use both my own example of past self-disclosure to clients (as outlined earlier in this chapter) and the fact that Albert Ellis (the founder of RET) also employs self-disclosure to show that competent RET therapists do self-disclose and that there seems to be little evidence that our clients generally see us as less competent (although some may have done so in the past).

The second reason RET therapists are reluctant to self-disclose is their need for their clients' approval. This is related to the need to be seen as competent; but here the therapist is more concerned with the approval of her clients than with their judgments of her competence. Again I suggest a double-barreled approach to this issue – helping the therapist first to identify and challenge her irrational beliefs before helping her to reevaluate the likelihood that her clients will disapprove of her if she does disclose to them some of her personal experiences.

Finally – and this is perhaps more true of novice therapists than more experienced ones – I find that some RET therapists have a dire need to see themselves as thoroughly mentally healthy. This is, in fact, a paradox, since if they demand that they *must* have perfect mental health, they are in fact disturbed because of the very existence of such a demand. This need to be problem-free stems partly from a misunderstanding of what it means to be a therapist. Being a therapist does not mean that one must be free of all psychological problems; rather that one has such problems, but can use RET techniques to overcome them. The approach to helping a therapist overcome this rigidity is quite similar to what has already been outlined in this chapter. I first encourage her to assume that her unrealistic expectation is true, namely that good therapists do not have any emotional problems. Then I help her to see that there is no reason why she *must* be a good therapist by this criterion and, if she is not, she can still accept herself and continue to overcome her problems. I then help her to reevaluate her unrealistic expectation and encourage her to see that being a good therapist does not mean being problem-free but means, in part, that one can apply what one is teaching others to oneself and one's own life situation. In using RET to help RET therapists in these ways, it is my experience that they become less anxious about disclosing themselves to their clients and do so appropriately and therapeutically during the process of RET.

References

Beck, A.T., Rush, A.J., Shaw, B.F., & Emery, G. (1979). *Cognitive therapy of depression.* New York: Guilford.

Bordin, E.S. (1979). The generalizability of the psychoanalytic concept of the working alliance. *Psychotherapy: Theory, Research and Practice*, *16*, 252–260.

Dies, R.R. (1973). Group therapist self-disclosure: An evaluation by clients. *Journal of Counseling Psychology*, *20*, 344–348.

Dryden, W. (1987). *Counselling individuals: The rational-emotive approach*. London: Taylor & Francis.

Ellis, A. (1972). Psychotherapy and the value of a human being. In W. Davis (Ed.), *Value and valuation: Aetiological studies in honor of Robert A. Hartman*. Knoxville: University of Tennessee Press.

Ellis, A., & Dryden, W. (1987). *The practice of rational-emotive therapy*. New York: Springer.

Moore, R.H. (1983). Inference as "A" in RET. *British Journal of Cognitive Psychotherapy*, *1* (2), 17–23.

CHAPTER 10

REASON AND EMOTION IN PSYCHOTHERAPY

Thirty years on

Journal of Rational-Emotive & Cognitive-Behavior Therapy, 12(2): 83–99 (1994)

In 1992, I was given a personal chair at what is now Goldsmiths, University of London. This made me Britain's first Professor of Counselling and I achieved this distinction 17 years after I began my first academic job at the University of Aston in Birmingham in 1975. One of the duties that new professors have to carry out is to give an inaugural lecture. After some reflection, I decided that since my award occurred 30 years after the publication of Albert Ellis's (1962) most influential book, *Reason and Emotion in Psychotherapy*, I would consider how REBT had changed since that volume's publication. The piece that follows is the text of my inaugural lecture on the subject. Two years after this lecture, Ellis (1994) published his revised and updated edition

References

Ellis, A. (1962). *Reason and emotion in psychotherapy*. New York: Lyle Stuart.
Ellis, A. (1994). *Reason and emotion in psychotherapy*. Revised and updated edition. New York: Birch Lane Press.

Albert Ellis founded rational-emotive therapy (RET) in 1955. His influence in the field of psychology is now such that in a survey of the American Psychological Association's clinical and counselling psychologists, published in 1982 (Smith, 1982), he was rated the second most influential psychotherapist (behind Carl Rogers, but ahead of Sigmund Freud). In another study (Heesacker, Heppner & Rogers, 1982), he was the most cited contributor of works published since 1957 in three major counselling journals over a twenty-seven year period, and a very recent study of Canadian clinical psychologists showed that Ellis was their most influential psychotherapist followed by Carl Rogers and Aaron Beck (Warner, 1991).

Reason and Emotion in Psychotherapy was Albert Ellis's first published book on RET as a system of psychotherapy. It appeared in 1962 and is still the most frequently cited reference on RET. Actually, the book is a collection of previously published papers and although Ellis worked on these papers to enable them to be published in book form, the text lacks the coherence of a work prepared especially for publication. Nevertheless, it is still recognised as a classic (Heesacker, Heppner & Rogers, 1982) and thirty years after its first publication merits detailed study. While many central features of RET theory presented in a book remain in place today, it is in the nature of the theory that it encourages flexibility. This quality has permitted a good deal of revision of the 1962 ideas—developments which have cleared up ambiguities and emphasised aspects of RET which Ellis only alluded to in 1962. This paper examines some major ideas presented thirty years ago, and points out developments which have modified and extended the theory of RET and its therapeutic applications.

Rationality

In 1962, Ellis defined his theory's central tenet of rationality. He said that rational means that which aids and abets human happiness, is consistent with reality, and is logical. Rational thinking, therefore, tends to greatly minimise emotional disturbance. In 1962, Ellis also set out how rational-emotive theory views emotional disturbance. He said that emotional disturbance results when individuals acquire and re-indoctrinate themselves with illogical, inconsistent and unworkable values. These three criteria of rationality and irrationality and their implications for human emotional disturbance remain current and basically unchanged since 1962.

Humanistic-existential emphasis

Besides the well-known cognitive-behavioural roots of RET, a humanistic-existential view is found in its concept of humans. RET sees humans as neither superhuman nor subhuman, and it considers all people equal in their humanity. While RET believes that biological and, to a lesser extent, social forces determine our psychological makeup, it argues that we retain much free will and choice in forming our emotional well-being. Moreover, we can increase our emotional health and happiness by adopting a policy of long-range hedonism. Long-range hedonists make decisions and act to increase their happiness over time. Short-range hedonists, on the other hand, strive for immediate happiness and gratification, opting to satisfy current frustrations at the probable expense of achieving future and longer-term happiness. Of these humanistic-existential foundations of RET, all are to be found in the 1962 text with particular emphasis being placed on the importance of striving for long-range hedonism. Today, the humanistic-existential roots of RET are more prominent and better integrated with its cognitive-behavioural features than hitherto.

Psychological interactionism

In 1962, Ellis noted that psychological processes such as cognition, behaviour and emotion are interrelated. This hypothesised interaction remains current in RET's understanding of human psychological functioning, although the complexity of relationships among these processes and their interaction with the environment is more to the fore now that it was thirty years ago (Ellis, 1991).

Frequently, people wrongly claim that RET maintains that cognitions cause emotions. This linear relationship, however, belies the complexity of the cognition-emotion interface, and RET has never considered it valid. Instead, certain cognitions and emotions are deemed in RET to overlap and are interrelated in such a complex manner that they become practically indistinguishable from each other.

In 1962, Ellis differentiated between cognitions which are calm, dispassionate appraisals of events, and those which are uncalm, strong, evaluative appraisals of events. The latter are called emotions. RET theory still considers this distinction applicable, but more modern terms are now used. Thus, calm, dispassionate appraisals of events are called cold cognitions, and uncalm, strong, evaluative appraisals of events are now termed hot cognitions. The concepts remain the same, but the descriptive terms are different. This distinction helps us to understand more clearly that it is hot cognitions which significantly overlap with emotional experiences.

Having made the point that from the outset Ellis stressed the inter-relatedness of cognition, emotion and behaviour, it is also true that he has always stressed the central role of cognitive processes in this trinity. To quote one of my students, Michael Neenan: "in RET theory, cognition is often primus inter pares—first amongst equals—in this holy trinity".

The role of evaluative thinking

One of the most significant changes in RET theory over the last thirty years clarified what type of beliefs is at the core of emotional experiences. In 1962, Ellis stated that a person's attitudes, interpretations of events, or what events mean to them, largely determine emotions. Note how general these cognitions are. As we shall see, Ellis is now much more precise about the type of cognitions that is involved in emotions. In addition, he occasionally mentioned in the 1962 book that situations or events themselves could directly determine emotions (e.g., "Married neurotics . . . tend to get upset by their mates' errors and stupidities" (Ellis, 1962, p. 208)). Given that Ellis was vague about the types of cognitions which are centrally implicated in emotion and given that he sometimes implied that cognitions are not important at all in determining emotion (i.e., by stating that situations or events can directly upset people), the reader of the 1962 book is bound to be confused about the precise determinants of emotional experiences. Readers of RET texts today are not likely to be confused by such contradictions.

Today, RET sees situations and a person's interpretations of events as less important in determining emotions than a person's *evaluative* beliefs. These evaluative beliefs are the hot cognitions discussed above. Ellis defines evaluations as judgements or appraisals about interpretations. So, for example, Mary says something unflattering about Jane, and Jane interprets this comment as insulting and becomes angry. According to current RET theory, Mary's comment does not cause Jane to become angry. Likewise, Jane's interpretation of Mary's comment, as insulting, does not cause her to become angry. Rather, Jane's evaluation of Mary's comment is the cognition that most clearly accounts for her anger. Jane's anger-producing evaluation probably goes something like this: "Mary absolutely must not say those things about me, and it is awful that she does. Further, her comments prove what a horrible person she is."

As seen, RET now differentiates between different types of thinking, or cognition. Current theory takes Ellis's original description of how people's cognitions determine their emotions, and further specifies it by dividing these cognitions into three levels (Wessler and Wessler, 1980). At the first level, descriptions occur. Here, for example, Jane notices that Mary spoke words and directed these words towards her. This type of cognition represents the descriptive level in that Jane only notes, or records, what occurs. At the second level of cognition, people make inferences about their recorded descriptions. For example, Jane determines what Mary's words mean about her (i.e. they are insulting). Note that up to now, RET hypotheses that this inferred insult does not fully explain Jane's anger. Her anger occurs at the third and final level of cognition called the evaluative level. At this level, Jane evaluates her inference of Mary's comment. She decides where it is positive, negative, or neutral, and as we shall see later, appraises the information flexibly or rigidly. So, compared to 1962, RET theory now more specifically delineates the cognitive processes which are involved in people's disturbances and keenly discriminates evaluations from inferences and descriptions. It also stresses the central role that evaluations play in colouring the inferences which people make about themselves, other people and the world (e.g. Dryden, Ferguson & McTeague, 1989).

Ellis describes this process from inference to evaluation to emotion as the ABC's of RET. In this model, A stands for an event or a person's interpretation or inference of that event, and the evaluation of this A occurs at B. A person's B, or evaluative belief, represents his or her judgement or appraisal about A. B then leads to C which stands for the emotional and behavioural consequences of holding the evaluative belief. Again, RET theory now places much more emphasis on the complex interactions between A, B and C than it did in 1962 (Ellis, 1991).

Ego disturbance and low frustration tolerance

Current RET theory distinguishes between two types of emotional disturbance and notes that these different types commonly interact. In 1962, Ellis noted that global, negative evaluations of the self lead to emotional disturbance. He later called this ego disturbance. Now, he and other RET therapists argue that an additional, central component of emotional disturbance exists called low frustration tolerance (LFT). People with a philosophy of LFT make themselves disturbed, for example, by believing that they cannot stand or bear frustration. They frequently sabotage their progress in therapy by not working to change themselves because they believe that such work is "too hard". A philosophy of LFT basically describes emotionally disturbing beliefs related to undesirable life conditions. Ego disturbance alone could not explain this area of emotional disturbance. The concept of LFT allows rational-emotive therapy to account for a much broader range of emotional disturbance than it could with ego disturbance alone. In 1962, the concept of LFT was mentioned only once (Ellis, 1962, p. 419) and an alternative term "I can't stand it" also appears only once—"Oh my Lord! How terrible this situation is . . . I positively cannot stand it!" (Ellis, 1962, p. 76). LFT (or discomfort disturbance—to give it its other name) has a central role in RET's current theory of psychological disturbance and this marks a significant development since the publication of *Reason and Emotion in Psychotherapy.*

The role of the musts

Throughout this article, I have noted that beliefs greatly determine emotional health. What do these beliefs contain, however, which lead to people making themselves emotionally disturbed? Ellis now states that evaluations lead to disturbed negative emotions particularly when they contain a must, and that these musts lie at the core of emotional disturbance. Musts are unconditional, dogmatic, absolutistic demands that the universe obey one's proclamations. They designate statements in which preferences and desires are transmuted to rigid commands which must, have to and absolutely should occur. Evaluative beliefs that are not rigid are preferential in nature and do not contribute to emotional distress, although they may lead to healthy negative feelings when one's desires are not realised, as we shall see later. Preferential evaluative beliefs also promote constructive behaviour leading to fulfilment of one's goals. RET currently states, therefore, that preferential evaluative beliefs maintain and promote emotional health. Escalating these preferences into musts results, however, in emotional disturbance. While this view appears in embryonic form thirty years ago, it is at the core of RET theory today.

In 1962, Ellis used the term "should" much more frequently than the term "must" to exemplify irrational beliefs, while the converse is true today. The reason for this shift concerns the fact that "should" has several different meanings while "must" clearly points to rigidity and demandingness. The word "should" can mean "preferably should", "empirically should" or "ideally should"; moreover, it can represent a recommendation and it can also point to demandingness. As Ellis saw more clearly that the essence of emotional disturbance was absolutism, rigidity and demandingness, he increasingly used the term "must" and decreasingly employed the term "should" to represent this essence.

Awfulising

In 1962, Ellis hypothesised a process known as awfulising as a major cognitive determinant of emotional disturbance and references to this process in *Reason and Emotion in Psychotherapy* are more frequent than references to the role of musts in such disturbance. However, it is probably true that in 1962, Ellis maintained that musts and awfulising have an equal role in explaining emotional disturbance. Sentences, therefore, such as: "I must be liked by everyone", and "It would be awful if everyone does not like me", would be seen by Ellis in 1962 as containing the same amount of power to produce emotional disturbance. Today, however, RET maintains that musts are primary in their ability to effect emotional disturbance and stemming from this "musturbatory" philosophy are secondary processes which people use to draw conclusions about themselves, other people and their lives. Ellis labelled the first conclusion or derivative as awfulising although he did not clearly define it in 1962. Currently, awfulising refers to evaluating an event as more than 100% bad—a magical and grossly exaggerated conclusion based on the musturbatory belief "This must not be as bad as it is." This distinction between musts and awfulising provides a precise and clear theoretical delineation of the nature of psychological disturbance and one that did not exist thirty years ago.

Ellis used the term awfulising less frequently than the word catastrophising in 1962. In fact, he saw awfulising and catastrophising as synonyms then. Today, however, RET therapists argue that human tragedies and catastrophes certainly exist. Just because they exist, however, does not require that people label them as awful. If they do, people make the unrealistic, illogical and self-defeating claim that something which does exist absolutely must not exist. This self-defeating escalation of a preference to a must leads to emotional disturbance rather than just intense, non-disturbed unhappiness over catastrophic situations.

Self-rating vs. self-acceptance

Most psychological models of personality propose a model of the self, and attempt to show how disturbances in one's view of one's "self" lead to emotional disturbance. RET put forth its model of the self thirty years ago, and this remains virtually unchanged today, although this view of the self is perhaps more coherent and consistent now than it was then. For the last thirty years, the primary theme in RET's model of the self has centered on suspending evaluation of the self. Ellis stated in 1962 that rating people can only yield meaningful information if humans are static, non-changing organisms and then, as today, he argued that people are too complex for a single rating to represent them accurately. RET sees peoples as constantly developing organisms who grow and change. One cannot legitimately label something that grows and changes because the label soon misrepresents what it attempts to describe. No label, therefore, can accurately represent hu-mans because they grow and change. Concepts such as self-rating and self-esteem involve the use of such global labels and are thus clearly illegitimate and inhibit the emotional growth of complex human organisms.

Since 1962, RET has viewed humans as fallible creatures who, by nature, cannot be perfected. Ellis maintains that humans would do well to accept themselves as fallible and try to learn from their mistakes. People who learn from their mistakes decrease the amount of time they disturb themselves and increase the time they involve themselves in constructive emotional problem solving, thereby leading happier lives. Humans would do well not to expect to prevent all mistakes because as long as people breathe, think and act, they will make mistakes. While rating themselves increases the chances that people will disturb themselves emotionally, rating their traits and behaviours from a position of unconditional self-acceptance helps them to focus on and change aspects of themselves that inhibit self-actualisation. As Ellis noted in 1962, people cannot try to be better, but can attempt to act better.

While RET's view of the self, laid out above, has remained basically unchanged for thirty years, Ellis later cleared up a major inconsistency present in his 1962 book. There, he stated that "true self respect . . . comes . . . from liking oneself" (Ellis, 1962, p. 62) and again:

> An individual who has a good ego or true pride does not have to keep protecting himself about the views of others . . . Generally he *likes himself so much* that he can be comfortable even when others disapprove his behavior. (Ellis, 1962, p. 270—emphasis added)

If you like your*self*, however, you are giving yourself a global rating. This smacks of theoretical inconsistency when one remembers that accurate self-ratings are not possible because (a) people are too complex to merit such ratings, and (b) they constantly change. To like your*self* does not make sense according to RET's view of the ever-changing self, as Ellis himself notes in the 1962 book (pp. 150–1). Saying that you like mastering a task, for example, but can accept yourself whether or not you master it, however, more closely describes a healthy view of the self and its vicissitudes. For current RET theory believes that deriving enjoyment from mastering a valued task will increase a human's chance of being happy. If people enjoy mastering a task, this does not mean that they have to like them*selves*. Rather, it means they rate their acts and through making such ratings can strive to improve their behaviour so that they can maximise happiness and minimise pain. Thus, rating aspects of ourselves is healthy but rating our "self" is not. This clarification makes RET's current view of the self more coherent and consistent.

Psychological health

Much of this article considers factors which lead to emotional disturbance, yet it is worth enquiring about RET's view of factors associated with emotional health. In 1962, Ellis delineated several criteria for psychological health. He stated that an emotionally healthy person demonstrates a health and enlightened self- and social interest, a commitment to creative pursuits and an adherence to long-range hedonism. Over the past thirty years, Ellis has added to this list of four criteria. Presently, this list additionally includes: self-direction, high frustration tolerance, flexibility, acceptance of uncertainty, scientific thinking, acceptance of self as a fallible human being, ability to take calculated risks, holding a non-utopian view of life, and taking responsibility for one's own emotional destiny. Ellis's expansion of his original criteria for psychological health reflects RET's commitment to extending the explanatory power of its theory.

Healthy and unhealthy negative emotions

Many people seeking psychotherapy wish to get rid of their negative emotions. Current RET theory does not advocate, however, extinguishing all negative emotions, for RET now distinguishes between two types of negative emotions: healthy and unhealthy ones. Ridding the client of unhealthy negative emotions rather than all negative emotions is a paramount goal in RET. Helping the client to identify and accept healthy negative emotions also becomes a goal during RET. Briefly, unhealthy negative emotions result from irrational beliefs and healthy negative emotions stem from rational beliefs. Examples of unhealthy negative emotions include anxiety, depression, shame and demanding anger, while their healthy equivalents are concern, sadness, regret and non-demanding anger (or annoyance). In RET, counsellors encourage clients to feel healthy negative emotions such as concern when facing an adversity. Emotions such as these serve as signals to people that they are in a situation they would do well to change. Healthy negative emotions act, therefore, as behavioural prompts and motivators to encourage people to maximise their happiness and minimise their hassles. Ellis did not clearly distinguish between these two types of negative emotions in 1962. Today, this distinction represents a more sophisticated account of negative emotions and provides therapists and clients with a guide as to which type of emotions to minimise, and which type to promote for profitable psychological adjustment and change to occur.

Acquisition and perpetuation of psychological disturbance

Any useful theory of psychological therapy is able to provide an account of how people acquire and perpetuate emotional disturbance. As we have already seen, Ellis stated in 1962 that situations can play a large part in how people acquire psychological problems. Thus, in several places in the 1962 book, Ellis indicated that people can be taught to be emotionally disturbed. For example, in talking to a client, Ellis (1962) says "You thought you would be terribly hurt by a girl rejecting you merely because you were *taught* that you would be" (p.256) and "so you were taught that being rejected is awful, frightful" (p.257).

Today, Ellis would tell this client that he brought his ability to disturb himself to these teachings and was not made disturbed by the teachings themselves. Indeed, a close reading of the book indicates that Ellis, at the time he wrote *Reason and Emotion in Psychotherapy*, was much more influenced by psychoanalytic thought than he is today. Thus in working with a client called Caleb, Ellis (1962) showed him "the connection between his psychosomatic symptoms and his father's stroke" and related "his symptoms to his mother's tendency to baby him when was physically ill and to his dislike of having to take over his father's factory instead of pursuing his own chosen career" (p.206). Ellis would now pour scorn on such psychoanalytically-oriented interpretations.

Today, RET states that people bring their innate tendency to disturb themselves to events and are not passively made disturbed by events. Parents and culture teach children which superstitions and prejudices to hold. They do not, however, create childrens' original tendency to unhelpful ritualism, spiritualism and dogmatism. Instead, Ellis maintains that children are *born* with these disturbance-creating tendencies. Today, RET adheres to the principle of constructivism which describes the idea that people create their own emotional disturbances (Ellis, 1990). Constructivism explains why Ellis has never articulated any elaborate theory of how such disturbances are acquired. For, experiences do not directly lead to disturbance, rather people bring their biologically-oriented demands to their experiences and disturb themselves emotionally in the process.

As seen, current RET theory places more emphasis on a biological explanation for human disturbance than on an environmental one. In fact, Ellis maintains now that biology accounts for 80% of psychological disturbance, while environmental factors contribute a role of only 20% (Ellis, 1978). In 1962, Ellis did not attempt to distribute the variance in this way. While the biological emphasis in RET theory was present thirty years ago, it is now more pronounced and an important paper published in 1976 showed Ellis's still current view on the extent to which biology influences acquisition of psychological disturbance (Ellis, 1976).

RET clearly regards biology, then, as the major factor in producing emotional disturbance. Ellis, however, gives people primary control of their emotional reigns in *perpetuating* this disturbance. To this day, and since its inception, RET maintains that people perpetuate their psychological disturbance because they lack three major insights concerning the nature of their problems. Insight number one states that unfortunate situational factors do not determine unhealthy negative emotions. Rather, absolutistic, musturbatory evaluations of situations lead to emotional disturbance.

People may have insight number one, but will still disturb themselves if they do not hold insight number two. This second insight maintains that people perpetuate their absolutistic beliefs by re-indoctrinating themselves with them in the present. Thus, a person may have disturbed himself in the past over some event. However, if he is still disturbed about it, it is because he is currently adhering to a set of irrational beliefs about the past occurrence.

While people may have insights number one and two, they will still disturb themselves if they lack insight number three. This final insight requires people to acknowledge that they must actively and repeatedly challenge and dispute their dogmatic beliefs if they are to overcome their emotional and behavioural problems. Unless people take up the Protestant work ethic and work, work and work at challenging and changing their irrational beliefs using cognitive, behavioural and emotive methods, they will continue to disturb themselves.

RET has always noted that people are not only highly adept at perpetuating their primary problems, but are also extraordinarily skilled at constructing secondary problems about their original problems. However, Ellis now places more emphasis on this disturbance-perpetuating factor than he did in 1962. An example of this factor occurs when clients make themselves anxious about their primary anxieties. Some people are even more talented at disturbing themselves. Thus, occasionally clients not only come up with secondary problems, but also tertiary problems (i.e. further problems about their secondary problems). For instance, a client came in because he was shoplifting (Problem 1). He was also ashamed of his shoplifting (Problem 2), and ashamed that he had to seek therapy over it (Problem 3). In addition, he berated himself for not working as hard as he believed he must to overcome his original problem (Problem 4). While Ellis alluded to clients' ability to disturb themselves about their original disturbances in 1962, this is given far more prominence in current RET theory and practice.

Since 1962, Ellis has identified other ways that humans perpetuate their psychological disorders. For example, RET therapists often ask clients to perform behaviours they are not used to doing (such as to act differently based on a newly acquired rational philosophy). Clients often report they cannot do these requested behaviours because they "feel like a phoney" or "I'm not like that, it's just not me." Some clients find it difficult to accept that it takes time for a person to grow accustomed to any "new" behaviour. Due to this, they do not perform the new, more constructive behaviour. Their refusal to feel like a "phoney" for a while, of course, perpetuates their problem.

Ellis also currently states that self-fulfilling prophecies perpetuate emotional disorders. For instance, an anxious person believes that she will make a fool of herself at a dance where she wishes to meet people. Due to her anxiety about acting foolishly, her thoughts freeze, she does not speak thoughtfully, and ends up actually acting foolishly. Needless to say, this serves to increase her anxiety because she then condemns herself for her foolish act. The role of self-fulfilling prophecies in the perpetuation process was not mentioned by Ellis in his 1962 book.

Finally, Ellis currently states that a philosophy of low frustration tolerance (LFT) perpetuates emotional disturbance. This philosophy was not emphasised in 1962. As mentioned earlier, people with a philosophy of LFT demand that change must not be "too hard" for them. Change requires, however, very hard work on the part of clients. Due to this requirement, people with LFT do not readily or easily change. They, thus, perpetuate their psychological problems by refusing to do the work necessary to overcome them.

The addition of LFT, self-fulfilling prophecies, and the role of phoney feelings to the list of factors preventing change, more fully develops RET's theory of the perpetuation process. In addition, awareness of these factors further assists clinicians and clients to anticipate and attack directly these problem-causing irrational beliefs in therapy.

Therapeutic change

In addition to providing an account of how psychological problems are acquired and maintained, a useful theory of therapy needs to account for therapeutic change. Currently, Ellis delineates various levels of therapeutic change which he did not articulate as comprehensively in 1962. He now distinguishes between philosophic (or evaluative) change, inferential change and behavioural change (Dryden & Ellis, 1988). In therapy, Ellis strives to promote philosophic change in clients whenever possible. Achieving profound philosophic change (sometimes called elegant change), requires clients to focus on their dogmatic or musturbatory ideas and to work steadily to change these beliefs to non-dogmatic preferences.

Ellis described another type of change, known as inferential change, which occurs when people alter their inferences about their experiences rather than their evaluations of these experiences. An example of inferential change occurs when a person decides, for example, that someone whom she thought was against her is, in fact, not against her. Rather, she concludes that the person concerned is either neutral towards her or, in fact, on her side.

Lastly, Ellis states that people can change their behaviour. Behavioural change often serves to alter the activating event—i.e. the A part of the ABC model. Dryden and Ellis (1988) maintain that achieving philosophic change frequently leads to inferential and behavioural change, whereas inferential and behavioural change less frequently lead to philosophic change. This explains why Ellis has always stressed the importance of trying to achieve philosophic change.

As already noted, Ellis did not differentiate these levels of change in his 1962 book. Rather, he just focused on philosophic change, although he did not call it this. Over the past thirty years, RET has, in my view, succeeded more than other cognitive-behavioural therapies (CBTs) in outlining how to achieve philosophic change. Other CBTs have mainly concentrated on how to achieve inferential and behavioural change, and have done so quite successfully. In my following comments, I will primarily focus on RET's pioneering methods of achieving profound philosophic change.

To effect philosophic change, Ellis states that clients first need to realise that they create, to a large degree, their own psychological disturbances. Secondly, they need to recognise fully that they have the ability to change significantly these disturbances. Third, they need to understand that emotional and behavioural disturbances stem largely from irrational, absolutistic beliefs. Fourth, they need to detect their irrational beliefs and discriminate them from their rational ones. Fifth, they need to dispute these irrational beliefs using the logical, empirical methods of scientific reasoning. Sixth, they need to work towards the internalisation of their new rational beliefs by employing cognitive, behavioural and emotive methods of change. Finally, they need to continue this process of challenging irrational beliefs and using multi-modal methods of change for the rest of their lives.

While this elaborate process of change can be found in the 1962 book, it appears there in quite a rudimentary form. Some parts of the process, though, did receive heavy emphasis then. For example, in 1962, Ellis stressed the importance of work and practice to effect change as much as he does now. However, other features of the change process that feature now were virtually absent then. Thus, his 1962 book contained only a few cognitive and behavioural change techniques whereas numerous such methods can be found in the current RET literature (Dryden and Yankura, 1993). In addition, Ellis did not include then any emotive or imaginal techniques which now feature prominently in the RET therapist's armamentarium. For example, Ellis (1987) now advocates the use of humour as an important emotive technique, whereas the RET of 1962 seems quite humourless by comparison.

As stated, Ellis did not discuss many techniques that an RET therapist could use in 1962; he did list, however, those not recommended for use. These included: abreaction, catharsis, dream analysis, free association, interpretation of resistance, analysis of transference, hypnosis, reassurance, reciprocal inhibition, and positive thinking. Ellis still recommends avoiding these techniques. Today, however, some RET therapists employ a few of these techniques as well as others derived from alternative therapeutic approaches, without adopting the theory which spawned these techniques. Methods borrowed from other orientations are used in a manner consistent with RET theory. Likewise, therapists do not employ techniques contraindicated by RET theory. This is an example of what I have called theoretically consistent eclecticism (Dryden, 1987a). In this form of eclecticism, theory guides technique selection which is not restricted to the limited number of techniques spawned by the theory itself.

The role of force and energy in change

As noted above, in 1962, Ellis encouraged people to work, work, work at changing their irrational beliefs. In 1992, he still encourages such work. However, he states that people do better when they use force and energy to change their irrational beliefs and behaviours. Thus, Ellis argues that people will challenge their irrational beliefs more successfully by questioning them in a vigorous manner, and by accentuating forcefully more logical, rational beliefs as alternatives. In addition, Ellis recommends that clients expose themselves as fully as they can to their fears. He thus favours the use of flooding rather than the use of gradual desensitisation techniques. So, instead of recommending that a social phobic phone one friend per week, he encourages them to phone five. The more recent ideas of force and energy in behaviour change and the use of full in vivo exposure clarify a central tenet of RET and extend its clinical application.

The therapeutic relationship

Of course, utilisation of any technique takes place within the context of a therapeutic relationship. In this relationship, client and therapist work together to help the client. How the therapist should act in this partnership is addressed in countless volumes in the literature on counselling and psychotherapy. Carl Rogers (1957) has described one of the most enduring and widely accepted models of how a therapist should interact with a client. In his model, he outlined a set of necessary and sufficient conditions for therapeutic change. Thirty years ago, Ellis said that Rogers' model was wrong. He maintained that Rogers' core conditions of empathy, respect and genuineness are desirable but neither necessary nor sufficient to effect psychological change. Instead, he stated that a therapist needs to act as a model and teacher to help the client change. Today, RET therapists place more emphasis on building and maintaining a therapeutic alliance with their clients than they did in 1962 (Dryden, 1987b). The role of the therapist as model and teacher, however, remains unchanged.

Summary

In summary, then, in 1962 RET displayed important features still current. These include the interrelatedness of cognitive, emotive and behavioural processes, the important role that cognition plays in psychological problems, its humanistic view of the self and the futility and dangers of self-rating. The emphasis on perpetuation rather than acquisition processes of emotional disturbance holds good now as it did then, and the core view of therapeutic change is essentially the same now as it was in 1962, despite further, more recent elaborations. Also, one can find the beginnings of a model of psychological health in 1962 that has been more fully developed since that time.

Significant change has occurred in RET since 1962 that updates several of Ellis's original ideas. These include the distinction between interpretations (or inferences) and evaluations, the primacy of musts in accounting for psychological disturbance, the clear distinction between healthy and unhealthy negative emotions and the greater role accorded to force and energy in the change process. Aspects of psychoanalytic theory, as well as conditioning theory featured in 1962 no longer appear, and a greater emphasis is placed on biological aspects of emotional disturbance now than thirty years ago. Finally, a greater range of cognitive, imaginal, emotive and behavioural methods are found in current RET literature than in *Reason and Emotion in Psychotherapy* where Ellis restricts himself to illustrating a few cognitive and behavioural techniques.

RET, then, has grown and developed over the past thirty years. In large part, this reflects the theory's flexibility and the competent people who have worked to make RET one of the most viable and widely used cognitive-behaviour therapies. Of these, I modestly include myself!

References

Dryden, W. (1987a). RET as a theoretically consistent form of eclecticism, in W. Dryden, *Current issues in rational-emotive therapy*. Beckenham, Kent: Croom Helm.

Dryden, W. (1987b). The therapeutic alliance in rational-emotive individual therapy, in W. Dryden, *Current issues in rational-emotive therapy*. Beckenham, Kent: Croom Helm.

Dryden, W. & Ellis, A. (1988). Rational-emotive therapy, in K. S. Dobson (Ed.), *Handbook of cognitive-behavioral therapies*. New York: Guilford.

Dryden, W., Ferguson, J. & McTeague, S. (1989). Beliefs and inferences: A test of a rational-emotive hypothesis. 2: On the prospect of seeing a spider, *Psychological Reports*, 64, 115–123.

Dryden, W., & Yankura, J. (1993). *Counselling individuals: A rational-emotive handbook*, London: Whurr Publishers.

Ellis, A. (1962). *Reason and emotion in psychotherapy*, New York: Lyle Stuart.

Ellis, A. (1976). The biological basis of human irrationality, *Journal of Individual Psychology*, 32, 145–168.

Ellis, A. (1978). Toward a theory of personality, in R. Corsini (Ed.), *Readings in current personality theories*. Itasca, IL.: F. E. Peacock.

Ellis, A. (1987). The use of rational humorous songs in psychotherapy, in W. F. Fry Jr, & W. A. Salameh (Eds.), *Handbook of humor in psychotherapy: Advances in the clinical use of humor*. Sarasota, FL.: Professional Resource Exchange.

Ellis, A. (1990). Is rational-emotive therapy (RET) "rationalist" or "constructivist"?, in W. Dryden (Ed.), *The essential Albert Ellis*. New York: Springer.

Ellis, A. (1991). The revised ABC's of rational-emotive therapy (RET), *Journal of Rational-Emotive & Cognitive-Behavior Therapy*, 9, 139–172.

Heesacker, M., Heppner, P. P., & Rogers, M. E. (1982). Classics and emerging classics in counseling psychology, *Journal of Counseling Psychology*, 29, 400–405.

Rogers, C. R. (1957). The necessary and sufficient conditions of therapeutic personality change, *Journal of Consulting Psychology*, 21, 95–103.

Smith, D. (1982). Trends in counseling and psychotherapy, *American Psychologist*, 37, 802–809.

Warner, R. E. (1991). A survey of theoretical orientations of Canadian clinical psychologists, *Canadian Psychology*, 32, 525–528.

Wessler, R. A., & Wessler R. L. (1980). *The Principles and Practice of Rational Emotive Therapy* San Francisco: Jossey-Bass.

CHAPTER 11

RATIONALITY, OUTRAGEOUS IDEAS AND SENSITIVITY

W. Dryden (Ed.) (1998) *Are you sitting uncomfortably: Windy Dryden live and uncut.* Ross-on-Wye: PCCS Books.

Over the years, as with most academics, I have been invited to give lectures at conferences and other events. I have tended to use these opportunities to present ideas that I have viewed as controversial, hoping to stimulate the audience to think about therapeutic matters in new ways. In 1997, I was invited to give a keynote address at the 1st International Conference on Counselling Psychology at Stratford-on-Avon and chose to show the shocking connotations of some of REBT's concepts, which need to be handled sensitively in the consulting room. I later developed this theme into a book (Dryden, 2010). I include this piece here as a good example of one of my controversial lectures.

Reference

Dryden, W. (2010). *Strange, but rational.* Ross-on-Wye: PCCS Books.

In my opinion this is one of the most controversial lectures that I have ever delivered. It was given as a Keynote Address on May 31, 1997 at the 1st International Conference on Counselling Psychology organised by the Division of Counselling Psychology of the British Psychological Society which took place at Stratford-upon-Avon. Nobody walked out of the talk and the discussion after the lecture was strangely muted. Either I overestimated the controversial nature of the lecture or the audience was dumbstruck!

In this talk, I am going to present some ideas that are derived from the theory of Rational Emotive Behaviour Therapy. If presented without explanation, these ideas will seem outrageous, but when embedded in the context of REBT theory they make perfect sense. I suppose at the outset I should issue a health warning, in that you may find some of what I say shocking and even offensive. You may even feel tempted to walk out. This is, of course, your prerogative. However, I would much prefer you to stay, express your displeasure and argue with me, so that we can have a dialogue about what I have presented.

While much has been written about desirable counsellor qualities and attitudes, little has been written about the ability of counsellors to hear all manner of things from clients without being shocked by what they hear. My view is that the unshockability of counsellors is a much under-rated therapeutic condition. If the counsellor conveys that she (in this case) will not be shocked by what the client says, then she will create a space where the client will dare to speak the unspeakable and think the unthinkable. In this spirit, I will say things that you thought you would never hear in a keynote address at a distinguished gathering. Allow me, for a brief period, to mention the unmentionable.

Beyond belief: the shocking ABCs of REBT

One of the core theoretical ideas of REBT is represented by the ABC model of human emotions. This can be summed up neatly by the statement: 'People are disturbed [at C] not by things [at A], but by their rigid and extreme views of things [at B].' For Albert Ellis, the founder of REBT, these rigid and extreme beliefs are at the very core of much psychological disturbance. As is now well known in the field of counselling and psychotherapy, dogmatic beliefs come in the form of 'musts', absolutistic 'shoulds', 'have-to's, etc., and are the breeding ground for three other irrational beliefs which are extreme in nature. These are known as: awfulising beliefs, low frustration tolerance beliefs, and beliefs where self, others and life conditions are deprecated.

The healthy alternative to these four irrational beliefs are essentially flexible and non-extreme in nature. These rational or healthy beliefs are known as preferences, anti-awfulising beliefs, high frustration tolerance beliefs and beliefs where self, others and life conditions are accepted.

Now the ABC model of REBT is not controversial until you begin to consider events at A which are highly aversive. Let's take rape, for example. The ABC model of REBT states as follows: women (in this case) are disturbed not by being raped, but by their rigid and extreme views of being raped. Now, I can well appreciate that for some of you this is a monstrous statement. A woman has been raped and now I (a man no less) am saying that this event did not cause her disturbed feelings, but that she made herself disturbed by holding a set of rigid and extreme beliefs about being raped. How insensitive and how inaccurate. Furthermore, you may think that I am blaming the victim and minimising the responsibility of the man committing the rape. I can understand if this is your reaction; for, stated in this stark manner, the idea that a woman causes her own disturbed feelings about being raped is insensitive and I would never put this in such a stark way to clients.

Imagine this scene. A woman has been raped and seeks counselling. She is sobbing uncontrollably, at which point the counsellor tries to show her that she is making herself disturbed about being raped. Is this insensitive? Of course it is, and no good REBT therapist would intervene in this way. A sensitive and empathic response is called for, and this is what the REBT therapist would offer. And yet, no matter how empathic and sensitive the counsellor is, this does not change the fact that the client *is* disturbing herself by the beliefs that she holds about the rape. But she is light years away from being able to hear this perspective. She is, however, closer to hearing that being raped can be said to be causing her distress.

REBT makes a crucial distinction between healthy negative emotions (or *distress*) and unhealthy negative emotions (or *disturbance*). Distress stems from rational beliefs and disturbance stems from irrational beliefs. Ruling out very unlikely reactions to rape such as pleasure and indifference, one can feel either distressed or disturbed about being raped. Now, given that irrational beliefs are dogmatic and extreme versions of rational beliefs, one can argue that it is highly likely that virtually everyone who is raped has a set of healthy beliefs about this very aversive activating event.

Thus, the woman in question is likely to have a very strong preference not to be raped, views it as something very, very bad and so on. These beliefs are so ubiquitous that we can say that being raped causes distress, whether this distress is overt or covert. But since irrational beliefs are rigid and extreme versions of these rational beliefs, they are not caused by the event (although I note in passing that the more aversive the rape, the more likely it is that the person will transform her rational beliefs into irrational beliefs); no, these rigid and extreme transformations of rational beliefs are the responsibility of the person who is raped.

This does not mean, of course, that we should blame the woman for her disturbance. It means that we are empowering her. I'll say that again. Helping the woman at a therapeutically sensitive time to acknowledge that she is responsible for her disturbance is an act of empowerment. It is empowering because it enables the client to free herself from her disturbed feelings. She may not get over her healthy distress (although this will probably lessen over time), nor should we want her to, for it is healthy for her to be distressed about such a highly aversive activating event as rape. But she does not have to be disturbed for an unduly long period about this event. She has the ability to transcend this experience in a healthy manner, and it is this realisation that is empowering.

She can accomplish this, according to REBT theory, by doing two things. First, she can rid herself of the rigid and extreme versions of her rational beliefs. Examples of such extreme versions are 'Being raped makes me a dirty, repulsive person' and 'My life is completely ruined.' Second, she can actively stay with the flexible, non-extreme beliefs that are at the core of her healthy distress (e.g. 'Being raped is a disgusting thing to have happened to me, but it does not define me as a person. I am not a dirty person: I am a person to whom a dirty thing was done' and 'My life has been badly affected, but not completely ruined. "Ruined" means that I cannot recover, but I can recover even though I may never forget it and may be somewhat influenced by it.'

Let me stress that it is probably normal for women (and men) who have been raped to be disturbed about it, but normal does not mean healthy. If we want to help people to overcome their disturbance, but not their distress, we can help them to remove what they themselves have added, i.e. the rigid and extreme beliefs which are not an intrinsic part of the rape. This needs to be done with great sensitivity at a time when the client is ready to benefit from it, and it should be emphasized that the client should not be blamed for needlessly, but understandably, adding irrational beliefs to the experience.

Finally, this work can be done without minimising either the aversiveness of the rape or the responsibility of the person who perpetrated the rape. Let me be perfectly clear about this. Rape is an act of violence and the person perpetrating the rape is to be held fully responsible for it. The position that I have taken with respect to the source of disturbance does not detract one iota from this point.

Taking offence at 'shoulds'

In REBT, as in life, the meaning of words is important. Unless I am clear about the meaning of a word that I am using, you may easily take offence at what I say and may even think that I am crazy for saying it.

Let me take the word 'should', for example. As I have already mentioned, REBT theory posits that rigid beliefs are at the core of much psychological disturbance. Such beliefs take the form of 'musts', 'got to's and 'have to's. They also take the form of 'shoulds', but only when these shoulds are absolute. The word 'should' has several different meanings in the English language, and this fact can lead to confusion at best, and to your taking offence and even my incarceration in a psychiatric hospital at worst.

Listen carefully to my next statement and note your immediate reaction to it. 'The Holocaust should have happened.' Have you taken offense at that statement? Are you angry at me for saying it? Do you think that I have taken leave of my senses or think that I am a member of the British National Party? I am neither mad nor a Nazi. All I have done is to use the word 'should' in a manner to convey one meaning, and you have reacted as if I have used the word 'should' in a way that conveys a very different meaning.

It follows therefore that when using language in REBT (or in any other approach to counselling) it is very important first, to be aware that a single word has different meanings and second, to take great care in differentiating and explaining these meanings when using these words with clients. This is precisely what I deliberately did not do when stating without any explanation that the holocaust should have happened. I mentioned earlier that timing of one's interventions is a mark of therapeutic sensitivity. Here I am arguing that the explanation of terms that might be otherwise misinterpreted without further elaboration is another hallmark of such sensitivity.

Let me now consider the different meanings of the word 'should' before returning to my statement about the Holocaust. The first meaning of the word 'should' that I want to consider is the absolute should. This is the only 'should' that represents an irrational belief. An example of an irrational, absolute should is as follows: 'You should not have treated me in this way.' What the person really means here is: 'You absolutely should not have treated me in this way.' In this example, the person is demanding or insisting that the other person not act in a certain way towards him. An irrational, absolute 'should' also leads the person to hold one or more further in irrational beliefs which Ellis (1994) views as being derivatives from this absolute ' should' (e.g. 'It's terrible that you treated me in this way', 'I can't stand the fact that you treated me in this way' and 'You are a swine for treating me in this way'). The absolute 'should' also leads to an unhealthy negative emotion, and in this example the person experienced demanding, condemnatory anger towards the other who treated him badly. As I mentioned earlier, the absolute 'should' is the only 'should' that represents an irrational belief and is thus the only 'should' that is the target for change in REBT.

The second 'should' that I wish to discuss is the preferential 'should'. This is the healthy alternative to the absolute 'should' and contains an implicit negation of it. If we make both the preferential nature of this 'should' and this negation explicit in our example, we get the following statement: 'You preferably should not have treated me in this way, but there is no law that states that you absolutely should not have done so.' As you can just hear this sounds very awkward, so the person is more likely to say: 'You should not have treated me in this way.' This is, of course, confusing, since it is exactly the same wording as was used to denote an absolute 'should'. However, a preferential 'should' leads to different effects from the absolute 'should'. First, it leads to a further set of rational beliefs (e.g. 'It's bad that you treated me in this way, but it is not terrible', 'It's difficult, but I can stand the fact that you treated me in this way', and 'You are not a swine for treating me in this way, but an unrateable fallible human being who has acted badly'). The preferential 'should' also leads to a healthy negative emotion, and in this example the person experienced non-demanding, non-condemnatory anger about the other person's mistreatment of him. As the preferential 'should' is healthy, it is not targeted for change in REBT.

The third type of 'should' is the recommendatory 'should'. Here, for example, you may recommend that a person take a particular course of action as in the statement: 'You should you put your money into a PEP.' Assuming that the person is acting in good faith, what she is saying here is that she thinks that it would be good for you to take out a PEP and this is what she recommends you to do. While the content of the recommendation may be questioned an REBT therapist would not question the recommendatory 'should' since it is not, by itself, dogmatic.

The fourth 'should' that exists is the predictive should. When you use the term ' should' in this way, you are predicting what will happen based on past experience. An example of this type of 'should' is found in the statement: 'The 6.05 from Waterloo should be five minutes late, since it usually is.' This type of 'should' is again not usually targeted for change in REBT.

The fifth 'should' that I wish to consider is the conditional 'should'. Here the person specifies the conditions that have to be met for an outcome to be achieved (e.g. 'If I study hard, I should pass my exams'). There is, of course, an element of prediction about this 'should', but its defining characteristic is in the specification of the conditions that have to be met for something else to occur. Conditional 'shoulds' frequently point to occurrences in the future, hence the overlap with predictive 'shoulds'. However, neither this 'should' nor the next is questioned in REBT since neither is implicated in psychological disturbance.

A sixth 'should' that exists is the ideal 'should'. This is really a special sub-type of the conditional 'should' and is more formally known as the ideal conditional 'should' in that it specifies a relationship between the meeting of ideal conditions and a particular outcome. 'The grey mare should win this race' is an example of the ideal 'should' in that the person is saying that, if ideal conditions exist, the grey mare should (or will) win the race.

A seventh 'should' is one that may be called the deserving 'should'. Here a person is specifying what 'should' occur on the basis of a sense of justice or fairness. 'He should be imprisoned for five years for what he did' is specifying a relationship between what the person did and what 'should' happen if justice is to prevail. It goes without saying that this sense of justice is subjective and will vary from person to person. 'He should get five years for what he did.' 'No, I think he should be hanged for it' is an exchange between two people indicating two different ideas of justice. Deserving 'should's are not targeted for change in REBT unless they are transformed into absolute 'shoulds'.

The eighth and final form of 'should' that I wish to consider is called the empirical 'should'. When the empirical 'should' is used, the person is indicating that she acknowledges that all the conditions were in place for what happened to have happened. Thus, when I use an empirical 'should' in the statement 'The Conservative Party should have lost the election', all I am saying is that all the conditions were in place for them to lose the election – nothing more, nothing less. I am not indicating my personal preference in this statement, nor I am appealing to any sense of deservingness. I am outlining what happened and stating that it should have happened because it did; i.e., all the conditions existed for it to happen. As such, the empirical 'should' is not the target for change in REBT.

Let me now return to my statement: 'The Holocaust should have happened.' In this statement, I am not saying that this is what I wanted to happen, nor am I saying that this was my recommendation. Furthermore, I am not saying that the Jews deserved their fate, nor am I saying that this is what ideally should have happened. All I am saying is that all the conditions were in place for it to happen – nothing more, nothing less. But, because my statement could have several different meanings, you can be forgiven if you thought that I was saying something very different. Because of this confusion over the meaning of the word 'should', I suggest that whenever possible we qualify the word when we use it and explain exactly what we mean. Thus, in my original statement what I meant was this: Tragically, catastrophically, unforgettably and shockingly, all the conditions were in place nearly sixty years ago for the Holocaust to have occurred, and thus, the Holocaust should have happened because tragically, catastrophically, unforgettably and shockingly, it did.

On thinking the unthinkable

As I have stressed several times, rigid beliefs can be expressed as 'musts', absolute 'shoulds', 'got to's and 'have to's. However they are expressed, they have many deleterious effects. REBT theory has focused a lot of attention on the impact of holding rigid beliefs on the way we feel and act. But it has also, more recently, studied the effects of holding these beliefs on the way that we think. I have referred to these latter effects as the *cognitive consequences* of holding dogmatic 'musts' and absolute 'shoulds'. Thus, with Frank Bond and others, I have discovered that if you hold a dogmatic demand you are much more likely subsequently to make a range of negatively distorted inferences than if you hold a flexible, healthy preference (Bond & Dryden, 1996).

If you hold a dogmatic demand, you are also more likely to develop a pattern of obsessive thinking, if you are so prone, than if you hold a non-dogmatic preference. Let me illustrate this with an actual case which I relate to you with the client's permission, as there is hardly any chance that the person can be identified from what I will tell you now. The two therapeutic factors that I wish to highlight here are counsellor unshockability and the importance of explaining to clients how they unwittingly help to create and elaborate their own obsessions. Without the presence of the former, clients will not disclose the true nature of their obsessions. Without the latter, they will remain scared that they will completely lose control of themselves, a fear that will prevent them from healthily resolving this problem.

This client, who I will call Sally, was a regular churchgoer. She had little sexual education and was a virgin. One day when she was in church her mind wandered and she found herself looking at a statue of Christ and in particular, gazing at Christ's nipples. She was horrified about this, primarily because she held the belief that while she was in church her thoughts had to be thoroughly pure. Given this demand, she tried not to look at the statue, but, typically in such cases, she began to have involuntary unwanted thoughts about the naked Jesus and started to look at Christ's crotch. She redoubled her efforts not to think about and look at Christ in this way, forbidding herself to do so in an absolute fashion. She also went to different churches, hoping that she could leave behind her growing obsession. She could not. At her latest church she began to have fantasies about having sex with Christ, and with every redoubled attempt to banish these thoughts and fantasies, they increased both in number and in vividness of sexual content. When I first saw her, it transpired – for it took her many weeks for her to tell me this – that she had begun to think about having oral sex with Christ while being taken from behind by the local vicar.

Using REBT theory, I helped this woman to understand how her thoughts and images had developed from innocently gazing at Christ's nipples to a scene more at home in the steamy world of explicit adult videos. Her task was to go back to church and to allow herself to think and imagine anything that she thought and imagined. She was to banish nothing from her mind. Of course, I told her it was healthy for her to be strongly desirous of not thinking and imagining such distasteful things, but there was no earthly (or heavenly) reason why she must be free of such cognitive phenomena. I also helped her to see the difference between having so-called shameful thoughts and being a shameful person. In short, I helped her to accept herself as a fallible human being who was not immune from thinking inappropriate and shocking things. It will come as no surprise to you that this woman believed that she always had to say and do the right thing as well as to think the right thoughts. She was a walking example of dogmatic moral correctness. Later in counselling I helped her to join the human race on this issue and surrender her wings.

Parenthetically, after the establishment of a working alliance, the judicious use of humour is particularly therapeutic in such cases. At the end of counselling Sally was back at her old church virtually free of her troubling thoughts. When she gets them she reminds herself of something that I want to leave you with: that sometimes it is therapeutic to go to church and think about giving Christ a blow job while being taken from behind by the local vicar.

Oedipus schmoedipus: why you don't have to gouge your eyes out when you have discovered that you have killed your father and married your mother

Most of you will be familiar with the story of Oedipus. For those of you who are not, let me briefly relate this tragic tale. The *Chambers Biographical Dictionary* (Magnusson, 1990: 1098) states that Oedipus was the

> *Greek legendary figure, who killed his father, Laius, and married his mother, Jocasta . . . An oracle had warned Laius, king of Thebes, that he would be killed by his son. Laius therefore exposed the infant Oedipus to die on the mountains after piercing his feet with a spike (hence the name Oedipus, which in Greek means 'with swollen feet'). The young Oedipus was rescued and adopted by Polybus, king of Corinth, and grew up with the belief that the rulers of Corinth were his parents. When told by an oracle that he was fated to kill his father and marry his mother, he left Corinth in an attempt to avoid fulfilling the prophecy. On his way through Boeotia, he was involved in a quarrel with his (to him unknown) father Laius, and killed him. He freed Thebes from the scourge of the Sphinx by solving her riddles, and in return married the now-widowed Jocasta, his mother, and became king of Thebes. At length, the terrible truth about his origins and parenthood was revealed to him. Jocasta took her life and Oedipus blinded himself.*

As you all know, this tale inspired Sigmund Freud, who coined the term 'Oedipus complex' to describe a young boy's longing to oust his father and have his mother for himself. I want to focus on a different part of the story and argue that Oedipus's act of self-blinding stemmed from an irrational belief. I am going to show you that there was no need for Oedipus to gouge his eyes out and no need for him to feel guilty about what he did.

Let's assume that I was alive at the time and practising REBT and that Oedipus, in an obvious state of disturbance, consulted me. This is how I would have endeavoured to help him.

Windy: OK, Oedipus, what's your problem?
Oedipus: I'm in a terrible state. I have committed two terrible sins.

Windy: What are they?

Oedipus: I've killed my father and married and slept with my mother?

Windy: Did you know that they were your mother and father before you killed the former and married the latter?

Oedipus: No, but that doesn't help me. People have tried to comfort me by reminding me that I didn' t know this, but I still want to gouge my eyes out.

Windy: OK, which crime shall we discuss first?

Oedipus: Let's start with the murder of my father, Laius.

Windy: OK, how do you feel about killing your father?

Oedipus: Very guilty.

Windy: Right. Let me put this into REBT's ABC framework. A, which stands for the activating event, is murdering your father, and C, which stands for your emotional consequence, is guilt.

Oedipus: What's B?

Windy: B stands for the beliefs that you hold about murdering your father which account for your guilt. In REBT, A (i.e. in this case your murdering your father), does not cause C, (i.e. your guilt): B does.

Oedipus: So what are my beliefs?

Windy: Well, let me put forward a couple of hunches and you correct me if I'm wrong. First, I think you are demanding that you absolutely should not have killed your father and second, I think that you believe that you are a thoroughly rotten person for killing him. Am I right?

Oedipus: That's exactly right. But aren't I a rotten person for killing my father?

Windy: Of course not. Let's leave aside for a moment that you didn't know that he was your father and accept that you did a rotten thing. How are you a rotten person for doing this rotten thing?

Oedipus: Well, I killed my father.

Windy: I'm not disputing that. Killing your father was wrong, it was a rotten deed, but how are you rotten through and through for doing this rotten thing?

Oedipus: I guess I'm not.

Windy: Why not?

Oedipus: Because as you say, one rotten deed does not make me rotten through and through.

Windy: That's right. If you were rotten through and through, you could never do anything good, but we know that you freed Thebes from the scourge of the Sphinx. Wasn't that a good deed

Oedipus: Yes it was.

Windy: But if you were a rotten person how could you have done such a noble deed?

Oedipus: You're right, I couldn't.

Windy: So if you aren't a rotten person, what are you?

Oedipus: I'm a fallible human being who can't be rated by my actions. Being fallible means that I can do good deed and bad deeds.

Windy: That's exactly right. Now, it's healthy to feel badly about your bad deeds, and consequently it would be healthy if you were to feel very remorseful about killing your father. But guilt is an unhealthy emotion which could lead you to blind yourself. Is that clear?

Oedipus: So remorse is healthy and guilt isn't.

Windy: That's right, remorse stems from your rational belief and guilt from your irrational belief. Now let's look at the other part of your belief: 'I absolutely shouldn't have killed my father.' Where is the law of the universe that states that you absolutely should not have done that?

Oedipus: Well it was very, very wrong.

Windy: You'll get no argument from me on that score, but being human are you immune from doing very, very, bad acts?

Oedipus: No, I don't have that immunity. But I was warned that I would kill my father. I absolutely should have known what I was doing and refrained from doing it.

Windy: Well, that would have been highly desirable, but does it follow that because it would have been highly desirable that you knew it was your father, therefore you absolutely should have known? Are you an oracle in your spare time?

Oedipus: Point taken.

Windy: And incidentally, if there was a law of the universe forbidding you from killing your father, there's no way that you could have killed him because you would have had to follow that law.

Oedipus: Right, reality should be reality however tragic it is.

Windy: Well put. Now I suggest that you go over these ideas for homework and next week I'll help you to get over your disturbed feelings about marrying your mother.

Oedipus: And also can we deal with my feelings of shame when others view me as an object of disgust?

Windy: We can indeed.

Oedipus: Great. How much do I owe you?

Windy: £85.

Oedipus: That's a small price to pay for saving my eyesight.

Windy: See you and be seen by you next week.

I wish to stress two points from this interchange. First, it is important that I agree with Oedipus that his 'crimes' were heinous. It is fundamental to REBT strategy that I do not try to show him what he already acknowledged, albeit intellectually: that he neither knew his father before he killed him nor knew his mother before he married her. Oedipus will be more open to this type of intervention once he has made strides in accepting himself for his 'crimes'. Second, it is important to distinguish between normal, understandable responses on the one hand and healthy responses on the other. While it is very understandable and statistically normal for Oedipus to condemn himself for his actions, this does not mean that it is healthy for him to do so. If I do not target for change his guilt-producing, self-condemnatory belief, he will remain vulnerable to deliberate self-harm.

Conclusion

In summary, I have discussed why being raped does not disturb you, why the Holocaust should have happened, why it is sometimes therapeutic to think about giving Christ a blow job while being taken from behind by the local vicar, and why it is not necessary to gouge your eyes out after killing your father and marrying your mother.

Before I close, let me provide you with an alternative summary. I have discussed the empowering nature of the ABCs of REBT, but stressed that this framework has to be used with great sensitivity, particularly when clients' activating events are very aversive. I have considered eight different meanings of the word 'should' and stressed the intended therapeutic benefits of differentiating these meanings to avoid the serious problems that can arise from misunderstanding the meaning of the word. I then argued that, when working with clients with obsessive thinking, it is beneficial to explain how thoughts spiral out of our control in direct proportion to our dogmatic attempts to control them and to stress the therapeutic benefits of thinking the unthinkable. Finally, I have discussed the unhealthiness of guilt and shown how to intervene to prevent its sometimes tragic consequences.

Rational Emotive Behaviour Therapy is based on a set of ideas that can be both enlightening and outrageous. I have reviewed some of these ideas and promise to review more in a future volume tentatively titled: *Strange, but Rational.*

References

Bond, F.W., & Dryden, W. (1996). Modifying irrational control and certainty beliefs: clinical recommendations based upon research. In W. Dryden (ed.), *Research in counselling and psychotherapy: practical applications*. London: Sage.

Magnusson, M. (ed.) (1990). *Chambers biographical dictionary*. Edinburgh: Chambers.

CHAPTER 12

UNDERSTANDING PERSONS IN THE CONTEXT OF THEIR PROBLEMS

A rational emotive behaviour therapy perspective

M. Bruch and F. W. Bond (Eds) (1998) *Beyond diagnosis: case formulation approaches in CBT*. Chichester: John Wiley & Sons (pp. 43–64).

While careful assessment of client problems has always been a feature of approaches within the cognitive-behavioural tradition of counselling and psychotherapy, case conceptualisation (also known as case formulation) is a more recent development in the that tradition. While Albert Ellis, the founder of REBT, was excellent at both assessment and case formulation, he rarely wrote at length on the latter topic. The piece that follows was written for an edited volume on case formulation in CBT and, as far as I can tell, was the first extended work on the use of case formulation in REBT.

I have grave reservations about the terms “case formulation” and “case conceptualisation” that are currently in vogue in cognitive–behavioural psychotherapy, and will explain why presently. Why then have I agreed to contribute to this book? For two reasons. First, because I think that coming to an overall understanding of a client in the context of his or her problems can enhance the effectiveness of therapy and second, because having an REBT-oriented contribution to this book will help redress the continuing marginalisation of REBT in the cognitive–behavioural literature.

My fundamental objection to the terms “case formulation” and “case conceptualisation” is that the use of these terms perpetuates the objectification of clients. In short, a complex, unique person is objectified as “a case” and I strongly object to this practice. For this reason, in this chapter, I will speak of understanding the person in the context of his/her problems (UPCP) instead of using the phrase “making a case formulation”. I do not know (or indeed care) whether or not other REBT therapists share my reservation about the terms “case formulation” and “case conceptualisation”. If this book is about nothing else it is about respecting the individuality of persons and as a person who is also an REBT therapist, I claim the same respect for myself. What I bring to this chapter, then, is an idiosyncratic approach to understanding persons (who happen to be clients) in the context of their problems based on REBT principles (Walker, 1997). I will approach this task as follows. First, I will present and discuss the framework that I use for UPCP. Second, I will apply this framework to highlight the work that I did with a particular client that is particularly relevant to the focus of this book. And finally, I will show how my UPCP guided my clinical thinking in treatment planning with a selected client. Let me stress at the outset that I have sought and received the permission of my client to do this as long as salient features of her situation are disguised. I have shown her the first draft of this chapter and she is satisfied with the modifications that I have made to protect her confidentiality.

This is not the place for me to discuss REBT theory in depth (see Dryden, 1994a; Ellis, 1994 for such a discussion). However, in order to understand what follows you will need to understand REBT's ABC assessment framework. Here is a thumbnail sketch of this framework.

"A" refers to the activating events that a person focuses on. These can be (i) actual or inferred; (ii) past, present or future or (iii) external or internal. "B" refers to the beliefs that the person holds about these events. As we will presently see, these beliefs may be irrational/unhealthy or rational/healthy. Finally, "C" refers to the consequences of holding these beliefs. These consequences may be emotional, behavioural and/or cognitive.

Before I consider the factors that need to be considered in developing a UPCP, I want to make the following point about its sequential place in the practice of REBT. Some approaches to cognitive–behaviour therapy consider that it is important to "formulate a case" before making therapeutic interventions. REBT does not advocate this position. Rather, it holds that it is equally possible and sometimes desirable to construct a UPCP after one has taught the client the ABC model of REBT and used this model to help the client with some specific problems. Indeed, I often find that teaching clients the ABC framework helps them to guide my UPCP since they are thus oriented to look for information that I need to formulate such understanding. However, other clients will respond more readily to REBT interventions once they have an overall understanding of themselves in the context of their problems. Thus, REBT adopts a flexible approach to developing a UPCP with respect to when this is done with different clients.

The factors that need to be considered in developing a UPCP

In this section, I will outline and discuss the factors that need to be considered. when understanding a person in the context of his or her problems. While these factors are heavily influenced by REBT theory, I do draw upon other cognitive–behavioural concepts. In the section, I will demonstrate how I developed a UPCP with a client using the factors which I will now discuss in general terms.

Basic information and initial impressions

If you receive referrals from GPs and psychiatrists, you will often receive basic information about clients before meeting them. While this information is second hand, it is important to consider because it will often contain relevant demographic information, family history and a developmental account of the client's past and present problems. If your clients are largely self-referred you will need to gather this information yourself. This information is important to consider in developing a UPCP since it places your client in a wider context.

You will also develop initial impressions when you meet your client and even when you speak on the phone to make an appointment. While you should regard such initial impressions tentatively, they can be useful in helping you to confirm or reject your beginning attempts to formulate a UPCP.

The importance of developing a problem list

I agree with Persons (1989) in her book on "case formulation" in cognitive therapy that it is important to develop a list of the client's problems when one is working to develop a UPCP. This is not an accepted practice in REBT, but I find it to be one of the ways that Beck's cognitive therapy has enhanced my practice as an REBT therapist. I also agree with Persons (1993) that it is useful to have these problems expressed in the client's own words whenever possible unless their words lack the necessary specificity for a working problem list. In this case, the therapist needs to paraphrase these problems in a way that more clearly elucidates them.

Having a clear idea of the range of problems the client wants to work on in therapy at an early stage, rather than working on a problem as soon as the client identifies one (an unfortunate practice, but a common one amongst novice REBT therapists) gives therapy a sensible direction based on an emerging UPCP.

Identifying goals for therapy

I have been very much influenced by Bordin's (1979) tripartite view of the working alliance in my practice of REBT. Bordin argues that one of the hallmarks of effective therapy is that the client and therapist have shared ides about the goals of therapy. However, there is another reason why asking for the client's goals is useful early in therapy. Doing so often reveals quite a lot about the client's problems, unhealthy beliefs and possible obstacles to therapy. Thus, if a client says that one of her therapeutic goals is never to be anxious again, this may reveal something important about her problem, her attitude to being in control (for example) and the likelihood of her becoming disillusioned with therapy (which in this case is very high).

Developing a list of problem emotions (or Cs)

The client's problem list may or may not contain specific information about which problematic emotions the client experiences. If this information is not provided in the problem list, then I find it useful to discover what these problematic emotions are at a fairly early stage of therapy since such a list will provide important clues about other aspects of the client's cognitive–affective–behavioural dynamics.

REBT theory clearly discriminates between healthy negative emotions (HNEs)—such as concern, sadness, healthy anger, remorse, disappointment, sorrow, healthy envy and healthy jealousy—and their unhealthy counterparts. These unhealthy negative emotions (UNEs) are anxiety, depression, unhealthy anger, guilt, shame, hurt, unhealthy envy and unhealthy jealousy.

At an early stage of therapy I like to know which of these UNEs are involved in my client's problems. I refer to these as the client's problem emotions. These occur at "C" in the ABC framework.

Developing a list of problematic critical As

As I mentioned earlier, As represent activating events in the ABC framework. In particular, REBT therapists are keen to identify those As about which clients disturb themselves. These are known as critical As (Dryden, 1995). These are best identified when the client's unhealthy negative emotions are known. There are twelve major ways of identifying critical As (see Dryden, 1995, for a discussion of these methods). In striving to develop an accurate UPCP, it is important to identify broad categories of critical As. Examples of these general categories are: disapproval, injustice, failure and uncertainty.

REBT therapists generally begin therapy by working on specific examples of client problems. However, in developing an accurate UPCP, I tend to ask a client who has identified a specific example of disapproval, for example, to what extent he experiences difficulties in dealing with disapproval in other areas of his life. For the purposes of developing a UPCP, I work from the specific to the general on each specific problem the client identifies.

Identifying core irrational/unhealthy beliefs

According to REBT theory, four irrational or unhealthy beliefs lie at the centre of psychological problems. These four beliefs are known as demandingness, awfulising, low frustration tolerance and depreciation of self, others and life conditions. In REBT practice, with its early focus on specific client problems, the therapist tends to identify specific irrational beliefs. However, as I have already mentioned, in working to develop an accurate UPCP, I tend to move quickly from the specific to the general in an attempt to gain an overall understanding of the range of my client's problems. Thus, I endeavour to discover which of the client's specific irrational beliefs are representative of more general core irrational beliefs. Identifying core irrational beliefs (which are unhealthy beliefs that the client holds in a variety of situations) tends to accompany attempts to identify general problem emotional Cs and general categories of problem–critical As.

In identifying core irrational/unhealthy beliefs, I strive to understand whether these beliefs reflect ego disturbance or non-ego disturbance. Basically, self-depreciation beliefs are a distinguishing feature of ego-disturbance and LFT and awfulising beliefs are distinguishing features of non-ego disturbance where self-depreciation beliefs are either absent or peripheral. As I have discussed elsewhere identifying demands on their own do not help the REBT therapist to judge whether the client's problem is an example of ego disturbance or non-ego disturbance (Dryden, 1996a).

Identifying dysfunctional behavioural Cs

Dysfunctional behavioural Cs are either actions or tendencies to act which accompany unhealthy negative emotions. As I have shown elsewhere (Dryden, 1995), certain classes of actions and action tendencies (defined as tendencies to act which may or may not be transformed into overt actions) accompany specific unhealthy negative emotions. While there are recurring actions and action tendencies which accompany specific UNEs, in developing a UPCP I am keen to identify the client's idiosyncratic dysfunctional behavioural Cs. These responses tend to be consistent with the UNEs and the unhealthy, irrational beliefs that underpin them.

Identifying the purposive nature of dysfunctional behaviour

REBT theory owes a debt to the work of Alfred Adler and the latter day Adlerians in that it recognises that behaviour can be purposive. My own work in developing a UPCP leads me to ask the person whether his or her dysfunctional behaviour helps:

1 to initiate an emotional state;
2 to stop an emotional state;
3 to avoid an emotional state;

4 to reduce the intensity of an emotional state;
5 to intensify an emotional state;
6 to maintain emotional state;
7 to elicit a response from the physical environment;
8 to elicit a response from the interpersonal environment or;
9 to act in a way that is consistent with personal values, standards and goals.

Identifying ways in which the person prevents or cuts short the experience of problems

It is a feature of human beings that because we find our problems painful, we are strongly motivated to prevent ourselves from experiencing them. We are also similarly motivated to cut short our problems once we have begun to experience them. In developing a UPCP, I actively probe clients to discover their idiosyncratic ways of preventing the onset of problems or cutting them short once they have begun to be experienced.

Without an understanding of these two categories of client functioning, I am disadvantaged in my planning of REBT treatment strategies.

Identifying ways in which the person compensates for problems

It also happens that clients may function in ways that help them to compensate for having their problems. A common example of such compensatory behaviour was identified by Adler (1927) who showed that striving for superiority can often be a compensation for feelings of inferiority. This mechanism and the two described above represents the client's "protective shell" which serves to protect the client from the unhealthy psychological pain that he would feel if he experienced the full impact of his problems.

Identifying meta-emotional problems

REBT theory has for many years held that people frequently experience meta-emotional problems, i.e. they experience emotional problems about their emotional problems. Thus, I want to find out how clients feel about each of their problem emotions. As I have discussed elsewhere (Dryden, 1990a), the presence of meta-emotional problems complicates the work that my client and I will do on their original problems. Identifying meta-emotional problems helps me to understand the type of obstacles I may experience in my work with the client's original problems. Such understanding helps me to plan to circumvent these obstacles.

Identifying the cognitive consequences of core irrational/unhealthy beliefs

In the ABC framework, "C" not only stands for the emotional and behavioural consequences of holding beliefs at B, it also stands for the cognitive consequences of these beliefs. When a person holds unhealthy, irrational beliefs then she tends to think in ways that are overly negative and distorted (Bond & Dryden, 1996). These cognitive consequences are generally inferential in nature and often serve as new "As" in subsequent ABC episodes. Furthermore, REBT theory holds that people implicitly bring their irrational or unhealthy beliefs to events at "A" with the result that these beliefs influence the inferences that are made at "A". Thus, a person who believes that he must succeed perfectly at important tasks brings this belief to performance-based situations, and may conclude that he has failed when objectively he can be said to have performed well, but not perfectly well, at the task in question.

In developing a UPCP, I look carefully at the cognitive consequences of irrational or unhealthy beliefs and see how they relate to inferences that the person makes in problem situations.

Identifying the manner of problem expression and the interpersonal responses to these expressions

It is a truism to say that people are social beings, but this can often be forgotten when one focuses on cognitive phenomena and, to a lesser extent, behavioural phenomena. When a client experiences a problem, I want to know how she expresses this when in the presence of others. Does she ask others for reassurance when she is anxious or does she put on a "brave face", for example?

Once I have discovered the client's routine ways of expressing her problems to others, I endeavour to identify how these others respond to these problem expressions. Do they, for example, offer reassurance when the client asks for it? And if the client puts on a "brave face", do others notice this and if so how do they respond? REBT is an interpersonal-oriented therapy, but this feature has not received as much attention in the REBT literature as it warrants. An understanding of the client's interpersonal world, as it is relevant to her problems, is important in two ways. First, this knowledge helps me to decide how much attention I need to place on helping the client to communicate her problems more functionally and second, it alerts me to the possible inclusion of one or more of the client's significant others in therapy.

Identifying the client's health and medication status

Clients are not only psychological beings, they are also biological beings and as part of developing a UPCP, it is important to understand their health and medical status. Thus, I want to know what their general health is like and whether or not they have any illnesses that may impact on their psychological problems.

I want to know whether or not they are currently taking medication, the daily dose of any such medication and their attitude towards taking these drugs. In addition, I determine whether or not their psychological symptoms warrant further psychiatric or physical investigations. Thus, some clients show biological signs of severe depression and are not currently on psychotropic medication. In these cases I refer the clients for a psychiatric evaluation.

Developing an understanding of relevant predisposing factors

As I have mentioned elsewhere (Dryden, 1996b), REBT does not have an elaborate theory of the acquisition of psychological disturbance. It argues that people are not disturbed by events, but bring their tendencies to disturb themselves to events. This being said, it is useful in developing one's UPCP to identify the predisposing factors that may have contributed to the origin of the client's problems.

The difference between contributory events (or what I call critical As) and predisposing factors is as follows. Contributory events are current events which trigger the client's unhealthy, irrational beliefs that underpin current problems, whereas predisposing events are usually past events which influenced (but did not cause) the development of his irrational beliefs. Predisposing factors are usually similar in theme to critical As.

Predicting the person's likely responses to therapy

I agree with Persons (1993) who argues that an important feature of her case formulation approach to cognitive therapy is to use this formulation to help her predict the client's likely response to therapy. I attempt to do this as well by drawing upon (i) the UPCP; (ii) the person's previous attempts to solve problems, including her utilisation of previous therapy and (iii) the person's interpersonal and learning styles as these are relevant to the therapy situation.

Negotiating a narrative account of the UPCP for consideration with the client

I also agree with Persons (1993) that it can be helpful to put one's UPCP in narrative form to the client for consideration, feedback and refinement. Sometimes I do this in writing, particularly when the UPCP is complex, but more often I do this verbally. Like Persons, I see the UPCP as fluid and open to refinement at any point in therapy. A rigid adherence to one's UPCP is not only bad therapy, it is also against the flexible nature of REBT.

Let me now show how I developed a UPCP with a particular client.

UPCP in action

Basic information and initial impression

Jane Smith was at the time I saw her a 36 year old single woman who was referred to me after a brief hospitalisation for anxiety and depression. The referral letter from her psychiatrist mentioned that she worked as a nursing sister in a rehabilitation unit and that she was regarded as a model practitioner and administrator. Jane had two younger brothers and her parents were still alive and constantly looked to her for emotional support. She was generally regarded as the strong person in the family and her two younger brothers often used her as a counsellor when life became too stressful for them. This was her first hospitalisation and she had no previous recorded history of psychological problems. She smoked thirty cigarettes a day, drank three units of alcohol a week and had no experience of taking mood-altering drugs.

When she called me to make an appointment she was very keen to know how long therapy would last. While this is a reasonable request for a client to make of a therapist (Dryden & Feltham, 1995), I was struck by the insistence with which Jane made her enquiries. I very much agree with Persons (1993) that all client communications are grist for the UPCP mill and while REBT and CBT therapists do not analyse their clients' every utterance for deeper meaning, as may be true of some of our more enthusiastic psychoanalytic colleagues, we certainly have our eyes and ears open for information which may help us to deepen our UPCP. Rather than develop a specific, albeit tenuous hypothesis about what Jane's insistence might mean, I noted the experience as potentially valuable for my UPCP.

Jane's problem list

I helped Jane to develop the following list of problems that she wanted to address in therapy. I should make clear that most of these items were developed in the first two sessions, but others were added as therapy proceeded.

1 unable to control my feelings;
2 overwhelmed with the demands of my job;
3 unable to say no to people in my work and in my personal life;
4 having to put on a brave face with people;
5 unable to commit myself to men;
6 afraid of falling in love;
7 unable to show weakness;
8 afraid of feeling anxious and depressed;
9 scared of falling apart;
10 expecting those I am close to to know how I feel without my having to tell them;
11 expecting others to know that I am stretched and not add to my burden.

Jane's goals for therapy

Jane's goals for therapy were as follows:

1 to be able control my feelings;
2 to develop healthy boundaries at work and in my personal life;
3 to be able to say no to people in my work and in my personal life;
4 to be honest about my feelings with people;
5 to be able to commit myself to men;
6 to allow myself to fall in love;
7 to be able to show weakness;
8 to deal constructively with feeling anxious and depressed;
9 to allow myself to feel out of control without being so scared of it;
10 not to expect those close to me to know how I feel if I don't tell them;
11 not to expect others to know when I am stretched if I don't tell them.

Jane's list of problem emotions (or Cs)

Jane identified the following emotions as being problematic for her:

1 anxiety;
2 depression;
3 shame;
4 guilt;
5 hurt;
6 unhealthy anger.

Jane's problematic critical As

Jane identified the following critical As as being problematic for her:

1 when I am not in control of my feelings;
2 when I am asked to take on more responsibility at work when I am stretched;

3 letting people down at work and in my personal life;
4 when I am asked if I feel all right when I am under stress;
5 if a man who I like asks me out;
6 thinking about being in a love relationship;
7 when I do not feel strong emotionally;
8 when I watch TV programmes when people have emotional problems;
9 when those close to me do not understand how I feel without my having to tell them.

Jane's core irrational/unhealthy beliefs

I helped Jane to identify her core irrational beliefs, by first helping her to analyse a number of specific ABCs and detecting a number of her specific irrational beliefs. I then took these specific irrational beliefs and asked Jane to consider to what extent she held these beliefs in other relevant situations. In particular, I asked her to use the items on her list of problematic critical As as a guide. In this way Jane and I developed the following list of her core irrational or unhealthy beliefs. In presenting these beliefs I have indicated which is an example of ego disturbance and which of non-ego disturbance.

1 I must be able to cope with anything that life throws at me and if I do not, I am a weak, defective person (ego disturbance belief).
2 I must feel in control and it is terrible if I don't have this feeling (nonego disturbance belief).
3 I must not appear to be weak to others and if I do, I am a weak defective person (ego disturbance belief).
4 I must have the approval of others and if I do not this means that I am inadequate (ego disturbance belief).
5 I must not be badly treated by others and if I am I can't bear it (nonego disturbance belief).

Jane's dysfunctional behavioural Cs

The following is a list of Jane's dysfunctional behavioural Cs grouped by her problem emotions:

1 When Jane feels anxious, she tends to:

  (a) smoke;
  (b) praise people who she thinks may disapprove of her;
  (c) hold on to things to steady herself;
  (d) distract herself with work-related activity.

2 When Jane feels depressed, she tends to:

  (a) smoke;
  (b) withdraw from others;
  (c) eat junk food.

3 When Jane feels ashamed, she tends to:

  (a) smoke;
  (b) withdraw from others.

4 When Jane feels guilty, she tends to:

(a) smoke;
(b) withdraw from others;
(c) blame herself in the presence of others.

5 When Jane feels hurt, she tends to:

(a) smoke;
(b) sulk.

6 When Jane feels unhealthily angry, she tends to:

(a) smoke;
(b) bang doors.

The purposive nature of Jane's dysfunctional behaviour

Jane's dysfunctional behavioural Cs served three major purposes:

1 To gain a sense of control

(a) smoking;
(b) holding on to things to steady herself;
(c) withdrawing from others;
(d) distracting herself with work-related activity;
(e) sulking.

2 To get rid of disturbing feelings

(a) smoking;
(b) withdrawing from others;
(c) distracting herself with work-related activity;
(d) eating junk food
(e) banging doors.

3 To ward off or neutralise interpersonal threat

(a) praising people who she thinks may disapprove of her;
(b) withdrawing from others;
(c) blaming herself in the presence of others.

How Jane prevents or cuts short the experience of her problems

In my work with Jane, I identified a number of ways in which she prevented or cut short the experience of her problems. While some of these methods are the same as those employed by Jane in the sections on irrational / unhealthy beliefs and dysfunctional behavioural Cs, the difference is that in those sections all the methods were behavioural in nature and were brought into play when Jane experienced the full force of her problems and associated feelings, while in this section the methods employed by Jane were a mixture of cognitive and behavioural and they were brought into play either to prevent the onset of her problems or to cut them short as soon as they had begun to be experienced.

Here are the methods that Jane employed to prevent or cut short the experience of her problems and associated feelings:

1 Behavioural

(a) smoking;
(b) withdrawing;
(c) immersing herself in work-related activities;
(d) volunteering for activities;
(e) agreeing to do whatever is asked of her at work;
(f) contacting others who have problems and helping them with these problems;
(g) going to the gym to work out;
(h) telling others who show concern for her that she is fine;
(i) turning down the offer of dates from men whom she finds attractive.

2 Cognitive

(a) imagining times when she felt strong and in control;
(b) thinking that she is tired or physically ill rather than emotionally disturbed;
(c) planning reorganisations at work;

How Jane compensates for her problems

The following are ways that Jane compensates for her problems:

1 taking on more work
2 being strong for others
3 teaching stress management classes at work
4 applying to join the Samaritans

Jane's meta-emotional problems

As discussed above, meta-emotional problems are emotional problems that the person has about her original problems. Here is a list of Jane's meta-emotional problems:

1 shame about not coping and feeling depressed;
2 anxiety about feeling anxious and not "feeling in control";
3 anger at herself for needing the approval of others.

The cognitive consequences of Jane's core irrational/unhealthy beliefs

The following are the cognitive consequences of Jane's core irrational/unhealthy beliefs. I have listed these under each core irrational belief.

1 I must be able to cope with anything that life throws at me and if I do not, I am a weak, defective person (ego disturbance belief)

(a) thinking that others will disapprove of me if I let them know that I am not coping;
(b) thinking of my emotional problems as weaknesses;
(c) when I am feeling out of control, seeing others as strong and myself as weak.

2 I must feel in control and it is terrible if I don't have this feeling (nonego disturbance belief)

(a) failing to acknowledge that I am under stress;
(b) when I do acknowledge that I am under stress, overestimating the chances that I will lose control and the degree of loss of control that I will experience;
(c) thinking that there are only two positions: being in full control or being out of control;
(d) underestimating my ability to cope with slight or moderate loss of control.

3 I must not appear to be weak to others and if I do, I am a weak defective person (ego disturbance belief)

(a) overestimating the negative consequences of "appearing weak" to others (e.g. being reprimanded at work or losing my job);
(b) overestimating the degree to which others view one negatively.

4 I must have the approval of others and if I do not this means that I am inadequate (ego disturbance belief)

(a) overestimating the amount of disapproval that I will experience from others;
(b) viewing objectively neutral responses from others as signs of disapproval;
(c) thinking that when others give me a positive response it is not honestly meant and that they have an ulterior motive. This is articularly the case when I do not think that I deserve the positive response;
(d) thinking that when I show a "weakness" in public everyone will notice and look down on me.

5 I must not be badly treated by others and if I am I can't bear it (nonego disturbance belief)

(a) thinking that if others treat me badly then I must have done something really bad to warrant it and will get into serious trouble as a result;
(b) thinking that if others profess to care about me, then they will be able to tell when I am under stress and treat me appropriately.

Jane's manner of problem expression and the interpersonal responses to these expressions

Jane's way of dealing with her problems was basically to internalise them. Since she was very adept at hiding her feelings and erecting a facade of being strong and coping, others did not realise that she was experiencing problems. Since she cultivated and successfully communicated an "I am strong" persona, people at work continually came to her with their problems and asked her to take on difficult problems because they were sure that she would be able to cope.

In her personal life it was a similar story. Jane was known in her family and among her friends as a "veritable rock" who could take everything that life could throw at her "and then some" as one of her friends put it. She was also known to be a good listener and to offer sound advice if needed. Consequently, her family and friends would seek her out if they had problems which was quite often. Since they saw her as a "veritable rock" it rarely occurred to any of her family or friends to enquire about her well-being other than a cursory "how are you?" Even when she was under extreme stress she used to answer such queries with an automatic "I'm fine". Later in therapy Jane and I humorously referred to this as meaning, "I'm Fragile, Insecure, Nervous and Edgy!"

Establishing Jane's health and medication status

Jane's health was generally good apart from periodic bouts of bronchitis exacerbated by smoking. The referring psychiatrist had not prescribed any medication for Jane's anxiety and depression partly because he did not think that her symptoms were severe enough after her discharge from hospital and partly because Jane was not keen to take drugs. This was not surprising given her core irrational belief that she had to be in control.

Jane's relevant predisposing factors

As I mentioned earlier, predisposing factors are of importance in my UPCP in helping to explain the past context for the development of the client's unhealthy irrational beliefs. They differ from contributory events in that the latter are present events which trigger her presently held irrational beliefs that underpin her current problems. I call these contributory events, critical As. Critical As (or contributory events) are usually similar in theme to predisposing factors.

Jane's predisposing factors were as follows.

1 From quite a young age, Jane's parents looked to her for her emotional support. This intensified as her two younger brothers grew up and began misbehaving both within the family and outside. In addition, Jane's brothers always looked up to her and frequently sought guidance from her. These predisposing factors were influential in leading Jane to see herself as the strong one in the family and the others as needing support. Early in therapy, Jane remarked that she developed the idea fairly early on that she had to be strong or the family would fall apart. REBT theory argues that these predisposing factors explain why Jane developed a keen desire to be strong, but we also have to take into account Jane's understandable human tendency to transform this strong desire into a devout demand.
2 From Jane's account it seems as if her parents compensated for their own problems and vulnerabilities by deriding others outside the family for being weak. Jane reported that for as long as she can remember, she had two beliefs about emotional vulnerability. First, it was to be despised as it proved that the person was weak, spineless and defective. This was the attitude that Jane developed towards herself and, to a lesser extent, to people that she didn't know. Second, when people in her family and those whom she knew showed that they were struggling to cope, they were to be understood and helped. This view contributed to Jane's compensatory strategy of proving to herself that she was strong by helping others who were not. She would not have helped them if she had despised them.

REBT theory argues that Jane introjected (i.e. believed without question) her parents' views about weakness and about some of those who display it and actively carried these ideas into her adult life.

It may be that Jane was temperamentally suited to be active and helpful to others, a factor which also has to taken into account when developing a UPCP. REBT theory has a bio-social view of the development and maintenance of psychological problems and does not only look for environmental predisposing factors but also for biologically based ones.

Predicting Jane's likely response to therapy

Given what I knew about Jane, I predicted that she would respond to therapy as follows:

1 Since one of Jane's core problems concerned "feeling" out of control and her need to be in charge, I predicted that she would be attracted to REBT because of its emphasis on self-help and its preference for forming egalitarian, adult-adult therapeutic relationships between client and therapist. Furthermore, investigations of her learning style indicated a good fit between her orientation towards independent learning and REBT.
2 However, since she abhorred the idea of not being in emotional control, being in therapy could be a constant reminder of her defectiveness about being weak. If this shame-based belief became strongly activated, then Jane might be tempted to terminate therapy prematurely. In any event, her cognitive dynamics would suggest that she would want a brief therapeutic contract. Corroborating evidence for this came from Jane's initial contact with me by telephone. If you recall, I was struck by her insistence to know how long therapy would last before we had even met.

Negotiating a narrative account of the UPCP with Jane

The following is a narrative account of my understanding of Jane in the context of her problems. The account is one that has been refined by the client and appears in the first person at the request of the client herself.

> My main problem is that I have a rigid attitude about being strong. This attitude leads me to be scared of losing control emotionally and to feel ashamed if I can't cope. I also need others to approve of me and think that they will not do so if I show that I can't cope and if they were to learn that I have emotional problems. In particular, this has meant that I have shied away from committing myself to men I like because I fear that they will reject me if they see the real me.
>
> The roots of these problems go back to the role that I took on in my family. I was seen as, and took on the role of, the strong one in the family and concluded that I had to be strong to keep the family from disintegrating. I need to rethink this role if I am to look after myself.
>
> I have developed a number of strategies to prevent myself from confronting what I see as my weak side. First, I take on too much work. This has the effect of leading me to feel overly stressed, but I do it to prove to myself and others that I can cope. Second, I feel strong when others turn to me for help even though it adds to my burden and creates more problems than it solves. Third, I have developed a number of ways to gain a sense of control and get rid of disturbed feelings. I recognise that these strategies don't work for me in the long term. Fourth, I have developed a number of ways of getting approval, but again these ways don't work for me in the long term.
>
> I recognise that I need to accept myself as a person who has strengths and weaknesses, and to tolerate feeling stressed long enough to deal with these feelings in more productive ways than I have managed at present. In particular, I need to develop healthy boundaries at work and in my personal life and to honestly admit to myself and others that I can't be strong all the time. I also

> need to take risks with people and particularly with men and to get over my fear of being rejected by them.
>
> While I want to help myself as quickly as possible, I recognise that therapy will take longer than this and I need to guard against bringing my "need to be strong" patterns to therapy.

You will note that while this narrative summary is fairly complete, it does not contain all the above elements of the UPCP. The purpose of the narrative summary is to paint a picture of the client's main problems and relevant associated factors rather than to include everything.

Before I discuss using the UPCP as a guide to therapy with Jane, let me say a few words about the relationship between the UPCP and psychiatric diagnosis. Basically, my view is the same as Persons' (1993) who has said that a psychiatric diagnosis may be useful for communicating with other clinicians, but it is insufficient for detailed treatment planning because it fails to describe the person's mechanisms underlying his or her problems in sufficient depth. It also fails to include the breadth of a person's problems. I also think that a psychiatric diagnosis unwittingly increases the risk that the client will become objectified and become equated with his diagnosis. In this vein, I frequently hear people described as "borderlines", for example. As I mentioned at the beginning of this chapter, I am passionately against anything that objectifies persons who seek therapeutic help and thus, I do not employ psychiatric classification systems such as the DSM-IV in thinking about my clients and as an aid to treatment planning and therapeutic intervention. It is for these reasons that I choose not to speculate about Jane's psychiatric diagnosis.

Using UPCP as a guide to therapeutic intervention with Jane

In this concluding section, I will show how I used the UPCP to guide my thinking about selecting therapeutic strategies and techniques with Jane. I will not discuss what I actually did with Jane in therapy since this falls outside the scope of this chapter; rather, I will outline briefly my therapeutic intentions and clinical thinking.

I believe that it is important to be explicit with clients about my clinical thinking so that I can involve them fully in therapy. I thus view therapy as a partnership between myself as therapist and my client. This view is particularly important in the work that I plan to do with Jane because my UPCP led me to conclude that she is likely to terminate therapy prematurely in that being in therapy is likely to be interpreted by her as evidence that she cannot cope and this will trigger her core irrational belief that she must be able to cope and if she doesn't, she is defective. As I noted above, one of Jane's characteristic ways of cutting short the experience of shame that accompanies the activation of this core irrational belief was withdrawal from other people, expressed here by terminating therapy prematurely. I plan to raise this issue with Jane early on in therapy and to check with her if she had such thoughts about cancelling sessions, for example.

As I have just expressed, it is my practice to involve clients in treatment planning. This does not preclude me from offering them my views about how we might best proceed. In this way, I strive to develop and maintain an effective working alliance between my clients and myself (Bordin, 1979). I thus plan to raise with Jane the possibility of working initially on her meta-emotional problems so that she can begin to accept herself as a fallible human being who has strengths and weaknesses and so that she can begin to tolerate more effectively the experience of being out of control without being overwhelmed by such experiences.

Early on in therapy, I plan to use bibliotherapy and I will suggest that Jane read one or two of the self-help books that I have written based on REBT principles. For example, I will probably recommend that she should read my book entitled *Ten Steps to Positive Living* (Dryden, 1994b) which is a step-by step guide to basic REBT principles. Later, I may suggest that she reads *Overcoming Shame* (Dryden, 1997) and certain key chapters from *Beating the Comfort Trap* (Dryden & Gordon, 1993) which focuses on non-ego disturbance problems.

This reading and the cognitive work that I imagine we will do in early sessions will underpin the behavioural changes that I will encourage Jane to make. For example, I plan to help Jane to begin to say no to unreasonable requests to take on extra workload and to withdraw from the role of being counsellor to her family members. This behavioural work will also be preceded by my helping her to challenge her core irrational belief about being approved.

In disputing her core irrational beliefs I plan to make liberal use of therapist self-disclosure. Thus, I plan to share instances of how I struggled with similar core irrational beliefs to Jane's, how I challenged these beliefs and the difference that changing these beliefs made to my own life. The reason why I think such self-disclosure may be particularly potent with Jane is that it will serve to equalise the relationship between us and ensure that her shame-based beliefs about being weak for having problems do not interfere with therapy. In using therapist self-disclosure it is very important to monitor the impact that these disclosures have on the client If it transpires that Jane reacts negatively to the first instance of such disclosure then I would not persist with this type of intervention (Dryden, 1990b).

As Jane makes progress in tolerating her feelings of not coping, I plan to encourage her to desist from using the strategies she employs to prevent, cut short and get rid of feelings of being out of control. In doing so, she will be able to use cognitive disputing of core irrational beliefs that I will have taught her before encouraging her to let go of these counterproductive strategies.

Then, I plan to teach her the effects that her core irrational beliefs have on her subsequent thinking and show her how she thereby creates many of her critical As. Once she has accepted and understood this point, I plan to encourage her to share with others when she is feeling vulnerable and to take risks in her relationships with attractive men. In addition, I plan to help her to challenge any negatively distorted inferences that remain. This last point is in keeping with REBT theory which states that it is important to challenge and change irrational beliefs at B before challenging and changing inferences at A. However, this sequence is not a rigid one and if it needs to be reversed in Jane's case, I will not hesitate to help her to correct some of her distorted inferences before working with her to replace her irrational beliefs with rational ones.

Conclusion

REBT therapists have written extensively on general strategies and techniques that can be used with a broad range of clients (Grieger & Boyd, 1980; Wessler & Wessler, 1980) and have been very explicit about how to work with clients on specific problems (Dryden, 1990a). However, there is a dearth of material in the REBT literature on how to understand clients in the context of their problems and how this understanding may inform the development of individualised treatment plans. It is my hope that this chapter will encourage other REBT therapists to take this important clinical topic further.

References

Adler, A. (1927) *The Practice and Theory of Individual Psychology*. New York: Harcourt, Brace.

Bond, F.W., & Dryden, W. (1996) Modifying irrational control and certainty beliefs: Clinical recommendations based upon research. In W. Dryden (ed.), *Research in Counselling and Psychotherapy: Practical Applications*. London: Sage.

Bordin, E.S. (1979) The generalizability of the psychoanalytic concept of the working alliance. *Psychotherapy: Theory, Research and Practice*, 16(3), 252–260.

Dryden, W. (1990a) *Rational–Emotive Counselling in Action*. London: Sage.

Dryden, W. (1990b) Self-disclosure in rational-emotive therapy. In G. Stricker and M. Fisher (eds), *Self-disclosure in the Therapeutic Relationship*. New York: Plenum.

Dryden, W. (1994a) *Invitation to Rational–Emotive Psychology*. London: Whurr.

Dryden, W. (1994b) *Ten Steps to Positive Living*. London: Sheldon.

Dryden, W. (1995) *Preparing for Client Change*. London: Whurr.

Dryden, W. (1996a) *Inquiries in Rational Emotive Behaviour Therapy*. London: Sage.

Dryden, W. (1996b) Rational emotive behaviour therapy. In W. Dryden (ed.), *Handbook of Individual Therapy*. London: Sage.

Dryden, W. (1997). *Overcoming Shame*. London: Sheldon.

Dryden, W. & Feltham, C. (1995). *Counselling and Psychotherapy: A Consumer's Guide*. London: Sheldon.

Dryden, W. & Gordon, J. (1993) *Beating the Comfort Trap*. London: Sheldon.

Ellis, I. (1994) *Reason and Emotion in Psychotherapy. Revised and Updated*. New York: Birch Lane Press.

Grieger, R. & Boyd, J. (1980) *Rational–Emotive Therapy: A Skills-based Approach*. New York: Van Nostrand Reinhold.

Persons, J. (1989). *Cognitive Therapy in Practice: A Case Formulation Approach*. New York: Norton.

Persons, J. (1993). Case conceptualization in cognitive-behavior therapy. In K.T. Kuehlwein and H. Rosen (eds), *Cognitive Therapies in Action: Evolving Innovative Practice*. San Francisco: Jossey-Bass.

Walker, A.P. (1997) Managing counter-transference and achieving appropriate self-disclosure: A new model from REBT. Workshop held at the annual UKCP conference (July).

Wessler, R.A. & Wessler, R.L. *The Principles and Practice of Rational–Emotive Therapy*. San Francisco: Jossey-Bass.

CHAPTER 13

MY IDIOSYNCRATIC PRACTICE OF REBT

Romanian Journal of Cognitive and Behavioral Psychotherapies, 1(1): 17–30 (2001)

I have been an REBT therapist since 1978 and have trained numerous therapists in REBT in many countries across the world. I observed quite early on that different REBT therapists practise REBT in different ways. When I was invited by Dan David, editor of the *Romanian Journal of Cognitive and Behavioural Psychotherapies*, to contribute a piece to the inaugural issue of the journal. I used this as an opportunity to reflect on what I termed "my idiosyncratic practice of REBT".

What sometimes happens with me is that such a piece serves as the germ of an idea for a larger project and this was the case here. (Another example of this occurred later when I was going to write an article on the distinctive features of REBT, an idea that turned into a book (Dryden, 2009) and then a book series called 'The CBT Distinctive Features' series published by Routledge.) I decided to invite other REBT therapists to write on their idiosyncratic practice of REBT and the book was published a year after the journal publication of the piece that follows (Dryden, 2002). The publishers of this book (PCCS Books) were also taken with the concept of 'idiosyncratic practice' and commissioned Suzanne Keys (2003) to edit a book on the idiosyncratic practice of person-centred therapy.

References

Dryden, W. (Ed.). (2002). *Idiosyncratic rational emotive behaviour therapy.* Ross-on-Wye: PCCS Books.

Dryden, W. (2009). *Rational emotive behaviour therapy: distinctive features.* Hove, East Sussex: Routledge.

Keys, S. (Ed.) (2003). *Idiosyncratic person-centred therapy: from the personal; to the universal.* Ross-on-Wye: PCCS Books.

Abstract

In this article, I concentrate on my idiosyncratic practice of Rational Emotive Behavior Therapy (REBT) and outline the reasons why I practise it in the way that I do. In particular, I discuss the importance of: (a) developing relationships with clients based on the principle of "informed allies"; (b) developing a "case conceptualisation" with complex "cases"; (c) developing an REBT-influenced problem and goals list with clients; (d) working with specific examples of target problems at the beginning of therapy; (e) identifying the critical "A" in the assessment process; (f) focusing on thinking "Cs" as well as emotional and behavioural "Cs"; (g) helping clients to develop and rehearse the full version of rational beliefs; (h) encouraging clients to voice their doubts, reservations and objections to REBT concepts and therapeutic process; (i) deliberately instructing clients in the skills of REBT; (j) encouraging clients to take responsibility for their change process; (k) using vivid methods to promote change; and (l) using humour to develop rapport and promote change. While this list of modes of practice is not designed to be an exhaustive account of my REBT practice, it is meant to indicate what I particularly emphasize with clients from an REBT perspective.

Introduction

To those outside the cognitive-behavioural therapeutic tradition, all cognitive behavioral therapies (CBT) appear the same. This, of course, is far from the truth and while CBT approaches share some important similarities, they also differ from one another in other important ways (c.f. Dobson, 2001). For example, while Rational Emotive Behaviour Therapy (REBT) is similar to Beck's Cognitive Therapy in some respects, it differs from it in others (Dryden, 1984; Haaga & Davison, 1991).

When we consider a specific CBT approach like REBT are we on safe ground in assuming that all REBT therapists practice REBT in the same way? The answer is: it depends. Thus, Robb, Backx, and Thomas (1999) found in their survey sample of REBT therapists on the Albert Ellis Institute referral list that when faced with clients who articulated the insight problem (i.e., "It makes sense, but I don't really believe it yet"), therapists generally responded with cognitive interventions. Warren and McLellarn (1987), in their earlier survey of the same listed therapists, found that "most RE[B]T therapists follow the philosophies and practices of RE[B]T as espoused and advocated by Ellis" (p.71). However, they also found that a "significant number of therapists .... disagree with Ellis in some of his philosophical views and appeared to adapt the practice of RE[B]T to their own preferred style" (p.71). On the latter point, Warren and McLellarn found that 36% of their sample reported using irrational belief inventories as an assessment procedure; 56% reported using rational role reversal with 38% of clients; and 46% suggest that their clients (38%) listen to audiotapes of therapy sessions as a homework assignment.

Given that REBT therapists do seem to practise REBT in different ways, while at the same time concurring on some of its main theories and practices, we need to know more about individual differences among REBT practitioners. In this article, then, I will take the lead and outline my own practice of REBT, focusing particularly on what I emphasize in my practice and why I do so. Space considerations mean that I am unable to discuss any of these points in depth and I will rarely have an opportunity to detail ***how*** I make the interventions I discuss (see Dryden, 1999; Dryden, Neenan, & Yankura, 1999 for a more detailed discussion on these points).

Developing relationships with clients based on the principle of "informed allies"

Although REBT employs a variety of cognitive, emotive, imaginal and behavioural techniques (Ellis & Dryden, 1997), it needs to be stressed that these techniques are used within the context of a therapeutic relationship and as such the development, maintenance and ending of this relationship needs to be considered. It is my view that the REBT literature has tended to underplay the importance of this relationship, a trend that I have tried to counterbalance in some of my own writings (Dryden, 1999; Dryden, 2001). In these writings and in my own practice of REBT, I emphasise a concept that I have called the principle of "informed allies". This concept comprises the principle of ***informed consent*** and the tri-partite idea of the working alliance first introduced by Bordin (1979) which I first introduced into the REBT literature in the late 1980s (Dryden, 1987). Bordin's conceptualisation of the working alliance highlights the therapeutic ***bond*** that develops between therapist and client, the ***goals*** of the enterprise and the therapeutic ***tasks*** that therapist and client undertake during the life of the therapeutic relationship to facilitate goal attainment.

I operationalise the "informed allies" concept in my practice of REBT in the following ways:

i) Early on in therapy, I outline the REBT model of psychological disturbance and psychological change to my client in bite-sized chunks to facilitate client understanding, using when appropriate the client's presenting problems. I also give them an idea of how I practice REBT and what this means for their participation in this process. I then ask them if they give their ***informed consent*** to proceed. Three outcomes are possible:

   (a) the client wishes to proceed, so we do;
   (b) the client is unsure. Here I usually offer a short-term contract so that the client can experience REBT in action and thus make a more informed decision to proceed or not; and
   (c) the client does not wish to proceed. Here I attempt to discover what therapeutic approach may "fit" the client better and effect a suitable referral.

ii) In practising REBT I attempt to develop a suitable ***bond*** with my client. There are a number of issues that I keep in mind in doing so:

   (a) *Informal vs. formal;* Clients differ with respect to their wishes for an informal or formal relationship with their therapists. As long as these wishes are healthy and do not unwittingly perpetuate the clients' problems, I am happy to meet their preferences on this point.
   (b) *Directiveness;* While REBT is an active-directive, persuasive approach to therapy, I tend to be less directive and less overtly persuasive with clients who are reactant in personality organisation and who react adversely to attempts to influence them. With these clients I am explicit about REBT concepts and emphasise their choice concerning whether or not they implement these concepts in their life.
   (c) *Humour;* Clients differ widely concerning their response to humorous interventions in REBT. While I prefer to practise REBT with a sense of humour (see below), I am quite happy to practise REBT in a more serious vein when this is required. I often have an intuitive "feel" concerning a client's "humour quotient", but when I am unsure about whether or not a client will respond well to my brand of humour, I offer "trial" jokes (in the same way that an analyst makes trial interpretations) and gauge his or her response to these. I also ask for feedback on my humour and adjust my therapeutic style according to the feedback I receive.

iii) In my experience as a supervisor of trainee REBT therapists, I often find that trainees lose sight of their clients' ***goals*** as they work with their clients over time (Neenan & Dryden, 2001). I am mindful in my own practice to keep my focus and that of my clients on their goals for change. In doing so, I consider that I am being a good role model since one of the ways in which clients maintain their psychological problems is lack of mindfulness about their healthy goals. I will discuss goals further later in this article.

iv) I mentioned earlier that the technical aspects of REBT are often highlighted in the literature. From a working alliance perspective, I am particularly concerned about the following issues concerning therapeutic ***tasks***:

   (a) that clients understand i) what their tasks are; ii) what my tasks are as an REBT therapist; and iii) the relationship between both sets of tasks;
   (b) that clients understand the relationship between their therapeutic tasks and their therapeutic goals;
   (c) that clients are deemed capable of executing their tasks before they are asked to carry them out;
   (d) that clients are trained to carry out their therapeutic tasks as appropriate;
   (e) that I carry out my therapeutic tasks with skill, care and enthusiasm; and
   (f) that I suggest the use of therapeutic tasks that are potent enough to help clients to achieve their goals.

Developing a "case formulation" with complex "cases"

Beginning with the pioneering work of Persons (1989), cognitive therapists have espoused the value of carrying out case formulations to aid therapeutic intervention. REBT therapists have not embraced this concept as readily and indeed, my work on the subject is the only publication that centrally addresses this issue from an REBT perspective (Dryden, 1999). Indeed, when I showed a pre-publication copy of this work to Albert Ellis, he questioned the efficiency of making case formulations prior to therapeutic intervention in REBT. His point was that therapists can waste valuable therapeutic time making such formulations and that they could better use such time helping clients to address and overcome their psychological problems. This would be true if therapists carried out lengthy pre-treatment case formulations with all of their clients, but I am not suggesting this, nor is it my practice. My view about conducting a case formulation is this. I will do one when:

i) *The referral is a complex one.* Once the client has given their informed consent to proceed with REBT and if it transpires that the client has complex problems, I will carry out a full case formulation before making any substantive change-based interventions since doing so will help me to understand the complexity of the client's "case" and help me to save time in the longer run. This meets Ellis's inefficiency argument.

ii) *The client isn't making progress as anticipated and/or I am stuck with the client.* When I predict that I can help a client, but the client doesn't make the anticipated progress or I get stuck and don't know why, I will then tend to do a full case formulation with that person. This often helps me to understand why the client isn't making the anticipated progress and/or why I am stuck and suggests avenues for intervention that had not previously occurred to me.

Let me now briefly present the factors that I consider when I do a formal case formulation. I call this doing a "UPCP" which stands for "*U*nderstanding the *P*erson in the *C*ontext of his/her *P*roblems" because I do not like referring to a person as a "case" (Dryden, 1999).

i) Obtaining basic information and utilising initial impressions
ii) Developing a problem list
iii) Identifying goals for therapy
iv) Developing a list of problem emotions ("Cs")
v) Developing a list of problem critical "As"
vi) Identifying core irrational beliefs
vii) Identifying dysfunctional behavioural "Cs"
viii) Identifying the purposive nature of dysfunctional behaviour
ix) Identifying ways in which the client prevents or cuts short the experience of problems
x) Identifying ways in which the client prevents or cuts short the experience of problems
xi) Identifying metapsychological problems
xii) Identifying the cognitive consequences of core irrational beliefs
xiii) Identifying the manner of problem expression and the interpersonal responses to these expressions
xiv) Identifying the client's health and medication status
xv) Developing an understanding of relevant predisposing factors
xvi) Predicting the client's likely responses to therapy
xvii) Negotiating a narrative account of the UPCP for consideration with the client

For more detailed information on how to conduct a UPCP together with a case example see chapter 5 in Dryden (1999).

The final point that I wish to make on "case formulations" is one that Ellis has made informally in many of his professional workshops. This is that competent REBT practitioners build up a working picture of their clients as they proceed in therapy and share this with their clients as a way of fine tuning these more informal case formulations. Albert Ellis is very good at this, as those who have witnessed him conducting therapy or been supervised by him will testify, but he has not written on this subject to any significant degree and this aspect of REBT has tended to be neglected.

Developing an REBT-influenced "problems and goals" list with clients

As I listed above, conducting a problem and goals list with clients is an important component of a "UPCP" or REBT "case" formulation. It is my practice is to develop such a list with virtually all of my clients (and not just when I am conducting a "UPCP") since this helps both of us to keep on track throughout the therapeutic process. This is probably common practice among REBT therapists. What may be different is the way in which I do this.

Rather than ask my clients to develop a problems and goals list in their own way, I encourage them to use a REBT-inspired formula in doing so (Dryden, 2001). Usually, I help them to use this formula in a session and then once they have understood it, I suggest that they complete it as a homework assignment. I will now provide this formula and illustrate its use with a client example.

Formula for specifying a problem

Problem = Type of situation + inferential theme + unhealthy negative emotion + unconstructive behaviour / subsequent unrealistic thinking.

Example of specified problem

Whenever my boss asks to see me (type of situation), I think he is going to criticise me (inferential theme) and I feel anxious about this (unhealthy negative emotion). I deal with this anxiety overworking so that he has nothing to criticise me for (unconstructive behaviour)

In helping clients to set goals, I encourage them in the first instance to keep the type of situation and the inferential theme the same and change the remaining factors. In doing so, I am being consistent with the traditional REBT approach which states that it is important at the outset *not* to change "A" until clients have achieved a fair measure of change at "B". Following, the tradition set by Wessler and Wessler (1980), "A" here incorporates the situation and the inference about the situation.

Formula for specifying a goal

Goal = Type of situation + inferential theme + healthy negative emotion (*rather than* the unhealthy negative emotion) + constructive behaviour / subsequent realistic thinking (*rather than* the unconstructive behaviour / subsequent unrealistic thinking)

Example of specified goal

Whenever my boss asks to see me (type of situation) and I think he is going to criticise me (inferential theme) and I want to feel concerned about this (healthy negative emotion) *rather than* anxious. I want to deal with this situation by doing the same level of work as if things were going well (constructive behaviour) *rather than* overworking.

Note in the goal formula and example that I encourage clients to specify their healthy emotional, behavioural and/or thinking goals as well as what they are going to strive not to feel, act and/or think; hence the emphasis on the phrase "*rather than*" in both formula and example.

I also help clients to distinguish between overcoming psychological problem (OPP) goals and personal development (PD) and to set both if relevant. Since this issue is outside the scope of this paper, I refer interested readers to Dryden (2001).

Focusing on specific examples of target problems at the beginning of therapy and working them through

In my view, one of the most common errors that trainee REBT therapists make at the beginning of the REBT therapeutic process is to work with clients at an abstract, non-specific level rather than at a specific level (Neenan & Dryden, 2001). Of course, I endeavour to avoid making this error whenever I can. I do so by encouraging clients to identify a problem from their problem list that they would like to work on. The selected problem is known as the "target problem". Then I encourage clients to identify a specific example of this target problem that we can work on and I explain why it is important for us to remain with this example and work it through. I explain that people make themselves disturbed in specific situations or when imagining specific situations and that given this, working with a specific example of their target problem will help us both to identify key elements of the ABC framework.

Thus, working with a specific example helps clients to identify with greater clarity than would be the case when working with abstract examples:

i) the aspect of the situation (actual or inferred) they particularly disturbed themselves about (known as the "critical A" – see below);
ii) their primary unhealthy negative emotion (emotional "C");
iii) their unconstructive behaviours or behavioural impulses (behavioural "C"); and
iv) their subsequent distorted thinking (cognitive "C").

I then encourage my clients to stay with this specific example until I have helped them to identify, challenge and change the specific irrational beliefs that they held in this situation, encouraged them to imagine themselves responding to the critical "A" while holding their specific rational beliefs and while acting constructively and thinking realistically. Finally, I encourage them to practise their rational beliefs and associated constructive behaviour and realistic thinking while facing the situation at "A" which contains the inferential theme under consideration. When clients have done this, I help them to capitalise on their progress by encouraging them to generalise their learning to other relevant specific situations. Finally, I contend that working with specific examples of target problems helps guard against REBT becoming an overly intellectualised enterprise which it can easily become if the therapist works with the client at a general, abstract level.

Identifying the critical "A" in the assessment process

In REBT theory, the concept of "A" (or activating event) is deceptively simple. As its name implies, it is an event that activates something. Now, of course, it does not activate the person's emotional, behavioural and thinking responses at "C" because that would be antithetical to REBT's ABC model of psychological disturbance and health. Rather, "A" activates the person's belief and it is this ' "A" × "B" ' interaction that accounts for the person's psychological at responses at "C". However, what actually constitutes an "A"? This is where the distinction between an actual event and an inference about that event becomes salient. One point is important here, Ellis could have used "A" to refer to an *a*ctual event, but he didn't. He clearly uses the term "*a*ctivating" when referring to "A".

To complicate matters a little further, some of us now use the term 'critical "A" ' (Dryden, 1995) to denote the core component of a situation that actually triggers the person's beliefs at "B". In using this term we recognise that there are many possible "As" in a situation, but only one triggers a belief, which accounts for a particular emotional-behavioural-cognitive response at "C". To make life even more complex for the REBT therapist, a client can experience several emotions in what Wessler and Wessler (1980) have called an emotional episode – an episode in which the client experiences emotions (and, I would add, behaviours and thinking responses as well) – and that each of these emotions are triggered by its own set of beliefs about a different critical "A".

As I noted in a previous section, when "As" are inferential they have recurring themes when paired with different emotions. This was noted 25 years ago by Beck (1976) whose thinking on this point has had a decided effect on my own with respect to the nature and role that "As" play in the ABC model. For instance, when a client reports anxiety, look for the inferential theme of threat or danger in their report; when depression is reported look for loss or failure, etc. (see Dryden, 1995 for an extended discussion of this issue).

In my view and experience, critical "As" are often inferential in nature. Given this, in identifying the critical "A" in a specific ABC I often merge the actual with the specified inferential theme in the client's account (e.g., I was most anxious about my girlfriend looking over my shoulder -actual situation- in case she found someone else more attractive than me -inferential theme-).

I have devised a number of different ways of identifying critical "As" (see Dryden, 1995) and now see the importance of distinguishing between inferences at "A" and inferences at "C" (see below). Thus, my practice of REBT features an emphasis on helping the client and myself to identify and work with the critical "A" in any highlighted emotional episode. This can often be a complex procedure and one, which novice REBT therapists struggle to do well and succinctly.

Focusing on thinking "Cs" as well as emotional and behavioural "Cs"

I mentioned above that inferences can occur both at "A" and at "C" in the ABC framework. When inferences occur at "C" in this framework they denote the fact that beliefs can not only have emotional and behavioural consequences, but thinking consequences as well. There are a variety of ways of dealing with thinking consequences in REBT. Thus, one can:

i) Deal with them as "As" rather than as Cs (e.g., as activating events for a subsequent ABC: "Let's suppose that everybody in the room does laugh at you, now how would you feel about that?" or as inferences as part of an inference chain: "and if everybody in the room does laugh at you what for you would be anxiety-provoking about that?");
ii) Challenge their distorted nature (e.g., "What is the likelihood that everybody in the room will laugh at you?"); or
iii) Educate clients about how they create them and to use them to identify the ABC in which they occur as a "C".

I find that while I do, at times, use the first two strategies listed above, I increasingly use the third strategy. Thus, if a client says that she is scared of speaking in public because she fears that everybody in the room will laugh at her, I show the client how they create this distorted inferential "C". I ask her questions such as "What would have to happen for you not to fear that everyone in the room will laugh at you?" If she says: "For me to have a sense of confidence about what I am talking about", I will show her that the opposite of this is likely to be her critical "A" and teach her how she creates the aforementioned thinking "C" by using the ABC framework. Thus:

"A" = "Not being confident about what I will be talking about to a group"
"B" = "I must be confident about what I am talking about and it is terrible if I'm not"
"C" emotional = Anxiety
behavioural = Urge to cancel the talk
thinking = "If I give the talk everybody will laugh at me"

Helping this client to dispute the irrational belief in the above example means that it is far less likely that she will create the thinking "C" than if the irrational belief remains unchallenged. If the thinking "C" persists then it can be dealt with by using the other two strategies listed above.

Finally, I want to note that it is a feature of my practice of REBT that I train my clients to identify the cognitive distortions in their inferential thinking so that they can treat these distorted inferences as thinking "Cs" rather than to challenge them as distorted inferences as cognitive therapists are more likely to do. In this way, my practice of REBT differs from the practice of cognitive therapy.

Helping clients to develop and rehearse the full version of rational beliefs

As is well known, according to the REBT theory of psychological disturbance and health, irrational beliefs are at the core of the former and rational beliefs are at the core of the latter. Consequently, it is a major task of REBT therapists to help their clients to identify, challenge and change their irrational beliefs and to replace them with rational beliefs which need to be rehearsed and acted on sufficiently often if they are to make a significant difference in the clients' emotional lives. So far, what I have said would feature in the practice of virtually all REBT therapists. What characterises my practice that might not be sufficiently present in the therapeutic work of my colleagues is the emphasis that I place on what I call full versions of rational beliefs.

As I have noted elsewhere (Neenan & Dryden, 1999), a rational belief normally has two components: one that asserts the presence of the partial rational belief and the other that negates the presence of the irrational belief. Thus, if my client holds the following demand: I must do well in my examination, I help him, in this case, to develop and rehearse the following alternative full preference: "I want to do well in my examination (asserted partial preference), but I do not have to do so (negated demand)." I strive to do this consistently with all forms of rational beliefs (full preferences, full anti-awfulising beliefs, full HFT beliefs and full acceptance beliefs). I have found that when I do so my client is less likely to transmute her rational beliefs back into irrational beliefs than when I work with the partial versions of rational beliefs (e.g., "I want to do well in my examination") [Dryden, 2001].

Encouraging clients to voice their doubts, reservations and objections to REBT concepts and to the REBT therapeutic process

One of the major features of REBT is that it has an explicit model of how people disturb themselves and what they need to do to undisturb themselves. Another major feature of this therapeutic approach is that it endeavours to teach this model to clients whenever possible and whenever appropriate. It is a feature of my practice to encourage clients to voice doubts, reservations and objections they have to any of the REBT concepts that I am teaching them or to any aspect of the REBT therapeutic process. My clinical experience has been that clients frequently harbour such doubts etc. and if these are not brought to light and examined with clients then they will have a decided negative influence on the therapeutic process. I have found it to be especially important to communicate to clients that I am very open to having REBT criticised in this way and to respond to these criticisms in a non-defensive manner. I also compliment clients for speaking their mind which is, I have found a good strategy for unearthing further doubts etc. later in the therapeutic process. Common doubts are too numerous to list here (see Dryden, 1995; 2001), but a few examples will suffice:

- Acceptance means resignation
- Accepting others means condoning their behaviour
- Musts are motivating
- Because preferences allow failure, they make it more likely that failure will occur. Musts, on the other hand, because they don't permit failure make failure less likely to occur
- REBT is simplistic
- REBT is brainwashing

From this illustrative list, the deleterious effect of such doubts on the practice of REBT can be clearly seen and reinforces the importance of encouraging clients to reveal their doubts etc. and the importance of dealing with them in a sensitive, but authoritative manner.

Deliberately instructing clients in the skills of REBT

I have always remembered a comment that Maxie C. Maultsby Jr. made at the very first workshop on REBT that I attended in 1977. He said that in essence effective therapy is self-therapy. In other words, clients will benefit from psychotherapy to the extent that they apply the principles of the therapeutic approach in their own lives. This fits very well with an educationally-oriented approach such as REBT and over the years I have elaborated this concept to the point that I have recently published a book entitled *Reason to Change: A Rational Emotive Behaviour Therapy (REBT) Workbook* (Dryden, 2001). While this is a self-help workbook, I use the material with my clients since it gives step-by-step guidance with examples on how to use some of the major REBT techniques. My practice is to devote a portion of each therapy session to the work that clients have done between sessions on the workbook and the rest of the session on clients' target problems. In this way, I can monitor the progress that my clients are making on their problems and on their REBT skill development.

Of course, not all clients take to the skills development emphasis of the *Reason to Change* workbook and thus flexibility is the watchword here (as elsewhere). With such clients, I suggest that they do not use the workbook at all and I take a non-workbook approach with them. However, I deliberately instruct most of my clients in the use of core REBT skills and therefore this is an identifiable and key aspect of my practice of REBT.

Encouraging clients to take responsibility for change

Deliberately instructing clients in the skills in REBT is part of a wider emphasis that I place on encouraging clients to take responsibility for change. Thus, at the outset I outline my tasks as an REBT therapist and their tasks as REBT clients (Dryden, 1995). These are basically as follows:

- Specify problems;
- Be open to the therapist's REBT framework;
- Apply the specific principle of emotional responsibility (i.e., acknowledge and act on the idea that I largely make myself disturbed by the holding a set of irrational beliefs;

- Apply the principle of therapeutic responsibility (i.e., acknowledge and act on the idea that in order to undisturb myself I need to dispute my irrational beliefs, rehearse and deepen my conviction in my rational beliefs and act and think in ways that are consistent with these developing rational beliefs and that I commit myself to doing this regularly);
- Disclose doubts, difficulties and obstacles to change.

In addition, I ask my clients, also at the outset of the therapeutic process how much time they are willing to devote to helping themselves *per day*. I point out to them that the best predictor of progress in the cognitive therapies is the regular completion of homework assignments.

Throughout therapy, I remind clients that I don't expect them to do my job and I am not able to do theirs. Once again, I want to stress that this emphasis on client responsibility for change is modified according to the client's present capability for taking such responsibility.

Using vivid methods to promote change

In the early 1980s, I published a series of papers (collated in Dryden, 1986) on what I called vivid RE[B]T. Vivid interventions are those that bring the therapeutic process to life and I argued then as I still do now that such interventions instigate change more effectively than non-vivid interventions. A good example of this is vivid representations of "As" where such "As" are presented in clear and emotionally impactful ways enabling clients' beliefs and feelings to be evoked and worked with in therapy sessions.

Thus, my work is still characterised by the use of such methods and I apply the same caveats as I described in the 1986 compilation (e.g., don't overuse vivid interventions in therapy sessions, don't use them with clients with a tendency towards a histrionic response and when you use them with clients use intellectualisation as a defense, introduce such methods gradually and at an initial "low dose" of vividness, increasing this "dose" if such clients respond well to the initial "dose" (see Dryden, 1986 for a fuller discussion of vivid REBT).

Using humour to develop rapport and promote change

The final distinguishing feature of my REBT practice that I want to discuss is my use of humour to develop rapport and to promote change. Although I mentioned the use of humour in the first mode of practice that I discussed in this paper, I wanted to include it separately since it is such a defining characteristic of my work.

I find it difficult to describe my use of humour in REBT. It is something that one has to observe to understand. However, it is a combination of puns, witticisms, bringing together disparate aspects of a client's experience in humorous fusion, self-mocking and jokes. I don't, on the other hand, make much use of rational humorous songs. Now, I don't want you to get the idea that my sessions are full of humour since this is not the case, I am serious when I need to be and often. However, I have found that my humorous interventions do lighten the therapeutic atmosphere to good effect, particularly in REBT group therapy. My experience is that humour is a therapeutic factor in that it helps clients to take themselves seriously, but not too seriously. It also serves to remind clients of a therapeutic point between sessions. My clients are wont to say that one of my humorous remarks came into their mind at an appropriate time and reminded them of a salient REBT concept that they were then able to translate into practice. In this sense, humour can also be seen as a vivid intervention.

I hope that I have conveyed in this chapter my idiosyncratic practice of REBT and that this encourages other REBT therapists to discuss their own particular way of practising REBT.

References

Beck, A. T. (1976). *Cognitive therapy and the emotional disorders*. New York: International Universities Press.

Bordin, E. S. (1979). The generalizability of the concept of the working alliance. *Psychotherapy: Theory, Research, and Practice, 16*, 252–260.

Dobson, K. S. (Ed.). (2001). *Handbook of cognitive-behavioral therapies*. Second edition. New York: Guilford.

Dryden, W. (1984). Rational-emotive therapy and cognitive therapy: A critical comparison. In M. A. Reda & M. J. Mahoney (Eds.), *Cognitive psychotherapies: Recent developments in theory, research, and practice* (pp. 81–99). Cambridge, MA: Ballinger.

Dryden, W. (1986). Vivid methods in rational-emotive therapy. In A. Ellis & R. Grieger (Eds.), *Handbook of rational-emotive therapy. Volume 2* (pp. 221–245). New York: Springer.

Dryden, W. (1987). The therapeutic alliance in rational-emotive individual therapy. In W. Dryden (Ed.), *Current issues in rational-emotive therapy* (pp. 59–71). London: Croom Helm.

Dryden, W. (1995). *Preparing for client change in rational emotive behavior therapy*. London: Whurr.

Dryden, W. (1999). *Rational emotive behaviour therapy: A personal approach*. Bicester: Oxon: Winslow Press.

Dryden, W. (2001). *Reason to change: A rational emotive behaviour therapy (REBT) workbook*. London: Brunner/Routledge.

Dryden, W., Neenan, M., & Yankura, J. (1999). *Counselling individuals: A rational emotive behavioural handbook*. Third edition. London: Whurr.

Ellis, A., & Dryden, W. (1997). *The practice of rational emotive behavior therapy*. Second edition. New York: Springer.

Haaga, D. A. F., & Davison, G. C. (1991). Disappearing differences do not always reflect healthy integration: An analysis of cognitive therapy and rational-emotive therapy. *Journal of Psychotherapy Integration, 1*, 287–303.

Neenan, M., & Dryden, W. (1999). *Rational emotive behaviour therapy: Advances in theory and practice*. London: Whurr.

Neenan, M., & Dryden, W. (2001). *Learning from errors in rational emotive behaviour therapy*. London: Whurr.

Persons, J. (1989). *Cognitive therapy in practice: A case formulation approach*. New York: Norton.

Robb, H., Backx, W., & Thomas, J. (1999). The use of cognitive, emotive and behavioral interventions in rational emotive behavior therapy when clients lack "emotional" insight. *Journal of Rational-Emotive & Cognitive-Behavior Therapy, 17*, 201–209.

Warren, R., & McLellarn, R. W. (1987). What do RET therapists think they are doing? *Journal of Rational-Emotive Therapy, 5*, 71–91.

Wessler, R. A., & Wessler, R. L. (1980). *The principles and practice of rational-emotive therapy*. San Francisco: Jossey-Bass.

CHAPTER 14

HOW RATIONAL AM I? SELF-HELP USING RATIONAL EMOTIVE BEHAVIOUR THERAPY

E. Spinelli and S. Marshall (Eds) (2001) *Embodied theories*. London: Continuum (pp. 28–42)

In my opinion one of the best books in the field is *Embodied Theories* edited by Spinelli and Marshall (2001), from which this chapter is taken. This book addresses the question: to what extent do practitioners live their lives according to the theory of psychotherapy that underpins their clinical work? I was honoured to be invited to contribute a piece to this volume which appears below. In my view, psychotherapy theory is not just something that is good enough for our clients, but not for us as people. If it is good enough for our clients should it not be good for us too? In my experience, the most effective REBT therapists are those who use it in their own everyday lives rather than as some group of techniques to be discarded once one has left the consulting room.

Despite the excellence of this book, it is not well known and, in my view, this is down to its esoteric title. People just do not seem to know what the book is about from its title. I would love to see it re-issued with a new title, one that makes it very clear what the book is about.

I first received training in rational emotive behaviour therapy (REBT) in 1977 and have practised it ever since. Before that I was trained in person-centred therapy and had some training in psychodynamic therapy, but neither of these therapeutic approaches resonated with me as much as REBT did, and still does. In this chapter I will consider:

1. Why I resonate personally with REBT theory and practice.
2. How I implement REBT successfully in my personal and professional life.
3. In which areas I struggle implementing REBT in my life.
4. Where REBT is not relevant in my life.

Let me stress at the outset that my account (and, if I may venture, that of my colleagues) is bound to be influenced by *post-hoc* rationalizations, and will therefore provide a more coherent narrative than is likely to be the case in reality. It will also be coloured by what I choose to disclose. On this latter point, my self-disclosure will not be as full as you, the reader, may wish. Since I do not know in advance how my revelations will be used in future, I will disclose as much as I feel comfortable about my professional life and particularly about my personal life.

While this chapter is decidedly not a chapter on the theory and practice of REBT, if you know very little about this approach then what I have to say will not mean that much to you. Consequently, let me first provide a thumbnail sketch of REBT so that you can understand to what extent REBT is for me an embodied theory.

The essence of REBT

Rational emotive behaviour therapy is an approach that is best placed within the cognitive-behaioural tradition of psychotherapy. It is based on a particular view of emotional disturbance which is summed up in a slightly altered version of a famous dictum, the original of which is attributed to Epictetus: people are disturbed not by things, but by their rigid and extreme views of things. In REBT theory, these views are known as irrational beliefs and take the form of demands (e.g. 'I must be loved by significant others'), awfulizing beliefs (e.g. 'It would be the end of the world if I was not loved by significant others'), low frustration tolerance (LFT) beliefs (e.g. 'I couldn't bear it if I was not loved by significant others') and depreciation beliefs where you depreciate yourself (e.g. 'If I am not loved by significant others then this proves that I am unlovable'), depreciate others (e.g. 'If significant others do not love me then they are no good') or depreciate the world/life conditions (e.g. 'The world is no good for allowing me not to be loved by significant others').

The basic goal of REBT is to help clients to change these irrational beliefs to a healthier set of rational beliefs which are flexible and non-extreme in nature. These take the form of full preferences (e.g. 'I want to be loved by significant others, but I don't have to be'), anti-awfulizing beliefs (e.g. 'It would be bad if I was not loved by significant others, but it wouldn't be the end of the world'), high frustration tolerance (HFT) beliefs (e.g. 'It would be difficult for me to bear not being loved by significant others, but I would be able to bear it and it would be worth bearing') and acceptance beliefs where you accept yourself (e.g. 'If I am not loved by significant others then this would not prove that I am unlovable. It proves that I am a fallible human being who is deprived of the love that I want, but do not need'), accept others (e.g. 'If significant others do not love me then they are fallible human beings who are depriving me of the love that I want, but do not need.They are not bad people') or accept the world/life conditions (e.g. 'The world is a complex place where good things happen, bad things happen – like me being deprived of the love that I want, but do not need – and neutral things happen. It is not a bad place just because I am not loved by significant others').

REBT is a structured, educational, active-directive approach to therapy where, within the context of a good therapeutic relationship, clients are taught a range of cognitive, imaginal, behavioural and emotive techniques.The purpose of these techniques is to enable them to internalize and integrate rational beliefs into their belief system so that they make a real difference to the way that clients feel, think and act both intrapsychically and interpersonally. In this sense, REBT encourages clients to adopt a self-help philosophy. For more details on the principles and practice of REBT, consult Ellis (1994).

Why I resonate personally with REBT theory and practice

Although I was originally trained in person-centred counselling and psychodynamic therapy, I did not resonate personally with either of these approaches. However, I did resonate with both the major theoretical principles of REBT and its practical ethos. For example, years before I became a counsellor I helped myself overcome my anxiety about the possibility of stammering in public by implementing what was in essence a typical REBT treatment approach. I heard Michael Bentine on the radio talk about how he coped with his stammer by convincing himself: 'If I stammer, I stammer, too bad.' I took this rational statement and made it more evocative by convincing myself: 'If I stammer, I stammer, fuck it!' Then I rehearsed this belief while using every opportunity to speak up in public without modifying what I said so that I did not avoid words over which I was highly likely to stammer. In doing so, I lost much of the anxiety that I experienced about speaking in public and, as a consequence of this anxiety reduction, I stammered less. I believe this example shows that I naturally resonated with the following:

1. That one can help oneself by actively confronting one's fears (the principle of behavioural change).
2. That one can influence the way one feels by changing one's beliefs (the principle of cognitive change).
3. That one can help oneself without being in counselling or psychotherapy (the principle of self-help).
4. That one can help oneself by changing current factors that maintain one's psychological problems without necessarily exploring the past (the principle of present centredness).

The question is: why do I resonate with these and other REBT principles? The short and uninspiring answer to this question is that REBT suits my temperament and character. These are factors which are largely biologically based, which I am easily drawn to and find natural to actualize. These factors are both intrapsychic and interpersonal in nature. Let me then explore some of the elements of my temperamentally based character and show how these lead me to be particularly suited to using REBT in my personal and professional life.

Activity level

I have always had quite a high activity level. I am easily drawn to areas where I can actively do something to help myself and others and where I can be actively involved in personally meaningful projects like writing professional and self-help material. When I reflect in depth on my experiences of personal therapy which have been largely psychodynamic in nature (and which fall outside of the scope of this chapter), I conclude that one of the main reasons why I found these frustrating and largely unhelpful experiences was that they didn't help me to do something active to help myself. Also, when I am not actively involved in personally meaningful projects, I get restless and easily bored. Thus, I have made several decisions to stop writing which I have broken because I miss this activity. So I have learned to go with my internal flow and give up making promises I really don't want, in my heart of hearts, to keep.

Self-discipline

Without wanting to blow my own trumpet, I will admit that I have rarely had a problem with self-discipline. Again this is largely due to my (in my view, largely innate) obsessive-compulsive traits.Thus, when I make up my mind to do something, I am very likely to persist until I have done it or until it becomes clear that I will not be able to do it. I almost always keep to deadlines and more often than not, I do things well before the deadline (like this chapter). Yes, I learned the value of self-discipline from my parents, but have very little difficulty putting it into practice. In short, it 'goes with' the grain of my temperament. In contrast, I learned the value of eating slowly from my parents, but have great difficulty doing so. This seems to 'go against' my temperamental grain. REBT stresses the need for humans to be self-disciplined and to view this as a lifelong project. I resonate with this view and have no problem with it (unlike the majority of my clients who initially view this with something akin to horror).

Self-reliance

Whenever I have had an emotional problem I have been drawn to help myself to overcome this problem. In the past I have failed to do so only because I lacked the knowledge of what to do to help myself, not because I have sought to be helped by others. I have, of course, sought help from others, but these help-seeking episodes have rarely borne substantial fruit largely because they failed to provide me with a sound and sensible course of psychological action to follow which would help me to overcome these problems. When I discovered REBT in 1977, it was as if I had 'come home' so to speak, so comfortable did I find it as a way of overcoming emotional problems. Yes, being an only child helped by providing me with an environmental context where I could easily express my tendency towards self-help, but I firmly hold that it did not originate this tendency. While many only children are natural self-helpers, many are not.

Cognitive and philosophic orientation

I mentioned above that I have a high activity level. I am also very much at home in the cognitive modality. Little wonder that I resonate with a cognitive-behavioural approach such as REBT. But why do I resonate more with REBT than with other cognitive-behavioural approaches? One of the reasons is that REBT has a decided philosophic emphasis. Far more than other cognitive-behavioural therapy (CBT) approaches, REBT outlines a philosophy of healthy living that is both realistic (e.g. it acknowledges that humans have a predisposition toward irrationality as well as toward rationality) and optimistic (i.e. it argues that humans can transcend even tremendous tragedy with their spirit shaken, but not broken). It is the combination of the realistic and optimistic that appeals so much to me and helps explain why I never truly resonated with person-centred philosophy (too idealistic for my realistic side) and psychodynamic philosophy (too pessimistic for my optimistic side). Other CBT approaches are either philosophically indifferent or philosophically poorly developed.

Humour

While others may disagree, I consider that I have always had a good sense of humour and fully agree with Albert Ellis (1987) who has said that psychological disturbance involves taking oneself, others and life *too* seriously. Not that I laugh *in*appropriately at myself, but I regard aspects of life that others cherish such as status, reputation and social standing as relatively unimportant. Thus, I am generally amused rather than angry when I hear of some rumour or other about myself that from time to time circulates in the counselling/therapy rumour mill. Even when I received a verbal warning at work for using profanity in the classroom (not, I hasten to add, for swearing *at* any of my students), I was amused as well as pissed off when contemplating the ease with which one or two of my students disturbed themselves about my language. Although this episode and its aftermath period had its trials, it also had its funny side as college wrestled with attempting to specify occasions when it is admissible to swear in class (apparently when you drop a heavy object on your foot and the expletive is involuntary). For me REBT is the Heineken of therapies, reaching humorous parts of myself that other therapies cannot reach.

Non-religious, anti-mystical orientation

I am also drawn to REBT because it resonates with my non-religious, anti-mystical side. While a number of REBT therapists have a religious faith, the theory does not encourage a 'faith unfounded on fact' view of the world and takes a decided stance against mystical, transpersonal ideas. The idea of a 'New Age' REBT is as likely as 'kosher bacon'. This suits me as I have never believed in God, reasoning quite early in my life that if there is a deity, why on earth (or heaven!) would he, she or it create Lot's wife a fallible human being and then turn her into a pillar of salt for showing her fallibility? No, I am an ethical humanist by persuasion and easily resonate with this aspect of REBT.

Lone pioneer

Finally, I am drawn to REBT because it is not popular (certainly not in Britain anyway). I am, I believe, Britain's leading proponent of REBT and have been beavering away to make it more accessible on this island. There is a part of me that resonates to my role as a lone pioneer struggling to make REBT's voice heard in a crowded market-place dominated by humanistic and psychodynamic practitioners. That part of me doesn't want REBT to be too successful. If it were, I would lose my lone pioneer role. While I don't make too much of this dynamic, it does exist in me.

Is there anything within REBT theory which resonates to this idea of the 'lone pioneer'? Yes, but in a way that is different from how this dynamic operates in me. I am referring here to the idea that it is important to pursue ideas which are personally meaningful even if it means incurring wrath and disapproval from others. REBT theory holds that it is self-defeating to believe that it is essential to be approved of by others; doing so will lead one to abandon one's pursuit of enduring meaning in favour of receiving approval which is transitory. I note that Albert Ellis himself pursued the promulgation of REBT in the face of severe criticism and personal abuse from the field in the mid-1950s and beyond. In those days he was a lone pioneer. But he did not waver from presenting his ideas whenever he could, because he did not need the approval of his peers.

Having speculated on why I am so drawn to REBT, let me go on to consider how I apply it in my life.

How I have implemented REBT successfully in my personal and professional life

The proof of the pudding of any therapeutic approach is in its eating. So how successful have I been in applying the principles of REBT to my personal and professional life? I think, in my biased view, that I have done so quite successfully and here are some examples of Dryden-centred REBT in action.

1 I practised the REBT principle of unconditional self-acceptance (Dryden, 1999) after I left my lecturing job at Aston University in 1983 and I failed to get any of the 54 jobs I applied for over a two-year period. 'That must have been very depressing for you,' people said when I told them about this period

of my life. 'Actually, it wasn't,' I replied, 'because I had 54 job rejections and no self-rejections.'

2 I implemented a high frustration tolerance (HFT) philosophy once I learned that I had high cholesterol by adopting a low-fat, low-cholesterol diet and forgoing many of the high-fat foods that I love. Whenever I am tempted to break this diet, I acknowledge that I am tempted, I recognize that I would like the high-fat food, but show myself that I don't need what I want. Not that I deprive myself of all high-fat foods. I have four squares of chocolate every Friday! I have also exercised five times a week for years now and again implement a similar HFT philosophy in doing so. Most of the time I don't want to get up and exercise, preferring to remain in bed, but I push myself to get up while reminding myself that I can stand the discomfort of getting up and it is worth it to me to do so.

3 Whenever I am in writing mode (which is fairly often) I resolve to write 500 words a day and very often exceed this figure. What if I'm not in the mood? In such cases, I remind myself that I don't need to be in the mood in order to write and push myself to get going. Most of the time I get in the mood after I have started, and even if I don't get myself in the mood I write anyway. In this way, I live a lifestyle which is rarely affected by procrastination (Dryden, 2000).

These three examples show that I am pretty adept at persisting through adversity as long as there is a point in doing so. As I said before, I believe that I have a temperament which facilitates this process, but I still have to push myself when the going gets tough.

Another good example of how I used REBT in action to cope with adversity concerns my reaction to the following episode. A number of years ago I wrote a self-help book entitled *Overcoming Shame*. As usual I finished this book ahead of schedule and effected a transfer of files from a memory card attached to my trusty Amstrad NC200 to a floppy disk. Unfortunately I wiped the files from the memory card before checking that they had been successfully transferred to the floppy disk and, yes, you've guessed it, the floppy was blank. I had lost the whole book because, as I discovered later, I had used one full stop too many while naming each of the files. Initially I went berserk, started throwing things around and calling myself all the names under the sun. I was furious with the world for inventing fucking stupid things called computers, and with myself for being such a fucking stupid individual. Dear reader, please don't be offended by my language. If you are a counsellor or therapist, hopefully you should not be shocked by profanity, and I'm trying to give you an honest account of my inner dialogue at that time.

Well, you might argue this doesn't seem very rational; throwing things about and cursing the world and yourself for making a mistake – a mistake albeit with serious consequences – but a mistake nonetheless. But let me finish the story. This inner-and outer-directed tirade only lasted for about a minute, for I stopped myself in mid-rant, acknowledged to myself that I was unhealthily angry, accepted myself for adding self-inflicted insult to injury, and reminded myself forcefully that my anger wasn't helping me to solve my practical problem.

After I had calmed myself down, I went on to tackle my self-depreciation. Yes, I reasoned, I had acted stupidly, but no, I was not a stupid individual. I was and remain a fallible human being capable of creativity such as writing a book on overcoming shame, and of a stupid act such as failing to institute simple checks that I 'know' I should ideally have done. That's human beings for you, I reminded myself, fallible and capable of fucking-up (I am using the actual words that I used with myself at the time because they did help me).

After accepting myself for my grave error, I then tackled my awfulizing belief. Yes, I acknowledged, the consequences of my stupidity were serious: six months of hard slog down the drain or into the ether, or wherever my damned data went.This was very bad, but awful, terrible or the end of the world? Hardly. I would always remember the incident, to be sure, but would I, I wondered, refer to this incident on my deathbed as the worst thing that happened to me, let alone the worst thing that *could* have happened to me? Definitely not, I exclaimed to myself. Yes, it's bad that I lost the book. I value my time, and the thought of devoting a good deal of it with nothing substantial to show at the end is difficult for me to tolerate. But losing the book is hardly awful and I can definitely tolerate it and, furthermore, doing so will help me to make the important decision concerning whether to rewrite the book or to give up on the project. Rehearsing these rational beliefs helped me to feel the constructive emotions of annoyance and disappointment rather than the unconstructive emotions of unhealthy anger and depression that I would have experienced over time if I hadn't identified, challenged and changed my irrational beliefs. These constructive emotions helped me to weigh up the pros and cons of rewriting the book, which I decided to do without complaint after I had concluded that this was what I wanted to do and that to do so was in my long-term interests. The result was the book *Overcoming Shame* (Dryden, 1997) in which I discussed this entire challenging but growthful episode.

The final area in which I have used REBT successfully again concerns self-acceptance. The REBT concept of self-acceptance is a profound one (Dryden, 1999). It encourages people to accept themselves for being fallible, unique organisms. I have already touched on how I used REBT to accept myself as a fallible human being for my angry reaction to losing an entire manuscript. Here I briefly want to focus on self-acceptance for being unique. I have a number of idiosyncratic interests. Earlier in life I might not have pursued some of them because I would have believed that a person of my intelligence and professional standing shouldn't be pursuing such interests (e.g. watching boxing and the soaps on television). Now I see that I am a person of complex diversity; that there is no need for me to attempt to fool myself into thinking that I am other than multi-dimensional. So, these days, I am more in tune with my 'real' self and hardly inclined at all to pigeon-hole myself.

Areas where I struggle to implement REBT in my life

Are there any areas where I struggle to implement REBT in my life? There most certainly are. Perhaps the area of personal difficulty that I struggle with the most is unhealthy anger. I very easily anger myself when others frustrate me in significant ways, when others get away with acting badly or when they receive advantages that (in my view) they do not deserve. I am well aware that when I make myself unhealthily angry I am holding strong demands about being significantly frustrated and about interpersonal unfairness, but I have great difficulty giving up these demands. I do so in the end, but it involves a great deal of forceful REBT-inspired effort on my part and often the effects only last until the next relevant episode.

Why do I struggle so much with unhealthy anger? Because in my view I have a strong genetic predisposition towards this unconstructive negative emotion. Virtually all the males on my father's side of the family have been quick to anger and this can be traced back over several generations. It's not that I fail to see clearly that unhealthy anger has far more costs than benefits, because I see this most clearly. It's just that on occasion (and sadly these occasions are becoming more frequent, the older I get), I experience a powerful push towards unhealthy anger. I am never violent and I do calm down fairly quickly, partly naturally and partly through using my REBT skills with myself very forcefully. But this doesn't stop me from making myself angry very easily the next time some significant frustration or unfairness impinges upon my personal domain. I usually express my angry feelings verbally, but very occasionally I have been known to throw the odd piece of furniture around (but not in the direction of another human)!

Another area in which I struggle to use REBT effectively may seem superficial, but it is important to me. As far back as I cremember, I have bolted down my food, often finishing a dish before the person I am lunching or dining with has half-eaten theirs. I find this habit frustrating because I would like to have a long lingering meal and I am sure that eating more slowly would have a beneficial effect on my digestion. Again, my felt experience is that I am struggling with a habit with a genetic loading behind it, but whether or not this is the case, it takes a great deal of mindful REBT-inspired effort for me to slow down my eating. Even though I may have done this on one occasion, the very next time I eat, I may well mindlessly wolf down my food again if I am not vigilant.

As I said earlier, I like to be active and I find it fairly easy to be self-disciplined. This is just as well because I do struggle when I have too much work to do. When this happens – and typically it occurs when I come back from holiday and have a great deal of post to deal with both at home and at work – I am vulnerable to stress because I try to deal with the pile of letters *too* quickly. Here, my implicit belief is that I have to be on top of things all the time and I can't stand it if I'm not. If I do not mindfully tell myself that I don't have to be on top of things at all times and that I can stand to work methodically rather than quickly, I will tend to try mindlessly to do several things at once and get myself quite stressed. This need to get things out of the way quickly has also led me on occasion to make impulsive decisions which I have later come to regret.

On thinking carefully about the issues that I struggle with, it seems to me that I find it much easier to tolerate the discomfort that is associated with making an effort and being disciplined than the more acute discomfort associated with not being on top of things and being frustrated.

Where REBT is not relevant in my life

REBT is a therapeutic approach which, like other therapies, has two basic goals: to help overcome disturbance and to promote psychological growth (Mahrer, 1967). In this chapter I have concentrated on showing how I have used REBT (or struggled use it) to overcome psychological disturbance, although I have also alluded to how I have used it to promote growth in the areas of self-discipline and self-acceptance. However, there are numerous other areas where REBT is not relevant in my life. Thus it has little or no impact on my political leanings and it has no bearing on what I find involving or interesting. For example, I enjoy football and am a season-ticket holder at Arsenal. Does REBT have an influence here? Decidedly not. It would be relevant if I disturbed myself about the grim fact that Manchester United beat us 2–1 at home this season (1999–2000). But I didn't, so it doesn't. Unlike psychoanalysis, REBT does not seek to take a position on a range of social, political and cultural issues. Rather, it sticks with what it is good at: offering a perspective on psychological disturbance and a set of procedures to help people overcome their disturbance and move toward psychological health.

In this chapter, I have outlined why I resonate with REBT, how I have used it successfully in helping me to overcome my own disturbance and to further my own development, and I have discussed areas where I struggle to use REBT effectively. In all other areas of my life, REBT has little or no relevance – and that, in my opinion, is as it should be.

References

Dryden, W. (1997) *Overcoming Shame*. London: Sheldon.
Dryden, W. (1999) *How to Accept Yourself*. London: Sheldon.
Dryden, W. (2000) *Overcoming Procrastination*. London: Sheldon.
Ellis, A. (1987) 'The use of rational humorous songs in psychotherapy', in W. F. Fry, Jr, and W.A. Salameh (eds), *Handbook of Humor in Psychotherapy: Advances in the Clinical Use of Humor*. Sarasota, FL: Professional Resource Exchange.
Ellis, A. (1994) *Reason and Emotion in Psychotherapy* (revised and expanded edition). New York: Birch Lane Press.
Mahrer, A. R. (ed.) (1967) *The Goals of Psychotherapy*. New York: Appleton Century Crofts.

CHAPTER 15

REBT'S SITUATIONAL ABC MODEL

The Rational Emotive Behaviour Therapist, 10(1): 4–14 (2002)

The ABCs of REBT are perhaps the most well-known part of this therapeutic approach. Based on Epictetus' well known dictum: 'People are disturbed not by things, but by the views they take of things', this framework has two parts: (i) 'People disturb themselves about the adversities of their lives by holding rigid and extreme beliefs about these adversities', and (ii) 'People can help themselves deal productively with these adversities by developing flexible and non-extreme beliefs about them.' There are actually quite a few versions of the ABCs of REBT used and in this piece, I wanted to make clear what I thought was the most accurate version of this framework based on an understanding of Ellis's and others views. About ten years later, I used this framework to consider the errors and confusions made about the ABCs by a variety of groups (Dryden, 2013).

Reference

Dryden, W. (2013). *The ABCs revisited: Perspectives on conceptualization.* New York: Springer.

Rational Emotive Behaviour Therapy (REBT) is an approach to counselling that can be placed firmly in the cognitive-behavioural tradition of psychotherapy, meaning that it particularly focuses on the way that we think and behave when understanding our emotional responses. REBT was founded in 1955 by Dr Albert Ellis, an American clinical psychologist who brought together his interests in philosophy and psychology which are still present in this approach over 45 years on. One of the hallmarks of REBT is that it holds that people can be taught and can learn the principles of good mental health.

In this article, I will present a situational version of REBT's 'ABC' model that Albert Ellis REBT first introduced over 45 years ago. There have been many versions of the ABC model (e.g. Grieger & Boyd, 1980; Walen, DiGiuseppe & Dryden, 1992; Wessler & Wessler, 1980; Woods, 1991) and before I present my situational ABC model, let me summarise its main features:

- It roots the ABC components in a specific situational context, thus underscoring that people tend to disturb themselves most in specific situational contexts
- It puts forward the view that the A that triggers B is best described as the critical A

- It thus distinguishes between a critical A and the situation in which the critical A occurs
- It makes clear that Cs can be emotional, behavioural and cognitive in nature
- It is very explicit in differentiating rational beliefs from irrational beliefs by making clear the different components of each
- It does not intend to be comprehensive and thus, for example, does not deal with core irrational beliefs and their core rational equivalents. It does not do so because these core beliefs are general in nature and span different situational contexts.

I will briefly describe the model in basic form before discussing each element in greater detail.

'Situation':

We do not react in a vacuum. Rather, we think, feel and act in specific situations. The term 'situation' in the 'ABC' model refers to a descriptive account of the actual event to which we respond emotionally and behaviourally.

'A' = Critical activating event:

Within this specific situation, when we have a significant emotional reaction it is usually to a key or critical aspect of this situation. This is known as the critical activating event (henceforth known as the critical A).

'B' = Belief:

It is a major premise of REBT that while our emotions are usually about a critical A, this A does not cause our emotional reaction. Rather, our emotions are primarily determined by the beliefs that we hold about the critical A.

'C' = Consequences of the beliefs at B about the activating event at A (there are three such consequences: emotional, behavioural and thinking).

When you hold a belief about a critical A, you will tend to experience an emotion, you will tend to act in a certain way and you will tend to think in certain ways. These three consequences of this A × B interaction. are known as emotional, behavioural and thinking consequences respectively.

Let me now discuss each of these elements in greater detail.

Situation

As I said earlier, emotional episodes do not take place in a vacuum. Rather they occur in specific 'situations'. Such 'situations' are viewed in the 'situational ABC' model as descriptions of actual events about which you form inferences (see below). 'Situations' exist in time. Thus they can describe past actual events (e.g. My boss asked me to see her at the end of the day), present actual events (e.g. My boss is asking me to see her at the end of the day) or future events (e.g. My boss will ask me to see her at the end of the day). Note that I have not referred to such future events as future actual events since we do not know that such events will occur and this is why such future events may prove to be false. But if we look at such future 'situations', they are still descriptions of what may happen and do not add inferential meaning (see below).

'Situations' may refer to internal actual events (i.e. events that occur within ourselves, e.g. thoughts, feelings, bodily sensations, aches and pains, etc.) or to external actual events (i.e. events that occur outside ourselves, e.g. your boss asking to see you). Their defining characteristic is as before: they are descriptions of events and do not include inferential meaning.

'A'

As I said above, 'A' stands for a critical activating event. This is the aspect of the situation about which you experience an emotional reaction. Let me make a number of points about 'A'.

i) An 'A' is usually an inference and needs to be differentiated from the 'situation' or actual event about which it is made.

An inference is basically an interpretation or hunch about the 'situation', whereas the 'situation' is purely descriptive. Let me provide you with an example to make this distinction clear.

Imagine that you receive a message from your boss to the effect that she wants to see you at the end of the day. You think that this means that she is going to criticise your work. The situation or actual event here is: 'My boss wants to see me at the end of the day', while your 'A' is: 'My boss is going to criticise my work.' As can be seen from this example the 'situation' is a description of the facts of the matter whereas the 'A' is a critical or key inference that you have made about the 'situation'. It is critical because it is the aspect of the situation to which you have an emotional response. When you have a significant emotional response to an event or 'situation', the 'A' represents the personalised inferential meaning that you give to the situation.

ii) Inferences that usually comprise the 'A' can be true or false and as such when you make an inference you need to evaluate it against the available evidence.

In the above example, it may be true that your boss is going to criticise your work when you go to see her at the end of the working day or it may be false. All you can do is to consider the available evidence and come up with the 'best bet' about what is going to happen at the meeting with the boss. This involves considering such factors as: a) what has happened in the past when your boss has asked to see you; b) the quality of the work that you recently submitted to your boss; and c) how critical or otherwise your boss is in general.

iii) An 'A' can also be about a past, present or future event.

When you have an 'A' about a past, present or future 'situation' or actual event you give that event inferential meaning. Thus:

Past 'situation' = My boyfriend did not return my call

'A' about past 'situation' = This proves that he doesn't care for me

Present 'situation' = My father is discussing the value of saving regularly

'A' about present 'situation' = My father is criticising me for overspending

Future 'situation' = The hospital will contact me with the results of my blood test

'A' about future 'situation' = The blood test will show that I am ill.

iv) An 'A' can be about an event external to you or about an event internal to you.

The defining characteristic of this 'A' is again its inferential nature. For example:

External 'situation' = Letter with a cheque in it has gone missing

'A' about external 'situation' = Somebody has stolen my cheque

Internal 'situation' = Intrusive thought about hitting someone

'A' about internal 'situation' = I am losing control

'B'

Beliefs are attitudes which can be rational (or healthy) or irrational (or unhealthy). You can hold beliefs about descriptive 'situations', but more often you will hold beliefs about the critical 'A's that you make about this more objective 'situation'.

Rational beliefs

REBT argues that there are four basic rational beliefs which have the following five major characteristics:

a) flexible or non-extreme
b) conducive to your mental health
c) helpful to you as you strive towards your goals
d) true
e) logical

Now let me discuss the four rational beliefs put forward by REBT theory.

i) Full preference

Human beings have desires and for desires to be the cornerstone of healthy functioning, they take the form of a full preference. A full preference has two components. The first component is called the asserted preference. Here you make clear to yourself what you want (either what you want to happen or exist or what you want not to happen or exist). The second component is called the 'negated demand'. Here you acknowledge that what you want to occur or exist does not have to occur or exist.

In short, we have:

Full preference = 'asserted preference' component + 'negated demand' component

ii) Non-awfulising belief

When your full preference is not met it is healthy for you to conclude that it is bad that you have not got what you wanted. It is not healthy to be indifferent about not getting what you desire. As with a full preference, a non-awfulising belief has two components. The first component may be called 'asserted badness'. Here you acknowledge that it is bad that you have not got what you want or that you have got what you don't want. The second component is called 'negated awfulising'. Here you acknowledge that while it is bad when you don't get your desires met it is not awful, terrible or the end of the world.

In short, we have:

Non-awfulising belief = 'Asserted badness' component + 'Negated awfulising' component

iii) High frustration tolerance (HFT) belief

When your full preference is not met it is healthy for you to conclude that it is difficult for you to tolerate not getting what you want, but that you can tolerate it. An HFT belief also has three components. The first component may be called 'asserted struggle' because you recognise that it is a struggle to put up with not getting what you want The second component is called 'negated unbearability'. Here you acknowledge that while it is a struggle to tolerate not getting your desires met it is not intolerable. The third component is called the 'worth tolerating' component and points to the fact that not only can you tolerate not getting what you want, it is worth doing so.

In short, we have:

High frustration tolerance belief = 'Asserted struggle' component + 'Negated unbearability' component + 'Worth tolerating' component

iv) Acceptance belief

When your full preference is not met it is healthy for you to accept this state of affairs. There are three types of acceptance belief: a self-acceptance belief where you accept yourself for not meeting your desires or for not having them met; an other-acceptance belief where you accept another person or other people for not meeting your desires and an acceptance of life conditions belief where you accept life conditions when they don't meet your desires.

There are three components to an acceptance belief which will illustrate with reference to a self-acceptance belief. The first component is called the 'negatively evaluated aspect' component. Here you recognise when you have not met your desires or that your desires have not been met by others or by life conditions and you evaluate this particular aspect negatively. The second component is called the 'negated global negative evaluation' component. Here you acknowledge that while you may have acted badly, for example or experienced a bad event, the whole of you is not bad. The third component is called the 'asserted complex fallibility' component. Whereas in the second component you negated the view that you are a bad person, for example, here you assert what you are: a complex fallible human being.

In short, we have:

Acceptance belief = 'Negatively evaluated aspect' component + 'Negated global negative evaluation' component + 'Asserted complex fallibility' component

Irrational beliefs

REBT argues that there are four basic irrational beliefs which have the following five major characteristics:

a) rigid or extreme
b) conducive to psychological disturbance
c) unhelpful to you as you strive towards your goals
d) false
e) illogical

Now let me discuss the four irrational beliefs put forward by REBT theory.

i) Demand

REBT theory holds that when you take your desires and turn them into rigid demands, absolute necessities, musts, absolute shoulds and the like, you make yourself emotionally disturbed when you don't get what you believe you must. Even when you do get what you believe you must, you are still vulnerable to emotional disturbance when you hold a rigid demand at the point when you become aware that you might lose what you have and need.

A rigid demand has two components. The first is known as the asserted preference and is the same as the asserted preference component of a full preference. Again, you make dear to yourself what you want (either what you want to happen or exist or what you want not to happen or exist). The second component is called the 'asserted demand'. Here you take what you want and you turn it into a 'rigid demand' (e.g. 'I want to do well in my examination and therefore I have to do so').

In short, wc have:

Rigid demand = 'asserted preference' component + 'asserted demand' component

ii) Awfulising belief

When your rigid demand is not met then you will tend to make the extreme conclusion that it is awful, horrible, terrible or the end of the world that you haven't got what you insist you must have. As with a non-awfulising belief, an awfulising belief has two components. The first component is the same as that in the anti-awfulising belief – 'asserted badness'. Here you acknowledge that it is bad that you have not got what you want or that you have got what you don't want. The second component is called 'asserted awfulising'. Here you transform your non-extreme evaluation of badness and transform it into an extreme evaluation of horror (e.g. 'Because it would be bad if I were to fail my exam, it would be horrible were I to do so').

In short, we have:

Awfulising belief = 'Asserted badness' component + 'Asserted awfulising' component

iii) Low frustration tolerance (LFT) belief

When your rigid demand is not met, you will tend to make the extreme conclusion that you cannot bear not getting what you demand. Unlike an HFT belief which has three components, An LFT belief tends to have only two components. The first component is again known as the 'asserted struggle' because you recognise that it is a struggle to put up with not getting what you must. The second component is called 'asserted unbearability'. Here you acknowledge that it is not just a struggle to put up with not getting your demand met, it is intolerable. Since you think that you cannot put up with not getting your demand met the issue of whether or not it is worth tolerating does not become an issue. You can't tolerate it and that's that.

In short, we have:

Low frustration tolerance belief = 'Asserted struggle' component + 'Asserted unbearability' component

iv) Depreciation belief

When your rigid demands are not met you will tend to depreciate yourself, depreciate others or depreciate life conditions. Thus, there are three types of depreciation belief: a self-depreciation belief where you depreciate yourself for not meeting your demands or for not having them met; an other-depreciation belief where you depreciate another person or other people for not meeting your demands and a depreciation of life conditions belief where you depreciate life conditions when they don't meet your demands.

There are two components to a depreciation belief which I will illustrate with reference to a self-depreciation belief. The first component is called the 'negatively evaluated aspect' component. Here you recognise when you have not met your demands or that your demands have not been met by others or by life conditions and you evaluate this particular aspect negatively. The second component is called the 'asserted global negative evaluation' component. Here you give yourself a global negative rating for not meeting your demands, for example. Thus, you may acknowledge that you have acted badly and then evaluate yourself as a bad person for acting badly.

In short, we have:

Depreciation belief = 'Negatively evaluated aspect' component + 'Asserted global negative evaluation' component

'C'

'C' stands for the consequences that you experience when you hold a belief at 'B' about 'A'. There are three major consequences which I will consider separately, but which in reality occur together.

Emotional 'C's

When your critical 'A' is negative and you hold a set of rational beliefs at 'B' about this 'A', your emotional 'C' will be negative but healthy. Yes, that's right; negative emotions can be healthy. Thus, when you face a threat, it is healthy to feel concerned and when you have experienced a loss, it is healthy to feel sad. Other healthy negative emotions (so called because they feel unpleasant but help you to deal constructively with negative life events) are: remorse, disappointment, sorrow, healthy anger, healthy jealousy and healthy envy.

When your critical 'A' is negative, but this time you hold a set of irrational beliefs at 'B' about this 'A', your emotional 'C' will be negative and unhealthy. Thus, when you face a threat, it is unhealthy to feel anxious and when you have experienced a loss, it is unhealthy to feel depressed. Other unhealthy negative emotions (so called because they feel unpleasant and they interfere with you dealing constructively with negative life events) are: guilt, shame, hurt, unhealthy anger, unhealthy jealousy and unhealthy envy.

Behavioural 'C's

When your critical 'A' is negative and you hold a set of rational beliefs at 'B' about this 'A', your behavioural 'C' is likely to be constructive. Such behaviour is constructive in three ways. First, it will help you to change the negative event that you are facing if it can be changed. Second, it will help you to make a healthy adjustment if the event cannot be changed and third it will help you to go forward and make progress at achieving your goals.

When your critical 'A' is negative, but this time you hold set of irrational beliefs at 'B' about this 'A', your behavioural 'C' is likely to be unconstructive. Such behaviour is unconstructive in three ways. First, it won't help you to change the negative event that you are facing if it can be changed. Indeed, such unconstructive behaviour will often make a bad situation worse. Second, it will prevent you from making a healthy adjustment if the event cannot be changed and third it will take you away from pursuing your goals.

Thinking 'C's

When your critical 'A' is negative and you hold a set of rational beliefs at 'B' about this 'A', your subsequent thinking (or thinking 'C') is likely to be constructive. Such thinking is constructive in two ways. First, it is realistic and allows you to deal with probable outcomes. Second, it is balanced and recognises, for example that you will get a range of positive, neutral and negative responses to your behaviour. As a result these thinking 'C's enable you to respond constructively to realistically perceived situations.

When your critical 'A' is negative, but this time you hold a set of irrational beliefs at 'B' about this 'A', your subsequent thinking (or thinking 'C') is likely to be unconstructive. Such thinking is unconstructive in two ways. First, it is unrealistic in that you will tend to predict the occurrence of low probability, highly aversive outcomes. Second, it is skewed in that you think, for example, that most people will respond to you negatively, a few may respond to you neutrally but nobody will respond to you positively. As a result these thinking 'C's interfere with your ability to respond constructively to realistically perceived situations.

Summary

Let me summarise below what I have discussed in this article.

Situational ABC model of psychological health

Situation = Objectively described event

Negative Critical 'A' = Aspect of the situation to which your respond emotionally, behaviourally and cognitively

'B': Rational belief = Full preference
Non-awfulising belief
High frustration tolerance belief
Acceptance belief

'C' = Consequences
Emotional (healthy negative)
Behavioural (constructive)
Thinking (realistic and balanced)

Situational ABC model of psychological disturbance

Situation = Objectively described event

Negative Critical 'A' = Aspect of the situation to which your respond emotionally, behaviourally and cognitively

'B': Irrational belief = Demand
Awfulising belief
Low frustration tolerance belief
Depreciation belief

'C' = Consequences
Emotional (unhealthy negative)
Behavioural (unconstructive)
Thinking (unrealistic and skewed)

References

Grieger R & Boyd J (1980). *Rational-emotive Therapy: A skills-based approach*. New York: Van Nostrand Reinhold.

Walen SR, DiGiuseppe R & Dryden W (1992). *A Practitioner's Guide to Rational-emotive Therapy*. Second edition. New York: Oxford University Press.

Wessler RA & Wessler RL (1980). *The Principles and Practice of Rational-emotive Therapy*. San Francisco: Jossey-Bass.

Woods PJ (1991). Orthodox RET taught effectively with graphics, feedback on irrational beliefs, a structured homework series, and models of disputation. In M E Bernard (Ed.), *Using Rational-emotive Effectively: A practitioner's guide*. New York: Plenum.

CHAPTER 16

THE PERSONAL THERAPY EXPERIENCES OF A RATIONAL EMOTIVE-BEHAVIOR THERAPIST

J. D. Geller, J. C. Norcross and D. E. Orlinsky (Eds) (2005) *The psychotherapist's own psychotherapy*. New York: Oxford University Press (pp. 98–113).

In our field it is almost mandatory for the psychotherapist to have his or her own personal therapy at salient points in our training and professional development. I am certainly no exception to this and, in the piece that follows, I chart my entire history with having personal therapy of one sort or another. If you have read the piece in Chapter 16, where I discussed how I used REBT in my own life, it will come as no surprise to learn that my REBT-based personal therapy experiences were the most helpful to me, even though they comprised informal therapeutic discussions with Albert Ellis and self-therapy.

In Britain today, most professional bodies require psychotherapists to have had personal therapy before being registered or accredited. While professional bodies representing different therapeutic approaches specify the length and frequency of such personal therapy, this is not the case with more general professional bodies. Both the British Association for Counselling and the Division of Counselling Psychology of the British Psychological Society now specify that accredited (in the first case) and chartered (in the second case) practitioners have to have a minimum of 40 hours of personal therapy. What is so magical about 40 hours? Neither body has given a convincing argument for this figure and certainly not one that stems from the research literature.

When I began my training as a counsellor in Britain (in 1974), there were few general accrediting professional bodies and there was very little guidance (outside the analytic tradition) concerning whether to seek personal therapy, let alone what type one should seek and how long and how frequently one should seek it. What follows, then, is an account of my personal therapy experiences from my contemporary position strongly in the rational emotive behaviour therapy (REBT) tradition.

In recounting my history of personal therapy I will cover experiences of individual and group therapy that I had before my training as a counselor and after I began training. I will also discuss the personal development groups that I attended, which were a mandatory part of three periods of my professional training. Finally, I will discuss instances of self-help because they illuminate why I derived so little help from consulting my fellow practitioners. After relating each episode (or related episodes) of personal therapy, I will comment on my experiences.

Three funerals and a wedding

The first time I entered personal therapy was at the end of 1974. I had just started my professional training as a counselor and, at the age of 24 years, was suffering from general feelings of unhappiness, a sense that my life was something of an effort even though I had clear vocational goals and was pursuing them. Had I completed the Beck Depression Inventory at that time, I would have scored in the mild to moderate range of depression. So I decided to seek personal therapy partly to deal with state of unhappiness but also because I thought that I *should* be in personal therapy, given that I was training to become a counselor. Even though there was no edict at that time from any professional body that I was associated with, there was a "feeling" that being in personal therapy was "a good thing," a view that was expressed by the various psychoanalytic associations. In Britain at that time (and to a lesser extent today) counseling was dominated by psychoanalytic and person-centered practitioners. The person-centered school recommended the inclusion of personal development groups in the therapeutic curriculum, and the psychoanalytic school recommended personal therapy as a mandatory activity, which had to take place away from the training institution where one was being trained.

I do not recall why I chose to seek a psychoanalytic personal therapist, but I do remember at that time uncritically accepting what I now consider to be a myth: that psychoanalytic therapy is "deeper" than other approaches.

Funeral 1

I am being somewhat unkind to therapists in this account by referring to my experience with them as *funerals*. What I mean to convey is that they were more or less ineffective from the point of view of helping me overcome my malaise. My first therapist was a middle-aged, male Jewish therapist (as I am now) and, I think, a Kleinian. My uncertainty stems from the fact that the person who referred me to him only said he was psychoanalytic by persuasion. My therapist certainly didn't tell me anything directly about his therapeutic orientation, and I didn't ask because at that time it never occurred to me to ask.

This therapist was not austere in his demeanor but neutral and strictly interpretative. Whenever I was speaking he buried his head in his hands, and on the infrequent occasions when he was about to say something, he would rock forward, take his hands away from his mouth, make an interpretation—which I usually found puzzling—and then return to his normal pose. My attempts to seek clarification about his interpretations were met by silence or by a further interpretation, along the lines that I wanted him to feed me (hence my guess that he was Kleinian). Indeed, as I recall, this was his favorite interpretation.

This therapy was unstructured and open ended. I had the sense that I could talk about whatever I wanted and that I could see him for as long as I wanted. Actually, the therapy lasted for about six months of weekly sessions because I was moving away from London and was reluctant to make the weekly trips back to London to see him. While I was not sorry to end, I have always wondered how (and indeed if) it would have progressed had I stayed. One thing was clear at the end of this episode of personal therapy: I still experienced the same sense of unhappiness.

Funeral 2

My second venture into personal therapy was with a psychiatrist who taught a module on "psychiatry" in the counseling program I had finished in July 1975 and in which I made the transition to lecturer in August 1975. I asked this man for a recommendation of someone who might take me on, since I still wanted to get to the bottom of my unhappiness. He suggested that he could see me himself in his National Health Service clinic at the local psychiatric hospital. I should add in his defense that the issue of dual relationships was not as sharply drawn as is now the case. I was just pleased at his suggestion and gratefully accepted his offer.

I knew that this second therapist was also psychoanalytically oriented, but he was far more interactive than my previous therapist. He also practiced psychodrama, and we used several psychodrama techniques over the time that I saw him. About five or six months after I had started to see him, he told me that he had to end the therapy because he was leaving his practice to work full-time as a senior lecturer in psychiatry. I understood this and experienced a good sense of closure, since he also arranged for me to see a colleague in the same clinic. My abiding memories of this second episode of personal therapy was that my therapist took voluminous notes at the beginning, which I found off-putting. However, he was quite happy to stop doing so when I asked him to. I also remember the psychodrama techniques and found them quite useful in getting me out of my head and more into my experience. My most vivid memory, as I look back on this experience, was that we both smoked cigars during therapy sessions but that his were longer than mine!

There was again no therapeutic contract at the beginning and, like my first experience, it had an open-ended quality about it. My feelings of unhappiness persisted.

Funeral 3

I was then referred to a man who was one of the few fully trained psychoanalysts working in the Midlands. However, he did briefer work in the clinic, where I had been seeing the second therapist and he had agreed to take me on at the request of that person. In all, I had eight sessions with this man, and it was an experience I found quite frustrating. Again, there was no therapeutic contract and no agreed time limit as part of this contract. In my innocence I was operating on the assumption that again the therapy would be open ended. My third therapist was neutral and cold. Looking back, I never experienced my first therapist as cold, even though he was strictly neutral. Somehow I sensed that he did have a concern for my well-being. However, this was not the case with my third therapist. I also remember that on one occasion I asked him whether what I was experiencing was transference and received quite a sarcastic reply. No, this man didn't show any concern for me as I look back, and this was also how I felt at the time.

I am drawn to books on therapy that seek to explore key therapy moments—crucial sessions and turning points in the therapeutic process—for I can still remember quite vividly the eighth and final session that I had with this man. He began the session by announcing that this was to be our last session. I am very sure, looking back, that we had not agreed on an eight-session contract (or any other time-limited contract), and my sense of shock and bewilderment at the time strengthens me in my retrospective view on this point. He then said, casually, and this is really clear in my mind, that if I wanted to continue to see him then I could do so in his private practice. I can't recall how I responded to this, other than to decline the invitation and to get myself out of his office as soon as I could. The lasting impression that I have of this man is that he was arrogant. I recall him being late for one session and offering no apology or explanation for his behavior. When I brought this up in the session, he dismissed my legitimate complaint and proceeded to interpret my reaction.

I remember to this day feeling dazed as I made my way home after the final session. I just couldn't believe what had happened. Had I imagined it? Had I offended him in some way? I was given no explanation for this abrupt termination except that this was to be the last session.

. . . and a wedding

Having been dismissed by this third psychoanalytic therapist, I decided to fall back on my own resources. Earlier in my life I had overcome my public- speaking anxiety, which I had developed due to my attitude toward a speech impediment, by implementing a technique that I heard described on the radio. In brief, I resolved to speak up at every opportunity—without recourse to the myriad of ways I had developed to prevent myself from stammering—while telling myself: "If I stammer, I stammer. Fuck it." Not only did I largely overcome my anxiety by this method, I stammered far less than previously.

Those who know anything about REBT will recognize this as an un-schooled version of one of its major techniques: the rehearsal of a rational belief while simultaneously confronting one's fears. Consequently, it will not come as too much of a surprise to learn that in 1976 I turned for inspiration to *A New Guide to Rational Living*, an REBT self-help book written by Albert Ellis and Robert Harper (1975). We had briefly studied REBT during my counseling program a year or so earlier, and I remembered resonating to Ellis's ideas about the theory and practice of psychotherapy, but I didn't have time to study REBT in depth because we were mainly concerned with the work of Carl Rogers.

On reading about the REBT perspective on psychological problems and their remediation, I quickly saw that my unhappiness was due to feelings of inferiority about various personal issues. I further realized that the reason I suffered from such feelings was because I held a number of irrational beliefs about myself in relation to achievement and approval. At last I had found what I was looking for: an approach that spelled out for me a perspective that I could make sense of and relate to (that I was unhappy because of the rigid and extreme beliefs I had about myself) and a way of overcoming these feelings (by identifying, challenging, and changing these beliefs using a variety of cognitive, imaginal, behavioral, and emotive techniques).

So my self-help therapy gave me what my therapist-delivered therapy failed to—clear information about a conceptualization of my psychological problems that I accepted and specific guidelines of how to overcome these problems. Not one of my three individual therapists had given me any kind of account of how they conceptualized my problems, and none of them gave me any guidelines at all concerning how to remediate those problems. I am not saying that all clients require such clarity, but I certainly did. If they had given me specific directions about conceptualization and treatment, I could have given my informed consent to proceed or decided that I did not want to continue.

You may be wondering whether I was not given this information because I was expected to know it, being a trainee counselor. I doubt this because (1) openness was not a feature of my therapists' behavior in other areas and (2) they did not even inquire of me whether I wanted this information. At any rate, if any of my therapists decided not to give me information about conceptualization and treatment because they thought I would know this already, then they were sadly mistaken.

Comments

None of my three therapists made any significant attempt to explain to me how they conceptualized psychological problems in general or my problems in particular. This is what Bordin (1979) considers a key therapist *task* and forms an important part of eliciting informed consent from the patient. Thus, none of my three therapists elicited my informed consent to proceed with therapy. While some would regard this as an ethical oversight, I will be charitable and say that my therapists were following the analytic tradition, where such explicit explanations are generally eschewed. Clearly, this lack of explanation did not meet my psychological "need" for explicitness. I am a person who likes to know clearly what help I am being offered so I can make my own mind up whether or not I wish to proceed. My attempts to elicit such clarity were either ignored, interpreted, or, in the case of my third therapist, ridiculed. Why did I not decide earlier that psychoanalytic therapy was not for me? Simply because I did not have the confidence in my judgment to do so.

Looking back, I thought that if I stayed in psychoanalytic therapy long enough, I would be helped by the process, despite evidence to the contrary. This taught me that clients may place too much faith in their therapists, who they think know what is best for them. As a therapist, I emphasize to my clients that what I have to offer them is one approach to understanding client problems and how to address them, and I stress that there are other approaches available. I tell them that if what I have to offer is not perceived as helpful to them then they are not to blame, and that I will make every effort to refer them to a practitioner who may be able to help them more effectively. As my friend and colleague Arnold Lazarus (Dryden, 1991) has said, making judicious referrals is a skill and a mark of therapist maturity. None of my individual therapists raised this as a possibility. Did they fail to do so because they knew I was a therapist-in-training and thought that I could be expected to know about their approach to the therapy they were practicing? Did they assume that I had already made an informed decision that I wished to proceed with therapy in each case? As I said earlier, I doubt that they had made such assumptions; even if they had, then they were in error. What I have learned from this is not to assume that therapists-in-training or even trained therapists have given informed consent to proceed without explicitly eliciting such consent first, unless there is powerful evidence to the contrary.

None of these three therapists discussed in this section explained to me what my tasks were in therapy or, for that matter, explained what tasks they were going to engage in during the therapeutic process. My guess is that either I was expected to know as a counseling trainee or, more likely, I was expected to just talk about whatever I was disturbed about at the time. It was all very unstructured and loose when I needed clarity and structure. The exception to this was the second therapist, who asked me if I wanted to try out some psychodrama techniques on several issues that I was exploring. My recollection was that this therapist introduced the possibility of using these techniques in a relaxed, nonpressuring way, and I was pleased with both the offer and how it was made.

Bordin (1979) has argued that it is important for therapist and client to agree on the latter's *goals* for change. This does not mean that the therapist uncritically accepts the client's goals. Rather, it means discussing openly the issue of goals so that agreed objectives emerge from such dialogue. It would have been helpful to me if my individual therapists had initiated such a discussion (for I do believe that it is the therapist's responsibility to do so). Willie I now understand the psychoanalytic position on goals, I did not realize this then, and therefore I was looking toward my therapists for guidance on this issue-guidance that never came. Even if I couldn't realistically have expected my therapists to change their practice to accommodate to my preference, was it too much to expect them to elicit my position so that they could judge whether I was suitable for their mode of treatment? I think not. Again, in my practice, I attempt to elicit my clients' views on this point, and I am clear with them concerning my position on eliciting goals for change.

It should be clear by now that none of my therapists understood what I thought might be most helpful to me from therapy. Such understanding forms one important part of what Bordin (1979) refers to as the *bond* component of the working alliance. Another aspect of the bond relevant to these personal therapies concerns the interpersonal connection between therapist and client. The relationship between the first therapist and myself was fairly neutral. Behind his steadfast interpretative stance, I sensed he was a fairly kindly man, but this was only a shadowy impression.

As I said earlier, I knew the second therapist in a different context, in that he taught in my counselor training program when I was a student and continued to teach this module during the time that I consulted him, when I was lecturing on the same course. So I knew him in other contexts and experienced him as someone who was reasonably caring. This side of him came to the fore after I had requested that he stop taking notes and give me greater face-to-face contact. Before this I sensed that he was hiding behind his psychiatrist role. He responded well to my request, and from that point I would characterize our therapeutic relationship as two colleagues, one senior and the other junior, working to help the latter toward some unspecified goal. Of all the individual therapists I consulted, he was the one who best understood my need to be active in therapy and suggested on occasion that we use psychodrama techniques. I would say that of the three therapists discussed in this section, I had the smoothest relationship with him and the most difficult relationship with the third therapist.

I didn't have the sense that the third therapist was listening attentively to me. He may have been, but as Rogers (1957) wisely said, for the core conditions to have a therapeutic impact on the client, the client has to experience their presence. If the therapist is listening attentively and the client does not experience this, then there will accrue no positive impact for the client. Indeed I experienced him as detached, uncaring, and somewhat arrogant. The way he abruptly and unilaterally terminated therapy, along with the offer that he could continue to see me as a patient in his private practice, showed the somewhat exploitative nature of this man's work with me and perhaps his greed. In brief, I didn't much care for him and sensed also that he didn't much care for me. By today's standards, I suppose one could argue that there were abusive elements to this relationship. I am thinking here of his unilateral announcement, without any prior warning, that he was terminating the therapy.

To be charitable, one might argue that in 1976 the importance of planning for termination was not as much appreciated as it is now, and the practice of moving patients from the National Health Service where therapy is free to the private (fee-paying) sector may not have been viewed as unethical, as it would be now. However, this man was a fully trained psychoanalyst, for goodness sake, and a full member of the Institute of Psychoanalysis, one of the most prestigious psychoanalytic institutes in the world. Even at that time, I am sure that his colleagues would have been shocked by his behavior toward me. The fact that I used this experience to very good effect should not be used to condone this behavior.

I described earlier how I gave up on therapist-delivered therapy and turned, with good results, to self-help. Why was this experience more effective for me than more than one year's therapy delivered by well-qualified practitioners? First,

I resonated much more with the REBT explanatory model than with the psychoanalytic one, such as I understood it. I liked the fact that when I read Ellis and Harper's (1975) *A New Guide to Rational Living*, the authors, from the very outset, made perfectly clear how they conceptualized emotional disorders. However, even if my therapists had clearly stated the psychoanalytic view of psychopathology, I would still have favored the REBT view. Why? Because it emphasized the role of cognitive factors, which struck a real chord with me in helping me to understand not only my own problems but also those of my clients. Up to that time, I was still practicing person-centered therapy, but my encounter with this REBT self-help book and my subsequent successful self-help efforts led me to decide to retrain in REBT, a decision I have never regretted.

Second, I resonated with the REBT's direct, clearly understood, and, some would say, no-nonsense approach to dealing with one's emotional problems. It was never really clear to me how talking in an open-ended way, as in my psychoanalytic therapies, would help me to overcome my sense of unhappiness, but it was crystal clear to me on reading Ellis & Harper's (1975) book what I needed to do to free myself of these feelings. I needed to identify, challenge, and change my irrational beliefs and act in ways that were consistent with me rational alternatives to these beliefs. Simple, but not easy, as we say in REBT.

For me, one of me problems with these individual therapies was that they were too open-ended with respect to goals. None of my therapists asked me what I wanted to achieve from therapy. When I began to use REBT with myself, I not only asked myself what my problems were, I asked myself where I wanted to be with respect to each of these problems. I saw that my problems at the time were to do with feelings of inferiority, and I wanted to be more self-accepting. The REBT position on unconditional self-acceptance (Dryden, 1999b) was a revelation to me. It encouraged me to view myself as equal in humanity to all other humans, to fully acknowledge my weaknesses as well as my strengths, and to appreciate that the existence of the former did not mean that I was inferior and that I could address them nondefensively. Carl Rogers's (1957) notion of unconditional positive regard did not have a similar impact on me, since it was, as I saw it then, encouraging people to prize rather to accept themselves.

Having a clear idea where I was headed on this issue, as well as how to work toward getting there, were key ingredients to the progress I made in overcoming my unhappiness. I should add that in my overenthusiasm I did not appreciate at the time that it is not possible to achieve perfect self-acceptance. I realize now that this is a lifelong process and that whereas I am far more self-accepting now that I was then, I still have my vulnerabilities in this area. This fact, however, does not discourage me.

It is perhaps strange to think of developing a bond with yourself, but in self-help that is precisely what happens. In helping myself overcoming my malaise, I developed a more accurate understanding of myself than my personal therapists had shown toward me. This was because I used the REBT perspective to understand myself. Note that I could not use the psychoanalytic perspective to do this, nor was I helped to do so by any of my personal therapists.

Finally, an important aspect of the therapeutic bond is pacing. All of my therapists worked too slowly with me, another feature of the psychoanalytic approach with which I did not resonate. By contrast, when I used REBT to help myself, I was able to do so at my own, quicker rate.

From all these experiences, I have learned the following, which I routinely implement my practice as a therapist.

1 I explain to clients exactly what REBT is and outline broadly the kinds of tasks I am likely to implement and the kinds of tasks they will be called upon to engage in. I elicit their reactions and, if they indicate that REBT is not the type of therapy they are seeking, I refer them to a therapist who is likely to meet their treatment preferences—as long as these preferences do not perpetuate the clients' problems.
2 I help my clients to specify their problems and what they want to achieve with respect to each of these problems. Then I focus therapy on helping my clients to achieve their goals.
3 I strive to develop the kind of bond that will facilitate the treatment process and if I consider that any of my colleagues can better develop a stronger bond with any of the people that are seeking my help, I do not hesitate to effect a suitable referral. I am fortunate that financial considerations do not compromise my position on this issue, since I am not dependent on my practice for my livelihood.

Having described and commented on my experiences of both therapist-delivered and self-help therapy, let me move on to my experiences of being a member of a therapy group that I joined in the final year of my undergraduate degree—before I began to train as a counselor.

One year of group therapy

The therapeutic experiences I have just related were not actually my first experience of being a client. In May 1970, toward the end of my second year of my undergraduate degree, I decided to stop working for my exams and to feign illness. I was sent to see the college psychiatrist, who decided that I needed to join a psychodynamic group that was being convened at the beginning of the next academic session in October 1970 that he was running with a psychiatrist colleague. In the interim, however, I finally got my act together and resat the exams in July, which I duly passed.

I dutifully joined the group, which was made up of about eight patients and two therapists, who both took a fairly inactive, interpretative role. I did admit to the group that I had feigned illness after about six months, but since I was well over my crisis by then, this disclosure didn't really help me.

Looking back, I think that my stopping working and feigning illness was an attempt to get out of something that I did not enjoy (second-year psychology topics are notoriously tedious), and I hoped that I could go into the final year of the course on the basis of my course work in lieu of passing the exams. Once I had tested the system and realized that I couldn't avoid the second-year examinations, I faced up to my responsibilities and studied hard from that point forward. My decision to take responsibility did not come from my participation in the group, since all this happened before I joined the group.

I did learn one thing from the group sessions that proved to be a valuable life lesson. I became friendly with one of the group members, and we started to meet socially (which, if I recall, was not prohibited by our group membership). This friendship turned out to be very one-sided; and if I did not contact him, he wouldn't contact me. Initially, I disturbed myself about this lack of reciprocity and even confronted him about it in the group. He apologized and promised to initiate contact, but didn't. At this point I remember changing my attitude about it. I reasoned that he was the person he was and not the person I expected him to be and if I wanted to be friends with him, I had to realize that I would have to initiate contact because he wasn't going to. Once I accepted this grim reality, I calmed down and decided to remain friends with the guy. He never did initiate contact, but I was undisturbed about it. Looking back on this episode, it occurs to me that I never shared my self-authored insight with the group since I tend to work things out in my head rather than through dialogue with other people.

So what else did I learn from being in the group? Precious little, other than that psychodynamically oriented groups were not for me. This was a lesson that I had to relearn several times, as I will presently discuss. Of course, some would say that being a member of the group helped me to come to this realization, and indeed this may be true, despite my protestations to the contrary. However, this hypothesis is impossible to disprove. All I can say is that it didn't seem to me either at the time or in retrospect that being in the group had a bearing on my adjustment to my friend's behavior.

Comments

Looking back, I really don't know why I was referred to this psychodynamic group. Certainly, when I saw the psychiatrist for an assessment interview and he made the recommendation that I join the group, he did not give me any kind of rationale for my joining. My impression is that he needed to get sufficient numbers for the group to be viable and there were no strong contraindications that would rule me out as a group member. At the time I was in awe of this psychiatrist (because of his status rather than his personality); if he thought that I needed to join a group for one year, then he must be right. After all, he was the professional and I was a mere undergraduate. Now, of course, I know different. As a practitioner, I regard giving clients a clear rationale for treatment as paramount, and I make sure that they think carefully about my treatment recommendations before accepting them.

One of the features of this group experience was the inactivity of the group therapists. Much of the work was done by the group members, who often gave each other fairly inept advice. When the therapists did intervene, it was to make interpretations, and if these were ignored, as they generally were, they remained silent. From what I could see, very few of the group members derived much benefit from the year of group therapy.

This experience taught me that it was important for a group therapist not only to encourage interaction between members but also to intervene frequently in the group process. This helps group members focus on their goals and presents a corrective force when they give each other bad advice. The way I do this as an REBT group therapist is to highlight any helpful aspects of the proferred advice and then to focus on the psychological issues that group members often overlook when they advise one another (Dryden, 1999a). In this way I strive to preserve the motivation of the group members to be helpful to one another, while focusing their attention to what they need to do psychologically to achieve their goals. As an REBT group therapist, I see myself as having a gate-keeping role, whereby I encourage fruitful interaction between group members, and an educative role, whereby I encourage members to use REBT techniques to help themselves and one another. The two group therapists running the group I have just described were rather poor gate-keepers, often allowing unhelpful interactions between group members to develop unchecked, and were poor educators in that they did not provide explanations for their interpretations.

Four tedious years of personal development groups

In all, I experienced four years of being in three personal development groups. Frankly, I found them something of a waste of time. Since they were composed of students who saw one another in other contexts (academic, supervisory, and social), most of us were on our guard concerning—what we said in the group about our lives and about our feelings toward one another. Not that such groups were unhelpful for everyone. From what I could see, they especially helped socially inhibited members, who learned that they could talk about themselves and even confront other group members and that nothing terrible resulted from such disclosures and confrontations. Since I already knew this, I decided to knuckle down and play the game, which seemed to be that one talked about oneself at length every five or six weeks and said something in every other group when others were talking at length. It seemed that unless you did this, you became the focus of the other group members, who wanted to know why you were silent or distancing yourself from the group.

I make no apologies for sounding cynical about these groups, but I do apologize to my past students for making them a mandatory part of counseling programs that I have run. I did so not because I thought that they were of any value but because professional accrediting bodies expect them to be a part of the training curriculum, and I didn't want to disadvantage my students by depriving them of this "mandatory" experience.

Comments

These personal development groups were, strictly speaking, not therapy groups but more like sensitivity groups. Group members were not seen as having personal problems for which they needed help but as developing professionals who needed to become more aware of themselves and their impact on other people. This is quite a reasonable activity for counselors-in-training to be engaged in, and I wouldn't have objected to attending one such group for a year. What I objected to was having to attend three such groups over a four-year period. My requests for exemption fell on deaf years, for a reason that I can understand, being a counselor trainer myself, but which ultimately cannot be justified, since the raison d'être of a personal development group (PDG) is the "personal development" of its individual members. It was thought that if trainees could exempt themselves from being a member of a personal development group, then this would produce a schism in the training cohort, which would split into "attenders" and "nonattenders." Trainers are very wary of permitting any practices that divide a training cohort and that deprive group members of a forum where they could discuss their feelings about the course and about other course members in a group facilitated by a person external to the course. However, I am not speaking against having a forum for course members to discuss the course, although in my view this needs to be done with the course director present.

It seemed, therefore, that my continuing membership in these personal development groups had more to do with promoting harmony (or at least minimizing conflict) in a cohort of trainees than with facilitating the personal development of individual trainees. My argument at the time was that my own particular personal development could have been better promoted outside the group setting, and I still hold to this view.

I mentioned that in my personal development groups many trainees were wary about what they said because they had to see their fellow trainees in other settings.

If membership in a personal development group is to be a mandatory training experience, it would be more sensible if such groups were made up of students from different training courses so that each group member of a PDG would only meet with other members in the PDG setting. The practice of putting trainees in patient groups addresses this issue but raises a number of other issues, a discussion of which is beyond the scope of this chapter. My suggested alternative would also mean that trainees who had previously attended a PDG would not be obligated to attend another. If this practice had been in operation when I did my training, I would have been spared three tedious years of attending PDG groups and would only have had to put up with one such year!

Preparing for a midlife crisis that never happened: two months of Jungian therapy

As I approached my fortieth birthday, I decided to reenter personal therapy to prepare for my midlife crisis. I should say that I wasn't experiencing a crisis at the time, nor have I subsequently had the crisis, but I was persuaded by the idea that preparing oneself adequately for a crisis is better psychologically than responding to that crisis after it happens. This time I deliberately chose a Jungian therapist, on the basis that Jung's work seemed especially suited to midlife issues, and I wanted to see a female therapist, merely because all my previous therapists had been male.

I remained in this therapy for about two months. It became clear to me fairly quickly and, I believe, also to my therapist that I was not suited to a Jungian approach. For one thing, I couldn't remember any of my dreams, which I think my therapist found somewhat frustrating, since it seemed to me that she liked to work with dreams. In addition, I found talking more helpful than her interventions, which, to some degree, took me away from my train of thought, but not in a productive way. So I decided to terminate—an ending that was mutually agreed, well-planned, and amicable. This ending enabled us to work together on a collegial, professional level much later. These contacts revealed her to be much warmer and humorous than she ever was as my therapist!

Comments

When I first entered individual therapy I had just begun to train as a counselor, and therefore it could have been said that I was naive in deciding to go into a psychoanalytic form of therapy. My knowledge of what was available in the therapeutic scene was fairly limited, and my major preoccupation was to find a therapist who came highly recommended. However, 16 or so years on, I could not be said to be naive. I had already had a good deal of therapy and had discovered that I was more suited to a cognitive-behavioral approach than a psychoanalytic one. So what possessed me to go into Jungian therapy? I have already given one explanation: Jung's approach was said to be particularly suited for those wishing to explore midlife conflicts and although I hadn't begun to be affected by such issues, I was taking preventative measures. I also wanted to see a woman.

But as I have engaged in writing this chapter, it is also clearer to me that I would not have made a very good client of cognitive-behavior therapy either, not in the early 1990s at any rate. If I had sought help from a cognitive-behavior therapist at this point, I would have had to curb my tendency (which, as I write, I see would have been clearly present) to supervise my therapist. If I may humbly say so, I have been a leading proponent of REBT in particular, and of cognitive-behavior therapy in general, for a number of years; I had obtained by the early 1990s a reputation in the field. I was probably Britain's leading REBT therapist and could not envisage consulting one of the very small band of trained British REBT therapists. First, I knew them all quite well and had trained most of them; second, I would have been sorely tempted to supervise them and correct their errors! In addition, I did not think of consulting a more generic CBT therapist, because that person would not have focused on my irrational beliefs but would have chosen instead to focus on my cognitive distortions and the like, which I would have found frustrating, as I did when I trained in Beck's cognitive therapy in 1981, after I had trained as an REBT therapist a few years earlier.

So it is a bit rich of me to criticize my Jungian therapist for practicing an approach which I must have known in my heart of hearts I would not resonate with. This, of course, turned out to be the case, and thus I do not feel inclined to be too critical of her.

I will only comment on one further thing. As I mentioned earlier, years after this therapy had ended, I met my ex-therapist in a professional activity and found her to be a charming, warm woman with a good sense of humor. These qualities were not apparent to me when I was her patient. This raises for me an interesting question. In adopting a fairly neutral therapeutic style, do psychodynamic therapists (and I include Jungians here) lose much of the therapeutic potency of their natural interpersonal style and qualities? My experience is that they probably do.

Consulting with Albert Ellis

The final personal "therapy" experience concerns the consultations I have had over the years with Albert Ellis, the founder of REBT and the person I most consider a mentor. For over 20 years I have made annual visits to what is now known as the Albert Ellis Institute in New York City. Whenever I go I arrange to see Albert Ellis, in what are known as his lunchtime and suppertime sessions. These are, in effect, his breaks between therapy sessions. While for the most part I have used these sessions to discuss matters relating to (1) finer points of the theory and practice of REBT; (2) problems I have had in my clinical practice of REBT; and (3) joint writing projects, I have on various occasions used these sessions to consult with Al on a number of personal issues. Normally, these have been issues where I have failed to identify a subtle factor that has eluded me and thus I have not been able to get to the heart of the matter. Invariably, Al has helped me to identify this factor and has trusted me to take remedial steps to deal with the clarified problem on my own.

Comments

Of all the therapist-delivered treatment I have had—and when I put together all of them, I am shocked to learn how much therapy I have had (with so little return!)—Albert Ellis, in the sporadic times when I have discussed a personal issue with him has been, by far, the best therapist I have ever had. Why is this so? First, our therapeutic discussions over the years have been in the context of him being more of a mentor than a therapist. This for me challenges the wisdom of implementing overly strict boundaries between therapy and nontherapy discussions with the same person. Such boundaries would be constructive for some, but would not have been for me.

Another aspect of therapy with Al Ellis that I appreciated was his use of self-disclosure. I would discuss a personal issue with Al, and he would tell me about a relevant experience that he had had with the same issue. Sometimes he would tell me how he had helped one of his clients with a similar problem. Rarely, if ever, would he practice formal, active-directive REBT with me. While I have never discussed this point with him, my sense is that he was quite aware that I knew REBT theory and practice very well and could trust that I had tried to use it with myself before discussing the issue with him. He respected my position as a knowledgeable REBT therapist, and he sought to help me in ways that I had perhaps not thought of. His indirect approach here was most beneficial.

As I write this, I am reminded of a remark that one of my REBT colleagues made about supervisory feedback he had received on one of his therapy tapes by an REBT supervisor he had sought help from. "He treated me as if I knew nothing about REBT," claimed my colleague, who found this approach to supervision patronizing and unhelpful. Al Ellis never once treated me in our therapeutic discussions as if I did not know REBT.

The other helpful aspect of having "therapy" with Ellis was that his style with me did not change according to the issue we were discussing. I contrast this with the discrepancy between my Jungian therapist's "inside therapy" style and her "outside therapy" style. Al was his humorous, raunchy, interesting self no matter what we were discussing. In a phrase, I experienced him to be genuine in all his dealings with me, and this "genuine informality" is a therapist quality that I find particularly helpful as a client and that I strive to achieve in my own work. I contrast this with the "nongenuine formal" style of my other therapists.

It is fitting to close this chapter with my therapy experiences with Albert Ellis since I owe him so much as a professional. It is also fitting that I have ended with a discussion of my one positive therapist-delivered treatment that I have had. Although I have been critical of my previous therapists (with the exception of Albert Ellis), I want to end by saying that I would not be a very easy client for most therapists. I have a clear idea of what is helpful to me and what is not, and I have a definite preference for self-help, which makes being in therapy a problematic experience for me if that therapy is not focused sharply on encouraging me to help myself.

And yet, so many of my therapists failed to discover this. As a result I have learned to consistently ask myself whether or not my REBT practice best suits the needs of the person who is seeking my help. If it does, then we can proceed; if not, I am prepared to refer this person to someone else. This is the lasting legacy of my personal therapy experiences and one that helps to keep my feet on the ground and helps me to remain dedicated and humble.

References

Bordin, E. S. (1979). The generalizability of the psychoanalytic concept of the working alliance. *Psychotherapy, Theory, Research and Practice*, *16*, 252–260.

Dryden, W. (1991). *"It depends": A dialogue with Arnold Lazarus*. Buckingham: Open University Press.

Dryden, W. (1999a). Friend or therapist? In S. Greenfield (Ed.), *Therapy on the couch: A shrinking future?* London: Camden Press.

Dryden, W. (1999b). *How to accept yourself*. London: Sheldon Press.

Ellis, A., & Harper, R. A. (1975). *A new guide to rational living*. Hollywood, CA: Wilshire.

Rogers, C. R. (1957). The necessary and sufficient conditions of therapeutic personality change. *Journal of Consulting Psychology*, *21*, 95–103.

CHAPTER 17

RESILIENCE AND RATIONALITY

Journal of Rational-Emotive & Cognitive-Behavior Therapy, 25(3): 213–226 (2007)

In the first decade of the twenty-first century there has been increasing interest placed on positive psychology and how to promote psychological health. I became involved in this movement when Michael Neenan and I wrote a book on life coaching (Neenan and Dryden, 2002) and I developed my interest in psychological health from that time till the present (see Dryden, 2011). The piece that follows considers what REBT has to say about resilience, one of the hallmarks of psychological health (see Neenan, 2009). In particular, I introduced the distinction between what I call an ideal rational resilience credo and a realistic rational resilience credo. The former is like self-actualisation, something to strive for, but rarely achieved, while the latter shows how one can be basically resilient even though one experiences blips along the way. Understanding the latter helps one to become self-compassionate when one falters, a topic I explore in greater depth in Chapter 22.

References

Dryden, W. (2011). *Understanding psychological health: the REBT perspective*. Hove, East Sussex: Routledge.

Neenan, M. (2009). *Developing resilience: a cognitive-behavioural approach*. Hove, East Sussex: Routledge.

Neenan, M. and Dryden, W. (2002). *Life coaching: a cognitive-behavioural approach*. Hove, East Sussex: Brunner-Routledge.

Abstract

In this article, I consider the relationship between rationality and resilience. First, I outline six responses to life's adversities: (a) a true disturbed response; (b) a feigned disturbed response; (c) a feigned indifferent response; (d) a true healthy response; (e) a feigned healthy response; and (f) a mixed response. These responses underpin two rational resilience credos, which will be then outlined: an ideal rational resilience credo and a realistic rational resilience credo. The implications of these credos for coaching will be explored.

Rational Emotive Behaviour Therapy (REBT) is a leading approach within the cognitive-behavioural tradition. Indeed, it can legitimately lay claim to be the earliest developed approach to CBT as it is accepted that it was founded in 1955 by Albert Ellis who is regarded as the grandfather of CBT. REBT was originally developed as an approach to psychotherapy, outlining an explanation of how people disturbed themselves about life's adversities, how they unwittingly maintained that disturbance and how therapists could help them address that disturbance effectively so that they could lead healthier lives. One of the strengths of REBT is how widely it has been applied in different helping contexts, with different client groups who have different helping "needs". The strength of this application is that a "potentially" helpful method is available to many people who want to live healthier lives free from the crippling effects of emotional disturbance. The weakness of this application is centred on the word "potentially" in the previous sentence. The application of REBT as a helping method has far outstripped efforts to carefully study its actual effectiveness under scientifically accepted conditions. While this is true for a large number of helping methods, this does not detract from the need for REBT to be rigorously tested more widely than it has been to date. Consequently, this article should be viewed as another promising attempt to broaden the application of REBT, which warrants empirical enquiry in this case to the field of resilience.

Resilience

The American Psychological Association (2004) has published a pamphlet entitled "The Road to Resilience" which, amongst other things, outlines the factors that comprise resilience. In this article, I will concentrate on one of these factors: the beliefs that underpin resilience, and will do so from an REBT perspective.

The term "resilience" conjures up a rock-like coping response. There is a scene in the film *Raging Bull* that typifies this. Jake LaMotta is fighting his old foe, "Sugar" Ray Robinson, and is losing. However, there is one thing about which Jake LaMotta has always taken pride and it has nothing to do with losing. No, he is more proud of the fact that he has never been knocked down. Towards the end of the fight with Robinson, LaMotta knows he can't win, but one thing he can do is to stay on his feet. So he urges Robinson to hit him and try to put him down which Robinson fails to do. At the bell ending the fight, LaMotta triumphantly says to Robinson, "You couldn't put me down, Ray. You couldn't put me down."

While rock-like coping can be seen as resilience, it is my view that there are dangers in so doing. First of all, it tends to have macho overtones. Jake LaMotta's pride in never being knocked down is in some ways more macho than if he'd taken pride in never being beaten. Second, it is somewhat perfectionistic. It does not allow for people to struggle and is therefore unrealistic. Third, it may also be dangerous in encouraging people to stand there and take it. There is something of this in the first half of the American Psychological Association's (2004: 2) definition of resilience in their pamphlet for the general public, mentioned above.

> Resilience is the process of adapting well in the face of adversity, trauma, tragedy, threats, or even significant sources of stress—such as family and relationship problems, serious health problems, or workplace and financial stressors. It means "bouncing back" from difficult experiences.

Perhaps a better metaphor for resilience is of the boxer who has been defeated and, unlike LaMotta, has been knocked down, but is not ashamed of that. He (in this case) can reflect on the knockdowns and learn from such experiences. He has an overall understanding of his skills as a boxer and of his vulnerabilities and will endeavour to play to the former and seek help with the latter. He may not bounce back from defeat immediately, but he will come back, chastened, having learned his lessons, but still with guarded optimism.

The second half of the APA's definition (2004: 2) reflects on this more human aspect:

> Being resilient does not mean that a person doesn't experience difficulty or distress. Emotional pain and sadness are common in people who have suffered major adversity or trauma in their lives. In fact, the road to resilience is likely to involve considerable emotional distress.

In this article, I will in due course present two rational resilience credos, which can loosely reflect the two ingredients of resilience discussed above. Before I present these credos, I will discuss six responses to life's adversities, which should be viewed as a framework for understanding the two credos.

Six responses to life's adversities

There are basically six responses to life's adversities:

- A true disturbed response
- A feigned disturbed response
- A feigned indifferent response
- A true healthy response
- A feigned healthy response
- A mixed response

Let me discuss these responses in more detail.

The true disturbed response

REBT's conceptualisation of the disturbed response to life's adversities can be summed up in a revised version of the following maxim attributed to Epictetus: "Men are disturbed not by things, but by their views of things." The REBT version is as follows:

> People are not disturbed by things. Rather, they disturb themselves by holding rigid and extreme beliefs about things.

Ellis (e.g., 1994) has consistently asserted that rigid beliefs (often couched in the form of musts, absolute shoulds, have to's, got to's, etc.) are at the very core of psychological disturbance and three extreme beliefs or conclusions are derived from these rigid beliefs. These three extreme beliefs are known as: awfulising beliefs, low frustration tolerance (LFT) beliefs and depreciation beliefs (about self, others and life).

The feigned disturbed response

Why might people feign a disturbed response to an adversity? In my experience, they do so for three main reasons:

- To derive a benefit (e.g., legal compensation in trauma cases, others feeling sorry for them and not imposing on them, to gain more time to do something such as completing an essay that they worry about not being good enough);

- To ward off a cost (e.g., a punishment or penalty that would be applied if the person was not in a disturbed frame of mind);
- To both derive a benefit and ward off a cost.

How can one tell if a person is responding unhealthily to an adversity? First, their belief needs to be irrational, their emotions negative and unhealthy, their behaviour unconstructive and their subsequent thinking very distorted. However, people may be adept at discovering these disturbed responses and feigning them and, consequently, clinicians may not be well placed to detect such feigned responses.

The feigned indifferent response

When people face life's adversities they try to convince themselves (and others) that they have no feelings or have mild, insignificant feelings about these negative events. This is usually an attempt at self-deception because they are likely to have disturbed themselves about the adversities and use indifference as a way of coping. As such, in my view, the indifferent response is virtually always feigned, be it witting or unwitting. For indifference beliefs to be true, people would have to believe in actuality that it really does not matter to them if adversities occur or not.

People may strive to develop indifference beliefs because they think that indifference is a healthy response to life's adversities or they think that indifference proves that they are being "strong" or "cool" in the face of such adversities and thereby hope to receive admiration from others.

The true healthy response

REBT's conceptualisation of the healthy response to life's adversities can be summed up as follows:

> People respond healthily to things by holding flexible and non-extreme beliefs about things.

Ellis (e.g., 1994) has consistently asserted that flexible beliefs (often couched in the form of non-dogmatic preferences, wishes, wants, etc.) is at the very core of psychological health in the face of life's adversities and three non-extreme beliefs or conclusions are derived from these flexible beliefs. These three extreme beliefs are known as anti-awfulising beliefs, high frustration tolerance (HFT) beliefs and acceptance beliefs (about self, others and life).

REBT is clear that while one may oscillate from holding rigid and extreme beliefs to holding flexible and non-extreme beliefs, a person cannot hold these two very different beliefs simultaneously. This is shown clearly in Table 17.1.

The feigned healthy response

As the heart of the REBT model of responding to life's adversities is a cognitive one, it is easy for a person to say that they are responding healthily to an adversity by claiming that their beliefs are rational (i.e., flexible and non-extreme).

So, how can one tell whether or not a person is responding to adversities in a truly healthy fashion? A person's self-report of their beliefs is problematic. It is perfectly possible for a person to say that they are holding a rational belief, but in

Table 17.1 Irrational and rational beliefs in REBT theory

Irrational belief	*Rational belief*
Demand × must (or must not happen)	Non-dogmatic preference I would like × to happen (or not happen), but it does not have to be the way I want it to be
Awfulising belief It would be terrible if × happens (or does not happen)	Anti-awfulising belief It would be bad, but not terrible if × happens (or does not happen)
LFT belief I could not bear it if × happens (or does not happen)	HFT belief It would be difficult to bear if × happens (or does not happen) but I could bear it and it would be worth it to me to do so
Depreciation belief If × happens (or does not happen) I am no good/you are no good/life is no good	Acceptance belief If × happens (or does not happen), it does not prove that I am no good / you are no good / life is no good. Rather, I am a FHB / you are a FHB, life is a complex / mixture of good bad and neutral

FHB = Fallible human being.
LFT = Low frustration tolerance.
HFT = High frustration tolerance.

reality they are not. The best way of judging this discrepancy is to consider how consistent the person is in their report. For a person to respond healthily to an adversity, their belief needs to be rational, their emotions negative but healthy, their behaviour constructive and their subsequent thinking realistic.

There may be many reasons why a person may feign a healthy response to an adversity. The two that follow are illustrative:

- They may feel ashamed of admitting (to themselves and/or to others) that they have responded unhealthily to an adversity because this means that they are weak or pathetic. Shame is a major determinant of defensiveness.
- They think that they will experience various negative consequences if it becomes known that they have responded unhealthily to an adversity such as jeopardising their promotion chances because they don't appear to have the "right stuff".

The mixed response

The mixed response to life's adversities is characterized by people first disturbing themselves about these adversities, then struggling to cope with their feelings; for example, by trying to make themselves feel indifferent or denying how they feel before eventually responding healthily. At the heart of the mixed response is realism and struggle as I will discuss later.

An ideal rational resilience credo

The Cambridge Advanced Learner's Dictionary defines credo as "a set of beliefs, which expresses a particular opinion and influences the way you live". In this part of this article, I will present two rational resilience credos, one ideal and one realistic. The ideal rational resilience credo, which I will present first, is a set of rational beliefs which promotes ideal resilient responsiveness in the face of adversity. It comprises the true healthy response outlined above.

I will present the ideal rational resilience credo in the first person. In doing so, I want to reiterate that this credo outlines the ideal towards which humans may strive, but not hope to achieve in any lasting sense. It is thus akin to the concept of self-actualisation (Maslow, 1968). Setting an ideal has its advantages and its disadvantages which I will discuss after presenting the credo.

> As a human being I recognise that I have many desires. I prefer certain conditions to exist in my life and other conditions not to exist. I also acknowledge that no matter how strong my desires are, sadly and regretfully, this does not mean that I have to have my desires met by myself, by others or by life conditions. When life adversities exist and I don't get my desires met, I will feel badly about this, even though I have accepted that I don't have to get what I want. These bad feelings are healthy. They are a sign that I have desires, that these desires are not being met when life adversities occur and they motivate me to change things if they can be changed and to adjust constructively if they can't be changed.
>
> I also recognise that when life adversities occur and my desires are not met, this is bad and unfortunate but not terrible or the end the world. I acknowledge that good can come from bad and even when my strongest desires are not met, I have other desires that can be met, if not now, at some time in the future.
>
> I also recognise that when life adversities occur and my desires are not met, it is a struggle for me to tolerate this state of affairs, but I can tolerate it and it is worth it to me to do so. Not having even my strongest desires met is not unbearable and if this happens, I do not lose my capacity for happiness and can gain this in other areas of my life; if not now, at some point in the future.
>
> When life adversities occur and I am largely responsible, I acknowledge that I am a fallible human being equal in worth to all other humans, although we differ in a myriad of different respects. I can see that this belief will help me to stand back and identify aspects of myself that I don't like and want to change, particularly with respect to my behaviour that helped bring about the adversities in question. I will work steadily to change those negative aspects of myself that can be changed and for those that I cannot change, I will strive to do my best to minimise their impact.
>
> When life adversities occur and others are largely responsible for this, I acknowledge that they are also fallible human beings who will sadly often do the wrong thing and, equally sadly, they will also often fail to learn from their errors. This is just the way it is and as such it proves that others are fallible and non-damnable for their behaviour even if their behaviour is heinous.
>
> When life adversities occur, I further acknowledge that life is a complex mixture of the good, the bad and the neutral and even when highly aversive events happen, this does not change the complexity of life. The complexity of life incorporates highly aversive events and joyous events as well as neutral events and I can accept life as such.
>
> While the above beliefs will help me to live resiliently in the world, I acknowledge that it is very unlikely that I will gain complete conviction in this credo and live fully according to its precepts. However, I can strive to do so. I

recognise that such striving involves much work and practice and I commit myself to doing this work on a regular basis.

As I work to internalise this credo, I accept that I will experience many lapses along the way. The best way of dealing with these lapses is to accept them, without liking them, learn from them and act on such learning in relevant future situations.

When I do disturb myself about life adversities I will refrain from disturbing myself about doing so, thereby avoiding giving myself a double dose of disturbance. Thus, I acknowledge that while it is desirable that I do not disturb myself, I am not immune from doing so. Then, I can undisturb myself before attempting to change the adversities. If I attempt to change the adversities while I am feeling disturbed, my attempts will be contaminated by my disturbed feelings and I will usually be less successful at changing the adversities. In fact, I may well make things more difficult for myself.

So what are the advantages and disadvantages of an ideal rational resilience credo? The advantages are as follows:

1 It gives people a clear indication of what to aim for in their quest for high level personal resilience
2 It can inspire and motivate some people in their quest for high-level personal resilience

However, there are disadvantages to the ideal rational resilience credo, although in truth this is more to do with how some people may misunderstand the purpose of the ideal credo and how yet others may bring their own irrational beliefs to the ideal. Nonetheless, the main disadvantages associated with the ideal rational resilience code seem to be:

1 It may demoralise some people who may conclude that they will never reach such dizzy heights of personal resilience and therefore it is not worth even trying to be a little more resilient. Thus, some people may develop a sense of hopelessness, particularly if they consider the credo as something that can be achieved rather than as a signpost to greater, but not ideal resilience.
2 People who may be doing well on the criteria of realistic resilience may dismiss their efforts because they seem to fall short of the ideal form of resilience. Again, such people misread the purpose of the ideal form of resilience and see it as an achievable state. As such they consider that they must achieve it and bring their perfectionistic attitude to the ideal. It is this attitude rather than the ideal that leads them to disregard their own more realistic resilience. REBT therapists are very familiar with clients who bring their rigidity to rationality. Here we are talking about a similar phenomenon: people who bring their rigidity to resilience!

A realistic rational resilience credo

The realistic rational resilience credo is a set of beliefs, which promotes realistic resilient responsiveness in the face of adversity. It comprises the mixed response outlined above and contains elements of the true disturbed response, the feigned indifferent response, the feigned healthy response and the true healthy response.

I will again present the realistic rational resilience credo in the first person. It outlines a non-utopian view of resilient responsiveness to adversities. As such it is within the reach of most people, unlike the ideal rational resilience credo, which outlines a level of responsiveness that is within the grasp of only a select few, e.g., Helen Keller and Viktor Frankl. Like its ideal counterpart, the realistic rational resilience credo has its advantages and its disadvantages, which I will discuss after presenting the credo.

> As a human being I recognise that I have many desires. I prefer certain conditions to exist in my life and other conditions not to exist. Particularly when faced with life adversities I tend to demand that the conditions that I want must exist and the conditions that I don't want must not exist. It is a real struggle for me to acknowledge that no matter how strong my desires are, sadly and regretfully, this does not mean that I have to have my desires met by myself, by others or by life conditions. In the journey towards believing this, I may well do many things to deal with my disturbed feelings which may help me in the short term, but not in the long term. Thus, I may well deny that I feel disturbed and say either that I am not bothered about what happened or that I am handling it well. However, I recognise that denial is not a good way and will use this as a cue to think rationally about life adversities as soon as I am able. While I recognise that I can do this, I also acknowledge that there are times that I won't. The path towards greater resilience is a rocky one. When I do eventually think rationally about life adversities, I will accept that when I don't get my desires met I will feel badly about this, even though I have accepted that I don't have to get what I want. These bad feelings are healthy. They are a sign that I have desires, that these desires are not being met and they motivate me to change things if they can be changed and to adjust constructively if they can't be changed. But I also recognise that it is very difficult for me to have desires about life conditions and to keep these desires flexible. As such I will return to disturbed negative feelings when I go back to holding rigid demands.
>
> I also recognise that when life adversities occur and my desires are not met, I tend to think that it is awful and the end of the world when this happens. When I do so, I cannot see any good in what is happening or acknowledge that there are other things in life that are important to me. It is a real struggle for me to accept that when my desires about life adversities are not met, this is bad and unfortunate but not terrible or the end the world. I can believe it, but I will oscillate between thinking it and thinking it bad, but not awful until the latter is stronger than the former. This will be interspersed by my attempting to deny that I feel disturbed about what happened. When I do eventually operate according to my anti-awfulising belief, I am in a better frame of mind to acknowledge that good can come from bad and even when my strongest desires are not met, I have other desires that can be met, if not now, at some time in the future.
>
> I also recognise that when life adversities occur and my desires are not met, I tend to think that it is unbearable when this happens and that I will never be happy again. It is again a real struggle for me to accept that when my desires about life adversities are not met, this is bearable and that I can bear it. I realise that I can believe this, but I will oscillate between believing that I can bear it and believing that I can't until the former is stronger than the latter. This will be again interspersed by my attempting to deny that I feel disturbed about what happened in order that I quickly get rid of my disturbed feelings When I

do believe that I can bear adversities, I am in a better frame of mind to see that I do not lose my capacity for happiness when they do occur and can gain this in other areas of my life; if not now, at some point in the future.

In the face of life adversities which I have brought about, I tend to depreciate myself and find it a real struggle to acknowledge that I am a fallible human being, equal in worth to all other humans although we differ in a myriad of different respects. I can eventually do this, but recognise that I will oscillate between depreciating myself and accepting myself interspersed with denial until my self-acceptance belief is stronger than my self-depreciation belief. When I do this I can see that this belief will help me to stand back and identify aspects of myself that I don't like and want to change. I will work steadily to change those negative aspects of myself that can be changed and for those that I cannot change, I will strive to do my best to minimise their impact. In striving to do this, I realise that I will often go back to depreciating myself and even when I basically accept myself I will occasionally depreciate myself.

In the face of life adversities when others are responsible for them, I tend to depreciate them and find it very difficult to acknowledge that they are fallible human beings who will sadly often do the wrong thing and equally sadly will also often fail to learn from their errors. I can believe this and will work towards doing so, but this is a real struggle for me because I easily condemn them and "feel" powerful and justified in doing it. As I strive to accept others, I will often oscillate between depreciating them and accepting them with periods of denial. When my other-acceptance belief is stronger than my other-depreciation belief, I can see that others acting badly is just the way it is and that as such they are fallible and not damnable for their behaviour even if that behaviour is heinous.

In the face of life adversities I tend to depreciate the whole of life and really struggle to accept that life is a complex mixture of the good, the bad and the neutral. When I do attain such acceptance, with the usual oscillations between life-acceptance, life-depreciation and denial in the face of highly aversive events, it may not be until a considerable amount of time has passed. Then I would see that the existence of highly aversive events does not change the complexity of life. The complexity of life incorporates highly aversive events, joyful events as well as many neutral events.

While flexible and non-extreme beliefs will help me to develop resilience, I recognise that even when I work hard to develop such beliefs, I will often return to thinking rigidly and in extreme ways. Similarly, I acknowledge that as I work to internalise this realistic credo, I will experience many lapses along the way. The best way of dealing with these lapses is to accept them, without liking them, learn specific things from them and act on such specific learning in relevant future situations.

When I do disturb myself about life's adversities, I will struggle with that and may well disturb myself for thus disturbing myself. I will strive to accept myself for disturbing myself about life's adversities and recognise that as I do so my efforts will oscillate between accepting myself, depreciating myself and various forms of denial. If I persevere, my self-acceptance will gain ascendancy and as it does so, I will also acknowledge that while it is desirable that I do not disturb myself, I am not immune from doing so. However, I will struggle with this too and at times will go back to demanding that I must not disturb myself about life's adversities. Once I have largely accepted myself for disturbing myself, I can then work on the original disturbance and then, and only when I have done this relatively successfully, will I attempt to change the adversities. If I attempt to change the adversities while I am feeling disturbed or disturbed about feeling disturbed, my attempts will be contaminated by my disturbed feelings and I will usually be less successful at changing the adversities. In fact, I may well make things more difficult for myself. However, being human I may well do the wrong thing and attempt to change the adversity when I am disturbed in the first place and disturbed about being disturbed in the second place. The best I can do is to catch myself doing so and work on not doing so. My successes here will be punctuated by lapses, as before.

So what are the advantages and disadvantages of a realistic rational resilience credo? The advantages are as follows:

1. It gives people a warts and all picture of rational resilience within the grasp of most people.
2. Even though periods of irrational thinking and denial are present in realistic rational resilience, there is still a clear indication of the rational thinking that people should aim for.
3. It can comfort rather than inspire and can thus motivate some people who value realism in their quest for greater personal resilience.

However, there are disadvantages to the realistic rational resilience credo:

1. It may legitimise disturbance and denial as necessary components of resilience whereas, in reality, they are frequently rather than inevitably occurring components.
2. It may discourage people who are capable of a more ideal form of resilience, i.e., one relatively free from disturbance and denial (as outlined earlier in the article) from striving to achieve it.

Implications for coaching

When clients are facing life adversities coaches are called upon to help them develop resilience in the face of these adversities before they encourage clients to attempt to change these adversities. As I said earlier, attempting to change such adversities is usually more effective when clients are relatively free from emotional disturbance than when they are actively emotionally disturbed about such events. REBT has a good framework to offer coaches who need to understand both non-resilient, emotionally-disturbed based responses to life adversities and resilient based responses to these same adversities.

Earlier in this article I outlined two rational resilient credos, one ideal, the other realistic. These credos detailed the attitudinal processes that lie behind ideal and realistic resilient responding. How can coaches who are working with clients facing life adversities use these credos? I suggest that they can do so in the following ways:

1. Coaches can assess their clients' history of dealing with adversity and determine which clients may benefit most from having ideal resilient responding as a goal and which are better suited to having realistic responding. Once they make their decision they can present the chosen credo to their clients and, if acceptable, the chosen credo can be used as a guide for the clients and for the work in coaching sessions. In particular, coaches can then break the credo

down into its constituent parts and these can be used to help clients develop the relevant specific rational beliefs that underpin the type of resilience related to the chosen credo.

2 Coaches could give their clients both credos to read and ask them which credo reflects the type of resilience they (a) would like to aim for or (b) are more capable of approximating. In doing so, coaches may also outline for their clients the advantages and disadvantages of each credo as presented earlier. Then the chosen credo would form the basis of the coaching work.

3 Coaches could give their clients both credos to read and ask for their preferences as above. Then they would disclose their opinion about which type of resilience they think would most benefit particular clients. A negotiation would follow where coach and client would come to an agreed position.

4 Coaches bring to the enterprise of coaching their own views about what is possible for clients to achieve in general. Some coaches, therefore, would be more idealistic in their work and these coaches would be more likely to advocate the ideal form of rational resilience than coaches who are more realistic in their views of what clients can achieve in adversity. These coaches would more frequently advocate the realistic form of rational resilience to their clients. Thus, the final implication of what I have presented on rationality and resilience concerns coaches being mindful of their own views and thus guarding against influencing the coaching process unwittingly by their unconsidered biases.

References

American Psychological Association (2004). *The road to resilience*. Washington DC: APA.

Ellis, A. (1994). *Reason and emotion in psychotherapy: A comprehensive method of treating human disturbances. Revised and updated*. New York: Birch Lane Press.

Maslow, A. (1968). *Toward a psychology of being*. New York: Van Nostrand Reinhold.

CHAPTER 18

THE IMPORTANCE OF CHOICE IN THERAPY

From the perspective of a, hopefully flexible, CBT practitioner

European Journal of Psychotherapy and Counselling, 11: 311–322 (2009)

The piece that follows was first delivered as a presentation at a conference at Whitelands College, Roehampton University in London in November 2008 entitled 'Against and for CBT: Towards a Constructive Dialogue?' This conference marked the publication of an edited book of the same name (House and Loewenthal, 2008). As I have argued in my introduction to this collection, in retrospect my work on REBT has been pluralistic in nature, always trying to modify its theory and practice by incorporating developments both within REBT and perhaps, more importantly from outside REBT. This chapter is perhaps my most explicitly pluralistic paper in this collection in that it promotes flexibility to the centre stage of my ideas and therapy practice.

Perhaps the tone of the conference was more "against" than "for", as evidenced in its title, but such antipathy does need to be understood in context as many practitioners were angry and feeling threatened by what they saw as the CBT-based agenda behind the Government initiative known as 'Improving Access to Psychological Therapies' (IAPT) in the NHS. This antipathy was also evidenced in another later publication by Loewenthal and House (2010) which comprised a number of people outside CBT critically engaging with CBT. I was asked to be a discussant of these papers, most of the authors of which were critical of a CBT that bore little resemblance to the therapeutic tradition that I know.

Interestingly, Loewenthal and House were later to be partly responsible for helping to awaken explicitly my interest in pluralism in psychotherapy at a conference they organised, again at Whitelands College, towards the end of 2011.

References

House, R. and Loewenthal, D. (Eds) (2008). *Against and for CBT: towards a constructive dialogue?* Ross-on-Wye: PCCS Books.

Loewenthal, D. and House, R. (Eds) (2010). *Critically engaging CBT.* Maidenhead, Berkshire: Open University Press.

The main purpose of this paper is to present a personal account of my therapeutic journey and to show how my practice of CBT is informed not only by orientation-specific variables (e.g. emphases on 1) attitude; 2) perpetuation of disturbance as opposed to its acquisition; 3) specificity; 4) the development of client self-help skills; and 5) homework), but by more general, trans-theoretical variables (e.g. rooting therapy in the bonds, views, goals and tasks domains of the working alliance and dealing effectively with threats to this alliance). In doing so, I hope to show that when practised well, CBT draws upon general principles that span different therapeutic approaches as well as on ideas specific to CBT.

The stimulus for the conference at which this paper was first presented was the debate that has been engendered by the Government's initiative known as 'Increasing Access to Psychological Therapies' (IAPT). In part due to the Layard Report (2006), but mainly as a result of guidelines laid down by the National Institute for Clinical Excellence (NICE), a significant amount of money has been given to the training of CBT therapists at two levels: the so-called 'low intensity' and 'high intensity' levels. This initiative has been underpinned by a certain reading of the research literature which clearly favours CBT therapies over most non-CBT therapies. This reading, and the initiative that it spawned, has led to a significant outcry in the wider field of counselling and psychotherapy. This outcry has two main thrusts: a 'research' thrust and a 'CBT is defective' thrust.

In the 'research' thrust, critics argue that a different reading of the research literature indicates that there is no superiority of any one approach over others and that non-approach-specific variables account for much of the effectiveness of the psychological therapies (Cooper, 2008; Wampold et al., 1997).

The second thrust has been to criticise CBT as being defective in three major ways. First, CBT is criticised as a state-sponsored intervention whose quantitatively scientific emphasis sits easily with a Government that likes to quote figures and statistics as a way of proving that it is doing a good job. Second, CBT is criticised as a superficial, quick-fix therapy which leads to short-term, symptom-based change rather than longer-term, more meaningful change. Third, CBT is criticised as trying to 'fix' 'sick' people when the real problem is the society that makes them 'sick' in the first place. These three thrusts are amply summarised in House & Loewenthal, 2008).

While CBT has always received its fair share of criticism dating back to the mid 1950s when Albert Ellis, a founder of the CBT tradition, first presented his ideas to the field, the current criticism is fuelled, in my view, by the threat to the professional standing and even livelihood of non-CBT therapists. For example, there have been more articles published on CBT (both for and against) in the BACP's house organ the 'The Therapist' post-IAPT than pre-IAPT.

The main purpose of this paper is not to engage with these criticisms, but to present a personal account of my therapeutic journey and to show how my practice of CBT is informed not only by orientation-specific variables, but by more general, trans-theoretical variables. In doing so, I hope to show that when practised well CBT draws upon general principles that span different therapeutic approaches as well as on ideas specific to CBT. My theme is similar to the title of one of Samuels' (1989) books: 'The Plural Psyche'. It is that as our psyches are pluralistic rather than singular, and we thus need to adopt a pluralistic perspective in healing these psyches. So while I am a CBT therapist, I have significant doubts about the IAPT initiative if it imposes a form of treatment on people who do not wish to engage with this treatment.

I will begin by recounting an incident that happened over 20 years ago, and remains with me to this day. I practise a form of CBT known as Rational Emotive Behaviour Therapy (REBT), first called 'Rational Therapy' (RT) when established by Ellis in the mid 1950s. In the late 1970s when I was working in Birmingham, I received a call from a man who wanted to consult me because he was told that I practised RT. I remember feeling a little perplexed at the time since the therapy was more commonly known as RET at that time rather than RT, but thinking that the man must have been informed by one of Ellis's early writings on RT I offered him an appointment. When we met he told me about the issues with which he was grappling and I responded with empathy before enquiring whether he would like to know how I intended to approach these issues. With his agreement I gave him a brief outline of the theory and practice of my approach as it pertained to his problems. He listened to me politely before telling me that he had never heard such a load of rubbish and what he was looking for was RT or Reichian Therapy. In Reichian Therapy problems are conceptualised as the result of energy blockages which need to be released through deep tissue massage and cathartic expression. I knew a Reichian Therapist who practised in Birmingham so I referred the man to this therapist and later heard that he derived a great deal from therapy.

This episode taught me a number of important things. First, people have different ideas concerning the conceptualisation of their problems and how they can best be addressed therapeutically. Second, it is important that the therapist is explicit about how he conceptualises the client's problems and how he thinks these could be best addressed therapeutically. Third, if the two agree on these issues they can proceed with therapy and if they can't then the therapist is advised to effect a suitable referral to a practitioner whose views on these issues more closely approximates those of the client.

I once saw an advert for a Gestalt therapist to join a University Counselling Service that was staffed only by Gestalt therapists. I wrote to the university concerned to protest about its advert, not because of any reservations I had about this therapeutic approach, but because I am against any service being staffed solely by therapists from one orientation whether this be Gestalt Therapy, Psychodynamic Therapy, Person-Centred Therapy or even CBT.

If the Government's present initiative leads to a kind of National Therapy Service where the only therapy on offer is CBT then I would be deeply worried since it would not accommodate people like the man from Birmingham who was seeking Reichian Therapy. CBT has much to offer people, but it is not for everyone.

Admittedly, there are many people who come to therapy without defined views on how their problems can be best conceptualised and addressed and would thus be open to a variety of therapies. Such individuals may be able to use CBT effectively and benefit from a cognitive-behavioural approach, however, not everyone is as amenable to this therapeutic stance. If there are no alternatives on offer for such people we are doing them a disservice in the same way as the university students who could or did not wish to make use of Gestalt Therapy were disadvantaged by a service that only employed Gestalt therapists.

Why I am a CBT therapist: a personal journey

Having expressed my concerns regarding the potential detrimental impact of the National Health Service adopting a predominantly CBT-based psychological therapies service, I now wish to outline why I am a CBT therapist, albeit one who is open-minded and flexible. I wish to emphasise at this point that what follows relates to my own personal experiences and observations. I am not making objective comments about the other therapeutic approaches that I mention.

Recent research helps illustrate why I am particularly drawn to CBT. This research shows that the personality traits of practitioners in part explain why they are drawn towards different theoretical orientations. Ogunfowora and Drapeau (2008) found in their study of practitioner and student therapists that 'conscientiousness' predicted preference for CBT in both samples. This confirms previous research that showed that CBT therapists tend to be orderly, conscientious and efficient (Arthur, 2000, 2001; Scragg, Bor, & Watts, 1999). Ogunforwora and Drapeau (2008) speculate that conscientious individuals may be drawn to the structured, goal-directed nature of CBT and in my case this rings true. However, it is not the complete story and as well as being conscientious I am loathe to commit myself wholeheartedly to any idea and this trait explains, to me at least, why I draw on other therapeutic traditions in my practice.

Early training in Person-Centred Therapy and a brief dalliance with psychodynamic therapy

I originally trained in what is now called Person-Centred Therapy and resonated with its theory. I liked the idea that personality growth could be facilitated by the personal qualities of the therapist as they are experienced by the client (i.e. empathy, respect and genuineness). However, as a practitioner of Person-Centred Therapy, I came to doubt the necessity and sufficiency of these qualities, although I have never doubted their importance. I then briefly trained in psychodynamic theory, but discontinued this because I did not resonate with much of its theory and practice. This does not mean that I do not have respect for psychodynamic practice. I do. But it was not for me. Parenthetically, these experiences led me to question years later the suggestion that trainees should be trained in therapeutic approaches that make little sense to them.

The principles that drew me to CBT

I resonated most of all to CBT and in particular to the theory and practice of REBT in which I trained in the late 1970s. I was especially drawn to the following principles.

Emphasis on attitude

Perhaps the main reason that I became a CBT therapist is because this approach puts attitude or belief at the centre stage of our understanding of psychological disturbance and does so in a clear manner. I have always resonated with Epictetus's dictum that people are disturbed not by things, but by their views of things and this statement neatly encompasses a basic CBT principle.

Emphasis on perpetuation of disturbance as opposed to its acquisition

I was and am still drawn to CBT because it argues that, in most cases, an understanding of how clients perpetuate disturbance is more important than an understanding of how they acquire it in the first place. My view is that I am willing to talk about whatever a client wishes to discuss and thus I have no problem at all talking about the client's past experiences. However, I hold that these experiences contribute to rather than largely determine the client's present disturbance since different people would react to these same experiences in different ways. I also hold that people bring their tendencies to think, act and feel to their past experiences and take from these experiences a complex interaction of these tendencies, what happened to them and how others responded to what happened to them. An understanding of this complex interaction is important if it helps the client deal more effectively with their problems in the present and in particular, with how they address the factors that serve to perpetuate these problems. However, if they can deal with these problems effectively in the present without such understanding, then I will not lead them back to exploring this past interaction.

Emphasis on specificity

I was also drawn to CBT and still am because it encourages clients to focus on concrete examples of their problems and helps them to understand the specific cognitive-behavioural-emotive mechanisms that underpin these problems which they need to address if they are to respond more effectively in the situations in which they experience these problems.

Emphasis on the development of client self-help skills

Helping clients to develop self-help skills which they can use in their own lives is more effective than hoping that clients will generalise their learning from therapy sessions to their everyday lives on their own accord. CBT takes this principle seriously and offers clients the opportunity to learn CBT-based self-help skills in a systematic way. I should add that this is an invitation and not something that is imposed on clients. I will develop this theme further when I discuss the relationship between CBT and the working alliance. My view now is that what has always attracted me to this principle is that it encourages autonomy, which is a key aspect of my own personality.

Emphasis on homework

The term 'homework' is unfortunate in that it conjures up memories of having to do school work out of school hours when one would be preferred to be engaged in more enjoyable pursuits. Leaving aside what you call such activities, one of the most robust research findings in CBT is that people get more out of the process when they do carefully negotiate between-session assignments than when they don't (Burns & Spangler, 2000). I was and am still drawn to CBT because it makes such activities an important component of therapy, although again in my view this is a desirable feature of the therapy rather than a mandatory one. However, I do say to clients who don't wish to incorporate the 'homework' tasks into their personal therapy, that the therapeutic process will take longer.

CBT and the working alliance

In 1978 I enrolled for a part-time MSc in Psychotherapy at the University of Warwick. By this time I was well into my training in REBT at what is now known as the Albert Ellis Institute. Two core values of this approach are flexibility and open-mindedness and these spurred me to enrol on this Masters programme precisely because it was eclectic in orientation and exposed me to other approaches. This course was remarkable in two major respects. First, all sessions were given by leading proponents of therapeutic approaches, modalities and ideas and second, there were only eight students on the course. We had a marvellously broad psychotherapeutic education and one which was very costly in terms of resources, but relatively cheap for the student. If such a course were to be run today, fees would be well over £10,000 a year to make it viable. Fortunately, the value of financial viability had not hit the university sector as we completed this course before the swingeing higher education cuts of the early 1980s. This course taught me to understand, value and respect a variety of different therapeutic approaches, modalities and ideas, and although my basic orientation has not shifted since then, I have retained a respect for other approaches which I hope is apparent in the Handbook that now bears my name (Dryden, 2007).

The idea that has most influenced my work since I finished the Warwick course is the Working Alliance Theory originally propounded by Ed Bordin (1979) and expanded by myself in 2006 (Dryden, 2006). I will proceed to summarise how I combine Working Alliance Theory with CBT in ways that I believe address some of the current concerns surrounding CBT.

Originally, Bordin (1979) argued that the working alliance between therapist and client can be understood in terms of bonds, goals and tasks. He said that therapy outcome is enhanced when the relationship between therapist and client is suitably bonded, when the two are working towards shared goals and when they both undertake mutually understood tasks designed to help the client achieve his/her goals. I will expand on this idea presently. But first, I will discuss a fourth element of the alliance neglected by Bordin which I have included in my expanded conceptualisation of the working alliance. I have called this element, 'views'.

The 'views' domain of the working alliance

Both therapist and client come to therapy with pre-existing views about many salient aspects of the therapeutic process, including how they both construe the client's problems and how these can be best addressed.

I have already discussed what happens when therapist and client hold divergent views of the determinants of the client's problems and how these can be best tackled. You will recall what happened when my Birmingham client sought me out because I practised RT only to discover that I practised RT and not Reichian Therapy. Clients who are offered CBT within IAPT will benefit from this therapy in part to the extent that the CBT-based explanation given to them of their problems and how these problems are to be tackled makes sense to them. My concern is, however, what happens when it doesn't? What provision is to be made for people who are bold enough to say: 'I don't agree with this way of conceptualising my problems? I think that my problems are (for example) more to do with unresolved conflicts in my past which can only be rectified by a thorough exploration of my past relationships in my family of origin.' CBT may be the best *empirically* supported treatment that we have, it may be NICE recommended but what if some people don't want it? This is my major concern about IAPT.

Clients may be prepared to be open to the therapist's view of the determinants of his/her problems and how best to deal with them no matter what the orientation of the therapist. However, this will only be the case when the therapist is explicit about these views. As I have already stated I am drawn towards CBT not only because I resonate with its views on such matters, but because it recommends that its practitioners are explicit about these issues.

Assuming that therapist and client agree sufficiently with respect to the conceptualisation of the client's problems and how these problems can be rectified, other elements of the working alliance come into play.

The 'bonds' domain of the working alliance

Any discussion of the bonds domain of the working alliance in a therapeutic approach has to outline the status in the approach of what have come to be widely known as the core conditions. In CBT the core conditions of empathy, respect and genuineness are considered to be important, but not sufficient for change to take place. They are regarded as the foundation without which the techniques of CBT would not have potency. However, on their own they are not seen as facilitating long-term cognitive, behavioural and emotive change. While I am largely in agreement with this view, I imagine that for some clients these conditions are necessary and for a smaller number they are necessary *and* sufficient for change to occur. Indeed, it may be that CBT is not indicated for such clients since the technical aspects of the therapy add no additional therapeutic value to what these clients need.

When you read of the therapeutic relationship in CBT much is made of the collaborative nature of this relationship. Although the focus here is on the therapist and client working together in formulating and addressing the client's problems, I agree with Ellis (1989) that there is something disingenuous about this view of the relationship in CBT. Ellis argued that the CBT therapist is the expert on CBT and the CBT change process while the client is expert on his/her experience. If they collaborate on this basis then this is more honest than seeing them as equal collaborators. They may be equal as humans, but they are unequal in terms of expertise on psychological change.

While on the subject of therapist expertise and the working alliance, I want to make the point that while some clients are more effectively influenced by the expertise of the therapist others respond better to the therapist when they like the person. Effective CBT therapists are able to modify their own behaviour to meet the influence preferences of their clients as long as they do so authentically. Lazarus (1981) refers to the therapist who can do this as an authentic chameleon.

Another aspect of the bond that is relevant to CBT is the concept of interactive style. Setting aside the issue of collaboration, CBT is perhaps known as encouraging its practitioners to adopt an active-directive interactive style with clients. Here the therapist is encouraged to be active in directing the client to the cognitive-behavioural dynamics involved in explaining how the client unwittingly perpetuates his/her problems.

A real danger of adopting an active-directive style is that it may render the client passive and directionless and if this is the case, I would argue that this is the fault of the practitioner rather than the approach. A skilled CBT therapist can adopt an active-directive style which both engages the client in the therapeutic process and preserves the client's autonomy.

There are a number of dimensions along which one can consider a therapist's interactive style: serious–humorous; formal–informal; structured–unstructured; self-disclosing–non-self-disclosing. Effective CBT therapists modify their interactive style according to the client with whom they are working. Again, I wish to reiterate that this modification needs to be done authentically. Thus, if a CBT therapist adopts a humorous, informal, unstructured, self-disclosing style with a client who would benefit more from working with a therapist who is more serious, formal, structured and non-self-disclosing, no matter how good technically the therapist may be, his effectiveness with this particular client will be impaired.

While CBT therapists generally favour an active-directive, structured style of therapy, its most competent practitioners are prepared to vary their behaviour on these key dimensions with certain clients throughout therapy and with all clients as therapy unfolds. In the first case, the therapist will be less structured and less active-directive with clients who either require a more exploratory style of therapy but still resonates with the 'views' expounded by CBT or who experience a structured, active-directive approach as a threat to their authority. In the latter case, as therapy unfolds the therapist will adopt a more prompting style of interaction in the service of encouraging clients to take increasing responsibility for using CBT skills of assessment and intervention in therapy both inside and outside therapy sessions.

The 'goals' domain of the working alliance

With respect to the goals domain of the alliance, CBT therapists generally encourage their clients to set 'SMART' goals, where 'S' stands for 'Specific', 'M' for 'Measurable', 'A' for 'Achievable', 'R' for 'Realistic' and 'T' for 'Time-bound'. However, this may not always be possible or desirable and effective CBT therapists prioritise preserving the alliance over working with such preferred goals. Thus, working towards client goals that both participants share is perhaps the most important ingredient here. With its emphasis on explicitness, CBT therapists are perhaps less likely to work towards goals unwanted by clients than therapists who are less explicit about goals in their therapeutic work.

The 'tasks' domain of the working alliance

The final aspect of the alliance that I wish to discuss is the task domain. I have left this to last to counterbalance the view that CBT is all about technique. It is not and I hope I have conveyed this point in this paper. However, of course, there are technical aspects of CBT and these have been well researched. From an alliance perspective, a skilful CBT therapist:

1 Helps his client to understand his/her own tasks and those of the therapist and how they relate to one another.
2 Helps his client to understand how carrying out their respective tasks will help the client to achieve his/her goals.
3 Trains the client where appropriate to carry out his/her tasks (Dryden, 2001; Greenberger & Padesky, 1995).

Some recent research has shown that the technical aspects of CBT have to be viewed within the broader context of the task domain of the alliance. I will mention two such studies. The first study, conducted by Delsignore, Carraro, Mathier, Znoj, and Schnyder (2008), demonstrated how patients perceive responsibility for change and the impact of this variable on engagement in therapy and outcome prediction in cognitive-behavioural group therapy for social anxiety. The researchers found that patients who considered that they were responsible for the success of their treatment engaged more in therapy and had a better outcome at three-month follow-up than patients who considered that the therapist was responsible for the success of their therapy. This shows that the potency of CBT techniques is mediated by important patient variables, and that general therapeutic principles of encouraging clients to take responsibility for change may be of equal or even greater importance than specific CBT techniques.

The second study examined the willingness of people aged 65 and over with anxiety and/or depression to engage with computerised CBT (cCBT), Elsegood and Powell (2008) found that almost half of this sample would be willing to engage and learn the necessary computer skills. However, just over half were not interested in engaging with CBT and the researchers identified six negative themes in the reasons given by this group: These were:

- lack of motivation to try computerised therapy due to depression;
- fear/rejection of technology;
- concern that cognitive abilities are inadequate for using a computer;
- concern that sensory and/or motor abilities are inadequate for using a computer;
- feeling too old to learn new skills; and
- preference for human contact.

CBT practitioners would deal with many of these patient concerns in an empirical way and would encourage such patients to test out their hypotheses by trying cCBT. However, this would only be the case if such patients would be willing to try this intervention. I am concerned for those who are not willing. Will the NHS offer them face-to-face CBT and if they are not willing to engage in this approach will the NHS offer them alternatives in the form of face-to-face psychodynamic, humanistic or systemic therapy?

If practitioners are drawn to specific theoretical orientations in part because of their personality surely this is the case with patients as well. If conscientiousness draws a practitioner to CBT, is this also the case with patients? We need research on the relationship between patient personality traits and theoretical orientation preferences. It may be that the NHS are providing CBT services that will largely benefit the conscientious

Dealing with threats to the working alliance: The art of therapy

Therapy rarely runs smoothly and the therapist as part of his training needs to be prepared to deal with threats to the working alliance if he is to be truly effective with a wide range of clients. My concern with the low-intensity and high-intensity CBT training that is being promoted as part of the IAPT initiative is that there is insufficient attention to the working alliance between patient and therapist and how to deal with threats to this alliance. The bulk of the training attention is on the tasks domain of the alliance where therapists are trained to conceptualise and deal with problems of anxiety and depression from a CBT perspective. But what if the client does not wish to approach their problems from a CBT perspective? What if they don't want to set specific goals or carry out homework assignments? Dealing with these threats to the alliance is the art of therapy and while the two levels of CBT training will no doubt increase the technical competence of therapists, I question whether they will increase their artistic competence to the same extent.

This having been said, CBT has been subjected to scientific scrutiny, a valuable asset in light of the fact that NICE values quantitative evidence over qualitative evidence. Non-specific variables may account for a good proportion of the variance in terms of therapeutic outcome, but it still behoves practitioners of non-CBT approaches to subject their approach to empirical study. In a recent article, Cooper (2008) highlighted two important points relevant to this discussion. First, he noted that greater evidence of effectiveness is not equivalent to evidence of greater effectiveness. Thus, although CBT has been studied more than non-CBT approaches, it does not follow that CBT is more effective than non-CBT approaches. However, he also said that the reason why non-CBT therapies are not considered effective for particular psychological problems is simply because no one has studied them yet. And I would add that it may be that CBT therapies may be more effective than non-CBT approaches when these studies are done. We just don't have sufficient data from well-controlled studies to judge. But it is not good enough for practitioners of non-CBT therapies to hide behind the Dodo Bird verdict that all have won and all must have prizes. Reichian therapists still have to prove the effectiveness of Reichian Therapy for this approach to be recommended by NICE and offered by the NHS.

In my view it is right that NICE should recommend CBT given its strong evidence base. It is wrong, however, if they *only* recommend CBT since many people may be unwilling or unable to engage with this therapeutic approach. It is ironic that at a time when diversity and plurality are being stressed in many walks of life that in relation to the funding of therapy by the NHS, a lack of diversity and plurality is so evident.

A call for greater respect

One of the byproducts of the IAPT initiative and the ascendancy of CBT in the NHS has been the criticisms levelled at CBT by non-CBT therapists. Whether these criticisms have stemmed from specific concerns about the approach, or from anxiety related to perceived or actual threats to one's professional standing and to one's livelihood, or even from envy, these criticisms have ranged from thoughtful points respectfully conveyed to points which have been far-fetched. People in the CBT community have experienced the latter as disrespectful. Respectful communication in our field is important if we are to serve as role models for our clients and with this in mind, I eagerly await the response to this paper.

References

Arthur, A.R. (2000). The personality and cognitive-epistemological traits of cognitive-behavioural and psychoanalytic psychotherapists. *British Journal of Medical Psychology*, *73*, 243–257.

Arthur, A.R. (2001). Personality epistemology and psychotherapists' choice of theoretical model: A review and analysis. *European Journal of Psychotherapy, Counselling and Health*, *4*, 45–64.

Bordin, E.S. (1979). The generalizability of the psychoanalytic concept of the working alliance. *Psychotherapy: Theory, Research and Practice*, *16*, 252–260.

Burns, D.D., & Spangler, D.L. (2000). Does psychotherapy homework lead to improvements in depression in cognitive-behavioral therapy or does improvement lead to increased homework compliance? *Journal of Consulting and Clinical Psychology*, *68*, 46–56.

Cooper, M. (2008). The facts are friendly. *Therapy Today*, *19*(7), 8–13.

Delsignore, A., Carraro, G., Mathier, F., Znoj, H., & Schnyder, U. (2008). Perceived responsibility for change as an outcome predictor in cognitive-behavioural group therapy. *British Journal of Clinical Psychology*, *47*, 281–293.

Dryden, W. (2001). *Reason to change: A rational emotive behaviour therapy (REBT) workbook*. Hove, East Sussex: Brunner-Routledge.

Dryden, W. (2006). *Counselling in a nutshell*. London: Sage.

Dryden, W. (Ed.) (2007). *Dryden's handbook of individual therapy* (5th ed.). London: Sage.

Ellis, A. (1989). Ineffective consumerism in the cognitive-behavioral therapies and in general psychotherapy. In W. Dryden & P. Trower (Eds.), *Cognitive psychotherapy: Stasis and change*. London: Cassell.

Elsegood, K., & Powell, D. (2008). Computerised cognitive-behaviour therapy (cCBT) and older people: A pilot study to determine factors that influence willingness to engage with cCBT. *Counselling & Psychotherapy Research*, *8*, 189–192.

Greenberger, D., & Padesky, C.A. (1995). *Mind over mood: Change how you feel by changing how you think*. New York: Guilford Press.

House, R., & Loewenthal, D. (Eds.) (2008). *Against and for CBT: Towards a constructive dialogue*. Ross-on-Wye: PCCS Books.

Layard, R. (2006). *The depression report: A new deal for depression and anxiety disorders*. London: London School of Economics.
Lazarus, A.A. (1981). *The practice of multimodal therapy*. New York: McGraw-Hill.
Ogunforwora, B., & Drapeau, M. (2008). A study of the relationship between personality traits and theoretical orientation preferences. *Counselling & Psychotherapy Research*, *8*, 151–159.
Samuels, A. (1989). *The plural psyche: Personality, morality and the father*. London: Routledge.
Scragg, P., Bor, R., & Watts, M. (1999). The influence of personality and theoretical models on applicants to a counselling psychology course: A preliminary study. *Counselling Psychology Quarterly*, *12*, 263–270.
Wampold, B.E., Mondin, G.W., Moody, M., Stich, F., Benson, K., & Ahn, H. (1997). A meta-analysis of outcome studies comparing bona fide psychotherapies: Empirically, "All must have prizes". *Psychological Bulletin*, *122*, 203–215.

CHAPTER 19

ALBERT ELLIS AND RATIONAL EMOTIVE BEHAVIOR THERAPY

A personal reflection

Journal of Rational-Emotive & Cognitive-Behavior Therapy, 29(4): 211–219 (2011)

In 2011, the journal that I edited from 2003 until 2012, the *Journal of Rational-Emotive & Cognitive-Behavior Therapy*, published a special issue entitled 'Albert Ellis and Rational Emotive Behavior Therapy's Influence: Past, Present and Future', guest edited by Kristene Doyle. Eight noted REBT therapists (including myself) were invited to reflect on their long-term relationship with the founder of REBT who died in June, 2007. While some of us had had difficult relationships with Ellis in the years immediately before he died, all of us gave testimony to the enormous influence that the man had had on our personal and professional lives. While writing such a reflection always runs the risk of straying into hagiography, I think I avoided doing so in my piece while at the same time giving credit where it was most properly due.

Abstract

I discuss what I consider to be Albert Ellis's ten most important contributions to the development of REBT. I also give a personal view on what we will miss on his passing and on what we won't.

Introduction

When Albert Ellis died on 24th June 2007, the world of psychotherapy lost one of its most influential, colourful and controversial characters. People in the REBT field have been speculating for years about what would happen to REBT after Al died, but it was thought unseemly to engage fully with this question while he was alive. He had, after all, threatened to outlive us all! But now that he has passed, it is important that we take stock and consider how REBT needs to develop in the future. In order to do this we need to base our discussions on (a) an appreciation of Ellis's contribution and (b) his strengths and weaknesses so that we can build on the former and minimise the latter from our future efforts to develop the approach. This paper represents my contribution to this debate.

Albert Ellis's best contributions to the development of REBT

It is well recognised and generally accepted that Albert Ellis made an unparalleled contribution to the professional fields of counselling, psychotherapy, sexual functioning and psychological education, to name just a few. Even when his influence has not been acknowledged, it can easily be discerned as discussed in a recently published collection of articles edited by Velten (2007). To do justice to all his professional contributions would take several volumes. What I will do here is to mention briefly ten of his contributions that have shaped REBT and have made it a distinct approach within the cognitive-behavioral tradition.

Irrational and rational beliefs

Perhaps Ellis's most profound contribution to our understanding of psychological disturbance and health in the face of adversity is his idea that such disturbance and health are underpinned by irrational and rational beliefs respectively. While Ellis's views of the nature of these beliefs have changed over the years, the most common expression of Ellis's views can be summarised in Table 19.1. Thus, from the outset, Ellis was not just putting forward the role of cognition in (a) people's psychological problems and (b) constructive solutions to these problems, he was also attempting to be quite precise in detailing the nature of these unhealthy and healthy cognitions.

We can see from Table 19.1 that Ellis focused on rigid and extreme beliefs (which underpin psychological disturbance) and flexible and non-extreme beliefs (which underpin psychological health). We can also see the relationship between both types of beliefs. Ellis's point here was that extreme beliefs are derived from rigid beliefs and non-extreme beliefs are derived from flexible beliefs. In this way, one of Ellis's core contributions is seen in the primary role given to rigid beliefs and flexible beliefs in people's belief systems.

Table 19.1 Rigid versus flexible beliefs and extreme versus non-extreme beliefs

	Rigid	Flexible	
	Demands	Non-dogmatic Preferences	
	V	V	
Extreme	Awfulising Beliefs LFT Beliefs Depreciation Beliefs	Non-Awfulising Beliefs HFT Beliefs Acceptance Beliefs	Non-extreme
	V	V	
	Psychological Disturbance	Psychological Health	

Extreme beliefs are derived from rigid beliefs. They both underpin psychological disturbance

Non-extreme beliefs are derived from flexible beliefs. They both underpin psychological health

Psychological interactionism

From REBT's beginnings, Ellis (1958) emphasized not only the important role that thinking plays in psychological disturbance and health, but also that thinking as a psychological process could not be separated from emotion and behaviour. This position of psychological interactionism pointed to the importance that the best way of changing irrational beliefs was by using cognitive, emotive and behavioural techniques in concert and *not* by using cognitive techniques alone. This point was not fully appreciated and occasioned the two name changes that Ellis initiated to make clear that his system of therapy neither neglected emotion (the change from RT to RET) nor behaviour (the change from RET to REBT).

Distinction between UNEs and HNEs

The REBT position on irrational and rational beliefs is that these are qualitatively different and do not exist on a continuum. For example, consider the irrational belief: "My boss must like me" (demand), and the rational alternative: "I want my boss to like me, but he doesn't have to do so" (non-dogmatic preference). The qualitative theory of beliefs states that while I might hold these two different beliefs at different times, I cannot hold both at the same time. It follows from this that that the negative emotions that stem from irrational beliefs (known as unhealthy negative emotions or UNEs) are qualitatively different from those that stem from rational beliefs (known as healthy negative emotions or HNEs). While the empirical data on REBT's qualitative theory of emotions is equivocal (David et al. 2005), it does represent a unique contribution to our understanding of emotions and their cognitive underpinnings. For me, the most important implication of this theory is that it is healthy for someone to have strong negative emotions about an adversity and that these feelings are healthy (if based on rational beliefs). Other approaches to CBT tend to advocate a quantitative theory of emotions where the goal of intervention is to reduce the intensity of negative emotions and where no distinction is clearly made between UNEs and HNEs.

Biological roots of human rationality and irrationality

Pelusi (2007) has made the important point that people do not object when a variety of theorists claim that humans are biologically prone to move towards self-enhancement and psychological growth, but they do object to Ellis's (e.g. 1976) notion that humans are also biologically prone to self-defeat and psychological disturbance. The biological hypothesis argues, for example, that people find it very easy to transform their preferences to demands especially when their preferences are strong. Therapeutically, it has two main implications. First, there is little to be gained from looking extensively at the social learning roots of psychological disturbance since such experiences are underpinned by a biologically-based tendency to disturb oneself. Thus, ten people with the same social learning roots will have different responses to these experiences. Second, while psychological change is possible (since we have a biologically-based tendency to think rationally as well as irrationally), it is predicated on much emotive, cognitive and behavioural work and practice. Cognitive insight alone rarely leads to lasting significant therapeutic change.

Acceptance

Ellis and Robb (1994) had long advocated acceptance as a prime mediator of psychological health. His conceptualisation of acceptance which predates the emergence of Acceptance and Commitment Therapy (Hayes et al. 1999) differs importantly from the way acceptance is used in ACT.

First, Ellis's view of acceptance was that it could incorporate the possibility of negatively evaluating what was to be accepted. This follows logically from Ellis's view (see above) that an acceptance belief was a derivative of a non-dogmatic preference about an adversity. Thus, I prefer this article to be universally praised in the REBT literature, but also hold that such praise is not essential to me (in other words my belief is a non-dogmatic preference). Consequently, if my article receives criticism, I will accept the existence of this criticism while disliking it. This, so REBT theory argues, enables me to be honest about my stance towards criticism, while opening up the possibility that I can examine it non-defensively and learn from it where relevant.

Second, Ellis (e.g. 2004) showed that the concept of unconditional acceptance can be applied to self (unconditional self-acceptance or USA), others (unconditional other-acceptance or UOA) and life conditions (unconditional life-acceptance or ULA). When it is applied in this way, it is a stance that is taken towards the whole (of a person—self or other—and of life) and towards an aspect of the whole. When taken towards the whole, it involves the person acknowledging that the object of one's acceptance (self, other or life) is too complex to warrant a single global evaluation and when taken towards the aspect, it involves acknowledging that the conditions were right for the aspect to exist, but it also involves a negative appraisal of this aspect. This is Ellis's preferred approach, but his back-up position was that one would not disturb onself if one gave oneself, the other person or life a global positive evaluation ("I am good", "You are good", "Life is good") as long as these global evaluations were unconditional. The real enemy of acceptance in Ellis's view is conditionality (e.g. "I will accept myself if I am loved" which implies that I will not accept myself if I am not).

Meta disturbance

Long before work on meta-cognitive processes appeared in the literature (Wells 2000), Ellis argued that clients frequently disturb themselves about their disturbances. Previously called symptom stress (Walen et al. 1980) and second-order disturbance, this process—which I refer to here as meta-disturbance—points to the fact that we can disturb ourselves about different aspects of our original disturbance, thus:

- Emotive ("I must not feel this way")
- Cognitive ("I must not think this way") and
- Behavioral ("I must not act this way")

Incidentally, meta-cognitive processes would be understood as inferences at "A" that clients make about cognitive experience (e.g. "I need to think the worst to protect myself from it happening"). Often, according to REBT theory metacognitive processes stem from irrational beliefs.

Early clinical emphasis on belief change

In line with his views on therapeutic efficiency, Ellis (1980) argued for an early clinical focus on irrational beliefs to help clients to identify them and to work towards changing them to rational beliefs. Getting to the heart of the therapeutic matter and helping clients understand why he was taking this stance characterized Ellis's best demonstration sessions (e.g. Dryden and Ellis 2003). However, if not done skillfully (i.e. by explaining to clients the rationale for this early focus and by eliciting agreement to proceed), it may, in fact, turn out to be inefficient. But when done skillfully, particularly when the therapist attends to salient aspects of the therapeutic alliance, it is an Ellis legacy that has probably saved much needless psychological pain for thousands of people.

Emphasis on work and practice in change

Even when clients can see clearly that their irrational beliefs are false, illogical and destructive and that the rational alternatives to these beliefs are true, logical and constructive, this intellectual insight is insufficient to uproot irrational beliefs. In order for them to achieve what Ellis (1963) first called emotional insight (i.e. the kind of insight that leads to change), they need to think and act in ways that are consistent with their rational beliefs and inconsistent with their irrational beliefs and do this many times for change to take place. When this "protestant ethic" approach is adopted by clients and applied with force and energy (see below), they can make profound changes in their lives.

Emphasis on force and energy in change

Ellis views irrational beliefs like very stubborn weeds which will not yield to gentle attempts at uprooting. Often irrational beliefs are held with strong conviction and weak disputing, for example, will not have much effect. Rather, Ellis (1979a) claims that a forceful and energetic approach to changing these beliefs is what is required. With respect to the therapist's use of force and energy in REBT, people have often thought wrongly that Ellis's style is the gold standard and should be emulated. This is not so. One can be forceful and energetic in many ways and REBT therapists are urged to marry these qualities with their own style rather than slavishly copy Ellis. Also, clients should be encouraged to use force and energy in ways that are both compatible with their own personality style and that promote a full engagement with their rational beliefs. Because the terms "force" and "energy" are easily misunderstood, perhaps the term "passion" is to be preferred.

One note of caution is needed here. Force and energy in the belief change process should only be used when clients have intellectual insight as described above. When therapists use forceful and energetic methods of change with clients who lack intellectual insight, this is a breeding ground for client resistance and is bad REBT.

Psycho-educational emphasis

REBT offers a particular perspective on psychological problems and how they can be best tackled and does so in a way that can be taught to clients. Ellis made much of teaching people how to be their own therapists and to this end he authored numerous self-help books—the first being *How to Live with a Neurotic* published over 50 years ago (Ellis, 1957)—and produced many audiocassettes and CDs which show people how they can apply REBT to a wide range of both clinical problems and non-clinical problems. Ellis's famous "Friday Night Workshops" conducted at the Albert Ellis Institute for over 40 years were a great example of REBT's psycho-educational emphasis where Ellis would interview two volunteers on their "Problems in Living" (this was the original title of what came to be known as the "Friday Night Workshop"). It has been found that the vast majority of these volunteers found the experience positive and helpful (Ellis and Joffe 2002).

While Ellis never published a step by step client manual showing clients how they can use REBT in a structured way to help themselves, I was inspired by Ellis's psycho-educational writings to produce two of my own (Dryden 2001, 2006).

What we will miss with Al's passing

Albert Ellis's main goal in life was the promulgation of the principles and practices of REBT. He often said that his work was his main priority and that other aspects of his life, like his relationships and his many non-work interests came second. His actions were certainly consistent with his words on this point. There is no suitably qualified and high profile person in the field of REBT who seems willing to make the promotion of REBT the main feature of their life. While this may be healthy for the individuals concerned, it means that unless there is a concerted group effort to take on Al's mantle in this promotional work we will lose what he gave us in this respect. In my view, he gave us the following:

- Ellis accepted every opportunity to write about REBT and every invitation to comment on others' REBT-based writings.
- Ellis was assiduous in writing rebuttals whenever he learned that someone in print had misrepresented some aspect of REBT theory or practice.
- Ellis wrote articles detailing the REBT perspective on current professional trends and issues, thus maintaining the profile of REBT when it could easily have become lost without his efforts.
- Ellis wrote articles showing how REBT would approach the treatment of a particular client groups or clinical problems. He thus showed that REBT had tremendous breadth and generalizability.
- Ellis travelled the world giving workshops on REBT to any professional group or association who would pay his reasonable fees (which he generously and unselfishly donated to the Institute that bares his name)
- Ellis continually looked to refine REBT principles and to find better ways of communicating them to both professional and lay people.

What we will not miss with Al's passing

While Albert Ellis did a tremendous amount that was good in promoting REBT, his contribution was not always positive. As he was a fallible human being, it is not surprising that he had his faults and failings which had a negative impact on the development of REBT. What will we not miss with Al's passing? In my view, we will not miss the following.

- Ellis's brazen, uninhibited and sometimes short-tempered style often alienated people who expected a more restrained, professional approach at his workshops. His honesty could be brutal and I remember one workshop in Mainz, Germany where in answer to a question about the mental health of the German people, he almost caused a riot by exclaiming that he thought that the Germans were "the most fucked up people on the planet."
- Ellis's emphasis on rational humorous songs and shame-attacking exercises was sometimes problematic. His intention with these techniques was laudable:

to show how people could take themselves seriously, but not too seriously. However, although popular with lay people, they had the effect of trivialising REBT in the minds of many professionals and interfered with them seeing the depth and richness of the approach.

- Ellis's style of doing therapy in public demonstrations, particularly in his latter years did not always provide a good role model of doing REBT within the context of a good therapeutic alliance. With Ellis, I published a book called *Albert Ellis Live* (Dryden & Ellis, 2003). This contained the transcripts and analysis of some of Al's best public demonstrations of REBT. In these interviews, Ellis showed a high level of technical skill married to a concern with the working alliance with his clients. These interviews show a master at the height of his powers. Sadly, towards the end of his life, Ellis's insistence on working "until I die in the saddle" meant that he showed his decreasing powers in his public demonstrations.

  Specifically, he displayed a penchant for playing to the crowd with an increasing emphasis on tired "rational" clichés and catch phrases and a greater emphasis on profanity than hitherto. Also, his previous emphasis on undertaking a quick, but accurate assessment on clients' problems was replaced with a rush to dispute irrational beliefs almost in the first couple of minutes of the interview without an accurate assessment.

  People have always tended to assume that all REBT therapists practise REBT in the style of Ellis. Those who saw Ellis practise REBT live in the latter years probably came away with an unfavourable impression of how REBT is generally practised which in reality is not the case.
- Finally, Ellis (e.g. 1979b) perpetuated the idea that there are two REBTs: specific (or elegant) and general (or inelegant). The former was regarded as superior to other approaches to CBT while the latter was regarded as synonymous with CBT. Ellis used whichever approach to REBT suited his current purpose with the result that some people became confused about the nature of the approach known as REBT and others became alienated by his statements about the superiority of elegant REBT. The terms "elegant" and "inelegant" were particularly problematic in this regard. Here, as elsewhere, Ellis's admirable honesty interfered with his greater purpose: to promulgate the theory and practice of REBT. It was difficult for some people within the tradition of CBT to appraise dispassionately the virtues of REBT while being told that they themselves practised an inelegant form of therapy.

Conclusion

In this paper, I have reflected on Ellis's phenomenal contribution to the field particular through his writings on REBT. I have given a personal view both on what we will miss and not miss with his passing. A1 was always very clear that he did not want us to grieve much when he died. Rather he wanted us to preserve his legacy, not for retrospective personal aggrandisement, but in order to make the world a more rational place in which to live. I, for one, will discharge my personal and professional debt to Albert Ellis by continuing to do just that.

References

David, D., Montgomery, G., Macavei, B., & Bovbjerg, D. (2005). An empirical investigation of Albert Ellis' binary model of distress. *Journal of Clinical Psychology*, *61*, 499–516.

Dryden, W. (2001). *Reason to change: A rational emotive behaviour therapy (REBT) workbook*. Hove, East Sussex: Brunner-Routledge.

Dryden, W. (2006). *Getting started with REBT: A concise guide for clients*. Hove, East Sussex: Routledge.

Dryden, W., & Ellis, A. (2003). *Albert Ellis live!*. London: Sage.

Ellis, A. (1957). *How to live with a neurotic: At home and at work*. New York: Crown.

Ellis, A. (1958). Rational psychotherapy. *Journal of General Psychotherapy*, *59*, 35–49.

Ellis, A. (1963). Toward a more precise definition of "emotional" and "intellectual" insight. *Psychological Reports*, *13*, 125–126.

Ellis, A. (1976). The biological basis of human irrationality. *Journal of Individual Psychology*, *32*, 145–168.

Ellis, A. (1979a). The issue of force and energy in behavioral change. *Journal of Contemporary Psychotherapy*, *10*(2), 83–97.

Ellis, A. (1979b). Rejoinder: Elegant and inelegant RET. In A. Ellis & J. M. Whiteley (Eds.), *Theoretical and empirical foundations of rational-emotive therapy* (pp. 240–267). Monterey, CA: Brooks/Cole.

Ellis, A. (1980). The value of efficiency in psychotherapy. *Psychotherapy: Theory, Research and Practice*, *17*, 414–419.

Ellis, A. (2004). *Rational emotive behaviour therapy: It works for me—it can work for you*. Amherst, NY: Prometheus Books.

Ellis, A., & Joffe, D. (2002). A study of volunteer clients who experienced live sessions of rational emotive behaviour therapy in front of a public audience. *Journal of Rational-Emotive & Cognitive-Behavior Therapy*, *20*, 151–158.

Ellis, A., & Robb, H. (1994). Acceptance in rational-emotive therapy. In S. C. Hayes, N. S. Jacobson, V. M. Follette, & M. J. Dougher (Eds.), *Acceptance and change: Context and content in psychotherapy* (pp. 91–102). Reno, NV: Context.

Hayes, S. C., Strosahl, K. D., & Wilson, K. G. (1999). *Acceptance and commitment therapy: An experiential approach to behaviour change*. New York: Guilford Press.

Pelusi, N. M. (2007). Albert Ellis's views on biological considerations in psychotherapy. In E. Velten (Ed.), *Under the influence: Reflections of Albert Ellis in the work of others* (pp. 163–171). Tucson, AZ: See Sharp Press.

Velten, E. (Ed.). (2007). *Under the influence: Reflections of Albert Ellis in the work of others*. Tucson, AZ: See Sharp Press.

Walen, S. R., DiGiuseppe, R., & Wessler, R. L. (1980). *A practitioner's guide to rational-emotive therapy*. New York: Oxford University Press.

Wells, A. (2000). *Emotional disorders and metacognition: Innovative cognitive therapy*. Chichester: John Wiley & Sons.

CHAPTER 20

ADAPTING CBT TO A BROAD CLIENTELE

W. Dryden and R. Branch (Eds) (2012) *The CBT handbook*. London: Sage (pp. 214–230).

In 2012, Rhena Branch and I edited *The CBT Handbook* for Sage (Dryden and Branch, 2012). In that book I decide to contribute a piece that showed the influence of Arnold Lazarus on my work. Lazarus (1989) coined the term 'bespoke therapy' to show that effective therapy often occurs when interventions have been designed with the uniqueness of the client in mind rather than as a standardised, 'off the peg' type of intervention. To some degree, then, this piece can be seen as critical of manualised therapy, although there are occasions where set therapeutic principles need to be implemented. The piece can also be seen as another example of how I adopt a pluralistic perspective in my work as a REBT/CBT practitioner.

References

Dryden, W., and Branch, R. (Eds) (2012). *The CBT handbook*. London: Sage.
Lazarus, A. A. (1989). *The practice of multimodal therapy*. Baltimore, MD: Johns Hopkins University Press.

Introduction

I will be discussing in this chapter how to adapt your approach to CBT when working with a range of different clients. The relevant issues will be considered and I will summarise my own views with regard to them. By summarising my position I do not wish to propose it as a model for good practice. Instead, it is intended to provide an illustration of one approach among many. The fundamental aim of this chapter is to explore a number of issues and allow you to reflect upon them.

'Bespoke therapy' was a term coined by Lazarus (1989) to identify an approach towards therapy based on the idea of 'tailoring'. The term 'bespoke' was used to focus on a customised approach to clinical work in contrast to a more fixed 'off-the-peg' style of therapy in which CBT is practised in an identical form, irrespective of who your client might be. In 'bespoke therapy', on the other hand, the approach is adjusted to fit the client and is developed out of an assessment of the particular variables in respect to your client. Later in this chapter I will examine a number of these variables.

Why your approach should be varied

In North American universities the first year 'Introduction to Psychology' courses (informally termed Psychology 101) usually commence by stating what appears to be obvious – that 'people are different!' If we apply this to CBT we can see clearly that all CBT approaches are based on the idea that clients are different. In fact, all CBT approaches encourage practitioners to treat each one of their clients as a unique individual. It therefore follows that as clients differ from each other and should be treated individually, you should respond as a therapist in a way that is most appropriate to each of your clients and that this should apply regardless of the particular form of CBT you practise.

What should you vary?

Assuming that you accept that you should give different responses to different clients as their therapist, regardless of what form of CBT you practise, what exactly will you be varying? In the following I will be responding to this question. As I have suggested above, my approach should be regarded as that of one CBT practitioner and I hope you will find your thinking stimulated in relation to your own practice on this issue.

I will be dealing with the following three major areas where customising your approach is important:

- customising CBT to fit your client's suitability for different therapeutic arenas;
- customising CBT to fit your client's stage of change on a problem;
- customising CBT to fit your client's relational style.

But first I will examine how the context in which you work may affect your CBT practice and I will begin by highlighting the fact that therapy does not occur in a vacuum.

How your work context may affect your clinical decisions

Many therapists may consider that they have high levels of independence and initiative. They do, but only within the framework and limits of their work context. This is clearly the case if you work in a clinic practice where several constraints may well be placed on CBT service delivery.

Case study

Alan works in the CBT-based voluntary sector. in the organisation in which he works, CBT is limited to eight sessions. Alan has to work within a strict set of exclusion criteria. The guidelines make it clear to whom he can and cannot offer CBT, but less clear for whom the service may be offered. Unfortunately, his is the only CBT-based service in the area. As a result, while on some occasions Alan offers eight-session CBT to clients with problems amenable to such short-term intervention, he often has to decide whether to offer this service to clients who need much longer intervention but who do not meet the exclusion criteria. Because he knows that if he turns away these clients, it is quite likely that they will receive no therapy of any kind, he offers them the service, which is a stance that affects his decisions regarding what they can usefully work on during the time they have together.

Even if you are in private practice, where to all intents and purposes you are self-employed, it probably means that constraints are set on your clinical decision-making when it comes to making any changes to your practice. In my case, although I work part-time in private practice, my office is not sufficiently large to allow me to run groups, so when a patient is referred to me whom I regard as most suited to a group therapy environment, I have to refer them to a CBT therapist who runs groups or to non-CBT group therapy, as I am not logistically able to run groups in my practice.

There is one further sense in which your work context may impinge on your work, and that is in relation to the process by which a client comes to see you in that setting. They may contact you and ask to be allocated specifically to you, but otherwise, if they have no preferences, how does a client get to see a particular CBT therapist? Some clients get assigned to a therapist according to the time both client and therapist have available for appointments; other clients may be allocated on the basis of what they have disclosed about themselves to a receptionist who decides on the allocation. To illustrate this, the following comes from a receptionist at the Albert Ellis Institute in New York:

> 'It should go without saying that when I do a telephone intake, I attempt to accommodate a potential client as best as I am able. If they request a specific therapist, time and/or day, fee or sex of therapist, I, naturally, comply with these wishes when possible.
>
> 'When a potential client who does not have specific requests calls, I generally begin by giving them my brief REBT and institute monologue. I have found that this is not only a constructive introduction for them, but it is also an opportunity for me to solicit reactions which are often indicative of who they will best work with. It seems to me that productive therapy (like productive learning) is likely to occur when the parties involved like and understand one another. So, as we (humans) tend to like and understand those people who are similar to ourselves, I will often endeavour to place a potential client with a therapist who might give me similar reactions to the REBT monologue as the client does. I do not mean with respect to what they say, but how they say it, what sort of accent they have, what sort of questions they ask.
>
> 'On the other hand, there are times when a client calls up and immediately it is evident that there is a specific problem. For instance, they are obviously stressed out and angry, a good candidate for stress and low frustration tolerance management or they are particularly passive and thus, a good candidate for assertiveness training. In a case like this, I throw what I have advocated in the previous paragraph out of the window and try to steer them in the direction of a therapist who works specifically in the given area.
>
> 'When all else fails, and I feel that it would not be inappropriate, I ask for a specific issue with which the client needs to deal and then try to match them with a therapist who works in this area. Incidentally, I do have a list which details therapists' specialisms. However, I seldom have to resort to this for some clients will immediately "spill their guts" to me, while most I am able to place without having to pry. On the very rare occasion when a person is extremely hesitant to comment or is simply scared out of their minds, the priority becomes getting them here, at least once, to see anybody.
>
> 'Of course, I wish that all telephone intakes ran as smoothly as I make them out on paper. However, these are the basic guidelines that I use for myself and so far, most intakes work out pretty well.'

Which therapeutic environments best suit clients in CBT therapy?

Now that a client has been referred to a CBT therapist, the best therapeutic environment for the therapy has to be decided. A therapeutic environment or arena is the interpersonal context in which therapy can ensue. The most common are: individual, couple, family and group. Ignoring the empirical issue concerning the effectiveness of different arenas for different client problems as it is too complicated to consider here, I would like to focus, in this section, on a number of criteria you may want to bear in mind when recommending a specific arena to a specific client.

I will start by providing the relevant criteria recommended by Albert Ellis, one of the originators of CBT:

> In regard to your question about placing people in individual, marital, family, or group therapy, I usually let them select the form of therapy they personally want to begin with. If one tries to push clients into a form of therapy they do not want or are afraid of, this frequently will not work out. So I generally start them where they want to start. If they begin in individual therapy and they are the kind of individuals who I think would benefit from group, I recommend this either quickly after we begin or sometime later. people who benefit most from group are generally those who are shy, retiring, and afraid to take risks. And if I can induce them to go into a group, they will likely benefit more from that than the less risky situation of individual therapy. On the other hand, a few people who want to start with group but who seem to be too disorganised or too disruptive, are recommended for individual sessions until they become sufficiently organised to benefit from a group.
>
> Most people who come for marital or family therapy actually come alone and I frequently have a few sessions with them and then strongly recommend their mates also be included. On the other hand, some people who come together are not able to benefit from joint sessions, since they mainly argue during these sessions and we get nowhere. Therefore sometimes I recommend that they have individual sessions in addition to or instead of the conjoint sessions. There are many factors, some of them unique, which would induce me to recommend that people have individual rather than joint sessions. For example, one of the partners in a marriage may seem to be having an affair on the side and will not be able to talk about this in conjoint sessions and therefore I would try to see this partner individually. Or one of the partners may very much want to continue with the marriage while the other very much wants to stop it. Again, I would then recommend they be seen individually. I usually try to see the people I see in conjoint sessions at least for one or a few individual sessions to discover if there are things they will say during the individual sessions that they would refuse to bring out during the conjoint sessions.
>
> On the whole, however, I am usually able to go along with the basic desire of any clients who want individual, marital, family or group psychotherapy. It is only in relatively few cases that I talk them into taking a form of therapy they are at first loathe to try. (Ellis, personal communication)

As this chapter chiefly concerns individual CBT, I will now provide a set of indications and contraindications for this particular arena. Before doing so, I would like to emphasise the fact that these decisions once made are not set in stone and may be changed during the course of CBT.

Nine indications for individual CBT

I will outline in this section indications for working with clients in the arena of individual CBT.

1 By its very nature, individual CBT offers clients more confidentiality than other therapeutic arenas. It is therefore preferable when clients need to reveal things about themselves in privacy without being anxious that others may use this information to their detriment. Some clients worry how other people might react to such disclosures – which might occur for instance in group counselling – and this kind of fear may prevent them from participating productively. Similarly, clients who would otherwise not reveal 'secrets' will find individual CBT the most appropriate therapy. However, as in other situations, transferring to other types of therapy, such as group or family therapy, may be more suitable later when these clients are more able and/or prepared to reveal themselves to others.
2 Because of its one-to-one nature, individual CBT affords an opportunity for a closer relationship to develop between therapist and client than may otherwise exist when other clients are present. This may be especially important for those clients who have not developed close relationships in their lives and who may initially find group therapy, for instance, too threatening.
3 One-to-one CBT can be performed in tandem with the client's pace of learning. It works particularly well therefore with those clients who, because of their present mental state or learning speed, need the full undivided attention of their therapist. This is particularly vital with clients who may be confused and might be distracted by the complex interactions that can sometimes occur in other therapeutic environments.
4 Similarly, if clients are feeling despairing and suicidal, they may benefit more from individual therapy by having the therapist's full attention: such sessions can allow the therapist to focus interventions more dynamically upon helping the client to emerge from suicidal crisis. It should be noted, however, that therapists are responsible for protecting the welfare of suicidal clients who may be at risk of self-harm. In some situations this responsibility may preclude individual outpatient CBT, such as when recommending psychiatric hospitalisation seems advisable.
5 Individual CBT is required when the major problems clients face concern their relationship with themselves rather than with others.
6 Individual CBT may be required for clients who wish for individual therapy separate from others; for instance, those who have decided to leave a relationship and wish to deal with the individual problems that ensue. In this case, however, some sessions in tandem with the partner may also be useful, particularly if it concerns conciliation (Gurman et al., 1986).
7 It can be useful for CBT therapists to vary their style of therapy with clients and thus minimise the risk of perpetuating the client's problems by responding in such a way that an inappropriate interactive style ensues. Individual CBT offers therapists an opportunity to vary their interactive styles with clients

without having to worry that such variation may have an adverse effect on other clients who may be present.

8 Individual CBT is particularly useful with clients who have deep problems regarding sharing therapeutic time with other clients.

9 Individual CBT may also be necessary for negative reasons. Clients may participate in individual CBT who may not benefit from having therapy in other arenas. Thus, clients who may monopolise a CBT therapy group or be too withdrawn within it to benefit from the therapy, or who are considered too vulnerable to benefit from family counselling, are often seen individually in CBT.

Four contraindications for individual CBT

In this section I outline contraindications for working with clients in individual CBT.

1 Clients who are likely to become overly dependent on the therapist, particularly when such a dependency becomes so intense that it leads to client deterioration, should not be given individual therapy. These clients may be more appropriately helped in group CBT where this kind of intense dependency is less likely to develop because the therapist has to relate to several other people.

2 Because individual CBT can be a close interpersonal encounter for the client, it is less likely to be indicated for clients who may find such a degree of intimacy, or the prospect of such intimacy, unduly threatening.

3 Individual CBT may not be considered appropriate for clients who find it too comfortable. Based on the assumption that personal change is often best effected in situations where there is a high level of stimulus, individual CBT may not challenge these clients sufficiently. In addition, Ravid (1969) noted that it may not be productive to offer individual therapy to clients who have already had a lot of previous individual therapy but who still require further therapeutic help.

4 Individual CBT may not be appropriate for clients for whom other types of therapy might be considered more beneficial. For instance, clients who are particularly withdrawn, shy and reluctant to take risks are more prone to benefit from group CBT (if they can be persuaded to participate) than from the less risky situation of individual CBT. Furthermore, partners who can use the conjoint situation of CBT couples therapy productively often benefit more from this arena than from individual CBT. This is especially the case when they have, to a major extent, conquered their disturbed feelings about their unproductive relationship and are dealing with issues relating to enhancing relationship satisfaction, which would particularly require their joint participation.

Tailoring CBT to fit the 'stages of change' model

Jim Prochaska and Carlo DiClemente made a highly significant contribution to substance abuse therapy a number of years ago (e.g. Prochaska & DiClemente, 1983) by arguing that people with substance abuse problems differ in relation to their 'stage of change' and any interventions should be tailored with this in mind. Before I describe the stages of change and show how I employ them to tailor interventions in a bespoke way with my clients, I would like to make the following general points.

Different interventions for different stages

The stages of change model chiefly indicates that you need to use different interventions with your clients depending on their stage of change. I discuss in the following how I use this principle in action. Clients may resist change because their CBT therapists are using interventions which are inappropriate for their stage of change, although appropriate for a different stage of change. CBT therapists may then make the mistake of assuming that their clients are either in a more advanced stage or less advanced stage than is actually the case.

Different stages for different problems

When clients come to CBT for help with more than one problem, it is important to understand that they may be in different stages of change for different problems (see Chapter 15). From this it should be appreciated that a client is only in a certain stage of change for a specific problem, not for all of her problems.

The stages of change

There are a number of versions of the 'stages of change' model. Here, I will present the one that informs my thinking and will show how it helps me to tailor my approach to different clients.

The pre-contemplation stage of change

If your client is in the 'pre-contemplation' stage of change, she is denying that she has a problem. The person may have been told or even ordered to come for CBT; or alternatively a referring agent – who has not taken time to explore whether the person actually wants CBT – may have sent her for help. From a technical point of view, this person would not be regarded as a client until she has given informed consent to proceed with CBT (see Chapter 22).

It is important with such clients not to have a judgmental view but to help them understand why they have attended the session and why other people consider they require CBT. While some types of CBT are essentially more persuasive than others, it is important to adopt a non-persuasive approach in helping the client in this stage of change to become involved in a discussion on why other people consider she requires help. In this context, motivational interviewing strategies can be helpful. These are strategies based on the 'spirit of motivational interviewing', as Rollnick and Miller (1995) called them. Such a spirit is characterised by the following ideas:

- 'Motivation to change is elicited from the client, and not imposed from without . . .
- 'It is the client's task, not the therapist's, to articulate and resolve his or her ambivalence . . .
- 'The therapeutic style is generally a quiet and eliciting one . . .
- 'The therapist is directive in helping the client to examine and resolve ambivalence . . .
- 'The therapist respects the client's autonomy and freedom of choice (and consequences) regarding his or her own behaviour.'

(Rollnick & Miller, 1995: 325)

As a consequence of this form of enquiry, the person may reach the decision that she does not have any kind of problem for which CBT could help her, or she may realise that she does have a problem and may start to think about whether or not she is prepared to address this issue. In the latter case, she has entered a stage of change which is called contemplation.

The contemplation stage of change

Clients in the contemplation stage of change start to realise that they have a problem, but they are in two minds about making any kind of change. In such cases, it is important for the therapist to accept this ambivalence and to encourage the client to accept it likewise as an overture to exploring the costs and benefits of the existing problem and any goals the client might be considering.

Most of my interventions at this stage are governed by cost–benefit analysis where I encourage the client to reflect on their situation in terms of a 2 × 2 × 2 matrix (see Figure 20.1) and to think about the costs and benefits of the problem and the goal, both to themselves and to relevant others, from (a) a short-term perspective and (b) a long-term perspective.

I generally invite clients either to assess these factors in a structured way (with written sheets) or in a less structured manner through dialogue but in such a way that their assessment is still being viewed against the matrix. Unless there is a good reason not to, I usually accept their preferences.

The preparation stage of change

When clients have reached the preparation stage of change, they have decided to change and are making plans to do so. At this stage I will explain the CBT model of change and the tasks that both the client and I will need to undertake during the necessary CBT therapy towards fulfilling her goals (Dryden, 2001, 2006). If the client indicates that she has a basic understanding of the CBT model and wishes to proceed on this basis, she may be considered to have given her informed consent to undertake the action stage of change.

The action stage of change

It is only when a client has reached the action stage of change that I begin what is most commonly understood as CBT therapy. It is at this point that I help the client to understand, question and change the dysfunctional attitudes and schemas underlying her problem. I can now assist her not only to formulate alternative functional schemas

Benefits				Costs			
Short-term		Long-term		Short-term		Long-term	
Self	Others	Self	Others	Self	Others	Self	Others

Figure 20.1 Cost–benefit analysis grid

that will allow her to achieve her goals but also to undertake a variety of thinking, behavioural and emotive assignments to strengthen her conviction in these functional schemas. The way in which I do this will depend on other factors (as discussed below), but this is the stage of change at which this is to be done.

The maintenance stage of change

Having reached the maintenance stage of change the client has achieved her goal or has made considerable progress towards it and is ready to consider how to maintain this change. At this point I help her identify vulnerability factors in order that she can deal with them; ideally, this will prevent lapses in progress (it would perhaps be best to regard these as hiccups in the process of change). I also help her manage the lapses that are bound to occur. I do this by encouraging her to accept herself for lapsing and from this to identify the factors which led to her lapse. By doing this, I will help her plan how to deal with these factors more effectively.

The relapse stage of change

A relapse is different from a lapse because it involves clients returning fully to older pre-CBT disturbed patterns of response. It tends to happen when a client has either ignored a series of lapses or not learned sufficiently from them. I consider my main tasks at this stage to be as follows:

- to encourage clients to accept themselves for relapsing;
- to respond to them therapeutically in such a way as to respect their *current* stage of change;
- to help them understand and learn from those factors that led to their relapse;
- to encourage them to work actively in the maintenance stage of change when they are in that stage.

Tailoring CBT to fit clients' relational styles and interpersonal preferences

If you were going to meet your MP for the first time it is most unlikely that your behaviour towards them would be the same as with your friends at the pub. We vary the way in which we relate to people depending on whom we are relating to and the context framing our interactions. Lazarus (1989) advises CBT therapists to vary their style of relating with different clients according to those particular clients' style of relating. This, he suggests, should be done in a genuine way and he comments that effective CBT therapists in this sense can be regarded as 'authentic chameleons'. In applying this concept to my own CBT work, I will now briefly discuss how I tailor my relational style to match three aspects of client relational functioning:

1. formal/informal relational style;
2. influence preferences;
3. degree of reactance and dependence.

Formality/informality in relational style

CBT may be practised in different styles. To demonstrate these style variations, I have chosen the relational style of formality and informality.

- With clients who tend to be informal in their style of relating, I prefer to adopt an informal style of practising CBT. This may involve, for instance, the use of humour and even self-disclosure in my interventions.
- With clients who are formal in their style of relating, I prefer to emphasise a formal style of practising CBT. In this case I would use more formal language, be more businesslike and ensure that humour and self-disclosure are kept to a minimum.

Varying the foundation of my influence

Some theorists (e.g. Dorn, 1984) regard CBT as a process of influence. From this point of view, the effectiveness of a therapist can largely be ascribed to the degree of benign influence they have on their clients. As to the issue of whom they might be most influenced by, different clients have different interpersonal preferences:

- Some clients are more influenced by me if I emphasise my expertise and will then listen, interact and be influenced by me. In such cases, I emphasise my qualifications, refer to my books and articles, and draw on my long, varied career in the field.
- Other clients, on the other hand, are completely unimpressed by my expertise and qualifications but if they like me, they are more likely to listen to, interact with and be influenced by me. With such clients, I emphasise my more likeable qualities, varying these like a good 'authentic chameleon' according to those qualities my clients find likeable.

Varying how I relate to clients according to degrees of reactance and dependence

Relating style and response to attempts to influence the client is brought into a single focus if we consider a client's degree of reactance and degree of dependence. I will begin by dealing with clients who are highly reactant.

Highly reactant clients

When a client is high in reactance, she (in this case) will tend to regard others' attempts to influence her as being attempts to control her or curb her freedom (see Beutler, 1983). She will respond to this by asserting her freedom in ways that demonstrate to herself and the others that she is free and cannot be controlled. As I practise an active-directive therapy (i.e. CBT), I am careful to avoid anything that highly reactant clients might view as a threat to their freedom. I will do so in the following ways:

- I will be as specific as possible about what I am aiming to do in CBT and to seek their permission in so doing;
- I will emphasise the idea that they may choose to believe whatever they wish to believe;
- I will refer to therapy as being self-therapy and describe myself as being a consultant in that process.

Once the client herself can see that negative thoughts and dysfunctional schemas underlie her problems and that realistic thoughts and functional schemas are healthy alternatives which will lead to her stated goals, they will work towards changing her negative thoughts and dysfunctional schemas, provided she is confident that she has reached her own conclusions independently and that her decision to pursue such realistic thoughts and functional schemas has not been influenced by me.

Highly dependent clients

Generally, conducting therapy with low-reactance clients does not tend to be problematic unless they are highly dependent. These clients are likely to want their CBT therapists to do their work for them and to agree with everything that their therapist says. In the beginning, it might appear gratifying to work with highly dependent clients – who are often complimentary – but it may well soon become obvious that they are not actually changing and that their true goal is to maintain the therapeutic relationship in order that they can depend on their CBT therapist for ongoing emotional support and decision-making. In customising CBT to such clients, I tend to do the following:

- If the question they put to me is one they can easily answer themselves, I encourage them to do so.
- I refuse to accept 'I don't know' for an answer, particularly when delivered as a knee-jerk response. Dependent clients, by instantly saying 'I don't know', stop themselves from thinking for themselves and by so doing, they are relying on their CBT therapists to think for them.
- I will help them identify, challenge and act against the underlying schemas that govern their dependency (for instance: 'I'm not strong enough to take care of myself'; 'It is easier to ask others to sort out my problems than for me to sort them out myself'). Since dependent clients are well known to be poor at completing homework assignments (or if they do complete them, they do it to please their CBT therapists), I spend considerable time working with them to commit themselves to carrying out these assignments and whenever they don't do them I will challenge them about this, unless their reasons for not completing the task are quite reasonable. My approach to CBT approach with such clients is based on the assumption that they are quite capable of taking the initiative to look after and help themselves.

How to decide what to vary

If you agree to the idea that it is important to vary your CBT approach with different clients, you may well have asked yourself how to decide what to vary. My own position is to follow George Kelly's famous principle: 'If you want to know anything, ask the client, he might just tell you.' The following are a few of the questions I ask clients to help me determine how best to customise my CBT approach with them in the areas discussed in this book.

General questions

- What have you found helpful in past therapeutic relationships – and why?
- What things could I do that would be particularly helpful to you – and why?
- Tell me about people in your past who have been helpful to you. What did they do that was particularly helpful to you?

Arena question

- Which therapeutic arena (individual, group, couple or family CBT) would be most helpful to you – and why?

Stages of change questions

- Who suggested that you come for CBT and why? If it was someone else's idea, what do you think of that idea?
- To what extent are you clear about which problems you need to tackle in CBT?
- How ready are you to address your problems?
- What reservations, if any, do you have about coming for CBT?

Relational-style questions

- Would you prefer it if I was relatively formal or informal in my interactions with you – and why?
- Would it help you or not if I told you things about my life experience that were relevant to your problems and how best to deal with them – and why?
- Do you think CBT therapists should show a sense of humour in CBT sessions or not – and why?
- How do you react when you feel that others are trying to influence you, even when you can see that they have your interests at heart?
- Would you rather someone else solved your problems for you or would you rather help yourself – and why?

Referral

I hope this has helped you see the value of varying your CBT approach with different clients. But supposing you decide that no matter how much you vary it you are just not the right person to help a client? I would like to end this chapter by discussing a subject that is seldom examined in the CBT literature, which is referral.

Both trained and trainee CBT therapists frequently find themselves pressured into seeing a client, even if for different reasons. If you are a trained therapist with a practice then your livelihood may be at risk if you keep referring clients to other CBT therapists. As a trainee therapist, you may be required to put in a certain number of CBT hours and this kind of pressure means that for every client you refer to someone else, you will be losing precious CBT hours needed to fulfil course requirements.

Now that I have made this point, it is still important for you to remember that your primary concern is to ensure that your client receives the best help available. If you decide that you are not the right person for your client, no matter which elements you vary, then you are required to refer the person to another practitioner who can better offer bespoke therapy, or, to put it another way:

'You may be a great tailor for most clients, but for other clients sometimes other tailors may make a better suit!'

To illustrate this, many years ago when I worked in Birmingham, a man rang me and asked if I practised an approach to therapy known as RT. The therapy I practise, which is known as Rational Emotive Behaviour Therapy (REBT), was originally called Rational Therapy (RT) and I decided that this man must be referring to REBT, though in its earliest form. On that assumption, I agreed to see him. After I had outlined the basics of REBT, he gave me a puzzled look and then said that he hadn't heard such intellectualised twaddle in a long while.

As it turned out, what he was actually seeking was Reichian Therapy (RT), a body-work oriented therapy which is completely different from REBT! Never forget that not all clients want or will benefit from CBT.

Reflection points

- If you object to the idea that you should vary your CBT approach with different clients, what are your precise objections to or reservations about this idea?
- if you are in favour of this idea, how do you currently vary your approach?
- What inclusion and exclusion criteria do *you* use for seeing clients in individual CBT?
- How do you vary your relational style with different clients and what leads to your decision to make such variations?
- How do you vary your CBT approach to work effectively with clients in different stages of change?

References

Beutler, L.E. (1983). *Eclectic Psychotherapy: A Systematic Approach*. New York: Pergamon.

Dorn, F.J. (ed.) (1984). *The Social Influence Process in Counseling and Psychotherapy*. Springfield, IL: Charles C. Thomas.

Dryden, W. (2001). *Reason to Change: A Rational Emotive Behaviour Therapy (CBT) Workbook*. Hove, East Sussex: Brunner-Routledge.

Dryden, W. (2006). *Getting Started with CBT: A Concise Guide for Clients*. Hove, East Sussex: Routledge.

Gurman, A.S., Kniskern, D.P. and Pinsof, W.M. (1986). 'Research on the process and outcome of marital and family therapy', in S.L. Garfield and A.E. Bergin (eds), *Handbook of Psychotherapy and Behavior Change*, 3rd edn. New York: John Wiley & Sons, Inc.

Lazarus, A.A. (1989). *The Practice of Multimodal Therapy*. Baltimore, MD: Johns Hopkins University Press.

Prochaska, J.O. and DiClemente, C.C. (1983). 'Stages and processes of self-change of smoking: Toward an integrative model of change', *Journal of Consulting and Clinical Psychology*, 51: 390–5.

Ravid, R. (1969). 'Effect of group therapy on long-term individual therapy', *Dissertation Abstracts International*, 30: 2427B.

Rollnick S. and Miller, W.R. (1995). 'What is motivational interviewing?', *Behavioural and Cognitive Psychotherapy*, 23: 325–34.

CHAPTER 21

DEALING WITH PROCRASTINATION

The REBT approach and a demonstration session

Journal of Rational-Emotive & Cognitive-Behavior Therapy, 30(4): 1–18 (2012, in press)

In 2008, the Albert Ellis Institute published a DVD of me in its Master Therapist DVD series working with a 'client' who had a problem with procrastination. (Although the client was an actor, he did have a genuine problem with procrastination for which he wanted help.) One of the professional activities that I particularly enjoy is demonstrating REBT in single one-off sessions in front of an audience. While this demonstration did not have a live audience, it does have an audience and I think that watching a skilled therapist practise 'live' is one of the most effective ways of learning how to practise therapy. I have been privileged enough in my career to have watched and served as co-therapist to such master therapists as Albert Ellis, Arnold Lazarus and David Burns and I am keen to help others learn how to practise REBT by observing my live demonstrations. The other professional activity that I enjoy is to analyse closely therapy sessions.

Thus, when Timothy Pychyl and Gordon Flett invited me to submit an article on the REBT approach to dealing with procrastination to their special issue on 'procrastination and self-regulatory failure' for publication in the *Journal of Rational-Emotive & Cognitive-Behavior Therapy*, I used this opportunity to indulge in these two favourite professional activities. So, after describing in general terms REBT's approach to the conceptualisation and treatment of procrastination, I provided a verbatim transcript of my session in the Master Therapist DVD series on overcoming procrastination and a commentary on my interventions in the session. This piece now follows.

Reference

Dryden, W. (2008). *Overcoming procrastination.* Master therapists DVD series. New York: Albert Ellis Institute.

Abstract

In this article, the Rational Emotive Behavior Therapy (REBT) approach to procrastination is outlined and demonstrated using the transcript of a session conducted in the REBT "Master Therapists" DVD Series (Dryden in Overcoming Procrastination: Master Therapists DVD series, Albert Ellis Institute, New York, 2008). A commentary provides links between the demonstration session and the general approach. The session provides particular emphasis on helping procrastinating clients develop an attitude of discomfort tolerance and the need to focus on specific examples of procrastination and the specific rational beliefs that must be acted on in order to replace procrastination with task engagement.

The REBT conceptualisation of procrastination

When people procrastinate, they put off doing a task that is in their best interest to do at a time when it is in their best interest to do it. The task and their best interest are judged by the people themselves rather than by any therapist or other interested person. In REBT, procrastination is seen as avoidant behavior at "C" in the "ABC" framework (Dryden 2000). What makes procrastination difficult to assess is that people do not often encounter the "A" or the emotional "C" due to procrastinating avoidance. Thus, it is typical when attempting to assess a person's procrastination problem that he[1] quite often does not know what he is avoiding or what his major emotion at "C" would be if he actually encountered what he is avoiding.

It follows, therefore, that when assessing a person's procrastination problem, the therapist needs to help the client to imagine encountering the "A" that he is avoiding and to predict the major emotional "C" he would experience if he actually encountered the "A." When this approach is taken, it emerges that people who procrastinate would experience the full range of unhealthy negative emotions if they allowed themselves to encounter their "A's" rather than avoiding them. In particular, people who procrastinate would experience anxiety, depression, unhealthy anger and shame, if they encountered the "A"s that they typically avoid. If therapists are successful at identifying such unhealthy emotions, these emotions suggest inferential themes at "A" that are present in specific examples of procrastination (Dryden 2009a). Alternatively if therapists are successful at identifying the inferential theme present in these specific examples, then these themes suggest the unhealthy negative emotions that the person would experience if he encountered rather than avoided his "A" (Dryden 2009a).

Thus, when a person anticipates experiencing anxiety if he encountered rather than avoided his "A", then the major theme present in the "A" would be threat, either to his self-esteem or broadly to his sense of comfort (Ellis 1979, 1980). When a person anticipates experiencing depression, then the major theme present in the "A" would be failure or some loss within the person's personal domain (Beck 1976). When a person anticipates experiencing unhealthy anger then the major theme present in the "A" would be that another person or state of affairs is curtailing the person's sense of freedom (Dryden 1996). Finally, when the person anticipates experiencing shame, then the major theme present in the "A" would be a major falling short of the person's ideal with an accompanying sense that others would look down on him (Dryden 1997).

Perhaps the main distinctive feature of REBT is the position it takes on the role of beliefs in psychological disturbance and health (Dryden 2009b). REBT argues that people do not procrastinate because they anticipate encountering threat, failure, curtailment of freedom and a significant fall from grace. Rather, they procrastinate because they hold rigid and extreme beliefs about these anticipated "A"s. These rigid beliefs often take the form of absolute musts, shoulds, got-to's and have to's and the extreme beliefs that are often derived from this rigid core take the form of awfulising beliefs, discomfort intolerance beliefs and depreciation beliefs relating to self, others or life conditions (Dryden 2009b).

People who procrastinate tend to adhere to a philosophy of low frustration tolerance (Ellis and Knaus 1977; Harrington 2005) and this is manifest in two major ways. First, they tend to avoid experiencing discomfort, particularly associated with the tasks that they do not want to do, but which is in their own judged best interests to do. Here, such people demand either that they must not experience discomfort or that they must only experience comfort. Second, they tend to be intolerant of experiencing emotional disturbance (Dryden 1999), and rather than experiencing such disturbance and working it through, they often choose to procrastinate and thereby avoid experiencing the disturbance. They do this because they demand that they must not experience disturbance or that they must only experience good feelings.

As with other emotional and behavioural problems, people who procrastinate then tend to focus on their procrastinating behavior and disturb themselves for procrastinating. While generally this is a legitimate target for intervention in REBT, it is important for the therapist to bear in mind one point. If she tackles this secondary problem first, then she may, unwittingly, reinforce the client's procrastination by putting off dealing with this primary problem in favour of dealing with the secondary problem.

The REBT treatment of procrastination

REBT therapists tend to deal with procrastination as they would with any other emotional or behavioural problem. Thus, she would begin with specific examples of the problem. However, as stated earlier, what makes dealing with procrastination particularly problematic is that the client does not get to encounter his "A" and therefore does not actually experience emotional disturbance at "C". Consequently, having taken a specific instance of procrastination, the therapist needs to encourage the client to imagine staying with the task and thus to predict what emotion he would experience if he did not procrastinate. Taking this approach will also help the client and therapist to assess more accurately the client's "A". With "A" and the emotional "C" assessed, it is fairly easy to assess the client's "B", since REBT theory states that a rigid belief and one or more extreme beliefs will underpin the person's procrastination. Formulation of the client's rational alternative beliefs is very important before any homework assignments are negotiated for without such alternatives, the client will find it only too easy to go back to his irrational beliefs since people do not live in a belief vacuum.

As in dealing with other problems, it is important to negotiate such homework assignments with clients. These should specify the task to be done, the time the client will start the task and, if necessary, where the task will be done. As will be seen in my session with Monty (below), for example, I negotiated with him that he would begin his task at a specific time (i.e., 3 p.m.) so that he would know he was procrastinating if by 3.01 p.m. he had not begun work on the selected task.

While eventually the therapist needs to help the client identify and work with more general core irrational beliefs, this general level of work should not be done until the client has demonstrated progress in acting on specific rational beliefs which result in task engagement rather than procrastination. People who procrastinate tend to be vague and abstract (e.g., McCrea et al. 2008) and need plenty of help dealing with specific examples of their problem before both therapist and client move to a more general level (Dryden 2009c).

People who have a chronic problem with procrastination tend to develop a number of rationalisations to deny to themselves and/or to others that they are not procrastinating when, in truth, they are. It is important that the therapist helps the client to identify a list of such rationalisations and to respond constructively to them if the client is going to fully commit himself to dealing with his procrastination problem over time.

People who have a chronic problem with procrastination also develop a set of justifications to explain to themselves the usefulness of procrastination (e.g., Neenan 2008; Spada et al. 2006). Common justifications include: "I need to feel anxiety to get going and therefore I will wait until I feel anxious before engaging in the task"; "I need to feel anxiety to be creative and therefore I will wait to feel anxious before engaging in the task"; "Even though I am not getting down to the task I am collecting the data I need to do the task. The longer I put off getting down to the task, the more data I will collect and the better I will do the task." As with rationalisations, it is important that the therapist helps the client to identify a list of such justifications and to respond constructively to them if the client is again going to fully commit himself to dealing with his procrastination problem in the longer term.

The demonstration session

The following transcript is of a session that I conducted in the REBT "Master Therapists DVD Series"[2] (Dryden 2008). The client was an actor but was asked to present a real problem that he had and that he wanted help with. In what follows, I provide a commentary on my interventions and provide a link between theory and practice.

Windy: Hello, Monty, thank you for coming in today. What problem would you like to present today?

Monty: Er, procrastination, very long term and sometimes large scale.

Windy: How do you define procrastination to yourself?

Monty: Well, it's putting off things that . . . putting off the thing, and this is just sort of putting off critical things, it's a sort of a total problem, putting off things till the last minute or past the last minute that I have plenty of time to take care of that leads me into being like chronically late for things, chronically like stressing out about something that has been on the plate for a long time and, yeah, sort of like creating massive problems for myself that didn't have to exist.

Windy: Yeah, I have a slightly different definition of procrastination. I see procrastination is putting off a task that is in your interest to do and putting it off beyond the time when it's in your interest to do it.

Monty: I like that definition.

Windy: Yeah?

Monty: I think that sounds like what I'm talking about.

[I find it useful to agree a definition of procrastination with clients so that we have a shared view of the problem under consideration (Dryden 2006).*]*

Windy: So maybe take an example of . . . maybe a current example, maybe a typical example . . . of a task that you're putting off doing that it would be in your interest to do at a time when it would be in your interest to do it.

[As is typical in REBT I ask Monty for a specific example of his procrastination problem.]

Monty: Sure, like in the last 24 hours there's two examples. One is I was supposed to have like the treatment of a script ready by the close of last week, there's a cast waiting on it, there's a pay cheque waiting on it . . . had a lot of time. The script is not finished, the treatment is not in and it was one of these things where I was moving up to start another project out of state recently and there were a few days before going up that I had kind of in my mind that I'm going to take care of this, it's going to be, you know, I should have enough hours to take care of it and it won't get . . .

Windy: So it would be useful to focus on that particular episode . . . you mentioned two?

Monty: Yeah, I was about to say the other one is a more general situation which sort of pops up continuously which is . . .

Windy: Which would be more meaningful for you to focus on?

Monty: Umm, yeah, actually now that I think about it, maybe the sort of the systemic as opposed to . . . the script is sort of a specific anomalous thing while the other thing I was thinking about is something that kind of comes up.

Windy: I still would like to take an example, if we go with the second one . . .

Monty: Sure.

Windy: . . . I'll be asking you for an example.

[Monty provides two examples, so to strengthen the working alliance between us I ask him to choose one of the two (Bordin 1979). *However, I stress the importance of Monty selecting a specific example of the problem whichever one he chooses.]*

Monty: Oh yeah, I've got this. It's most recent but it's part of a long and endless system.

Windy: So do you want to go with the systemic one and take an example of that?

Monty: Yeah. This is like . . . as an actor pretty much everything is . . . everything is time sensitive, like extremely time sensitive, and just recently, again, it's the most recent example is there is like a theatre company that I did some work with sort of by accident very recently and the Artistic Director and everything was like "great job", we need you to send in your head shot and all of the standard actor stuff, and . . . did not do it.

Windy: It is still something that you're putting off?

Monty: It's still something I'm putting off.

Windy: Okay, so . . .

Monty: It's like, I mean, I could have done it yesterday before coming here.

Windy: Can I ask you then . . . if I were to ask you to define a time where you would agree with yourself, perhaps later on today, that you're going to sit down and do this task and yet you suspect that at that time you might put it off even having made that agreement with yourself, when might that be, would it be later on today?

Monty: It would be like later on today.

Windy: What time would you say?

Monty: Like, you know, 3.00 p.m.

[As I mentioned earlier, the therapist can maximise her impact with the client if she helps the client select a specific example of his problem that is imminent with a specified starting time. This helps both assessment and intervention and additionally provides the client with an immediate opportunity to deal constructively with his problem.]

Windy: So let's take 3.00 p.m., let's take 3.00 p.m. and what I want to do is to try and get a flavour of how you procrastinate. So you have agreed with yourself, right . . .

Monty: Yeah.

Windy: . . . you're going to do this task, and the task involves what, by the way?

Monty: Yeah, getting to the computer, printing out a cover letter . . .

Windy: Okay, so come three o'clock you have an agreement with yourself, you're going to sit down on this computer and get this cover letter done . . . and yet you are beginning to procrastinate. Can you imagine really focusing on that as a situation?

Monty: Absolutely.

Windy: Now, what do you think is going on at that point, what would it . . . what do you think might be going through your mind at that point that might lead you to break that agreement with yourself?

[My use of the general question "what do you think might be going on in your mind . . ." was deliberate in that I wanted to encourage Monty to look at his thinking as a relevant source of his procrastination. I will use REBT's specific formulation of procrastination later.]

Monty: At some level there is a "ooh, I've got a little bit more time" so there are some other things that I could sneak in there. But there's also like a certain level of . . . I mean, it's, it's like a, like I don't want to have to do it at that time.

Windy: You don't want to have to do it at that time, right.

Monty: If that makes any sense . . .

Windy: So the first one it sounds like you're beginning to kind of create a story which would . . .

Monty: Justify why . . .

Windy: . . . justify and that's what we call a rationalisation.

Monty: I'm good at those.

Windy: You're good at those?

Monty: Yeah.

Windy: Okay, and the other one, it sounds like you're beginning to experience some emotion which you are then moving away from. Would you say that would be correct?

[Monty's response indicates that he would rationalise not beginning the task ("I've got a little more time . . .") and that his procrastination would be motivated by an avoidance of feeling. I acknowledge both, but decide to assess the avoided "emotional C".]

Monty: Yeah.

Windy: What do you think that emotion would be, that if you really allowed yourself to feel it that you might experience?

Monty: It's like it's something like a, it's like a fear or something but it's . . .

Windy: Fear?

Monty: Yeah, it's the first word that comes to mind but it's . . .

Windy: I'll tell you what the first word that came to my mind when I was listening to you and, listen, the point of this is that I may very well be wrong . . .

Monty: Yeah.

Windy: . . . okay, and correct me if I'm wrong, but I kind of got a sense that you might be starting to feel, if you actually started to kind of do it, some kind of anger or resentment?
Monty: Yeah, that's resentment towards it.
Windy: Resentment?
Monty: Yeah, absolutely.
Windy: Right.

[Here, I asked the Monty what he would feel at "C" if he allowed himself to stay with the task and not procrastinate and he says "fear". However, he says it in such a tentative way and his response seems to be at variance with what he said earlier (i.e. "I don't want to have to do it at that time") that I put forward an alternative emotion that more likely goes along with the sense of doing something that he does not want to do, i.e. "resentment" which Monty resonates with better than with "fear". At this point in the session I was looking for consistency between the language that he used and the feeling that he came up with and did not find such consistency. In putting forward my hypothesis about his emotional "C", I was careful to give him the opportunity to disconfirm my hypothesis by saying "correct me if I'm wrong".]

Windy: Can you see that that resentment is somehow connected to your procrastination?
Monty: Yeah.
Windy: In what way would you say?
Monty: I mean, it's a . . . I mean the worst part of this is having to slog through like endless amounts of outreach letters.
Windy: Even though it's in your interest?
Monty: Even though . . . I mean, because even though you know it's part of the . . . it's like that's not . . . like I don't think anybody gets into any of the creative fields, acting especially, like looking forward to do a whole lot of like outreach letters. I mean, even in spite of the fact that it's very clearly connected to the thing, I mean it's, yeah.
Windy: You mentioned fear and I kind of noticed resentment. What do you think that in this episode that you're talking about, three o'clock, do you think the fear is the feeling that's going to stop you or the resentment?
Monty: It's the resentment.
Windy: It's the resentment, okay. Who or what are you resentful towards? Is it a person, is it you, is it life conditions or . . . what's the object of your resentment?

[Having agreed that resentment is Monty's avoided emotional "C", I begin the search for "A".]

Monty: That's a good question and the general result is that I get angry at myself for procrastinating that's the immediate after effect.

[This is an important choice point in the session. In response to my question concerning the object of his resentment (which would be his "A"), Monty responds by providing a secondary problem (anger at himself for procrastinating). While REBT encourages therapist to look for and work with such problems when these interfere with work on the primary problem, it would have been a mistake for me to have done this. As I

pointed out earlier in the article, working on the secondary problem may be colluding with the client's own tendency to put off dealing with his primary procrastination problem. Also, by changing the focus at this point, I would be providing a poor role model for Monty who shifts focus both in the session and when there is a task to be done. This "shifting focus" is characteristic of those who have a chronic problem with procrastination and the therapist should endeavour to model "retaining the focus" for the client.]

Windy: Well, listen, if we went with that we'd be putting off dealing with the problem.
Monty: (laughter) I know that.
Windy: Sure.
Monty: I mean, I think that the resentment is . . . I think it's definitely targeted at the, I don't know, the sort of the . . . the . . . I mean, not the specific people that I'm sending it to.
Windy: It's not . . .?
Monty: I mean, it's not like I think of like the Artistic Director who gave me the job the other day and was like sending in some extra work. It's not like specifically like how can you make me send this in, it's more like I just wish that wasn't the case that I have.
Windy: Yeah.
Monty: You know, I guess it's one of those things like you must do this and not only must I do this on this day, but you have to send in the head shots, the agents who aren't going to look at the thing, there's like a general level.
Windy: So it kind of sounds that you're experiencing and, again, correct me if I'm wrong, that somehow you are in a situation where your freedom is being curtailed.
Monty: Definitely.
Windy: Yeah?
Monty: Definitely.
Windy: And would you say that you are angry about being put in that situation?
Monty: Definitely.

[Here I have assessed the "A" which is I am being put in a situation that is curtain my Freedom.]

Windy: So what do you do to prove that you are a free man at that time?
Monty: I will like play video games.
Windy: Right, okay. "I'm a free man"!
Monty: And pretty much anything that I can find, at the lowest level. It's like when I'm at the computer and like Word is open, it can be like turn on some kind of –
Windy: Yeah, so somehow, as long as you are kind of resentful about having your freedom curtailed and you are in a situation, you're going to prove to yourself that you are a free man, you are going to continue to procrastinate. Is that correct?
Monty: That sounds spot on.

[Here I help Monty to see that from his perspective engaging in non-task behaviour helps him to restore his sense of freedom at that time, which he later calls "Monty time".]

Windy: Okay, so what would you like to do instead?
Monty: At?
Windy: At three o'clock.
Monty: Like today?
Windy: Yeah.
Monty: That's a good question, rather than writing this up?
Windy: No, I mean . . .
Monty: I would really like to get the letter out of the way . . .
Windy: Yeah.
Monty: . . . that's, I mean, I'd like it to be gotten out of the way because that's the thing that like, I would really like to work with this company in the future and –
Windy: Can I just feed back something to you about your language?
Monty: Yeah, you don't like the way [laughs].
Windy: Well, 'I'd like it to be gotten out of the way, rather than you doing it' [laughs]. Well, let's face it, you're not going to like to do it . . .
Monty: No.
Windy: . . . but would it be more accurate to say well look, I'm going to choose to do it even though I don't want to do it because I want the outcome?

[In this section, I address the issue of goals with Monty and in particular, I give him feedback about his use of passive language: "I'd like it gotten out of the way". Instead, I emphasise the active, choice-based nature of him engaging with the task instead of procrastinating: "I'm going to choose to do it even though I don't want to do it because I want the outcome".]

Monty: Yeah.
Windy: Okay. Now, in order to do that I guess we're going to have to help you to have a different attitude towards having your freedom curtailed. Because, you see, it sounds like, you know, I mean, I personally don't like having my freedom curtailed and yet I actually don't procrastinate that much because while we are grappling with the same issue here, I have an attitude that states that while I don't like having my freedom curtailed, I don't have to be exempt from that. I can actually choose to do something that I don't want to do to get the result I do want to want and in a funny sense I'm actually freer because in a strange sense it sounds like you have to do the video games to prove how free you are. And that's a bit of a dilemma because when you say you have to you are not free . . .

[There are a number of ways to make what REBT therapists call the "B"–"C" connection (Dryden and Branch 2008). *I choose to do so here by engaging in therapist self-disclosure* (Dryden 1990). *Here I show Monty the relationship between my rational belief about curtailment of freedom and my non-procrastinating behaviour. Additionally, I show Monty that by attempting to prove to himself that he is free by not doing what is in his interest to do, he is paradoxically not free. As his response below shows, this is a point with which he particularly resonates.]*

Monty: Yeah [laughs]. Ah bright light of day.
Windy: Oh yeah bright light of day. Exactly.
Well, look, I reckon that there are three possible attitudes you can have towards having your freedom curtailed and let's have a look at them and

let's have a look at the consequences of them and let's have a look at what's in your interest and let's have a look at... and then we can examine them.

The first one, and this is going to sound a bit strange but it's a theoretical possibility, but it does involve you lying to yourself, and that is the idea of what we call indifference and that would go something like this. "I don't care one way or the other whether my freedom is being curtailed or no. It is a matter of indifference to me."

Now, is that kind of something that appeals to you?

Monty: I am not . . . I mean, it's definitely like it's an active, like I am gonna to do something that is my choice.

Windy: I'm going to do something that is my choice because I have to prove what?

Monty: I don't know if it's . . . I don't know if these are the thoughts of I've got to prove something. I don't know, maybe that is . . . it is definitely like, and this extends into a lot of different areas, but if there's definitely one thing it's like I just need to go to ground for a second . . .

Windy: You need to go to ground?

Monty: Go to ground as in like I need to go and just have Monty time and like not . . . even though Monty time includes specifically not doing the things that I need to do.

Windy: Monty time is in your mind, free time?

Monty: It's my brain's sort of interpretation of like personal freedom.

Windy: Yeah, so it's like a positive, yeah. So let's come back to the other two possible attitudes that you can have towards the curtailment of freedom is this, look, "I must not have my freedom curtailed, I really must not" or "I don't like it if my freedom is curtailed but, sadly and regretfully, that doesn't mean I'm exempt from that."

Now, which do you think you implicitly believe that leads to your resentment and procrastination?

[Here I more formally present the REBT model of resentment-based procrastination by outlining the three possible beliefs Monty could hold in this situation with respect to his "A" i.e. having his freedom curtailed: an indifference belief, a rigid demand (irrational belief) or a flexible, non-dogmatic preference (rational belief). I then ask him which beliefs underpins his resentment/procrastination. This approach is known as the theory-driven approach to assessment in REBT (DiGiuseppe 1991a).*]*

Monty: I mean, on an emotional level, definitely A.

Windy: Where it is a must?

Monty: Yeah.

Windy: Okay.

Monty: I understand that I really need to do these things but I feel that I should really, you know, take them on and do something . . .

Windy: But as long as you believe, or act as if you believe, because in a way you never actually get to . . . you see, the thing about procrastination is it's basically a problem of avoidance, right, and therefore what you are avoiding is dealing with the issue of having your freedom curtailed.

You never get there. But, even though you never get there, you are reinforcing through your behaviour the idea that you have to have your freedom at that time. Your behaviour is strengthening the very attitude that is leading to your procrastination.

Monty: Yeah, I'll buy that.

[Monty can see that is his irrational belief that underpins his procrastination. I capitalise on this by showing him that his procrastination also reinforces his irrational belief.]

Windy: Yeah, okay. So the other alternative is to say well look, "I don't like having my freedom curtailed, but sadly and regretfully, I don't have to be immune from it or exempt from it and, therefore, I can choose to do what I don't want to do to get the results that I do want to have."
And I put that to you, Monty, that that is true freedom. I put that to you that what you're doing is that you are a prisoner of your own must and musts don't give you freedom to manoeuvre. So when you think you're free, you're really a prisoner of your own musts. What do you think of that idea?

Monty: I think it seems to hold water.

Windy: Okay, so let's see if we can't rewind and put it into a situation that we will actually have at three o' clock, right? Typically speaking, what will happen today at three o'clock, your motivation would be to have this thing out of the way, right?

Monty: Correct.

Windy: So presumably, if a little fairy came along and did it for you, you would not object?

Monty: Absolutely not. I spend a lot of time thinking that.

Windy: Okay, so typically you are acting on the belief "oh, I'm being made to do something which I see is a curtailment of my freedom. I must not have this curtailment, I'm going to prove that I'm a free man, I'm going to have Monty time, I'm going to do what I want to do, prove I've got a free mind."
If you act out what you normally do, that would happen, is that correct?

Monty: Yeah.

Windy: Okay. So let's go back, let's really focus on this one. I'm going to play the must, right, and let's see if you can answer it back and see where we go.

Monty: Okay.

Windy: It's three o'clock and I'm . . . it's a bit like when you see Mickey Mouse and Donald Duck, I'm going to be the little Monty devil.

Monty: Nice idea [laughs].

Windy: Monty, listen, your freedom is being curtailed, you know, that mustn't happen to you, you need Monty time. Now, how are you going to respond to that?

Monty: That Monty time will be richer in the future if I have Monty time on stage.

Windy: Yeah, but "I must not really have this curtailment now, I've got to get rid of this negative thing right now."

Monty: Bear with me, we'll take care of this and there will be Monty time later.

Windy: Yeah, but, Monty, how are you going to . . . what attitude are you going to take to this curtailment of your freedom?

Monty: I'd suck it up, I guess.

Windy: Suck it up?

Monty: Yeah.

Windy: Which means what?
Monty: Just . . .
Windy: I'm a poor British . . .
Monty: Yeah, let's say that's Americanese for take it on the chin, keep on. . .
Windy: Take it on the chin?
Monty: Keep on going.
Windy: What attitude towards the curtailment of freedom does that represent?
Monty: Again, it's not a constructive attitude.
Windy: Isn't it?
Monty: No.
Windy: Okay, so . . .
Monty: It's not the choice and I guess the choice is, again, as you've said, it's just like this is the choice that . . .
Windy: Yeah.
Monty: . . . like Monty time is creating the present and future for myself in which success in my craft which leads very obviously to personal happiness for myself and my loved ones is the priority as opposed to like immediate . . .
Windy: But let's kind of really zero in on the attitude, lets have a look at those two attitudes . . . we are going to ditch the indifference belief.
Monty: Yeah.

[In retrospect, I made the wrong decision here. Being keen to show viewers of the DVD a more emotive approach to disputing irrational beliefs, I assumed the role of devil's advocate. Here, I voice his irrational belief and encourage him to dispute it. I then backtrack and use a less emotive, but more focused approach to disputing which appears below (see DiGiuseppe 1991b). Here, you will see that I encourage Monty to keep his focus on his irrational and alternative rational belief at the same time and ask him to assess their empirical and pragmatic status. There are many ways of disputing beliefs, but I have found this approach to be particularly useful with many clients.]

Windy: Let me go over them and have them side by side. The first one is saying "I . . . okay, my freedom is being curtailed, I must have freedom, I can't bear to have this curtailed."
Monty: Right.
Windy: As opposed to "Look, I don't like this but I don't have to be exempt from it, it's bearable, I can tolerate it and it's worth it."
Monty: Yeah.
Windy: Which of those beliefs is true and which is false? Is there a law which says that Monty must be free . . .?
Monty: Free now, not so much. I mean, like, I don't know, it's at the point . . . at a certain level where it's like I remember having that time or something and maybe like it's a, yeah, and I don't know if I have ever read a law that says there has to be.
Windy: No, exactly.
Monty: Well, even if there was an unspoken law it's like –
Windy: Actually, paradoxically, if there was a law you couldn't go against it. You'd be a prisoner of it.
Monty: There it is.
Windy: That's it and that's the ironic thing, because when you are a prisoner you're not free. You're not free to choose at the moment when your

attitude is "I've got to get rid of this state of affairs right now where I am faced with doing something that I don't want to do even though it is in my interest to do it."

So . . . but is it true, let's break it down, is it true that you would, at the time when your freedom is being curtailed is it true that you don't like that?

Monty: Yeah.

Windy: Okay, and is it also true "but there's no reason why I have to be exempt from that"?

Monty: That's also true.

Windy: Okay, so if you put that together it would be "Look, I don't like this but I don't have to be exempt from it, it's true and the idea that I must be exempt from it, I must get rid of it, I must not be, you know, have my freedom curtailed, that's not true."

Which of those two is healthier for Monty?

Monty: I mean, it's definitely choosing to go non-exempt.

Windy: Okay, which would you like to commit yourself to working on at three o'clock?

Monty: Definitely the choice of not being exempt.

Windy: Right, but now we're going to have to deal with one other issue which I think is in there and that is, when you make that choice you're going to be uncomfortable.

Monty: Yeah.

Windy: Do you know why?

Monty: Because it's a change from the norm.

Windy: Because there's freedom over here, there's videos over here which is Monty time and over there there's doing what you don't want to do even though it's in your interest. So you're actually going to feel uncomfortable because you've chosen to do what you don't want to do when there's an option of doing what you do want to do, right?

Monty: Yeah

Windy: Right, so, I guess, what would you typically say about that discomfort that might lead you to go to the video games, what attitude do you think you might be acting on, the idea that I've got to get rid of it or –

Monty: I mean, absolutely. It's definitely the thing like I'll be working on the thing for real and be like man, this is like what a pain in the ass and then I will just temporarily just jump in here for a second so that I can feel like I'm having some of my time and then come back.

Windy: Well, you see, you could still say this is a pain in the ass and still stick with it.

Monty: Right.

Windy: But in order to do that you have to see that again you have a rigid idea about lack of freedom because you're telling yourself, I'm hearing, I've got to get rid of this discomfort right now. Oh look, there's a very good way of doing it.

Monty: Yeah, the click.

Windy: The click, as opposed to, let's be honest, "I'm uncomfortable right now but I don't have to be free of that, I can tolerate the discomfort and see what happens", you see?

So I would suggest perhaps a little homework assignment, we kind of suggest these things, and it would be at three o'clock, right, recognise that you made like a contract with yourself, right, recognise that when you sit down, you are going to have an urge, and it could be backed up by rationalisation, oh I've had a hard time, you know, things like that or even Professor Dryden is making me do it which I'm not, it's just a suggestion. So at that point you can either choose, and I'd suggest that you can rehearse this in your mind, "I don't like this curtailment feeling, I don't like this discomfort but I'm going to stick with it, it's in my interests. I don't have to be free right now in the way that I want freedom but I can have true freedom and choose to do something that I don't want to do when it's in my interest to do that because when I am going to the video games I'm not free because I believe I have to get rid of these other things."

[In the above part of the session, I am working with Monty on his attitude to discomfort. While people procrastinate for different reasons, most clients with a chronic procrastination problem have great difficulty engaging with a task when they feel uncomfortable. So, I bring up the topic of handling discomfort with Monty even though he has not explicitly mentioned it. I would go as far to say that if REBT therapists do not help their procrastinating clients to develop an attitude of discomfort tolerance then these clients will be particularly vulnerable to relapse.

It is worth noting again the specificity of the homework assignment that I negotiated with Monty. People who procrastinate need a clear marker for when they are procrastinating. So Monty knows that he is procrastinating if he has not begun work by 3 pm that afternoon. I have found that the more specific clients can be with themselves in terms of when they are going to do something and in which context, the more likely it is that they will do it. Also, I think that the sooner after the session clients agree to carry out a negotiated homework assignment, the more likely again they are to do it.]

Windy: Now, can you imagine doing that?
Monty: Yeah.
Windy: Okay, now imagine you're doing that and imagine you've started to type, what happens then?
Monty: I mean, even now just thinking about it, I can . . . like the images of like, man, but that game is right there.
Windy: Okay.
Monty: Immediately popping up.
Windy: Okay, fine. That's fine. That's realistic and there's nothing that I can do or say that's going to stop you from having that thought pop up in your mind. Now, the question is, how are you going to respond to that thought?
Monty: The response to the thought is yes, there's the thought but here's the thing. I mean, it's definitely true in personal experience that like when I succeed in pushing through like projects, be they late or whatever, it's always the feeling is a thousand times better than any, you know, temporary like stop gap.
Windy: But it sounds like at that point, you see, having . . . it's almost like you back yourself into a corner and there's nowhere for you to go, that's what happens when you come at the last minute.
Monty: Yeah.

[I have missed an opportunity to help Monty to develop and rehearse a rational belief concerning dealing with the immediate lure of the video game.]

Windy: Do you also have a sense that, in a way, you work better under pressure at the last minute?

[Here I help Monty to identify a justification for continued procrastination. Note below how I suggest that he needs to test this hypothesis rather than assume that this is true.]

Monty: Absolutely.
Windy: Yeah.
Monty: That's definitely . . .
Windy: How do you know that since you haven't tested that? [laughs]
Monty: [laughs] Because that is generally the way I work.
Windy: Must be good because I do it [laughs].
Monty: I'm not sure what you mean [laughs].
Windy: The point is you may well be right but you can experiment so the question is, let's just come back to that thought. Yes, there's a video game in here and the response towards that is "Yes, there is! But what am I going to choose to do?"
Monty: Let's leave it there.
Windy: "Yeah, okay, and I don't want to do it but I want . . ."
Monty: I want it done.
Windy: "I want it done and since . . ." I suppose you could get somebody to do it for you but that's not going to be . . .
Monty: Not at this level.
Windy: Not at this level. So is that a realistic image, that you are now at your desk. At what point do you think . . . is there a slight over the hump, that after a while once you get into it you'll get into the letter?
Monty: Absolutely.
Windy: Yeah.
Monty: There's even like periods of time where I'm sort of easier on . . .
Windy: You see, I often find that. It's really . . . it's like getting over the hump . . .
Monty: Yeah.
Windy: . . . when you . . . first of all, you know, what happens typically in your case is you approach the task, as you approach in your mind, curtailment of freedom, I've got to get rid of that, I need Monty time, rationalisation, okay. You've got you through that and then you've started to do it and then there's still a part of your mind that says hey . . .
Monty: Right.
Windy: Yeah, there is, okay. Now, as you get into it the chances are you might still get those thoughts but the more you get into it they probably will lessen.
Monty: Yeah.

[This is another error. It would have been better if I helped Monty to focus more on his implicit irrational belief about being tempted to engage in non-task behaviour and to help him develop a rational alternative belief. While the point I do actually make is a valid one – that if Monty starts work on his dissertation and continues to work on it no matter what thoughts crop up that encourage him to seek short-term

satisfaction, then he will get into the task and continue to work on it – my focus is not sufficiently on Monty's beliefs. It would have been better for me to encourage Monty to first rehearse his rational belief i.e. "I may want to play that video game right now, but I don't have to do so" and then begin work on his agreed task while noticing but not engaging with the thoughts that tempt him to procrastinate.]

Windy: Alright. Now, what about trying that . . . well, actively committing yourself to do that at three o'clock this afternoon?
Monty: Absolutely.
Windy: Okay, it would be very interesting to see what happens to you.
Monty: Okay, thanks a lot.
Windy: Thank you.

As this was a one-off demonstration session showing how an REBT therapist endeavours to help someone who has a procrastination problem, I do not know whether or not Monty carried out his agreed homework assignment. If this was regular therapy, I would have begun the following session by checking his assignment with him. If REBT therapists do not routinely check agreed homework assignments with clients in the following session, they communicate that these assignments are not really that important, an attitude detrimental to helping clients deal effectively with procrastination.

However, I think that this session does show REBT's distinctive approach to the assessment and treatment of procrastination as outlined in the early part of this paper.

Notes

1 In this paper, the therapist is female and the client is male.
2 The verbatim transcript appears here by kind permission of the Albert Ellis Institute.

References

Beck, A. T. (1976). *Cognitive therapy and the emotional disorders*. New York: International Universities Press.
Bordin, E. S. (1979). The generalizability of the psychoanalytic concept of the working alliance. *Psychotherapy: Theory, Research and Practice*, *16*(3), 252–260.
DiGiuseppe, R. (1991a). The rational-emotive model of assessment. In M. Bernard (Ed.), *Using rational-emotive therapy effectively* (pp. 151–172). New York: Plenum.
DiGiuseppe, R. (1991b). Comprehensive cognitive disputing in rational-emotive therapy. In M. Bernard (Ed.), *Using rational-emotive therapy effectively* (pp. 173–195). New York: Plenum.
Dryden, W. (1990). Self-disclosure in rational-emotive therapy. In G. Stricker & M. N. Fisher (Eds.), *Self-disclosure in the therapeutic relationship* (pp. 61–74). New York: Plenum.
Dryden, W. (1996). *Overcoming anger: When anger helps and when it hurts*. London: Sheldon Press.
Dryden, W. (1997). Overcoming shame. London: Sheldon.
Dryden, W. (1999). Beyond LFT and discomfort disturbance: The case for the term "non-ego disturbance". *Journal of Rational-Emotive & Cognitive-Behavior Therapy*, *17*(3), 165–200.
Dryden, W. (2000). *Overcoming procrastination*. London: Sheldon.
Dryden, W. (2006). *Counselling in a nutshell*. London: Sage.
Dryden, W. (2008). *Overcoming procrastination: Master therapists DVD series*. New York: Albert Ellis Institute.

Dryden, W. (2009a). *Understanding emotional problems: The REBT perspective*. Hove, East Sussex: Routledge.
Dryden, W. (2009b). *Rational emotive behaviour therapy: Distinctive features*. London: Routledge.
Dryden, W. (2009c). *How to think and intervene like an REBT therapist*. Hove, East Sussex: Routledge.
Dryden, W., & Branch, R. (2008). *The fundamentals of rational emotive behaviour therapy: A training handbook* (2nd ed.). Chichester: Wiley.
Ellis, A. (1979). Discomfort anxiety: A new cognitive behavioral construct. Part I. *Rational Living*, *14*(2), 3–8.
Ellis, A. (1980). Discomfort anxiety: A new cognitive behavioral construct. Part 2. *Rational Living*, *15*(1), 25–30.
Ellis, A., & Knaus, W. J. (1977). *Overcoming procrastination*. New York: Institute for Rational Living.
Harrington, N. (2005). It's too difficult! Frustration intolerance beliefs and procrastination. *Personality and Individual Differences*, *39*, 873–883.
McCrea, S. M., Liberman, N., Trope, Y., & Sherman, S. J. (2008). Construal level and procrastination. *Psychological Science*, *19*, 1308–1314.
Neenan, M. (2008). Tackling procrastination: An REBT perspective for coaches. *Journal of Rational-Emotive & Cognitive-Behavior Therapy. Special issue on cognitive-behavioural coaching*, *26*(1), 53–62.
Spada, M. M., Hiou, K., & Nikcevic, A. V. (2006). Metacognitions, emotions and procrastination. *Journal of Cognitive Psychotherapy: An International Quarterly*, *20*, 319–326.

CHAPTER 22

UNCONDITIONAL SELF-ACCEPTANCE AND SELF-COMPASSION

M. E. Bernard (Ed.) (2013, in press) *The strength of self-acceptance: Theory, research and practice.* New York: Springer.

This last piece was written in response to a general invitation from Michael Bernard to contribute to his edited volume on self-acceptance – a key concept in REBT theory. After much thought, I decided that I would write a piece on the relationship between unconditional self-acceptance (USA) and self-compassion, a concept that is very popular in the mental health field at the time of writing (May 2012). This piece is a good contemporary example of me demonstrating how a concept that was developed outside REBT (self-compassion) can be related to a concept that was developed within REBT (like USA) to create a more sophisticated understanding of how to help people more effectively, in this case with problems of self-criticism and low self-esteem.

Introduction

This book is largely concerned with one stance that it is possible to take towards the 'self' – self-acceptance. However, it is possible to take a number of other productive stances towards the 'self' and in this chapter, I will consider the relationship between unconditional self-acceptance (USA) and one of these other stances: self-compassion (SC). In doing so, I will draw upon the ideas of several major theorists in these respective fields. Thus, in discussing USA, I will draw upon the work of Albert Ellis (2005), Maxie Maultsby (1984). Paul Hauck (1991) as well as those of my own (Dryden, 2003) and in discussing SC, I will draw heavily on the ideas of Kristin Neff (e.g. Neff, 2003a). While this chapter is based on the proposition that it is best to develop USA before SC, I will argue that these two concepts can be integrated both conceptually and practically. It is my basic thesis that the two concepts augment one another and that a therapeutic strategy based on the two together will be more productive than one based on each alone.[1] I will begin by defining precisely what I mean by unconditional self-acceptance and self-compassion.

The definition of unconditional self-acceptance (USA)[2]

A number of theorists have over the years been critical of the concept of 'self-esteem' as a primary determinant of psychological health and well-being (e.g. Baumeister, Smart and Boden, 1996). A variety of alternative concepts have been proposed which do not appear to have the unintended consequences of raising self-esteem, i.e. increasing levels of narcissism and self-absorption (e.g. Seligman, 1995). One such concept is unconditional self-acceptance (USA), which has been extensively represented in the work of Albert Ellis for over 50 years (e.g., Ellis, 1962; 2005). While Ellis has presented a number of different definitions of USA over the years (see Ellis, 2005), one which is most consistent with the views expressed in this chapter is as follows: 'I do not have intrinsic worth or worthlessness, but merely aliveness. I'd better rate my traits and acts, but not my totality or "self". I fully accept myself, in the sense that I know I have aliveness and I choose to survive and live as happily as possible, and with minimum needless pain. I require only this knowledge and this choice – and no other kind of self-rating' (Ellis, 1999: 6).

The term 'unconditional self-acceptance' is comprised of three elements and I will consider these in the following order: the 'self', 'acceptance' and 'unconditional'.

1 The 'self'

There are many definitions of the self (e.g. Hauck, 1991). However, rather than using any one such definition here, I will outline a number of defining attributes that comprise the 'self' (Dryden, 2003, Ellis, 2005, Hauck, 1991). First the 'self' is highly complex. It includes your characteristics, traits, actions, feelings, thoughts, images, sensations, and bodily aspects. As such, complexity is a defining attribute of the 'self' which together with another of its intrinsic aspects – that it is in flux – means that the 'self' cannot validly be rated. For example, if we take the process nature of the self (by which I mean that the 'self' is not fixed, but fluid over time), any global rating of the 'self' that is made would very soon be out of date as the 'self' at the time of the evaluation would not be the same as it would be after it is made. Indeed, the very nature of the evaluation would change the 'self'. As we shall see, you can validly rate discrete aspects of your 'self', but you cannot, validly, rate your entire 'self'. There are three further defining attributes of the 'self'. The first is that it is human. The second is that it is fallible. You are prone to error and this proneness cannot be eradicated. As Maxie C. Maultsby (1984) has said, all humans have an incurable error-making tendency. Finally, you are unique. There has never been and never will be, as far as we know, another you. Even if you were cloned, you and your clone would have different experiences and this would not invalidate your uniqueness.

2 'Acceptance'

In this, chapter, when I use the term 'acceptance', I mean acknowledgment of the existence of something in the form in which it currently exists (Dryden, 2003). The term can also be understood by what it does not refer to. Thus, it does not involve evaluation, either positive or negative, of you as a person and it also does not preclude change in what is being accepted.

3 'Unconditional'

By the term 'unconditional', I mean that which is without conditions or not contingent upon anything (Dryden, 2003).

Putting these three aspects together, we have the following definition: 'Unconditional self-acceptance involves you acknowledging that as a person you are human, unique, complex, in flux and fallible and that this is true about you no matter what conditions exist in the world. As such your "self" cannot be validly rated, but can be accepted unconditionally on the basis of the above ingredients.'

Example

Marie was an actress who attended a very important audition, but did a poor job and failed it. Instead of condemning, herself, Marie acknowledged that it was bad that she messed up, but that this failure did not define her. Rather, she acknowledged that she was a fallible human being who was not immune from failure and that even if she passed the audition this would not change her 'self'.

The definition of self-compassion (SC)

Neff (2003a) has also argued that the concept of self-compassion was proposed as one of a number of alternatives to the concept of self-esteem in outlining what would constitute a healthy attitude to oneself without the unintended negative consequences associated with attempts to raise self-esteem noted above. The proposal of self-compassion as a healthier alternative to self-esteem was also part of psychology's increasing interest in what Eastern philosophies, and in particular Buddhism, have to offer our understanding of psychological well-being (e.g. Epstein, 1995).

Neff and Lamb (2009: 864) have argued that as a particular stance towards the 'self', self-compassion has three components:

1 self-kindness – extending kindness and understanding to oneself in instances of perceived inadequacy or suffering rather than harsh judgment and self-criticism;
2 common humanity – seeing one's experiences as part of the larger human experience rather than seeing them as separating and isolating;
3 mindfulness – holding one's painful thoughts and feelings in balanced awareness rather than over-identifying with them in an exaggerated manner.

Putting these three aspects together, we have the following definition: 'Self-compassion involves showing yourself kindness, recognizing that you are connected to other humans and mindfully accepting your negative experiences without actively engaging with them.'

Example

Marie, whom we met above, talked kindly and supportively to herself even though she was disappointed in her behaviour which resulted in her failing the audition. She understood that she probably messed up because she was trying too hard and recognized that many other actors and actresses have done the same over the years. This helped her to learn from the experience without dwelling on it.

Similarities and differences between USA and SC

In this section, I will consider together the concepts of unconditional self-acceptance (USA) and self-compassion (SC) and reflect on some of the similarities and differences between them.

1 Absence of self-judgment

As can be seen from the foregoing, when you accept yourself and show yourself compassion, you refrain from making a negative judgment about yourself and this lack of negative self-judgment is what is common between these two stances.

However, while it is clear that Neff (2003a) considers negative self-judgment to be incompatible with self-compassion, it is not clear what her view is concerning positive self-judgment. As I have already shown, in the concept of unconditional self-acceptance employed in this chapter, both negative self-judgment and positive self-judgment are regarded as overgeneralizations about the 'self' and therefore to be avoided, not because they are merely overgeneralizations, but because of the negative impact that self-evaluation has on mental health and well-being. This position follows logically from the definition of USA with its emphasis on the complexity of the 'self'. This 'complexity' component appears not to be emphasized in SC.

2 Fallibility

In the stance known as USA, the concept of the 'self' as fallible plays an important role. Thus, in exhorting clients to develop unconditional self-acceptance, clinicians implementing this concept are often heard encouraging clients to see themselves as 'fallible human beings'. It is clear that in USA, the concept of fallibility is an attitude that clients are urged to apply to themselves. Thus, it is basically an intra-personal concept, an attitude towards the 'self' that the person applies to himself or herself irrespective of the actual or inferred global judgments that others make of that person's 'self'.

When the focus of therapy shifts to the person's attitude towards others where this attitude is the source of the person's disturbance, then that person is likely to be encouraged to develop unconditional other-acceptance (UOA). This involves seeing others as human, unique, complex, in flux and fallible and that this is true about them no matter what conditions exist in the world. Only when the person develops USA and UOA at the same time does he (in this case) see his own situation in a wider human, interconnected context.

By contrast, in the stance known as SC, the component known as 'common humanity', or interconnectedness, where one is encouraged to 'see one's experiences as part of the larger human experience rather than seeing them as separating and isolating' (Neff and Lamb, 2009: 864) plays an integral role.

3 Kindness

If one considers the stance of USA carefully, it involves adopting what one might call an 'acknowledging' attitude towards the 'self'. As I have already stated, when you accept yourself unconditionally, you acknowledge that your 'self' has a number of features which do not change: uniqueness, complexity, being in flux and fallibility. This accepting/acknowledging attitude is the only attitude made explicit in USA. By contrast, if one considers the stance of SC carefully it is clear that one of the main attitudes being advocated is that of kindness where the person takes a fair-minded, empathic and supportive attitude towards 'self'. As I will discuss later in this chapter, developing an unconditionally self-accepting attitude helps you to develop a kindly attitude towards your 'self', but the latter is not an integral part of the former as currently conceptualized.

4 Acceptance, compassion and change

As I will discuss later in this chapter, clients often resist developing the stances of USA and SC because of the negative constructions they place on these stances. This phenomenon can also be found in the professional literature. Thus, Neff and Lamb (2009: 865) say that '. . . while self-acceptance may theoretically entail passivity towards personal shortcomings, self-compassion involves the desire to alleviate one's suffering, and is therefore a powerful motivating force for growth and change'. Actually, this statement is confusing as it is not clear whether Neff and Lamb (2009) mean that such passivity is part of the theoretical concept of self-acceptance or whether they mean that it is possible for self-acceptance to be taken as promoting such a passive stance.

If Neff and Lamb mean that USA inherently involves passivity, then they are incorrect, since Ellis (e.g. 2005) has often made the point that USA does not promote passivity, but may actually promote change. Developing USA for a personal shortcoming does two things. First, it protects the person from self-disturbance and second, it frees the person to focus on the shortcoming and think how best she (in this case) can address and change it. To use Neff and Lamb's (2009: 865) own words, but made by them about self-compassion, unconditional self-acceptance 'involves the desire to alleviate one's suffering, and is therefore a powerful motivating force for growth and change'.

However, if Neff and Lamb (2009) mean that it is possible that USA may be seen as promoting passivity then they are correct, although this also applies to self-compassion.

In conclusion, USA and SC actually promote change, although they may both be incorrectly seen as promoting passivity.

5 Mindfulness

Neff (2003a) makes clear that mindfulness is one of three major components of SC, the other two being self-kindness and common humanity. By contrast, mindfulness is not seen as an integral part of unconditional self-acceptance but as a consequence of it. According to rational emotive behaviour theory, USA is a stance towards the 'self' that is derived from a more primary, flexible rational belief. The hallmark of this primary flexible belief is that the person articulates her (in this case) desire, but acknowledges that this desire does not have to be met. As Dryden (2009) has noted there are three consequences of rational and irrational beliefs: emotional, behavioural and cognitive. In the face of an adversity, when the person holds a rigid belief and a self-depreciation belief that is derived from it, then the cognitive consequences of these irrational beliefs are likely to be highly distorted and skewed to the negative. Given the compelling nature of these highly distorted thoughts, it is very easy for the person to over-identify with them in an exaggerated manner and thus to ruminate on them. By contrast, in the face of the same adversity, when the person holds a flexible belief and a USA belief that is derived from it, then the cognitive consequences of these rational beliefs are likely to be a mixture of thoughts that are realistic (albeit negative) and distorted. This will help the person to be more able to hold these in balanced awareness than if they are predominantly highly distorted and thereby not ruminate on them.[3] This holding in balance awareness is a main feature of mindfulness as outlined by Neff (2003).

In conclusion, mindfulness is seen as an integral part of self-compassion, whereas in Ellis's (2005) view, it is seen as a state that stems from and best engaged with when the person holds a USA belief.

People tend to resist developing USA and SC

The concepts of unconditional self-acceptance and self-compassion are often subject to misconceptions and criticised wrongly on the basis of such misconceptions. Consequently, people may resist developing USA and/or SC because they construe these concepts negatively. Here are six examples of such misconceptions to which I will provide a corrective response:

- 'I don't deserve to accept myself or to show myself compassion'
Response: This objection rests on an attitude of self-criticism which has been shown to be a major resistance to self-compassion (Gilbert *et al.*, 2011). Here it is helpful to show the person that she would not hold that view towards a loved one and thus she could choose not to hold it about herself.
- 'USA and SC lead to passive resignation and do not promote change'
Response: As discussed above, both USA and SC promote change in that they help the person to focus on a personal shortcoming without self-disturbance, understand it in a compassionate context and think about ways of changing it when she sees that it is in her interests to do so and it can be changed.
- 'USA and SC absolve people from taking responsibility for their actions'
Response: This is not correct. You can accept yourself and show compassion to yourself while still taking responsibility for your actions. Assuming such responsibility will be without self-blame, however.
- 'USA and SC lead to smugness'
Response: Again this is incorrect. Smugness implies that you rest on your laurels in a self-satisfied manner. Neither USA nor SC encourage such an approach. As mentioned above both USA and SC motivate you to change what you can change about yourself.
- 'USA and SC lead to self-indulgence'
Response: Here, you think that if you know that you can accept yourself and show compassion for yourself then you can afford to indulge yourself in activities that are not good for you. This view is incorrect because it ignores the fact that self-indulgence tends to stem from a philosophy of short-range hedonism and selfishness rather than from a stance towards the self that emphasizes unconditional acceptance or compassion. Dealing with this philosophy is difficult as it involves self-regulation failure. USA and SC can actually help you to learn from such failure and can help you to work towards greater self-discipline rather than to greater self-indulgence, by freeing you to identify, question and change one's particular short-range hedonistic philosophy.
- 'USA and SC reinforce a preoccupation with the "self" '
Response: Actually, the reverse tends to be the case. When you judge yourself, criticise yourself or in other ways reject yourself these stances towards the 'self' lead you to become preoccupied with whatever it is you are rejecting yourself for. USA and SC actually help to free you from self-preoccupation since they tend to promote constructive change wherever possible and help to minimise the rumination that accompanies self-preoccupation.

An investigation of items comprising the self-compassion scale with implications for USA

In this part of the chapter, I will consider the items on The Self-Compassion Scale (SCS) that have relevance for USA and its possible integration with SC.

The Self-Compassion Scale (SCS) is a 26 item scale that has six sub-scales: self-kindness vs. self-judgment, common humanity vs. isolation, mindfulness vs. over-identification. Each item is rated on a five-point scale with the scores on negative subscale items – self-judgment, isolation, and over-identification – reversed (Neff, 2003a; 2003b).

The main issue that arises from the content of this scale that is relevant to the theme of this chapter concerns the stance taken towards the 'self'. From the perspective of unconditional self-acceptance (USA), it is important to distinguish between the attitude that a person takes towards his entire 'self' and the attitude that he takes towards aspects of his 'self'. Thus, a person may dislike and make a negative judgment of an aspect of his 'self' (e.g. his procrastinating behaviour), but still accept himself unconditionally for his behaviour. When we look carefully at the items on the self-kindness and self-judgment sub-scales, this distinction is not always made.

Looking at the self-kindness items first (Neff, 2003b), three of the items describe a kindly attitude towards the 'self' (Item 5: I try to be loving towards myself when I'm feeling emotional pain; Item 12: When I'm going through a very hard time, I give myself the caring and tenderness I need and Item 19: I'm kind to myself when I'm experiencing suffering) while two outline a similar attitude towards aspects of the 'self' (Item 23: I'm tolerant of my own flaws and inadequacies and Item 26: I try to be understanding and patient towards those aspects of my personality I don't like).

Second, considering the self-judgment items (Neff, 2003b), three outline a negative judgment of the 'self' (Item 8: When times are really difficult, I tend to be tough on myself; Item 16: When I see aspects of myself that I don't like, I get down on myself and Item 21: I can be a bit cold-hearted towards myself when I'm experiencing suffering), while two outline a similar attitude towards aspects of the 'self' (Item 1: I'm disapproving and judgmental about my own flaws and inadequacies and Item 11: I'm intolerant and impatient towards those aspects of my personality I don't like).

It may be that from the perspective of self-compassion theory (Neff, 2003a), the distinction between adopting a compassionate stance towards the 'self' as a whole and aspects of the 'self' is not crucial, but it is from the perspective of the theory underpinning USA. It means that attempts to integrate USA with SC have to be made with due care when considering attitudes towards the 'self' as a whole as opposed to its aspects.

Integrating USA and SC with respect to therapeutic change

In this section of the chapter, I will outline how I think that self-compassion and its elements can be integrated with the concept of unconditional self-acceptance to make the latter a richer concept and one that may be more acceptable to theorists and clients alike with respect to therapeutic change.

However, first let me review how USA has been conceptualised in relationship to therapeutic change (see Figure 22.1).[4] Developing USA enables a person to focus on a negative aspect of himself that he wants to change without self-disturbance. Once the person has focused on this negative aspect without self-disturbance, he can initiate attempts to change[5] it if he can change it or to accept matters if he cannot change it (the latter is known as stasis).

One of the issues that concerns clients about the concept of unconditional self-acceptance is that it does not allow them to develop a positive attitude towards the 'self' when they wish to do so. Ellis (2005) was aware of this and offered such people an alternative concept that I refer to as 'unconditional self-esteem'. Applying this concept, you would again acknowledge that you were human, unique, complex, fallible and in flux and that these conditions are unchangeable, but this time you

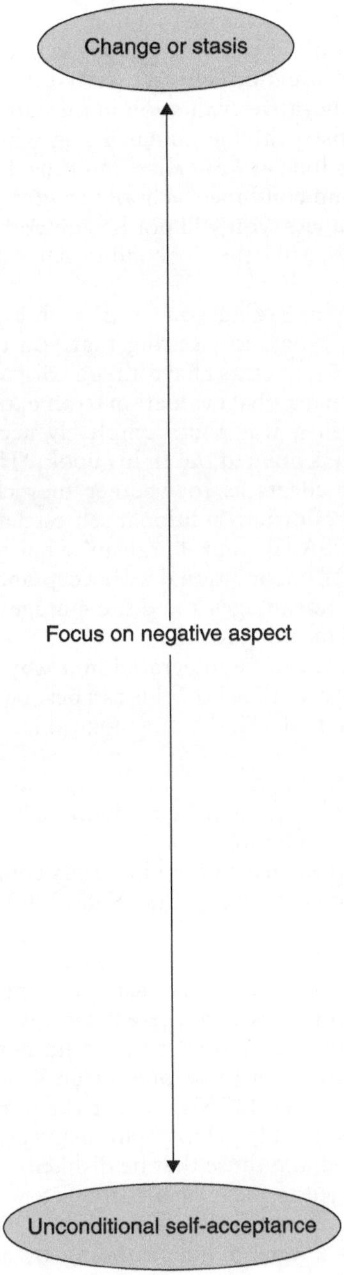

Figure 22.1 The impact of unconditional self-acceptance on attempting to change a negative aspect of oneself

would choose to give yourself a positive rating (e.g. 'I recognise that I am a unique, complex, fallible human being who is in flux and that these conditions are constant as long as I am alive and thus, I choose to like myself and/or to regard myself as a good or worthwhile person'). Now, Ellis (2005) was well aware of the arbitrary nature of such a positive evaluation. He argued that it would be equally justifiable for you to give yourself a negative evaluation in this circumstance (e.g. 'I recognise that I am a unique, complex, fallible human being who is in flux and that these conditions are constant as long as I am alive and thus, I choose to dislike myself'). However, if you choose and continue to choose to give yourself a positive evaluation under these circumstances, you will not be vulnerable to ego disturbance (e.g. low self-esteem) because of the unconditional nature of your positive self-evaluation.

Note, however, that by awarding your 'self' such a positive evaluation, albeit one that is unconditional, you are asserting that you can give yourself a global rating as a human being. However, as I have already discussed, it is just not possible, in any valid sense, to assign a global evaluation to an extremely complex organism, and one that is in flux, in a way that completely accounts for that organism. However, as Ellis (2005) has pointed out in his book, 'The Myth of Self-esteem', it is a matter of choice for clients as to whether they choose unconditional self-acceptance (as defined here) or unconditional self-esteem. As will discussed in the forthcoming section on 'USA, SC and Pluralism' what is important is that clients understand the concepts of unconditional self-acceptance and unconditional self-esteem together with their advantages and disadvantages and choose to implement the concept that has most meaning for them.

In my view, USA and SC can be integrated in a way that preserves the best of both concepts and I will now outline how this can best be done. While the following order is only notional it is, perhaps, the most logical (see Figure 22.2).[6]

1 The person would be encouraged to accept himself unconditionally as a unique, complex, fallible human being who is in flux and that cannot be validly given a global evaluation.
2 He would also be encouraged to see himself as connected to other humans – this is the common humanity aspect that Neff (2003a) highlights as an integral part of SC.
3 He would adopt a balanced attitude towards any reverberating disturbed emotional and cognitive states. This means that he would be aware of such states, understand that they will be present for a while until he has more fully digested the attitude of USA and thus he would not engage with such states. Rather, he would allow them to be present until they fade away. This is the mindfulness aspect that Neff (2003a) sees as the third integral part of SC.
4 The person would then be able to look at his many aspects and would acknowledge those that he liked and those that he disliked.
5 He would be encouraged to focus on a particular negative aspect and to do so with kindness – this is the self-kindness aspect that Neff (2003a) also says is an integral aspect of SC – and with understanding and see if he could change this aspect and how best to do so.
6 Whether or not he is able to effect change in this area, the person would be encouraged to develop a balanced awareness towards any residual states of emotional and/or cognitive disturbance and not to engage with these states as in point 3 above.

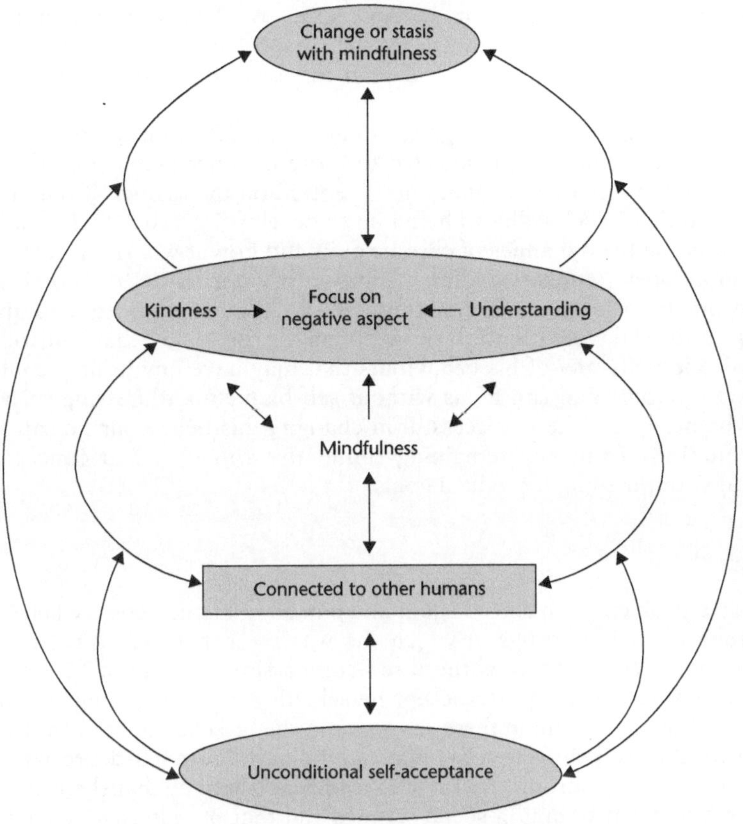

Figure 22.2 Integrating self-compassion with unconditional self-acceptance and the subsequent impact on attempting to change a negative aspect of oneself

Interestingly, in response to an enquiry from me concerning the relationship between USA and SC, Neff (personal communication, 27th December, 2011) said the following which is consistent with Ellis's (2005) position on the importance of developing USA before SC: 'I think self-compassion and self-acceptance are highly related, and that self-compassion basically requires self-acceptance. The main difference would be that self-compassion includes elements of active self-soothing, a sense of common humanity, and mindfulness (although self-acceptance can be seen to be embedded in mindfulness).'

Integrating USA and SC: how best to deal with chronic guilt

Chronic guilt is a problem where a person tends to blame himself for whatever goes wrong within the sphere of his involvement (Dryden, 1994).[7] Attempts by a therapist, for example, to encourage the person to stand back and take a self-compassionate attitude when he feels guilty may tend to fail or be short-lasting. Generally, it may be the case in such instances that the person needs to develop USA first and here it is important to elicit and respond to any doubts, reservations and objections that the person has to the concept of USA. If the person is blaming himself he will tend to resist efforts to encourage him to develop SC.

Once the person has made progress at developing USA, he is more open to the idea that his experiences are connected to those of other people and that he can begin to detach himself from ruminations centred on the theme: 'If only I did this or did not do that.' USA will also help him to develop a greater level of objectivity in understanding the dynamics of chronic guilt and how it works. At this point, he is much more open to understanding the impact of external variables on his behaviour and on the behaviours of others involved. Also, he can begin to apply the compassion that he would tend to show others for the same behaviour to himself. He can also identify any of his behaviours that may have unwittingly contributed to the bad outcome and can focus without self-blame on addressing such behaviours. Whether or not he is successful in changing his behaviour he can learn to detach mindfully from any remaining ruminative thoughts and concentrate on getting on with pursuing his valued goals.

Example

Teresa had a problem with chronic guilt and tended to blame herself when anything went wrong in social settings in which she was present. In using the concept of unconditional self-acceptance without self-compassion (see Figure 22.1) the therapist would encourage Teresa to accept herself for any wrongdoing (i.e. negative aspect) she thought she did in these settings and then to change her behaviour. The therapist would also help Teresa to understand that the core self-depreciation belief that underpinned her chronic guilt would lead her to assume that she was to blame when anything went wrong in social settings and that her alternative core unconditional self-acceptance belief would lead her to see that there might be other reasons why such things went wrong which did not involve her.

In integrating self-compassion with USA (see Figure 22.2), the therapist would do the same as above, but he would also do the following:

- He would encourage Teresa to see that others felt the same way as she did in holding the same belief.
- He would help Teresa to understand that even when rehearsing her USA belief, she might still think that she was to blame for things going wrong. He would teach her how to acknowledge the existence of such thoughts without actively engaging with them.
- He would help Teresa to understand some of the factors that may have contributed to the development of her chronic guilt problem and to view herself with kindness as she grappled with this problem. In doing so, he would encourage her to be empathic with herself, support herself through the process and, if necessary, to soothe herself.
- In assuming temporarily that she did contribute to things going wrong socially, he would not only help Teresa to accept herself for this negative aspect, but to view herself kindly and with understanding as she addressed this behaviour.
- Whether or not Teresa effected a positive change, the therapist would encourage her again to adopt a mindful attitude to any reverberating cognitive and emotional states.

USA, SC and pluralism

Up to now, this chapter has been based on the principle that it is best to think rationally about oneself before addressing such matters as connecting one's experiences to those of others, showing oneself kindness and holding a mindful attitude towards residual disturbed emotional and cognitive states (Ellis, 2005). Although as is shown in Figure 22.2, USA is deemed to interact with these three components of self-compassion, it is nevertheless seen as a foundation of compassionate-based change or stasis.

An alternative view of the relationship between USA, SC and change/stasis comes from a pluralistic perspective on counselling and psychotherapy and I will conclude this chapter by considering what a pluralistic perspective on USA and SC might involve. This perspective is underpinned by the following viewpoints (Cooper and McLeod, 2011):

1 There are multiple pathways to therapeutic change.
2 If we want to know what is likely to be most helpful for an individual client, we should start by exploring it with them.
3 It is vitally important to develop with clients a way of talking about therapy and to collaborate with them on its implementation.

Adopting these principles means, in this context, that clients may hold different views to the ones outlined in this chapter concerning the best way to use the concepts of unconditional self-acceptance (Ellis, 2005) and self-compassion (Neff, 2003). Some clients may not find the concept of USA valuable, while others may not consider SC to be a helpful concept.[8] Some may agree with Ellis (2005) that they need to develop USA before SC, while others may hold the opposing viewpoint. Pluralistic practitioners take their clients' views very seriously even if they disagree with them and attempt to resolve such disagreements empirically rather than referring to expert authority—their own or that of others. Such practitioners wisely hold that while a principle may hold true in the general case, it may not hold true with specific clients at specific times. In this way, pluralistic practitioners take their clients' views as seriously as they do their own theory and the research that supports this theory.

Questions concerning the effectiveness of a theory-driven approach to the development of both USA and SC versus a pluralistic, client-driven approach remain to be investigated.

Conclusion

In this chapter, I outlined the concept of unconditional self-acceptance based on the ideas of Albert Ellis (2005) and others including my own (Dryden, 2003) and discussed its relationship with self-compassion based on the work of Neff (e.g. Neff, 2003a). In doing so, I considered the similarities and differences between the two concepts and showed how integrating self-compassion with unconditional self-acceptance can lead to a richer understanding of clinical phenomena with consequent healthier results for clients with self-esteem problems. I demonstrated this briefly in the treatment of chronic guilt. I concluded the chapter by offering a pluralistic perspective on the relationship between USA and SC.

The rationale of this book is to explore how the concept of self-acceptance contributes to positive well-being. I hope how I have shown how integrating unconditional self-acceptance and self-compassion can enhance and enrich this project.

Notes

1 This, of course, is an empirical question that needs investigation.
2 In this chapter, much of what I have to say about USA is based on the views of Albert Ellis (2005), the founder of rational emotive behaviour therapy (REBT).
3 It should be made clear here that mindfulness involves holding in balanced awareness negative thoughts whether these are realistic (albeit negative) or highly distorted without actively engaging with these thoughts. My point is that it is easier for people to be mindful of negative thoughts if they are a mixture of the realistic and the distorted than if they are predominantly highly distorted.
4 In Figure 22.1, by 'negative aspect' I mean either an internal aspect (e.g. negative personal characteristic or behaviour) or external aspect (e.g. an outside adversity).
5 Such attempts at self-change are facilitated when the person is able to tolerate the ensuing discomfort. This is known as discomfort tolerance.
6 In Figure 22.2, by 'negative aspect' I again mean either an internal aspect (e.g. a negative personal characteristic or behaviour) or an external aspect (e.g. an outside adversity)
7 Most theorists in the field now distinguish shame from guilt and see shame linked to some global judgment of self and guilt focused on behaviour. I see them both as based on self-judgments where shame is linked to the idea that the self is defective, diminished or disgusting and guilt is linked to the idea that the self is bad in some respect (Dryden, 2012).
8 I accept the point that clients may hold misconceptions about USA and SC and that these need to be addressed by their therapist. However, after such discussion clients may still hold doubts, reservations or objections to these concepts and these need to be taken seriously in jointly planning and implementing a therapeutic programme

References

Baumeister, R. F., Smart, L., and Boden, J. M. (1996). Relation of threatened egotism to violence and aggression: The dark side of self-esteem. *Psychological Review*, 103: 5–33.

Cooper, M., and McLeod, J. (2011). *Pluralistic counselling and psychotherapy*. London: Sage.

Dryden, W. (1994). *Overcoming guilt*. London: Sheldon Press.

Dryden, W. (2003). *Managing low self-esteem*. London: Whurr.

Dryden, W. (2009). *Rational emotive behaviour therapy: distinctive features*. Hove, East Sussex: Routledge.

Dryden, W. (2012). *Dealing with emotional problems using rational-emotive cognitive behaviour therapy: a practitioner's guide*. Hove, East Sussex: Routledge.

Ellis, A. (1962). *Reason and emotion in psychotherapy*. Secaucus, NJ: Lyle Stuart.

Ellis, A. (1999). *REBT diminishes much of the human ego*. Revised edition. New York: Albert Ellis Institute.

Ellis, A. (2005). *The myth of self-esteem*. Amherst, NY: Prometheus.

Epstein, M. D. (1995). *Thoughts without a thinker*. New York: Basic Books.

Gilbert, P., McKewn, K., Gibbons, L., Chotai, S., Duarte, J., and Matos, M. (2011). Fears of compassion and happiness in relation to alexithymia, mindfulness, and self-criticism. *Psychology and Psychotherapy: Theory, Research and Practice*, published online 8 November 2011.

Hauck, P. (1991). *Hold your head up high*. London: Sheldon.

Maultsby, M. C. Jr. (1984). *Rational behavior therapy*. Englewood Cliffs, NJ: Prentice-Hall.

Neff, K. D. (2003a). Self-compassion: An alternative conceptualization of a healthy attitude toward oneself. *Self and Identity*, 2: 85–101.

Neff, K. D. (2003b). The development and validation of a scale to measure self-compassion. *Self and Identity*, 2: 223–250.

Neff, K. D., and Lamb, L. M. (2009). Self-compassion. In S. Lopez (Ed.), *The Encyclopedia of Positive Psychology*. Oxford: Blackwell Publishing (pp. 864–867).

Seligman, M. E. (1995). *The optimistic child*. Boston: Houghton Mifflin.

INDEX

Note: Page numbers in bold type refer to main articles; page numbers in italic type refer to figures and tables.